FINDERS, KEEPERS

FINDERS, KEEPERS

FINDERS OF TRUTH, KEEPERS OF FAITH

366 Daily Devotionals for Overcomers

ROBERT KLOUS

R.W. Klous Publishing

Finders Keepers by Robert Klous
No part of this publication may be reproduced, stored in a retrieval system, or transmitted in any form or by any means—electronic, mechanical, phototocopy, recording, or any other—except for brief quotation in printed reviews, without the prior permission of the publisher. All rights reserved.
All Scripture quotations, unless otherwise noted, are taken from the New American Standard Bible. Copyright, 1960, 1962, 1963, 1968, 1971, 1972, 1973, 1975, 1977 THE LOCKMAN FOUNDATION. (Used by permission. (www.Lockman.org).
All devotional readings and quotes placed before them originate from the author unless attributed to another author or designated as unknown or anonymous.
Copyright @ 2015 by Robert Klous
R.W. Klous Publishing
All rights reserved.
Cover Design by: Richard Ike
Interior Design by: CreateSpace
To order copies of this book please contact: www.amazon.com or https://www.facebook.com/rklous
Library of Congress Cataloging-in-Publication Data:
Klous, Robert, 1952-
        Finders Keepers/Robert Klous—First edition.
        Pages cm
Includes subject index.
ISBN …..(trade paper)
ISBN…..(ebook)
ISBN: 1515341860
ISBN 13: 9781515341864
1. Devotional 2. True Spirituality 3. Personal development 4. Revival
Printed in the United States of America

We all know some things are missing is the typical Christian life. Where is the daily quite time devotion? Where is biblical literacy? Where is truth found and the faith worth keeping?

King David: "One thing I have asked from the LORD, that I shall seek: That I may dwell in the house of the LORD all the days of my life, to behold the beauty of the LORD, and to meditate in His temple" (Ps 27:4). "Tremble, and do not sin; meditate in your heart upon your bed, and be still, Selah." (Ps 4:4).

Jesus: "and you shall know the truth and the truth shall make you free" (Jn 8:32).

Paul: "Fight the good fight, keeping faith and a good conscience which some have rejected and suffered shipwreck in regard to their faith" (1 Tim 1:19).

TABLE OF CONTENTS

DEDICATION

This book is dedicated to all Christians, called out of darkness by the Lord of lords to be saints, to be light and God's holy and royal priests, to function as living stones in His holy temple, under the Lordship of Jesus Christ for such a time as this.

PREFACE

This devotional arose out of my awareness that something is seriously wrong with contemporary Christianity. Popular religion has replaced private devotion. Doctrinal ignorance has replaced biblical literacy. Many are caving in to fear rather than stepping out and keeping the faith. More and more are following after falsehood rather than finding truth. Christianity is being attacked on every side, by hostile enemies without and by professing Christians within. Many are leaving contemporary Christianity whether they be the DONE's who are done with institutional religion or the NONE's who denounce any affiliation with any denomination.

The good news is that a faithful remnant is obeying the call and meeting the challenge; those who understand the times and are willing to take a stand for such a time as this. The Finders Keepers devotional was conceived and produced to help encourage and equip true believers to experience powerful personal revival, to expedite a spiritual revolution and to a exemplify a radical return to biblical Christianity.

Because modern Christianity is plagued with biblical illiteracy, fifty shades of sin and increasing falsehood, this book is devoted to those who want to be biblically wise, finders of truth, keepers of faith and devoted to God. There has been a proliferation of New Age and contemplative devotionals and books containing questionable communications with God and mindless meditations on some inner guide or god within. Therefore there is need for a biblically based devotional that encourages biblical meditation on the God of the Bible, who reigns from above. Biblical meditation is superior to New Age contemplation. Filling the mind with truth is wiser than emptying the mind of thoughts. Calling on the God above is safer than connecting with some New Age god within. Holy Spirit illumination to God's tested and proven inspired revelation is vastly superior to new and novel revelations inspired by men.

Prayerfully this devotional has been created with the intent to enhance the spiritual disciplines of biblical literacy and a devotional life. It seeks to accomplish this purpose by being a devotional solidly backed by Scripture in its content, relevant to the times, and motivational in its quotes and writing style. The devotional contains over 5,000 scripture references to enhance spiritual growth and a subject index to enable the reader to locate appropriate daily devotionals that will address the immediate challenges facing one's spiritual walk.

Robert Klous

INTRODUCTION

This book is written for those who want more of Jesus and who are bored with and don't buy what American Christianity is selling. Reading, meditating, digesting and practicing these daily devotional readings will equip you to BE the Church in these religious times. They will motivate you to persevere and keep the faith in these trying times. They will enable you to find, know and experience the truth that will set you free to experience the abundant life in these deceptive and depressing times.

The great and final reformation, or spiritual revolution, will be the restoration of the first century style overcoming Church. The early Church was not conformed to the world but upset the world. It did not preach to tickle ears but to pierce hearts. This spiritual revolution will be experienced by and expanded in areas where two or three are gathered in Jesus' name, not in man's name, to advance the Kingdom of God, not man's agenda, to do the business of the Father, not of the devil. There will be a restoration of righteous, peace and joy accomplished by the empowering presence of God, the Holy Spirit (Rom 14:17). This spiritual revolution will not eradicate all evil nor snatch the world that is sinking in sin out of the hands of the devil. Rather it will warn sinners not to fall into the hands of an angry God and help saints be received and embraced by the hands of their loving Father. Christ-minded, Spirit-led, God-fearing and Bible believing Christians will be the lights that expose evil, by having Jesus who is the Light of the world, shine through them. They will shine before the world by being separated from the world. They will not be conformed to the world but will be overcomers of the world, for they will not be of the world though they are in the world.

This household of God and assembly of true believers will proclaim and practice the Good News of the Gospel in demonstration of the Spirit and of power (1 Cor 2:4). This final and true reformation will surely happen for the Lord is coming back to perform a marriage that is undefiled and not redefined. The heavenly Bridegroom will be wed to a virgin Bride, refined by fire and dressed with holy attire and who has made herself ready, clothed in fine linen, bright and clean; for the fine linen is the righteous acts of the saints (1 Pet 1:2-9; Rev 19:7-8).

The Lord is returning for a virgin Bride, not a religious harlot and unrepentant and professing church. It will take such a first century Holy Spirit empowered and faith overcoming Church, not the 21st century powerless and plagued church, to overcome and persevere what is soon coming. It will become more and more apparent to the wise that such a true revival will not be brought about by the ingenious efforts of the religiously educated professional seminarians, church growth experts and a proud, flesh anointed clergy cast. No, it will be brought about by the indwelling Holy Spirit of God operating supernaturally through average and ordinary believers, God's holy and royal priesthood (Acts 4:12-13; 1 Pet 2:5,9), as well as Spirit-anointed pastors, and everyone who is determined to become an overcome rather than be overcome. And this true personal revival will occur wherever its condition, true repentance, is practiced. The extent of its reach depends on the number of its partakers. The duration of its existence depends on the commitment to its conditions.

Such revived and overcoming saints will walk in newness of life (Rom 6:4), laboring with God's sanctifying grace (1 Cor 15:10; Tit 2:11-12) and abiding in Christ who is their life (Col 1:27; 3:4; Jn 15:1-8). To help facilitate this last day reformation this devotional has been produced in order to help every Christian to find truth and keep faith in these deceptive and trying times. It isn't necessary to be a spiritual superman with a Ph.D to understand and advance the Kingdom of God. One only has be a God Empowered Disciple, a GED (Acts 1:8; Matt 4:19).

God empowers ordinary people to do extraordinary things. The Lord uses the weak to shame the strong, the foolish to shame the wise, the spiritual to rebuke the religious and the Spirit-led to rescue the purpose-drunken. It is the spiritually blessed who delivers prosperity victims and the heart-pierced who leads the ear ticked back into BEING the Church. We need more Christ minded and godly role models and overcomers, not the carnal minded and world conformers, who will experience this true personal revival. The Lord has been "waiting" for His faithful remnant to wake up, sober up, shape up, stand up, suit up and wrap up this last hour, hastening His coming (2 Pet 3:11-12), waiting until His enemies be made a footstool for His feet (Heb 10:13).

These devotional readings should not only to be read devoutly and practiced daily, but should also be studied diligently and digested completely. By giving ample Scriptural references, it is designed to be a discipleship tool as well as a devotional resource; useful both in private devotions as well as in group discussions in home fellowships and in Sunday school classes. The Subject Index provides practical and easy access to devotional readings which may help readers find the appropriate devotionals that will address the immediate challenges to their spiritual growth. The quotations at the beginning of each devotional introduce the reader to other saints of God, and often present a spiritual idea quite different from the daily devotion, providing another daily truth that may enhance one's devotional life. All quotations not specifically credited to another person or are designated unknown are those made by this author.

The militant (aggressive) and triumphant (overcoming) Church, the assembly of saints and God's household is assured that neither the gates of hell nor the striking of man's gavel will overpower her, nor the threats of the wicked will prevail against her (Mt 16:18). For the Lord's overcoming saints have not been sent on a "mission impossible" but on a mission invincible. All that is needed for righteousness to triumph is for God's saints to do something, and that something is to BE His Church

JANUARY 1

To exit and leave earth with its dirt is no dread for those who are prepared to enter heaven with its glory.

STAY WITHIN FOUR WALLS OR GO TO THE FOUR CORNERS

A church may quickly be built by market-driven strategies, church growth principles, and downloaded spirituality and rest on the foundation of institutional religion. But when Satan's winds begin to blow and God's judging quakes begin to rumble, the man-made church will quickly crumble back to its foundation of sand and to rubble (Heb 12:25-29). You may be in a church building but are you "in Christ"? Are you in the church HE is building (Mt 16:18)? The true Church is built with living stones who are ignited by a love for God, united by the Lord, and empowered by the Holy Spirit, (1 Pet 2:5; Jn 13:35; 1 Jn 4:19). The real temple of God is not a pile of dead bricks and old mortar hiding behind four walls, stationary on a street corner. Rather, it is the living Temple of God taking the Gospel to the four corners.

In a day when god-haters laugh, the proud strut about, the liberals lie, the religious kill, the depraved pervert, judges malpractice, preachers entertain, and prophets deceive, it's nice to know that the day is soon coming when the great Judge, King, Prophet, Shepherd and Ruler, the Lord Jesus Christ will return to have the last laugh, declare the last verdict, set the record straight, exalt the humble, reward the holy and will be glorified amidst His own (Ps 110).

JANUARY 2

How much better it is to ascend to the New Jerusalem,
the city built upon the Rock than to dwell in earthen
cities falling on the rocks; to enjoy God the righteous
judge of all than endure the enemy, the accuser of all.

THE CROSS OF CHRIST SOLVES EVERY CRISIS. NO WONDER THE DEVIL HATES IT SO.

It is easier to bear the Cross when you realize that it can bear you up. When you feel the weight of the Cross, have faith that it will lift you up.

When the world's trials take your happiness, let heaven's Cross give you peace.

The Lord was crucified on the Cross so that the Cross would crucify your Self.

The Lord surrendered His life and died so we would surrender our life and live.

Victory, peace and well-being do not come from wearing a cross, but by bearing the Cross

You can't truly love Christ and loath His Cross.

A life endured with Cross pain, makes for great gain.

JANUARY 3

Some who serve God can only kneel, wait and go to God in
prayer; others serve who can stand, march and go to war.

THERE IS A WAY THAT SEEMS RIGHT...

There is a way which seems right to a man, but its end is the way of death (Prov 14:12). Those who are called by God and follow Him will not be consumed with being purpose driven. They will be Spirit led (Rom 8:14). Trust in your finite self and be let down, trust in the infinite God and be lifted up (Prov 3:5). Trust in your abilities and you will hit the wall, trust in God's gracious enablement and you will leap over walls (2 Cor 3:4-6; Ps 18:29). Those striving for personal fame may very well go down in flames, but those exalting His name will go up to heaven.

Those led by the Spirit of God will not have to worry about discovering the purposes of God. They have a heavenly GPS, God's Positioning Spirit, teaching God's own how to abide in Christ (1 Jn 2:27), how to finish the race (1 Cor 9:24-27) and how to enter His kingdom (2 Pet 1:5-11; Acts 14:22; Rom 8:16-17). They will bear much fruit (Jn 15:8) and reach their destiny. Those who are driven by purpose most likely are in the driver's seat frantically following their worldly GPS, the newest bestseller at the nearest Christian bookstore.

When the Lord is in the driver's seat, His Spirit will position the Lord's servants where He intends them to go. There is a way which seems right for a man, but its travelers often go the wrong way. They fail to read the road signs, God's warnings and follow the road map, God's Word. They are so busy texting they have no time for praying; so busy talking, to hear God calling; so busy going, yet getting nowhere. But once all this ends and silence is restored, God's voice is heard and true direction begins. There is a way that is surely right for man, and it brings the abundance life now and eternal life then.

JANUARY 4

"Everyone who has responded to His call to 'come' is responsible to His command to 'go'". Wesley Duewel

Christians need to stop hiding as skeletons in dark closets and come out, clothed with the Lord Jesus Christ, empowered by the Spirit of God, fattened up on the Word of God, and walk as obedient children of the Father of Lights.

We need to keep the lamp filled, the flame burning, the Light shining, the Gospel going and the devil on the run. We have the keys to lock up the thief who comes to steal, kill and destroy (Jn 10:10a; Mt 16:19). So why lock ourselves inside a church building which has no testimony, to practice a religion which has no power, serving a god who has no clout, and laboring for that which has no reward?

We will never engage the devil on the battlefield as long as we are entertained by his fun and games in the church house. It's time to mourn not laugh; to pierce hearts, not harden them; to have hearing ears, not itching ears; to have feet shod with the Gospel of peace, not feet running after a gospel of prosperity; to speak sound doctrine, not tolerate demonic doctrine; to boldly shine the Light of Truth and proclaim His name, not hide in darkness behind compromise, fear and shame. Only when the true Church rises up and speaks out, will the devil shut up and get out. The Great Shepherd cleansed the temple and cast out demons. Today's false shepherds corrupt His Temple and invite them in.

JANUARY 5

*"No erudition, no purity of diction, no width of
mental outlook, no flowers of eloquence, no grace
of person can atone for lack of fire. Prayer ascends
by fire. Flame gives prayer access as well as wings,
acceptance as well as energy. There is no incense without
fire; no prayer without flame." E. M. Bounds*

PRAYERS THAT DON'T BOUNCE BACK

Do you ever wonder why prayers are often powerless, answers are few and problems persist? They seem to bounce back off the ceiling rather than reach God's throne.   Sin will certainly hinder prayer as clearly stated in Scripture (1 Pet 3:7; Jn 9:31).   And it is written in the Psalms: "If I regard wicked in my heart, the Lord will not hear" (Ps 66:18). Isaiah says: "Your iniquities have made a separation between you and your God, and your sins have hidden His face from you so that He does not hear" (59:2).

In Proverbs we read: "He who turns away his ear from listening to the law, even his prayer is an abomination" (28:9). But God will hear the prayer of the righteous (Prov 15:29).   For the prayer of the upright is His delight (Prov 15:8).   In the New Testament we learn how John instructed believers in prayer saying: "Beloved, if our heart does not condemn us, we have confidence before God, and whatever we ask we receive from Him, because we keep His commands and do the things that are pleasing in His sight" (1 Jn 3:22). James says: "Draw near to God and He will draw near to you. Cleanse your hands, you sinners; and purify your hearts, you double-minded" (4:8).

The author of Hebrews clearly lays out God's protocol in prayer: "Let us draw near with a sincere heart in full assurance of faith, having our hearts sprinkled from an evil conscience and our bodies washed with pure water" (10:22). Thus, it is the effective prayer of the righteous that accomplishes much in the heavenlies rather than bouncing off our ceiling (Jam 5:16; Rev 8:3, 4). Fortunately, when we get back in line through confession and renouncing of sin, God gets back online.

JANUARY 6

*As the eye which has gazed at the sun won't see earthly things;
as a man who beholds the mighty ocean isn't impressed
with a dirty pond; so the mind which contemplates the
eternal will not be content to dwell on the temporal.*

Lord, turn my eyes to Thee that so that I will not focus on me (Heb 12:2). Help me to dwell on the heavenly, not on vanity (Col 3:1-4; Phil 4:8). Fill me with pure intention and help me with sin prevention, so that I may walk in newness of life and attain to resurrection (Phil 3:11; Rom 6:4). Help me to see who I am in You, a new creation of the great I Am, so that I will not return to the old man I was (Eph 1:3; 2 Cor 5:17; Col 3:8-10). Help me to resist the raging tides of the world, enticing temptations of the flesh, hidden traps of the devil, and contrary thoughts of the mind. Help me to take the kingdom of heaven by force, so I will not be taken by vice (Mt 11:12). Help me to rejoice and not fear when I suffer for righteousness and share in the sufferings of Christ (1 Pet 3:14, 4:13-14). For the more I fear to suffer, the more sufferings I will need to bear.

JANUARY 7

*Prayer is our most powerful weapon. Prayer invites
God in to work things out, instead of relying
on our strength just to make it through.*

TRIBULATION BRINGS TRIUMPH

The Son of God learned obedience from the things He suffered (Heb 5:9). Likewise, O son and daughter of the Lord, you can consider it all joy when you encounter various trials, knowing that the testing of your faith produces endurance. And let endurance have its perfect result, so that you may be perfect and complete, lacking in nothing. (Jam 1:2-4). "For through many tribulations we must enter the kingdom of God" (Acts 14:22b), which is righteousness, peace and joy in the Holy Spirit (Rom 14:17). If we suffer with Him we will also be glorified with Him (Rom 8:17). For you have need of endurance, so that when you have done the will of God, you may receive what was promised (Heb 10:36). And this is the promise which He Himself made to us, eternal life (1 Jn 2:25). "After you have suffered for a little while, the God of all grace, who called you to His eternal glory in Christ, will Himself perfect, confirm, strengthen and establish you" (1 Pet 5:10).

Weeping may last through the night while the sun has set, but a shout of joy comes in the morning, when the Son and Morning Star rises. (Ps 30:5; 2 Pet 1:19; Rev 22:16). If your tribulation season of life has you "hitting the wall", your Deliverer is right around the corner, "and by my God I can leap over a wall" (Ps 18:29b).

The darkness does not comprehend the Light. The carnal does not like the Holy. The cold and lukewarm are uncomfortable with the Hot. The religious are opposed to the Spiritual. Sinners are hostile to Saints. No wonder the followers of Jesus are few and their battles are many. But the one who endures tribulation will enjoy triumph.

JANUARY 8

Be loving to those whom the Spirit is convicting so you will not chase off those whom the Son is drawing.

PERSEVERING BY THE WORD

In these last days the Word of God is being rewritten by proud scribes, censored by the depraved, paraphrased beyond description, peddled for profit and adulterated by compromise. It is divided asunder rather than rightly divided. Often it's thrown on a shelf to collect dust rather than treasured in the heart to dispose of sin. Where there is no acknowledgment of its inspiration, no appreciation for its wisdom, no agreement to its teaching, no wonder of its power and no tolerance of its commands you find the good, the bad and the ugly all thinking they are perfectly fine. They prefer pleasant words of men that tickle the ears and soothe their conscience.

But praise the Lord that many Christians are becoming spiritually awakened and prepared to not only to persevere but also to prevail and overcome in these last difficult days. It seems that the majority are content with merely professing Christ, sleeping in the pews and stumbling in darkness. Rather than being filled with the Spirit they are intoxicated with the world, with their heads in the sand and their lives in the gutter. Yet, the Lord Jesus Christ is raising a mighty army and faithful remnant who confess Him as Lord, who magnify Him and proclaim His mighty name, having their eyes fixed on Him and their mind preoccupied with Him.

JANUARY 9

Too many are addicted to superficial movements
of strange spirits upon their emotions because
they are too little accustomed to the supernatural
working of the Holy Spirit in their life.

THE DEVIL DESPISES THE PROMISES OF GOD

Cash in on the promises of God and the devil will have to check out. It is by claiming the promises of God that we continue on the road to holiness and partake of divine nature, becoming holy as God is holy (1 Pet 1:15, 16). "He has granted to us His precious and magnificent promises, in order that by them you might become partakers of the divine nature, having escaped the corruption that is in the world by lust (2 Pet 1:4). So what are some of these magnificent promises?

God's unlimited power is available for us, (Acts 1:8, 10:38; Eph 1:19, 3:20; Phil 2:13; Heb 13:20-21).

Resist the devil and he must flee, (Jam 4:7; 1 Pet 5:9; Mt 4:10).

We can overwhelmingly conquer in overwhelming circumstances, (Rom 8:37; 2 Cor 2:13-14; Ps 37:7-18; Ps 149).

Our Mission Assignment to destroy the works of the devil as Jesus did, (1 Jn 3:8; Acts 10:38; Jn 14:12; Mt 12:28; Gal 3:5; Eph 5:11; Acts 26:18; 2 Tim 2:25, 26).

In us lives Christ before whom demons tremble and are tormented, (Gal 2:20; Mk 3:11, 5:7; Acts 19:15).

The Spirit of God is greater than the devil, (1 Jn 4:4; Mt 12:28; Acts 6:3, 8:5-7).

The Holy Scriptures make us adequate and equipped for every good work, (2 Tim 3:16, 17).

By the power of the Holy Spirit and by practicing the Word of God, we can cleanse ourselves from all defilement of flesh and spirit, (Ps 119:9, 11; Rom 8:13, Gal 5:16; 2 Cor 7:1).

Being seated with Christ at the right hand of God, far above all rule and authority and power and dominion (Eph 1:20-21, 2:6), and having been enlisted as His soldiers and sent out as His ambassadors, we have divine authority and power to rule and take dominion away from the devil, expanding the Kingdom of God by force, (Mt 11:12; Mt 28:18; Lk 9:1,2; Eph 2:6, 6:12f; Rom 5:17; 8:37; 2 Cor 5:20; 2 Tim 2:3, 4).

JANUARY 10

Pray and expect, don't play and neglect.

TEN SPIRITUAL ENDOWMENTS

There are ten spiritual endowments offered to born again Christians that fully equip them to experience heaven on earth. And we are not talking about angel feathers, gold dust, portals of heaven, awakened angels, contemplative prayer, prosperity religion or quantum spirituality. These ten true spiritual endowments are: the inspired Word of God (2 Tim 3:16-17);

the great and magnificent promises of God (2 Pet 1:3-4); the Armor of God (Eph 6:10-18); the Holy Spirit of God (Jn 7:37-38; 1 Cor 6:19-20); the Name of Jesus (Acts 3:16, 4:12, 8:12; Jn 1:12, 16:23); authority over evil principalities and powers (Lk 10:17-19; Mt 10:1); the grace of God (Jn 1:16; 1 Cor 15:10; Tit 2:11-12; Col 2:6; 1 Pet 5:12); a new holy calling (2 Tim 1:9; 1 Pet 1:15); a new identity and nature (Gal 2:20; Phil 3:20; Col 1:13; 2:10; 2 Cor 5:17; 1 Pet 2:9), and a new destiny (1 Pet 5:9; 1:3-5; Rom 8:28-29; 2 Thess 2:14; 2 Tim 2:10).

JANUARY 11

It's far better to be prayed up than preyed upon,
to be stirred up rather than stressed out; to BE the
church, rather than play church; to preach repentance,
rather than accept compromise; to perform the signs
of a true apostle with godly fear, rather than to
perform before an audience to tickle an ear.

DON'T FALL FOR HYPER GRACE

Endurance in grace is not effortless grace (1 Cor 15:10). The Christian race is not "effortless spirituality", a jog through the park or relaxing in a bed full of roses (1 Cor 9:24-27); Heb 12:1, 4). God's true grace is both a saving and a sanctifying grace. It saves from eternal damnation and it delivers from present sin contamination. God's true grace offers the eternal solution to sin's condemnation as well the effective sin management in those who carry His cross.

On the other hand, hyper or modern grace is a man-made grace, tailored for those who chose not to stand on and labor with God's true grace (1 Pet 5:12; 1 Cor 15:10). Beware of deceived believers who distort the true grace of God. The devil's new game today is "effortless spirituality". Relax, don't labor. Pursue happiness, not holiness. Confess your righteousness not your sin. God is happy with you no matter what you do, for He is so near sighted that He doesn't see your sin, but only Jesus seated beside Him who paid for your sin. They do not see the importance and necessity of laboring by God's grace to live sensibly, righteously and godly in this present age (1 Cor 15:10; Tit 2:11-12).

Wise and Spirit taught believers work out their salvation with fear and trembling (Phil 2:12). They know that true spirituality often comes with Holy Spirit conviction (Rom 9:1; Phi 3:15; 1 Jn 2:27; 3:24, 4:13), Fatherly discipline (Heb 12:4-11) and sharing in the sufferings of Christ (2 Cor 1:5-7; Col 1:24; Phil 1:29; 1 Pet 4:13, 5:1).

JANUARY 12

The Lord is calling on all pastors to become overcomers not undertakers, to disciple their sheep rather than lead them out to pasture among wolves.

IN CHRIST WE ARE COMPLETE, SO WHY COMPLAIN?

In Him we have been made complete, so there is no need to complain (Col 2:10; 2 Cor 3:4-6). We have been raised up with Christ so no need to be bent over (Eph 2:6a). In Him we have blessed with every spiritual blessing, so no need to feel spiritually impoverished (Eph 1:3), nor seek a prosperity gospel.   In Him we are free from the curse of religion, so no need to be accused by the religious (Gal 3:10-13). We have been rooted in Him who is the Truth, so no need to be deceived by falsehood (Col 2:7; Jn 14:6; Eph 5:6; Col 2:8). In Him we have been born again to abundant life, so no need to be bored to death in this temporal life (Jn 3:3,5, 10:10b). In Him we are seated in the heavenlies, so no need to lay in the world's gutters (Eph 2:6b). We are united with Christ, the Head of the Body and Light of the world, so no need to mindlessly walk in Satan's darkness (Col 1:18; Jn 8:12, 12:35). We are called to walk in resurrection life rather than follow the walking dead (Col 3:1-3; Rom 6:4; Mt 8:22). We have been adopted by our heavenly Father who freely gives, no longer to be a captive child of the devil who steals (Jn 10:10a). We have the mind of Christ who came to destroy the works of the devil, so no need to be clueless and worked over by the devil (1 Cor 2:16; 1 Jn 3:8).

JANUARY 13

"I have said for many years that what the world calls fanaticism and much of the church calls extremism, God calls normal." Michael L. Brown

NORMAL CHRISTIANITY IS SUPERNATURAL

The time will come when sanctified believers and mighty followers of the Lord will lay aside religious trinkets and lay hold of the Lord

Jesus Christ who is the greatest Treasure. They will love God with all their heart, soul, strength and mind (Lk 10:27). Therefore, they will enjoy the abundant life to the fullest (Jn 10:10b), even in the midst of tribulation (Phil 1:29; Acts 14:22; Rom 5:3-4; 8:36-37). They will die to self and to sin and thus walk in newness of life, with Him (Rom 6:4, 11; Gal 2:20; Phil 1:21; 1 Pet 2:24). They will not allow their minds to be corrupted by invading and novel religious slogans (2 Cor 10:4-5), seeking religious anointings, mantles and tokens. Instead, they will renew their minds with truth, be set free and advance the kingdom of God in word and in power, exposing the evil deeds of the kingdom of darkness (Rom 12:1-2, Jn 6:31,32,36; 1 Cor 4:20; Eph 5:11; Jn 7:7). They will engage the true enemies of the cross rather than be entertained by them. They will be the faithful remnant who have not bowed their knees to Baal nor opened their minds to deception (Rom 11:5; Mt 24:4). They will proclaim the true gospel of the Kingdom in demonstration of the Spirit and of power, walking in the supernatural works which God has prepared beforehand that we walk therein (1 Cor 2:4; Eph 2:10).

JANUARY 14

Who shall ascend into heaven but he who has a child-like faith, believing and seeing the God who is, not conceiving and contemplating on a god who isn't.

FAITH THAT OVERCOMES

How great it is to see God who is exalted above all yet ministering to people who have hit rock botton. "For thus says the high and exalted One who lives forever, whose name is Holy, 'I dwell on a high and holy place, and also with the contrite and lowly of spirit in order to revive the spirit of the lowly and to revive the heart of the contrite'" (Is 57:15). He does this to those who believe. "For without faith it is impossible to please Him, for he who comes to God must believe that He is and that He is a rewarder of those who seek Him" (Heb 11:6). Those who truly believe will see the invisible God do the impossible. For they remember Jesus' statements: "All things are possible to him who believes (Mk 9:23) and "All things you ask in prayer, believing, you will receive" (Mt 21:22). They believe that God is able to do exceeding abundantly above all that they ask or think, according to the power that works in them (Eph 3:20).

They are fully assured that what God has promised He is able also to perform (Rom 4:21). Faith is "the assurance of things hoped for; the conviction of things not seen" (Heb 11:1). The gospel is the power of God for salvation to everyone who believes (Rom 1:16). True believers believe that God "gives life to the dead and calls into being that which does not exist" (Rom 4:17). Such ones have observed that "the word of God performs its work in those who believe (1 Thess 2:13). "Faith comes from hearing, and hearing by the word of Christ" (Rom 10:17). So knowing the Word is essential to the one who expects to see God do the impossible.

JANUARY 15

If you flee from those who speak truth, you will fly into the traps of those who speak falsehood.

THE GREAT FALLING AWAY

The great falling away is happening today. Too many play, too few pray. Too many are living to be happy, while others are just happy to be living, and fewer are those living to be holy (Rom 12:1). Too many organize, too few agonize. Many are quick to laugh, slow to mourn; love to shake, but hate to break. Many go to church, few ARE the Church. Many are being lured to sleep and carnality by ear tickling wolves dressed in sheep clothing. They will not enjoy facing the Righteous One dressed in glory. The glorious Bridegroom is returning for a holy bride dressed in fine linen, bright and clean, not for a harlot bride dressed to kill (Rev 19:7-9).

If the Church of God had remained loyal to its original design, being a House of Prayer (Mt 21:13), and remained filled with those who had not abandoned their first love (Rev 2:4) nor were prevented from exercising their priesthood (1 Pet 2:5,9); and had they continued their devotion to the apostles teaching, and to fellowship, to the breaking of bread and prayer (Acts 2:42), churches today would not have deteriorated into houses of play and buildings of clay, but would have remained standing high and strong, as temples of living stones (1 Pet 2:5).

JANUARY 16

Christians who are taught by the Spirit of Truth will be nourished on the Word of God and will possess the mind of Christ. They will be less inclined to listen to words of men and be blown about by every wind of doctrine. They sail with the Spirit and walk on water rather than shipwreck on the shore or drown at sea.

WHAT IS YOUR DIET?

Jesus stated that man cannot live on physical bread alone but must live by every inspired word of God (Mt 4:4). The God inspired Word brings spiritual growth (1 Pet 2:2) and spiritual equipping (2 Tim 3:16-17). When practiced it brings discernment (Heb 5:14) and blessing (Jn 13:17). When despised it bring indebtedness (Prov 13:13a). And of course, being sincere about doing the will of God is required to obtain true understanding of the teachings of God (Jn 7:17; Ps 119:66).

Is the Bible an ornament on your table or is it a lamp unto your feet and a light to your path (Ps 119:105)? "All Scripture is inspired by God and profitable for teaching, for reproof, for correction, for training in righteousness; that the man of God may be adequate, equipped for every good work" (2 Tim 3:16-17). The psalmist said: "If Your law had not been my delight, then I would have perished in my affliction" (Ps 119:92). "Those who love Thy law have great peace, and nothing causes them to stumble" (Ps 119:165).

Those who understand the supernatural nature of God's revelation appreciate its value. "Now to Him who is able to establish you according to my gospel and the preaching of Jesus Christ..." (Rom 16:25). "My eyes anticipate the night watches, that I many meditate on Your word" (Ps 119:148). "At midnight I shall rise and give thanks to You because of Your righteous ordinances" (Ps 119:62). "Seven times a day I praise You, because of Your righteous ordinances" (Ps 119:164).

The word of God, not religious traditions of men, is the mighty sword for true warriors (Eph 6:17; Mt 15:9). Of course it has to be used under the guidance of the Holy Spirit, since it is a sharp two edged sword (Heb 4:12), one edge to cut out sin, the other edge to cut off the enemy. This is where many get into trouble and get wounded or killed in battle or taken captive by the enemy: they wield the sword in their own power as they see fit, often injuring fellow soldiers instead of fighting the true enemies of God.

JANUARY 17

Many so-called "church growth" experts don't realize that the stone which the builders rejected is still the Stone that crushes and the Cornerstone that remains.

THE CHURCH OF THE CARPENTER

Churches which exalt Jesus as Lord and Savior; where God is worshiped in spirit and in truth; where the Holy Spirit is invited to minister in power; where Savior friendly saints assemble who are hungry for solid food and sound doctrine, rather than fast food religion and pastoral pastries; where believers crave to be filled with living water rather than bottle fed.... there we will see true believers BEING the church inside, regardless of what denominational sign may appear outside. Wherever faithful believers assemble to be equipped to evangelize the lost with compassion but without compromise; to proclaim the full Gospel with boldness, yet without hesitation; where sin is exposed with love, yet without condemnation; where true disciples are made rather than pew dwellers counted; where true repentance is preached with clarity, yet without regret; where God's kingdom and righteousness is pursued above all, without hypocrisy, there we will see the true Church in action, not being tossed here and there by every wave of the sea.

JANUARY 18

"The world may frown—Satan may rage—but go on! Live for God. May I die in the field of battle." James B. Taylor

DON'T JUST LAY THERE, GET UP AND GET DRESSED FOR WAR

Every Christian has been called to spiritual warfare (Eph 6:10-18; 2 Tim 2:3-4; Jam 4:7; 1 Pet 5:8-10). Spiritual warfare began for us when, at salvation, we were born from above by the Spirit and turned from darkness to light and from the dominion of Satan to God (Acts 26:18). It involved God delivering us from the domain of darkness and transferring us to the kingdom of His beloved Son (Col 1:13). It was a victory battle when we became freed from slavery to sin and became slaves of righteousness and enslaved to God (Rom 6:18, 22). It was a supernatural rescue mission whereby we escaped from the snare of the devil, having been held captive by him to do his will" (2 Tim 2:26).

It also consists of being delivered out of the world's system, much like when God called Moses to lead Israel out of Egypt. And spiritual warfare continues for Christians as they invade Satan's dark kingdom, rescuing his captives so they can enter the kingdom of God, which is righteousness, peace and joy in the Holy Spirit (Rom 14:17). It is much like, when God sent Joshua to invade Canaan. It involves taking down spiritual enemies, like when David downed Goliath, and later when Joshua and Caleb overcame those who stood against them. They did not see their enemies as giants and themselves as grasshoppers, but saw them as they really were, forces to be defeated at God's command (Joshua 1:1-9). Likewise, the Christian's spiritual enemies have been disarmed and defeated by the Savior's Cross (Col 2:15).

The Church received the Holy Spirit at Pentecost to make her a bold, holy and conquering army, not to make her a blessed, happy and comfortable assembly; to make her invincible, not invisible, aggressive, not defensive. We are not to build a bypass around Satan's kingdom, but a highway through his kingdom. We are not to "hold the fort" until Jesus returns to rapture us, but to storm the gates of Hades because Jesus lives in us (Mt 16:18; Gal 2:20). Demons who bowed down before Him before, (Mk 3:11), still bow down to Him who lives in us (Gal 2:20).

We are in the final hour to see God's miracle power revealed, His purposes realized and His enemies routed. Don't cower when the devil, like a lion, roams about and roars. You are covered by the blood of the Lamb, the Lion of Judah who reigns. With God's doubled-edged sword in your hand (Heb 4:12; Eph 6:17), with God's praise on your lips (2 Chron 20:20-22; Ps 149:5-6) and with Satan crushed under your feet (Rom 16:20), begin to tread upon his serpents and scorpions and over all the power of the enemy (Lk 10:19), refusing defeat. "Through God we will do valiantly, and it is He who shall tread down our adversaries" (Ps 108:13).

JANUARY 19

In these last difficult and evil days, the health of a church will be measured by the caring "one another" Bible based ministry among its members.

SPIRITUAL DISCIPLINES FOR TRAVAILING TIMES

There are biblically mandated spiritual disciplines that must be mastered if one is to prevail in these travailing times. The Father of glory and our Abba in heaven searches for and is pleased with and delights in all who practice them. So practice these biblical disciplines, and not false teachings, and you will also be delivered from self-condemnation, defeat, hopelessness, aimlessness and sense of unworthiness and rejection.

These spiritual disciplines are:

Pursuit of holiness (2 Tim 2:21; Heb 12:4, 14; 1 Pet 2:24)

Proper knowledge and skillful use of Scripture (2 Tim 3:16-17; 2 Cor 17, 4:2; 2 Tim 2:15)

Fear of God (Eccl 12:13; Prov 1:7, 98:13, 9:10; 2 Cor 7:1; 1 Pet 1:17)

Love in deed and truth (1 Jn 3:18; Jn 13:34; 1 Cor 13)

Fellowship with the Holy Spirit (2 Cor 13:14)

Relying on the true (not hyper/modern) grace of God (1 Cor 15:10; Col 2:6; Tit 2:11f)

Fully suited with the armor of God (Eph 6:11-18; 1 Thes 5:8; 2 Cor 6:7)

Devotion to biblical prayer (Col 4:2; Eph 6:18; James 5:16)

Obedience (Eccl 12:13; 1 Sam 15:22; 1 Pet 1:1-2; Heb 5:9; Jn 3:36)

Exaltation of the Lord Jesus Christ (Jn 16:14; Col 1:18-29; 2 Cor 4:5; Phil 1:21, 3:8-11; Acts 4:12, 8:12)

Possessing persecution readiness (1 Pet 4:12-16; Phi 1:29; Rom 8:17; Acts 14:22)

These disciplines are primary. Other spiritual disciplines of the Christian life will fall under these major categories. For example, evangelism would fall under obedience, spiritual gifts under love, worship under the fear of God, sin management and exposing evil under holiness etc. etc.

JANUARY 20

"If we are to better the future we must disturb the present." Catherine Booth

THE LAST MOVE OF GOD

The last move of God will be led by those who pursue the God of heaven, who please Him, proclaim His Gospel, seek His Kingdom and make certain their calling and election (2 Pet 1:10-11). Those who continue to sleep in and follow after the modern politically correct, spiritually corrupt and biblically compromised version of Christianity offered by the god of this world will be in for a rude awakening. They will not be able to stand in the difficult days ahead, having one foot in the world and the other foot in their mouth, denying their Lord by their talk as well as their walk.

To advance this true move of God, more Christian soldiers and bravehearts are needed who aren't in the popularity contest to win friends and influence people, but are compassionate to equip an army to fight the good fight and to win the real war. The professing church needs to return to its first love and to its original spiritual heritage and heed biblical exhortations such as recorded by Jeremiah: "Thus says the LORD, 'Stand by the ways and see and ask for the ancient paths, where the good way is, and walk in it; and you shall find rest for your souls" (Jer 6:16a). The professing church has said: "We will not walk in it" (Jer 6:16b). So apostasy is returning today: "For My people have forgotten Me. They burn incense to worthless gods and they have stumbled from their ways, from the ancient paths, to walk in bypaths, not on a highway, to make their land a desolation, an object of perpetual hissing. Everyone who passes by it will be astonished and shake his head. Like an east wind I will scatter them before the enemy; I will show them My back and not My face, in the day of their calamity" (Jer 18:15-17).

The winds of Eastern religion, Emergent, NewAge and contemplative spirituality are now blowing through the church, causing people to vainly search for the god within while rejecting the God above. And the day of calamity is right at the door. Jesus came to be Lord as well as Savior. Too many are consumed with going within, or concerned about going without, when they should be committed to going on with HIM. The best life now is when the only life is Him. The race will be won by those who make Him number One.

JANUARY 21

The spirit is willing but the flesh is weak. Though God's Spirit is still striving the institutional church is sick.

WE LIVE IN A UNIQUE AND GREAT TIME

Sinners are growing tired of hearing how God hates them. The devil's captives are growing weary of coping with the world. The pew dwellers are leaving main line churches, becoming bored of the weekly entertainment shows and stale pastoral pastries. God seekers are becoming more reluctant to jump on smelly religious band wagons covered with cow chips, wood, hay and straw. The youth are turned off by powerless religion marketed by aimless, careless, clueless and worthless preachers and religious icons. The intellectuals are growing bored and unfulfilled debating theological trivia, while atheists question how fulfilling it is to spend their whole life denying a god they say does not exist.

The old are afraid of dying. The young are afraid of living. Citizens are afraid of aliens. The governed are afraid of governments. Many today are afraid of tomorrow. The devil knows his days are short. Demons are terrified of the new warrior on the scene, the militant Church, which doesn't play church. So now is the time for the Spirit filled, Bible believing, Christ following, God fearing, non compromising militant Church to arise, afraid of nothing, proclaiming the only Good News in bad times, hopeful in everything and purposeful in all things.

JANUARY 22

*The seminaries and church growth experts may have
given us their Authorized Church Version. Unfortunately,
their version is unauthorized according to Jesus,
heaven's authorized and perfect church builder.*

THE CHRISTIAN'S NEW SELF IMAGE

Christians who know who they are in Christ don't have to worry about what they are not in the eyes of the world. They are not bothered by a poor self image, knowing that they are new creatures in Christ, who is the image of God (2 Cor 5:17; Heb 1:3). Their old self is crucified and they walk in newness of life (Rom 6:4-6). As the apostle Paul said: "And such were some of you; but you were washed, but you were sanctified, but you were justified in the name of the Lord Jesus Christ, and in the Spirit of our God" (1 Cor 6:11). The children of God are led by the Spirit of God to think and walk as sons of God, new creatures in Christ, having the mind of Christ (Rom 8:14; 1 Cor 2:16). They take every thought captive to the obedience of Christ and destroy all lies and accusations of the evil one (2 Cor 10:3-4). They are truly dressed for success, fully clothed with divine armor and fully equipped with inspired Scripture to win souls and encourage the saints (Eph 6:11; 2 Tim 3:16-17).

Jesus revealed four distinguishing characteristics of those who walk with Him who is their Life, and magnify their witness of Him who is the Way. These are: unity (Jn 17:21,23), love (Jn 13:35), fruitfulness (Jn 15:8) and continual abiding in His Word (Jn 8:31). All four of these spiritual qualities are produced by the Holy Spirit: unity (Eph 4:3), love (Rom 5:5), fruit (Gal 5:22-23) and abiding in Christ (1 Jn 2:27). No wonder the apostle gave equal importance to the love of God, the grace of the Lord Jesus Christ and the fellowship of the Holy Spirit (2 Cor 13:14). No wonder Jesus many times promised the coming of that divine Helper, the Holy Spirit, the empowering presence of God and the only drink that satisfies.

JANUARY 23

"Satan is so much more in earnest than we are—
he buys up the opportunity while we are wondering
how much it will cost." Amy Carmichael

TRUTH PREPARES FOR THE FUTURE WHICH COUNTS

The kingdom of God often comes near, yet most don't care nor fear. They would rather live in the present rather than prepare for the future. The bad news is that in day of judgment they will regret that they neglected God's Good News, in this day of grace. "For the grace of God has appeared bringing salvation to all men, instructing us to deny ungodliness and worldly desires and to live sensibly, righteously and godly in the present age" (Tit 2:11-12). This same costly grace that brings salvation, also instructs believers in sanctification in which they are set apart and made holy, looking for the blessed hope and the appearing of the glory of our great God and Savior, Christ Jesus (Tit 2:13; 1 Cor 15:10). For He gave Himself for us, that He might redeem us from every lawless deed and purify for Himself a people for His own possession, zealous for good deeds (Tit 2:14).

Yet, most are unwilling to receive Him as Savior and believe and obey Him as Lord so that they may have eternal life (Jn 5:40; 1:12, 3:16, 18, 36; 5:40). They are more concerned with having their "Best Life Now". They delight in lawlessness by living in sin (1 Jn 3:4) and disdain holiness by thinking lightly of repentance. Those who reject the love of the Truth, "Thy Word is Truth", and choose not to obey the Lord who is the Light of the world, (Jn 17:17, 8:12), have their eyes blinded to the Light by Satan, the god of this world. (2 Cor 4:4). For he who rejects the words of the Son who is the Truth, rejects the Father who sent Him and will not be taught by the Spirit of Truth sent by them (1 Jn 2:27; Jn 14:26, 15:26). God gives their minds over to believe what is false, so as to enjoy false peace with their friendly adversary, the devil, the father of lies (Lk 10:10-12; Jn 8:44; Jn 3:18; 2 Thes 2:10-12; 1 Pet 5:8).

JANUARY 24

*It seems that many Christian leaders today are
admired because of how fruity they are, not
by how much spiritual fruit they bear.*

IMPORTANT "I NEED TO'S" FOR THE OVERCOMING CHRISTIAN

The important "I need to's" for the overcoming Christian in these challenging times are:

To spend more time in prayer and in the Word.

To guard the mind for it is the battlefield.

To seek out and fellowship with likeminded believers so as to reduce isolation, disconnection and disunity within the Body.

To consider how to work out one's salvation in the midst of a lost world.

To long for holiness and the laying aside of the sinful stronghold that so easily entangles and is so often ignored (Heb 12:1).

To get in a mindset that anticipates, prepares and will sustain one through upcoming persecution.

To covet and cultivate fellowship with the Holy Spirit, which Scripture emphasizes along with the grace of our Lord Jesus Christ and the love of God (2 Cor 13:14).

To increase in faith by studying of God's Word (Rom 10:17).

To appropriate the promises of God and experience their provisions, by obeying their conditions (2 Pet 1:3-4).

To become more detached from worldly involvement which steals one's time, hinders one's walk and resists one's spiritual advancement.

To beware of deception and false teaching that is pandemic in contemporary Christianity.

Discernment is needed in these last days of widespread religious deception. And discernment comes from hearing and practicing the solid food of sound doctrine (Heb 6:14) and desiring and digging for spiritual treasures hidden in Jesus, in whom are hidden all the treasures of wisdom and knowledge (Prov 2:1-11; Col 2:3).

JANUARY 25

Faith removes mountains, doubt creates them.

If Jesus is the Head of the Church and the Great Healer, why is contemporary Christianity so sick?

Today many elevate personal experience over revealed truth. Many prefer visions and dreams over the written Word of God, ears tickled rather than hearts pierced, pulpiteers rather than prophets, living for self rather than dying to self. Modern day Christianity is plagued with a repentance without change, prayer without faith , faith without works, preaching without passion, teaching without action, conversions without commitment, religion without power, houses of entertainment instead of houses of prayer, demonic deception rather than divine discernment.

Consequently, we see Christians treading in the water up to their neck, rather than walking on the water, crushing Satan under their feet. There needs to be a serious reconsideration of Paul's exhortation: "Do not be deceived, God is not mocked; for whatever a man sows this he will also reap" (Gal 6:7). Soon the devil's game will be over, for the great Judge is coming to declare "Checkmate" to His defeated foe. Until then we have a battle to fight, a race to run, a course to finish and a war to win. Those who know their God will display strength and take action (Dan 11:32). Those who falsely claim to know the Lord will be in for a rude awakening (Mt 7:21-23).

Paul said: "Now those who belong to Christ Jesus have crucified the flesh with its passions and desires" (Gal 5:24). The New Covenant describes Christians as saints who occasionally sin, not as sinners who occasionally confess. Born again, Spirit regenerated believers are new creatures in Christ, the old things passed away; behold, new things have come" (2 Cor 5:17). How can a newly created citizen of heaven continue to live according to the sinful course of this world? (Eph 2:2; Phil 3:20; 1 Pet 2:9-12)? True born again Christians have been delivered from the dominion of Satan, from the domain and authority of darkness, and have been transferred to the kingdom of God's beloved Son (Acts 26:18; Col 1:13). They are in the Kingdom of God business of righteousness, peace and joy achieved by the Holy Spirit but not without a spiritual fight (Mt 6:33, 11:12; Rom 14:17).

After all, our citizenship is in heaven, from which we also eagerly wait for the Savior, the Lord Jesus Christ (Phil 3:20). Our citizenship is not in this world which lies in the power of the evil one (1 Jn 5:19). The Lord doesn't look on His own as sorry duds and dirt clods but as royal priests and living stones (1 Pet 2:5, 9). "For we are His workmanship, created in Christ Jesus for good works, which God prepared beforehand, that we should walk in them" (Eph 2:10). Christians are empowered by the Holy Spirit to build up and BE His Church (Mt 16:18), not to sit in churches built of dead brick and mortar.

JANUARY 26

*The one who is seated above with the great Shepherd should
not be bothered by barking dogs and roaring lions below.*

THE SUPERNATURAL LIFE

The God of heaven illuminates our problems by His presence, bears our burdens by His compassion, comforts us by His promises, guides our steps by His precepts, sustains our hope by His providence and secures our future by His sovereignty. The inept devil and god of this world only darkens, deceives, devours and delights in false religion.

God's Word isn't imprisoned and effective prayer can never be thwarted. His Word never returns void and biblical prayer brings answers. The promises of God are never invalidated, by those who claim them along with their conditions. Those who fear God enjoy His lovingkindness. Those who fellowship with the Holy Spirit enjoy His leading. Those who serve the Lord and Shepherd enjoy His care. Those who practice biblical Christianity, enjoy its unique blessings, privileges and promises.

JANUARY 27

*The best church service is the one which serves, for it is
more blessed to give of one's self than to receive for oneself.*

DOCTRINAL DECEPTION: WHY ARE THOU?

Doctrinal deception is rampant in society because many of God's people have forsaken the truth. Jesus said: "Thy Word is Truth" (Jn 17:17b). Rather than being sanctified by this Truth, most leave it setting on their table collecting dust. Christians not possessing the mind of Christ and not having their minds renewed, taught and empowered by the Spirit, often find their minds becoming spiritual minefields (Rom 12:2; 1 Cor 2:16; Eph 3:16). Vain speculations, unbiblical thoughts and lies from the prince of the power of the air enter such unguarded minds.

Likewise, demonic doctrines become more entrenched in those who do not take seriously this spiritual warfare occurring in the battlefield of the mind. Often the mind is not protected from incoming piercing accusations and destructive lies of the evil one (2 Cor 10:3-5; Mt 16:23; Acts 5:3-4; 2 Cor 2:10-11). Many prefer to wear the hat of popular religion or "effortless" Christianity that accommodates the world, rather than the helmet of salvation that confronts the world (Eph 6:17; Acts 2:36, 40). In many Christian assemblies, many carry a butter knife to slice pastoral pastries, rather than use God's sharp two-edged sword to judge the preaching, as Bereans (Acts 17:11). They fail to sweep clean the mental minefields.

They pursue happiness, not holiness, and prefer to play than pray, to live in sin rather than die to sin (Rom 6:11-12; 1 Pet 2:24; 1 Jn 3:9-10). Though they make frequent trips to the altar, they seldom die on the altar (Rom 12:1).

They proudly stand on whitewashed, sinner-sensitive hyper grace, rather than stand in God's blood-bought sanctifying grace (Tit 2:11; 1 Pet 2:18, 5:12). And instead of running the race set before them, they fall in disgrace before Him. Though they may publically claim Jesus as Savior, they practically deny Him as Lord. (Acts 2:36; 2 Cor 4:5; Rom 10:9; Col 2:6; 1 Pet 3:15). So it was prophesied in these last days: "But the Spirit explicitly says that in later times some will fall away from the faith paying attention to deceitful spirits and doctrines of demons (1 Tim 4:1)...."But evil men and impostors will proceed from bad to worse, deceiving and being deceived" (2 Tim 3:13).

Jesus also warned of this last day deception. When asked by His disciples, "what will be the sign of Your coming, and of the end of the age" (Mt 24:3), Jesus replied: "See to it that no one misleads you" (Mt 24:4). Thus, John later writes, instructs, and warns against deception, sin and unrighteousness: "These things I have written to you concerning those who are trying to deceive you...Little children, let no one deceive you; the one who practices righteousness is righteous, just as He is righteous; the one who practices sin is of the devil " (1 Jn 2:26, 3:7-8a).

JANUARY 28

*Today we have too many private interpretations
and too few powerful proclamations.*

HEAVENLY BRIDEGROOM AND HOLY RECEPTION

Early faithful Christians were not content with merely acquiring knowledge about God. They were committed to intimately knowing God (Phil 3:8; Jn 17:3). They were consumed with advancing the kingdom of God, which is righteousness and peace and joy in the Holy Spirit (Rom 14:17), which often involved spiritual warfare (Mt 12:28). They obediently and properly preached the good news about the kingdom of God and the name of Jesus Christ (Acts 8:12). They preached Jesus as the sinner's only Savior (Acts 4:12) and the believer's only Lord (Col 2:6; Rom 10:9; 1 Pet 3:15), who "will appear a second time for salvation without sin to those who eagerly await Him" (Heb 9:28).

They didn't preach about themselves, but about Christ Himself. Paul said: "we do not preach ourselves but Christ Jesus as Lord" (2 Cor 4:5b). Nor did they preach a distorted gospel offering a salvation to those who saw no need to work out their salvation with fear and trembling (Phil 2:12) and who saw no need for repentance nor any obligation to serve Jesus as Lord.

They didn't know of a repentance which didn't involve changed behavior (Mt 3:8; Acts 26:20; 1 Thess 1:9; Rev 2:5; Eze 14:6), or of a new creation that didn't walk in newness of life (2 Cor 5:17; Rom 6:4).

They didn't preach a gospel without power (1 Cor 2:5; Rom 1:16), or a form of godliness without power (2 Tim 3:5), or a kingdom of God without power (1 Cor 4:20), by those who are powerless and overcome by defilements of the world (2 Pet 2:18-20).

They didn't practice preaching without passion, teaching without action, conversions without transformations, and altar decisions without after devotions.

The early Church which overcame just wouldn't fit it with today's popular church which is overcome; overcome by the sensitive seeker, repentance avoiding and sinner friendly hyper grace. The early church would not feel easy with today's easy believism, prosperity loving and purpose drunken and emergent church. Jesus, heaven's mighty Church builder, is not impressed with many of the world's last day megachuches, mega-dosed on pastoral pastries, prophetic dribble and demonic doctrines, submerged in darkness and deception. Rather, this coming heavenly Bridegroom is looking forward to presenting to Himself the Church in all her glory, having no spot or wrinkle or any such thing and for that holy marriage reception (Eph 5:27).

JANUARY 29

Lordship would not have to be debated if the Lord's command to make disciples was obeyed.

A NEW SONG FOR A NEW DAY

"This is the day which the LORD has made; let us rejoice and be glad in it" (Ps 118:24). "The LORD has established His throne in the heavens, and His sovereignty rules over all" (Ps 103:19). "God reigns over the nations, God sits on His holy throne" (Ps 47:8). When we feel like we are falling into a pit of destruction, we can rest assured that He has set our feet on the Solid Rock, the sure foundation of His true Church (Ps 40:2; Mt 16:15-18; Eph 2:20). Though the God of heaven is shaking all the nations, His holy nation receives a kingdom which will never be shaken (Heb 12:28; 1 Pet 2:9). "For the kingdom of God is righteousness, peace and joy in the Holy Spirit" (Rom 14:17). The LORD puts a new song in our mouth, a song of praise to our God; many will see and fear and will trust in the LORD (Ps 40:3).

We sing a new song because we belong to and serve Him who sits on the throne who is already making all things new (Rev 21:5). Those who are have received the new birth and overcome will receive a new name and enter His new kingdom (Jn 3:3, 5; Rev 2:17). Being in Christ we are a "new creature; the old things passed away; behold, new things have come" (2 Cor 5:17). God says: "Do not call to mind the former things, or ponder things of the past. Behold, I will do something new, now it will spring forth; Will you not be aware of it? I will even make a roadway in the wilderness, rivers in the desert" (Is 43:18-19).

We will receive a new inheritance which is imperishable and undefiled and will not fade away, reserved in heaven for us (1 Pet 1:4) who have not stored up treasures on earth, where moth and rust destroy, and where thieves break in and steal (Mt 6:19). We possess a new mind, the mind of Christ, in whom are hidden all the treasures of wisdom and knowledge (1 Cor 2:16; Col 2:3). We have a new citizenship in heaven (Phil 3:20) because we are aliens and strangers to this world (1 Pet 2:11). We are adopted into the new family as children of Abba, our heavenly Father (Rom 8:14-16), no longer children of the devil and father of lies, in bondage to sin and carrying out his desires (1 Jn 3:10; Jn 8:44; 2 Tim 2:26).

God has given us a new spirit of power and love and discipline, re-placing the spirit of timidity and fear (2 Tim 1:7; Heb 2:14-15). Being united with the risen Christ, we walk in newness of life, no longer walk-ing according to the course of this world which lies in the sphere of the evil one (Rom 6:4; Eph 2:2; 1 Jn 5:19). We are blessed by the New Covenant of God that secures our eternal redemption and inheritance. Our conscience is cleansed from former dead works of religion to serve and enjoy a new relationship with God (Heb 8; 9:12-15). We possess new hope, the anchor of the soul, a hope both sure and steadfast which enters the very presence of God in heaven (Heb 6:19-20), no longer hopeless and without God in the world (Eph 2:12). So we sing a new song for a new day.

JANUARY 30

"The man whose little sermon is 'repent' sets himself against his age, and will for the time being be battered mercilessly by the age whose moral tone he challenges. There is but one end for such a man—'off with his head!' You had better not try to preach repentance until you have pledged your head to heaven." Joseph Parker

NO NEED TO WAIT FOR REVIVAL, WHEN REPENTANCE IS FOR NOW

Those affected by church scheduled revivals usually return to their old ways; whereas those affected by true repentance move toward His new way. Revivals may remove sin temporarily, repentance removes sins permanently. The Holy Spirit is hopefully present at revivals; He is powerfully present in repentance. Personal revival will follow true repentance, but lasting repentance will not follow one seeking only revival. Repentance requires death to the old self; revival often settles for a mere beating of the old self. The battered self always recovers and life goes on as it was. In repentance, the old self is buried and the life of Jesus lives on anew. While revivals can make one happy, repentance will make one holy. Isn't it time we start praying for the real thing and stop playing the church game?

JANUARY 31

*Some are too quick to judge because they don't take
the time to discern. They love being right more
than they love the commandment to love.*

HAD ENOUGH YET?

Have you had enough of the Best Life Busts, Purpose Drunken Placebos, Prosperity Promises, Contemplative Confusion, Harlem Shakes and Sinner-friendly Hyper-Grace? They leave you in disgrace, aimless, and poverty stricken, holding a bag of bounced prosperity checks. Are you tired of ear scratching sermonetts that leave you crying in your bassinet for another bottle of stale milk and crusty pastoral pastry and barely able to crawl from the pew to the almighty altar for you weakly confession?

The Master and Captain of your soul is looking for brave-hearted soldiers who will pause long enough to contemplate His cause; who will run long enough to finish the course; and who will fight long enough to win the war. He is looking for mighty man and women of valor who understand the times, who will redeem their time and give their adversary the devil no time.

The LORD of Hosts is looking for those willing to pray, not wishing to play; who will fight the good fight, heeding the holy call, not running away in flight ignoring His call. He is looking for committed disciples who will follow Him, becoming fishers of men rather than following after every whim and sinking in sin. Though the institutional church may sleep on through the darkness of night, we will march on through in the light of day in Holy Spirit might.

Christians are to run toward the spiritual enemies of God who have invaded His land not run away in fear of them. Prevail, not wail. We are not grasshoppers, but demon stompers. God has our back so we can go forward, having put on the breastplate of righteousness and the rest of the armor of God. The devil only flees when resisted.

FEBRUARY 1

The quicker we can get done with lip service at the altar,
self-service behind the pulpit and no service in the pew, the
quicker we can get on with the Lord's business in our life.

THE SON HAS RISEN TO DISPEL THE DARKNESS

GOOD MORNING AMERICA, THE SON HAS RISEN: "The people who were sitting in darkness saw a great light, and those who were sitting in the land and shadow of death, upon them a Light dawned." From that time Jesus began to preach and say, 'Repent for the kingdom of heaven is at hand" (Mt 4:15-17). Radical Christianity like this may help bring release to the captives, restore life to a dead contemporary churchianity and morality to a postmodern depraved culture. Jesus would say: "Unbind him, and let him go" (Jn 11:44). Jesus is in the business of raising those dead in sin, giving them new life, unbinding them of the wrappings of sin and freeing them to go and tell and demonstrate the Good News.

The Good News is that we can be clothed with His righteousness and walk in freedom and holiness (Rom 13:14; 2 Tim 1:9; 1 Pet 1:15-16). Don't let the religious naysayers keep you bound up in sin and entangled with the world. The thief from below comes to steal your heavenly blessings, to kill your joy and to destroy your soul (Jn 10:10a). Don't let his foot inside the door and his demons in your house or you may find yourself hiding in the closet sitting in darkness. Keep the Light shining and the door shut to the evil solicitors of your soul.

FEBRUARY 2

The devil is a master at getting his non-resisters
attracted to his world, addicted to its idols, inspired
by his role models, accustomed to mediocrity,
and alienated from true spirituality.

Take care what you listen to, for the devil is the prince of the power of the air. The airwaves are filled with his devilish noise which many take for music, his demonic doctrines which many receive as truth, and his distorted gospels which many understand as being politically correct, culturally relevant and spiritually superior. Whether it comes from the stage or from the pulpit, it may sound nice to the ears but is damaging to the heart. It may be desirous to the flesh, but is destructive to the soul.

Beware of strange winds and demonic doctrines that are blowing through the church house (Eph 2:2, 4:14; 1 Tim 4:1). These winds come not from above, but from below, blowing wisdom that is earthly, natural and demonic. They breed jealousy, selfish ambition, disorder and every evil thing (Jam 3:14-16). However, the wisdom from above is "first pure, then peaceable, gentle, reasonable, full of mercy and good fruits, unwavering, without hypocrisy" (Jam 3:17).

Unfortunately, in much of contemporary Christianity, what is preferred is experience over exposition, personal opinion over eternal truth, what is in style rather than what is inspired, what tickles ears rather than what pierces the heart and entertainment over equipping (2 Tim 4:3; 3:16-17). Thus many fail to discern the direction of the winds and end up being tossed about by every wind of doctrine (Eph 4:14), originating from wayward preachers, preaching hot air into itching ears rather than solid truth into convicted hearts.

Don't allow strangers in the pulpits and strange fire in the sanctuary. Or else you may get burned from fire below, instead of being baptized with the fire from above. Be on fire with Him wherever you go. Let your lamp will be filled with Holy Oil and you will shine brightly. Demons will flee in torment when the Jesus the King sits on the throne; when you sanctify Christ as Lord in your heart (1 Pet 3:15). Put on His helmet of salvation and you will guard your mind from demonic invasion (2 Cor 10:3-5).

Remember the devil is a liar and is defeated. He only prevails when we lay down our armor and run. His demons can invade the minds with strange doctrines, paranoia thoughts, demeaning accusations, and other novel ideas, even religious ones, contrary to the ways and words of God (2 Cor 10:3-5). Citizens of heaven should never let the god of this world get his foot in the door. Give him a foothold and he plants in you a stronghold.

FEBRUARY 3

*He who has ears to hear truth will hear from the
God of heaven, but he who has ears only to be tickled
will surely hear from the god of this world.*

May there be a day this week when you can be the Church, where two or three are gathered in Jesus' name (Mt 18:20), so that He may be present. And may we consider how to stimulate one another to love and good deeds (Heb 10:24), rather than to assembly in the name of some celebrity or to promote a denomination, or flaunt our good works, which only brings glory to man (Jn 5:44). We are to gather to celebrate His name, the only name given under heaven by which we must be saved (Acts 4:12).

For He declared Himself to be "I am" (Jn 8:24, 58) and the Son of God, making Him equal with God (Jn 5:18, 10:33). For in Him all the fullness of Deity dwells in bodily form (Col 2:9). He is the radiance of God's glory and the exact representation of His nature (Heb 1:3). He life and work has fully explained God (Jn 1:18). He said: "He who has seen me has seen the Father (Jn 14:9). Calling Himself the Son of God, was admission to being God (Jn 5:18). So, He was either liar, lunatic or the LORD. Let's quitting beating around the bush, being ashamed of His name but proclaim it (Acts 8:12; Col 1:28). Let's stop running from His presence, but kneel before the Burning Bush and Tree of Life and get baptized with His Holy Spirit and fire (Jn 3:11).

FEBRUARY 4

*Too many contemporary Christians have left their
first love, Him who first loved them, to love the world
which hates them. Now how smart it that?*

MIGHTY SOLDIERS OF VALOR OR LITTLE BABES IN THE PARLOR?

Mighty Christians of valor are hard to find in these last days of easy believism, modern hyper grace and "effortless" Christianity. Too many remain sleeping in bed with the world, covered up with their false security blankets. Instead of being equipped for service and fed sound doctrine (Eph 4:11; 2 Tim 3:15-16; 1 Tim 4:6), too many are ensnared by contemporary Christianity, sucking their thumbs and waiting to be cuddled and bottle fed with milky sermons and spoon fed with pastoral pastries. Only until they quit playing with their idols and crying for things and begin to hunger for God and His word and cry out in repentance will they escape the coming refining fires.

But they can experience His kingdom, which is righteousness, peace and joy in the Holy Spirit (Rom 14:17) when they wake up, rise up, grow up, and run the race set before them, with self-discipline and endurance (1 Cor 9:24-27; Heb 12:1). Only until their dirty religious diapers are changed through repentance and they put on the Lord Jesus Christ in obedience and put on full armor of God completely (Rom 13:14; Eph 6:11-18), will they begin to walk as the new creatures they are in Christ, boldly (2 Cor 5:17; Acts 13:46). Then they will become the mighty men and women of valor for the King as they ought, victoriously (1 Chron 12:21, 22 , 38; 2 Tim 2:3-4).

FEBRUARY 5

We are saved by responding to the God's prevenient grace,
and we are sanctified by relying God's on perfecting grace.

WHAT IS IT WITH THE SUPER APOSTLES AND
ANOINTINGS; SUPER PROPHETS AND MANTLES?

Nearly two thousand years ago, through Christ Jesus our Lord, His disciples "received grace and apostleship to bring about the obedience of faith among all the Gentiles for His name's sake" (Rom 1:5). Jesus authorized, commanded and commissioned them saying: "Go ye therefore, and teach all nations, baptizing them in the name of the Father, and of the Son, and of the Holy Ghost; teaching them to observe all things whatsoever I have commanded you: and lo, I am with you always, even unto the end of the age" (Mt 28:19-20). They would not lack anything since Jesus would send His Spirit to baptize, indwell and empower them to be witnesses and martyrs. Then they could die to self and become living sacrifices for Him (Acts 1:8; Rom 12:1; 2 Cor 4:10-11).

They would be given everything needed for their job in seeking and proclaiming the kingdom and the Gospel of God. After all, they had been blessed with every spiritual blessing in the heavenly places in Christ (Eph 1:3). Believers have been made complete in Christ (Col 2:10); have been granted God's precious and magnificent promises to escape the world's corruption and to become partakers of divine nature (2 Pet 1:4). They are adequate and equipped for every good work having been entrusted with the inspired Scripture (2 Tim 3:16-17). They would be empowered to live for Christ and be taught to abide in Him by the

Holy Spirit of truth (Rom 8:11; Lk 24:49; Acts 1:8; Eph 3:16; Jn 15:26; 1 Jn 2:27).

Having received the anointing of the Holy Spirit they would not need anointings of men (1 Jn 2:20). Having been baptized and clothed with Christ, the Righteous One, they would not need to seek baptisms and mantles from religious ones. And in case anyone may still question God's full provision, the apostle Paul reminded the believers: "He who did not spare His own Son, but delivered Him over for us all, how will He not also with Him freely give us all things?" (Rom 8:32). So what is lacking now is not that believers are lacking, but they are slacking.

FEBRUARY 6

Many Christians hate God's true grace being expounded
because it exposes the sins which so many love to embrace.

THE TRUE PROSPERITY GOSPEL WON'T ROB YOU BLIND

Christians alone are privileged to be blessed with every spiritual blessing in Christ (Eph 1:3), are created as new creatures in Christ (2 Cor 5:17), are made complete in Him (Col 2:10), in whom are hidden all the treasures of wisdom and knowledge (Col 2:3), and are blessed to be empowered by the Spirit of God (Acts 1:8, Eph 3:16). We have been granted everything needed pertaining to life and godliness, as well as God's precious and magnificent promises (2 Pet 1:3-4).

His inspired Scripture makes each one adequate and equipped for every good work (2 Tim 3:16-17). We possess all divine authority needed to proclaim the gospel, to set captives free and to make disciples (Mt 28:18-20; Lk 9:1, 10:1,17; Acts 8:6-7, 12-13). We have given the full armor of God for spiritual victory (Eph 6:11-18). Even the glory which the Father gave to Jesus, He has given His own (Jn 17:22a). We are seated in the heavenlies with Christ as citizens of heaven, awaiting His return to receive immortal and glorified bodies to spend eternity with the true God (Phil 3:20; 1 Cor 15:51f). These are just a few of the unfathomable riches of Christ for those who are in Christ, who have received and believed the true Prosperity Gospel.

FEBRUARY 7

To depart from the inspired word of God is to
commit the highest treason against heaven and to
display the most depraved reason on earth.

CHRISTIANITY IS FOR LOSERS

Christian haters love to say: "Christianity is for losers." Of course Christianity is for losers, those who have forsaken earthy trinkets in order to gain heavenly treasures, as poor yet making many rich, as having nothing yet possessing all things (2 Cor 6:10). True Christianity is practiced by those who acknowledge they are dead in sin and lost without Him, yet are now overcomers in Him and will be winners in the end. The apostle Paul who said "I am a nobody (2 Cor 12:11) and "it is no longer I who live" (Gal 2:20), also said: "I can do all things through Him who strengthens me" (Phil 4:13). He counted it all joy to lose the temporal in order to gain the eternal: "I count all things to be loss in view of the surpassing value of knowing Christ Jesus my Lord, for whom I have suffered the loss of all things, and count them but rubbish, so that I may gain Christ" (Phil 3:8).

The Lord's winners and those exalted by Him are those possessing true humility and those dead to self. Or to say it another way, true humility is demonstrated when God is given 100 percent credit for the work "we" do. Our "work" in working out our salvation is really our willingness to allow God to "work in us, both to will and to work for His good pleasure (Phil 2:13). After all, we have been crucified with Christ; and it is no longer we who live, but Christ who lives in us (Gal 2:20). He who is most crucified with Christ is the least likely to rise up in pride and fall down in disgrace. Such a one chooses rather to stand in His grace (Rom 5:2; 1 Pet 5:12).

FEBRUARY 8

Bless Him for all as well as for the awful.

Our calling is sure, our trumpet is loud, our message is clear and our mission is biblical. It is not to win friends and influence people, but to encourage the saints and win the war. Our colors are bold. They are not gay, but glorious: Red, White and Blue and more importantly, Purple, the color of royalty, Our King (Mk 15:17).

Christians should labor with all who are committed to first things first: obeying Jesus' commands, making disciples, pursuing holiness, devoted to prayer, resisting the devil, preaching the true Gospel, and loving in deed and truth. There isn't time to get entangled with those who get bent out of shape over what doesn't matter or who twist out of recognition what is truth or who fight over religious issues which aren't essential.

They will fight the good fight with all believers who reign as citizens of heaven, raised up with the Lord Jesus Christ, flying as eagles. They will not run about in the world like chickens with ruffled feathers. Together they resist the roaring lion so he will flee, serving the Reigning Lion who conquers; rather than running away like scared dogs, from the devil who devours. They will advance the kingdom of God as good soldiers by not being entangled in the affairs of everyday life. They will overwhelmingly conquer with all who are Bravehearts, who are Christ-minded and have a backbone, leaving behind the timid souls, carnal minded and those clutching to a wishbone.

FEBRUARY 9

How is it that we often give God second or third place in our hearts and life, when He holds first place in the universe? He who holds all things together, can't He help us keep it together?

Surely we, as Christians and citizens of heaven, are aliens and strangers to this world which is becoming more wicked by the day and the world's religious are becoming more deceived by the hour and its wicked more depraved by the moment. But praise God of heaven who is in control every second. God is sovereign over all. For it is written: "The LORD has established His throne in the heavens; and His sovereignty rules over all" (Ps 103:19). Therefore we can rest assured that God "is able to do exceeding abundantly beyond all that we ask or think, according to the power that works within us" (Eph 3:20). We are strengthened with power through His Spirit in the inner man (Eph 3:16).

We can be assured that "God causes all things to work together for good to those who love God, to those who are called according to His purpose" (Rom 8:28), even in the midst of suffering and trials when living for God. The apostle Paul conveyed such confidence saying: "For this reason I also suffer these things, but I am not ashamed; for I know whom I have believed and I am convinced that He is able to guard what I have entrusted to Him until that day" (2 Tim 1:12). By the presence, power and ministry of the Holy Spirit we can guard the spiritual blessings in Christ which have been entrusted to us (2 Tim 1:14).

These blessings are many, consisting of the gospel, spiritual gifts, the grace of God, and our holy calling and mission and much more. And to make our mission easier and successful during our temporary stay on earth, God has sent the promised Holy Spirit to indwell His own, transforming them into holy and royal priests in His Church and overcomers in the world, for greater is the Spirit who is in us that the evil one who is in the world (1 Pet 2:5, 9; 1 Jn 4:4). The Holy Spirit brings glory to Christ who lives in us when the character of Christ is produced in us and when we possess the mind of Christ (Jn 16:14; 2 Cor 3:3; Gal 4:19; 1 Cor 2:16).

FEBRUARY 10

What the Holy One calls the Christian to do, He will carry him through. But what the religious one commands another to do, will likely do him in.

In these last days evil men and impostors will proceed from bad to worse, deceiving and being deceived (2 Tim 3:13). We see the broad way filled with the wicked as well as with the religious, Christian in name only, worshiping a god of their own making, living a life of their own choosing, believing a gospel of their own imagination, and enjoying it to their own damnation. They are energized by the evil prince of the power of the air, the devil (Eph 2:2), being ensnared and held captive by him to do his will (2 Tim 2:26). They are ever opposing the truth, never coming to their senses and to true repentance by God's grace (2 Tim 2:25). Instead, they choose to live in sin, not cleansed by the blood of redeeming grace, but whitewashed by a novel and an unbiblical sinner-friendly hyper-grace. Instead of running the race to win, before witnesses in heaven, they choose to live in disgrace, lives full of leaven.

On the contrary, the Bible speaks of the true saving and sanctifying grace: "The grace of God has appeared bring salvation to all men, instructing us to deny ungodliness and worldly desires and to live sensibly and righteously and godly in the present age" (Tit 2:11-12). On the day of Pentecost, Peter kept on exhorting in his sermon: "be saved from this perverse generation" (Act 2:40). How can one be holy in a perverse generation without the sustaining, purifying grace of God and the Spirit of God? How can one be spiritually taught about Jesus, full of grace and truth (Jn 1:14) without the Spirit of truth? How can one be helped and empowered for service without the Divine Helper? How can one cast out evil spirits without the Holy Spirit? Ask the typical modern day pastor and he will say: I never heard of such a Spirit. And we wonder why the world has turned the professing contemporary church upside down. Much of the Americanized man-built church has become purposed drunken, entertainment addicted, and sin enslaved. Whereas, the true Church Jesus is building is Spirit led, Scripture fed, supernaturally equipped and free.

FEBRUARY 11

*The most effective way to mortify sin in our life is to
hate it. And the more we understand its harmful and
enslaving effects on us, the more we will hate it.*

NEW LIFE SPELLS ACTION NOT BOREDOM

Spiritual ACTION, not religious ACTING, is the certain and expected fruit evidencing the spiritual resurrection life of truly born again, new creatures and children of God. Such ones exercise an active and overcoming faith in the living God, laying hold of the living hope set before them (1 Thess 1:3; Heb 6:18). With spiritual action we grow in true grace, not wallow in hyper-grace. We fight the good fight of faith, not frolic around in an "effortless" Christianity. We make time to pray, not waste time in play. We run the race to win heaven's prize, not run a contest to win man's praise. Who says being spiritual is boring?

As long as preachers are obsessed with counting noses and nickels, wearing the cross instead of bearing the cross, in securing decisions rather than in making disciples, inviting sinners to merely pray at the altar, rather than to die on the altar, the religious game will only continue on. The religious circus wagons will continue to roll in and the roaring lion will continue to roam about. Demons will continue being entertained and their pulpit thieves will leave their sheep without (Jn 10:10a; 2 Pet 2:19). Fortunately, the Lord's faithful remnant will not indulge nor be deceived by such nonsense in this late hour, but will wisely possess the mind of Christ and proclaim His gospel in demonstration of the Spirit and of power.

FEBRUARY 12

The sun is more appreciated when its effects are
more clearly seen. Likewise, the Son is more
adored when His graces are more explored.

Church doors are being opened wide to the devil and his demons to
come in and party with the sheep in all denominations. The deceiver
loves to buddy up with all pastors who refuse to worship God in spirit and
truth; who give mere lip service to the Lordship of Jesus; who are bankrupt
in holiness, and in bed with the world. The devil knows he can advance his
kingdom of darkness with clergy who desire to make a name, rather exalt
His Name, who are purpose driven to do their thing, rather than Spirit led
to advance God's kingdom.

Such ones minimize prayer and forsake discipleship and are more interested in the best life now than in the eternal hereafter. Many exchange the
unfathomable riches of Christ for a damnable worldly prosperity. Discerning
Christians will exit such doors and attend a God fearing assembly if they
can find one. Until then they will continue BEING the church, proclaiming Jesus who is the Door and giving the devil his due. The devil hates such
Christians who are sold out to do God's business, God's way with God's
power, having Jesus as their model, the Bible as their guide and the Holy
Spirit as their Teacher.

Those committed to BEING the Church do not seek Jesus for what He
can offer, but serve Him for what He has done. They do not labor for that
which is temporary nor fix their hope on the uncertainty of riches, but on
God who richly supplies all things (1 Tim 6:17). Jesus said: "Do not work

for food which perishes, but for the food which endures to eternal life". He said earlier: "My food is to do the will of Him who sent Me and to accomplish His work" (Jn 4:34). Such heavenly food is necessary for those who labor in God's vineyard and endure to inherit eternal life. The hyper grace dieters prefer to "practice" their "effortless" Christianity in the world as they dine on pastoral pastries and fast food religion instead of being nourished on the Living Mana from heaven and sound doctrine.

FEBRUARY 13

Wielding the Sword of God by the power of the Spirit is Satan's greatest fear and praying the Word of God in the Spirit is Satan's greatest nightmare.

Don't be intimated, controlled, deceived nor taken captive by lustful shepherds, lying prophets, flesh anointed apostles, liberal theologians, lukewarm churches nor luring church growth practices. Every Spirit-filled, Jesus following, Bible nourished, God worshiping Christian is a holy and royal high priest and commissioned soldier and sent ambassador of the King of kings and Lord of lords (1 Pet 2:5,9; 2 Cor 5:20; 2 Tim 2:3). Every child of God has received all authority, possesses the greatest power, has been divinely anointed and totally equipped to go and proclaim the Good News, in demonstration of the Spirit and of power (Mt 28:18-20; 1 Cor 2:4). Every child of God and citizen of heaven has been given the keys of heaven to unlock worldly prison doors and liberate Satan's captives, as the Lord continues building His Church, His Temple of living stones (Phil 3:20; Mt 16:18-19; 1 Pet 2:5).

Christians are not to be secret agents, but bold ambassadors. They should stand out as a peculiar people, as strangers and aliens to this fallen world (1 Pet 2:11; Rom 12:1). For "those who belong to Christ Jesus have crucified the flesh with its passions and desires" (Gal 5:24). Jesus said: "So then, you will know them by their fruits" (Mt 7:20). "For whoever does the will of My Father who is in heaven, he is My brother and sister and mother" (Mt 12:50). If Jesus was present today cleansing the Temple, He would perform a great "down sizing", as He did before. "For the gate is small and the way is narrow that leads to life, and there are few who find it" (Mt 7:14). One must consider what god it is that is attracting the religious masses today.

FEBRUARY 14

*Because of their greed for the dollar sign they give no heed
to the warning signs. Because there is no fear of God in
their heart there is no fruit of godliness in their walk.*

50 SHADES OF ABOMINATION

You exist for such a time as this: when the devil devours, demons deceive, sinners mock and the church hides. It is time for true Christ followers to stand up, come out and "call a spade a spade" and not keep their heads buried in the sand. Otherwise, we will see an increasing flood of political correctness promoting corruption, spiritual corruption condoning compromise and unjust judges authorizing lawless government and immoral laws. Today's pagan Christian culture is diseased with the plagues of prosperity preaching, Scripture peddling, purpose drunken madness, contemplative confusion, sinner-friendly hyper-grace, power-less religion, fruitless repentance and false conversions. While biblical Christianity of old was the pillar and support of the truth, the light to the world (2 Tim 3:15; Eph 5:8; Mt 5:14), modern compromising Christianity could aptly be called "Fifty shades of abomination". The enemies of God continue to rejoice when repentance and holiness is replaced by sinner-friendly hyper grace, workless faith, and an "effortless" Christianity. While Jesus stands outside knocking on the church door, the devil is in-vited in with open arms.

The overcoming Christian soldier will not be entangled with the af-fairs of this world but will engage the enemy of this world (2 Tim 2:4). The kingdom seeking saint will fight the good fight, not sit on cushioned chairs. He follows the Great Shepherd and is not led astray by devilish shepherds (Jn 10:14, 27). He will keep the faith, not give up the hope; persevere to the end, rather than let the devil do him in. He is empow-ered by the Spirit of God, instructed by the Word of God, advancing the Kingdom of God, because he possesses a healthy fear of God. Thus, he is an overcomer, not overcome; a bright light piercing the darkness, not a flickering lamp losing its oil; a fruit-bearing branch of the True Vine, not a dry and fruitless twig cast away; salt that has not lost its flavor and a true saint serving his Savior.

FEBRUARY 15

*The discipline of reverently praying the Lord's Prayer,
totally relying on the Spirit's power and faithfully
claiming the Father's promises are three strikes that will
put the devil back in the dugout where he belongs.*

Christian soldiers and bearers of the cross do not behave as secret agents of the Kingdom but as bold soldiers and ambassadors, commissioned and sent out by the King (Mt 28:19; 2 Tim 1:7, 2:3-4; 2 Cor 5:20). They are not double agents used by the devil to sit on the religious fence trying to serve two masters in a conformist Christianity. No. They are called to be single minded and Christ-minded special agents and supernatural forces of God serving their true Master (Rom 8:14; 1 Pet 3:15; 2 Cor 4:5). Empowered by the Spirit of God (Acts 1:8, 8:13; Gal 5:16; Eph 3:16), they walk in the works which God prepared beforehand (Eph 2:10) and do the miracles Jesus prophesied before His ascension (Jn 14:12).

This walking in newness of a supernatural life is done not by the man's might or power, but by the Holy Spirit whom Jesus sent (Zech 4:6; Jn 16:7; Rom 6:4). The greatest miracle is seeing sinners dead in trespasses and sin being made alive in Christ (Jn 3:3, 5; Eph 2:1-5), former captives and servants of the devil becoming slaves of God and righteousness (2 Tim 2:25-26; Rom 6:18, 22), those ransomed and delivered saints becoming disciples, pursuing holiness and remaining holy in a wicked world (Mt 28:19; Col 1:28-29; Matt 6:33; Jam 1:27; 2 Cor 6:14-18; Heb 10:10).

FEBRUARY 16

"Are the things you're living for, worth Christ dying for?" Leonard Ravenhill's epitaph

WE ARE LIVING ON BORROWED TIME, LOANED FROM GOD

We all live on borrowed time; time to use, not abuse; time to ponder, not squander; time to reap, not sleep. Time is short and we need to do as much as we can, as quick as we can, to all that we can, while we can. As the apostle Paul said, "Awake sleeper, arise from the dead…walk as wise men, making the most of your time, because the days are evil" (Eph 4:14a, 5:16). Paul again said: "Therefore, be careful how you walk, not as unwise men, but as wise, making the most of your time, because the days are evil" (Eph 5:15-16).

"Teach us to number our days, that we may present to You a heart of wisdom" (Ps 90:12). Teach us to cleanse our minds of deception so that we can present to You the mind of Christ. Empower us to lay aside the deeds of darkness so we may be offered to You as living and holy sacrifices. Purge our prayers of demonic intrusion so our prayers may ascend to Your throne and their answers bring them confusion. Life is like a grain of sand in an eternal hour glass. Make the most of your time while you have the time, for one day you will slip into eternity with no clock to watch but only a Savior to address, and then hopefully, the true God forever to worship.

FEBRUARY 17

Saving souls and making disciples is not mutually exclusive but totally inclusive. A saved soul who isn't discipled is a happy meal ready to be eaten by the roaring lion.

WEARINESS OF HEART DOESN'T DISCOURAGE BRAVEHEARTS.

Weariness of heart and soul comes with the calling as a true servant, saint, prophet and soldier of God. "Yet those who wait for the LORD and will gain new strength. They will mount up with wings like eagles, they will run and not get tired, they will walk and not become weary" (Is 40:31). "For by You I can run upon a troop; and by my God I can leap over a wall" (Ps 18:30). King David was convinced that foreigners and enemies who opposed him would "fade away, and come trembling out of their fortresses" (Ps 18:45). The prophet Micah said: "I will watch expectantly for the LORD; I will wait for the God of my salvation. My God will hear me. Do not rejoice over me, O my enemy. Though I fall I will rise; though I dwell in darkness, the LORD is a light for me" (Micah 7:7-8).

The apostle Paul also was confident, even during difficult times, that his Lord would deliver him. He said: "The Lord will deliver me from every evil deed, and will bring me safely to His heavenly kingdom; to Him be the glory forever and ever. Amen" (2 Tim 4:18). For the resurrected Christ, the Light, and Holy Spirit, the Oil, forever indwells our person and enlightens our path. We are lifted up to soar as eagles over the battlefield, with the enemy crushed under our feet, while we sit seated in the heavenlies. When we have to engage the spiritual enemy in hand to hand combat, we do so with the sword, "the word of truth, in the power of God and by the weapons of righteousness for the right hand and the left and the full armor of God (2 Cor 6:7; Eph 6:10-18).

Don't let the prince of darkness and roaring lion have you for lunch on the battlefield as his undeserved meal. Instead, hand him his deserved reward: a rebuking in the name of the Lord. And in the power of the Spirit of God, with the authority of the Son of God, and by the Sword, the Word of God, resist this enemy of God. Destroy his plague of lies, expose his crafty deceptions, extinguish his paralyzing threats and spring his ensnaring traps.

FEBRUARY 18

It is not play time, bed time or night time for the
overcoming Christian. But rather, it is high time to
engage our enemies: the world, the flesh and the devil;
to be sober minded and spiritually alert; to walk in the
light of Christ exposing the unfruitful deeds of darkness.

The sooner the Church gets to stepping out the sooner the Lord will begin stomping out. The sooner the Church gets to trotting, the sooner God will get to treading. The sooner God's people begin "looking for and hastening the coming of the day of God", the sooner the King of kings and Lord of lords will return and show all who is Boss. The sooner the reigning Lion of Judah returns, the quicker the roaring lion will be put in his cage. "Through God we will do valiantly, and it is He who shall tread down our adversaries" (Ps 108:13). "Work out your salvation with fear and trembling; for it is God who is at work in you, both to will and to work for His good pleasure" (Phil 2:12b-13). "For we are His workmanship created in Christ Jesus for good works which God prepared beforehand so that we would walk in them" (Eph 2:10).

How amazing it is that the sovereign God of the universe has chosen to work through finite creatures to accomplish His mighty purposes. He has given each believer who is now a new creation in Christ a certain calling and purpose in life and fully equips each one to carry out that purpose. And such is accomplished not by our strength but by His power, not by our expertise but by His grace, and not so much by our ability but by our availability (Zech 4:6; Phil 4:13). "For consider your calling, brethren, that there were not many wise according to the flesh, not many mighty, not many noble; but God has chosen the foolish things of the world to shame the wise, and God has chosen the weak things of the world to shame the things which are strong, and the base things of the world and the despised, God has chosen, the things that are not, that He might nullify the things that are, that no man should boast before God" (1 Cor 1:26-29). "And such confidence we have through Christ toward God. Not that we are adequate in ourselves to consider anything as coming from ourselves, but our adequacy is from God" (2 Cor 3:4-5).

"For thus says the high and exalted One who lives forever, whose name is Holy, 'I dwell on a high and holy place, and also with the contrite and lowly of spirit in order to revive the spirit of the lowly and to revive the heart of the contrite" (Is 57:15). It is God's mighty grace that makes all this possible. Just as we were saved by His grace so we must walk in His grace (Col 2:6). We must not receive it in vain: "And working together with Him, we urge you not to receive the grace of God in vain" (2 Cor 6:1). Remember, those who "receive the abundance of grace AND of the gift of righteousness will reign in life through the One, Jesus Christ" (Rom 5:17). Those who do not may find themselves ruined in this life. But praise the Lord that His grace labors within us and instructs us. As Paul confessed: "But by the grace of God I am what I am, and His grace toward me did not prove vain; but I labored even more than all of them, yet not I, but the grace of God with me" (1 Cor 15:10). "For the grace of God has appeared, bring salvation to all men, instructing us to deny ungodliness and worldly desires and to live sensibly, righteously and godly in the present age" (Tit 2:11-12). "Who is wise? Let him give heed to these things, and consider the lovingkindnesses of the LORD" (Ps 107:43). "A good understanding have all those who do His commandments" (Ps 111:10).

FEBRUARY 19

*Beware of common altars that give false assurance to false
confessors; altars that accept remorse over repentance,
where many bend the knee but never amend their soul,
where many may knell at the altar, but often don't die on
the altar, they come as they are and leave as they were.*

MOUNTAINS OR MOLE HILLS?

Sometimes we come upon mountains of temporary difficulties so God can bless us with present victories and eternal rewards, "for momentary, light affliction is producing for us an eternal weight of glory far beyond all comparison" (2 Cor 4:17). We are to assail them in faith as if they were mole hills. God can and will carry you through mountains, because He is the Lord and sustainer of heaven and earth (Col 1:17; Heb 1:3). He says: "I will make all My mountains a road, and My highways will be raised up" (Is 49:11).

The devil prefers that we see in life formidable mountains and challenging road blocks. However the overcoming, Spirit-filled, prayed up, Jesus following, Bible nourished, God worshiping, Jesus following believer does not see obstacles but opportunities. "The path of the upright is a highway" (Prov 15:19b), and "by my God I can leap over a wall" (Ps 18:29b). They march on forward carrying heavens' victory banner as co-workers with God (2 Cor 6:1), co-laborers with the Son (Mt 9:37-38) and co-intercessors with the Spirit (Eph 6:18).

Contrary to a popular view of an "effortless" Christianity, Scripture exhorts Christians to keep the faith, fight the good fight, finish the course, resist the devil, take every thought captive and destroy ungodly speculations and thoughts contrary to the true knowledge of God (2 Tim 4:7; Jam 4:7; 2 Cor 10:3-4). By the Holy Spirit's power and fruit of self-control, they can exercise the needed self-discipline for godliness. And by being taught by the Holy Spirit of truth they test the spirits so as not to be misled but rather abide in Jesus who is the truth (1 Jn 2:27, Jn 14:6). They abstain from every form of evil, die to self and walk in newness of life (Rom 6:4, 8:13; Gal 5:23). They are convinced that God will make a tunnel through the mountain to the Light at the end. And though true Christianity is not "effortless", a piece of cake, a walk in the part, or a bed of roses, the one who is nourished on truth knows God will turn their mountains into ant hills, their tunnels into triumphs.

FEBRUARY 20

The more highly we think of ourselves the lower
we descend into ourselves and into our former
ways. The more highly we think of Him the higher
we ascend with Him in newness of life.

One cause of depression is the absence of communion with the living God. Even King David who had much to be stressed over said: "Thou wilt make known to me the path of life; in Thy presence is fullness of joy; in Thy right hand there are pleasures forever" (Ps 16:11).

The devil, hell's psychiatrist, prescribes his solutions whether they be entangling sins and enslaving idols or intellectual falsehoods and spiritual deceptions. Soul sickness and depression awaits the one who rejects the Great Physician's treatment. Suicide and depression are often the devil's most effective long term prescription. His other prescriptions only give temporary relief.

Suicide often occurs when one listens to the destructive lies of the evil one, the devil himself, who comes to steal, kill and destroy (Jn 10:10a). But Christ minded believers will take every such thought captive and destroy such lies of hopelessness, defeat, regret, remorse and despair (2 Cor 10:3-4). Those who deny the reality of spiritual warfare which is so prevalent in the Bible often prefer to ignore biblical counsel and run unknowingly first and foremost to the god of the world for his supposed "solutions". And he often works through doctors, drugs and triggers. But it is far wiser and healthier to rely first on the grace, care, blessings and refuge of the Great Physician and His divinely inspired prescriptions.

FEBRUARY 21

If the devil can keep you looking back he
can keep you from moving forward.

SEVEN MOUNTAINS OR ALL THE WORLD?

Jesus Christ is to have preeminence over every mountain, not just seven of them. Jesus clearly made His will known two thousand years ago to His apostles and prophets pertaining to the summing up of all things in Christ (Eph 1:10, 20). This will be ultimately realized when, Christ, who is all and in all, returns (Col 3:11). But until then, the will and kingdom of God is to be sought and practiced by all the saints whose have died to the old life and whose new life is hidden with Christ in God (Col 3:3-4). Such ones are taught by the Spirit of Truth, not by a new breed of super anointed apostles and prophets (1 Jn 2:27). So Paul instructed: "Whatever you do in word or deed, do all in the name of the Lord Jesus" (Col 3:17). Some seek to take dominion of seven mountains, others overcome the world.

FEBRUARY 22

Christians must not let their light be diffused in a dark and confused society, becoming fifty shades of gray.

PROSPERITY PREACHING PROFITS LITTLE

A bankrupt person who had a millstone of debt around his neck would not delay long in using blank checks signed by a millionaire and donated to him for his distress. Why then do many heavenly blessed Christians not cash in on God's 'exceeding great and precious promises' (2 Pet 1:3-4) which have already been signed by His hand and are contained in our checkbook, the Bible? In the distressing and dark days ahead many "believers" will stand with blank looks wondering why their coveted promissory notes signed by Prosperity Preachers bounced in heaven and failed to deliver on earth. Instead of being lights shining brightly in the world, they will increasingly become conformed to the world; lampshades offering fifty shades of gray, to victims walking in darkness.

However, believers filled with the Holy Spirit, their lamps full of oil, will be vessels which will expose the unfruitful deeds of darkness (Eph 5:13, 14, 18). As followers of Christ, who is the Light of the world (Jn 8:12), they will shine upon those who sit in darkness and the shadow of death, to guide their feet into the way of peace (Lk 1:79), to Him who is our peace (Eph 2:14), to the Christ living in them, the hope of glory (Gal 2:20; Col 1:27). It is time for shady Americanized religious Christians to come out of dark closets, to descend from idolatrous stages and come out from behind compromising pulpits and go the altar in repentance and for a refill of divine power, sanctifying grace and true spiritual prosperity. Then they will understand that they have already been blessed with every spiritual blessing in the heavenly places in Christ (Eph 1:3), and have been granted everything pertaining to life and godliness (2 Pet 1:3). They will see that "the LORD God is a sun and shield; the LORD gives grace and glory; no good thing does He withhold from those who walk uprightly" (Ps 84:11).

FEBRUARY 23

Powerless preachers hate the book of Acts which displays
the mighty acts of saints. And those doing nothing
are convicted by not doing the Acts of the saints.

BIBLICAL CHRISTIANITY VS. CHURCHIANITY

The Holy Spirit is mobilizing an army of active Christian soldiers who understand the times and who understand spiritual warfare. Only those most separated from the world, nourished on the Word, suited up with divine armor, obedient to God's calling, committed to His Kingdom, and willing to be Spirit led and Christ governed, will overwhelmingly conquer their enemies on the battlefield. The rest will continue playing games with the devil, being entertained by his demons and deceived their doctrines.

The Spirit of Truth will not be silenced nor the God of creation be caged. The Word of God cannot be imprisoned or the Kingdom of God suppressed. The Light of the Gospel will never be darkened nor the Good News censored. Only deceived fools believe such fantasies for they serve the prince of darkness and spew demonic even religious gospels of defeat, destruction and destitution. God will never be mocked, but His mockers forever will.

In days ahead, more and more victims of the twentieth first century powerless, dehydrated and junk food nourished, yet emaciated churchianity will be delivered and become devoted to first century Christianity. In those glorious early days sinners became saints in practice, mighty acts were performed not explained away, demons were expelled not entertained, the world was overcome not loved, disciples were made not decisions, true conversions were experienced not shallow confessions, Christ was exalted, not the antichrist spirit of the age.

FEBRUARY 24

"How shall I feel at the judgment, if multitudes of missed opportunities pass before me in full review, and all my excuses prove to be disguises of my cowardice and pride." W.E. Sangster

GOOD NEWS EVANGELISM

How about this method for evangelism: The greatest Evangelist said it this way: "The Spirit of the LORD is upon Me, because He anointed Me to preach the gospel to the poor. He has sent Me to proclaim release to the captives, and recovery of sight to the blind, to set free those who are oppressed, to proclaim the favorable year of the LORD" (Lk 4:18-19). In Scripture it is written: "For God did not send the Son into the world to judge the world, but that the world might be saved through Him" (Jn 3:17). "Sing to the LORD a new song; sing to the LORD, all the earth. Sing to the LORD, bless His name; proclaim good tidings of His salvation from day to day. Tell of His glory among the nations, His wonderful deeds among all the peoples. For great is the LORD and greatly to be praised; He is to be feared above all gods. For all the gods of the people are idols, but the LORD made the heavens" (Ps 96:1-5). The GOOD News of the Kingdom of God and the unique and only saving Name of Jesus Christ should be preached to all those whom the Lord is drawing (Jn 12:32), whom the Spirit is convicting (Jn 16:8) and whom God is teaching (Jn 6:45).

The only kind of evangelism that will reverse the downward spiral of "progressive", feel good, self-centered contemporary Christianity that is so attractive to Millennials will be biblical evangelism. That is, evangelism that demonstrates the life changing and supernatural power of God, reconciling sinners to the holy God. They will experience the true peace of God and be motivated to accomplish the purposes of God. They will rely on the full provision of God and claim the great and magnificent promises of God. They will see no value or reason to compromise truth, to tolerate evil, to live in sin, nor to embrace powerless religion, church growth marketing or pop theology. They will no longer be impressed by feel good spirituality nor give lip service to religious traditions of men. They will reject Satan's not-so-good news, preferring the Savior's Good News instead. They will carry the Cross on their back, rather than wear the cross of an "effortless" Christianity around their neck. They want the real thing and will thus experience lasting revival. They will stand on true grace rather than fall for modern hyper grace.

FEBRUARY 25

*The devil, the father of lies, prowls about like a
roaring lion seeking to steal, kill and destroy. He is
relentless and sleepless, while too many professing
Christians are sleeping and repentless.*

THE EXCHANGED LIFE OF THE TRUE CHRISTIAN

True Christians are all exchange students, citizens of heaven living as aliens and strangers in the world (1 Pet 2:11). Christians are to be discipled and taught by the Holy Spirit send from above, rather than being deceived and taught by the wicked god of this world. We have been called to live an exchanged life. "If any man be in Christ, he is a new creature: old things are passed away; behold, all things are become new" (2 Cor 5:17). Paul described the new life this way: "I have been crucified with Christ: and it is no longer I who live, but Christ lives in me; and the live which I now live in the flesh I live by faith in the Son of God, who loved me and gave Himself up for me" (Gal 2:20).

John reminds us: "And ye know that He was manifested to take away our sins; and in him is no sin…For this purpose the Son of God was manifested, that he might destroy the works of the devil" (1 Jn 3:5, 8b). God made the Son "to be sin for us, who knew no sin; that we might be made the righteousness of God in Him" (2 Cor 5:21). So it is high time that professing Christians live the exchanged life.

Upon graduation on earth where will many go, into eternal punishment and eternal fire which has been prepared for the devil and his angels (Mt 25:41, 46), away from the presence of God and from the glory of His power (Mt 25:46; 2 Thess 1:9), or to heaven to enjoy God and forever in His presence? One may pursue the best life here and miss out on the eternal life thereafter. And one may be purpose driven now and prove never to have been heaven bound then. Those who walk by the Spirit are overcomers, not overcome; victorious not victims. They turn the world upside down, rather than let the world turn them inside out. Such ones the Bible calls saints, not sinners; Christ followers not men pleasures.

FEBRUARY 26

"The greatness of a man's power is the measure of his surrender." William Booth

JESUS: ABIDE IN HIM AND WIN

Nothing is too hard for Jesus. No man can work like Him. He who abides in Him will surely win.

Nothing is hidden from His eyes. Everything done in darkness will be exposed when He returns in the skies.

The proud may strut and boast, but only until He returns with His heavenly host.

Then Christians will rule the world, even judge angels, when they reign with Him, the Creator of the world and Holy One adored.

We will dwell in God's House forever blessed, while the man-made church house will be forever cursed.

Who can be stressed out who is on the winning side, with the King of Kings so soon to trumpet His victory shout?

His inauguration speech will be heard by all, no media will black out that holy upward call, when the great God and Shepherd returns for His sheep, He who rules over all.

We overwhelmingly conquer through God who loves us, by the Son of God who lives in us, by the Spirit of God who empowers us, by the Word of God which instructs us, and by the armor of God which protects us. But those without God in this world are in a world of hurt.

FEBRUARY 27

The gifts of the Holy Spirit are most often practiced
where heaven's Gift, the Lord Jesus Christ, is supremely
exalted. For the Holy Spirit was sent to glorify the
Son and the gifts were given to edify His body.

HOW CAN YOU?....YOU CAN'T!

How can you be filled with the Spirit when so full of self (Eph 5:18)? How can you have ears to hear having ears that lust (2 Tim 4:3)?

How can you see God when not pure in heart (Mt 5:8)?

How can you enjoy the presence of God with disobedience that excludes His presence (Jn 14:21, 23)?

How can you taste and see that the LORD is good while feasting on the world's goods (Ps 34:8)?

You can't. But you can do all things through Him who strengthens you (Phil 4:13). For "every good thing bestowed and every perfect gift is from above, coming down from the Father of lights, with whom there is no varia-tion or shifting shadow" (Jam 1:17), enabling every believer to become a good servant of Christ Jesus.

Every Christian is to be a good servant of the Lord, separated from the world, a walking citizen of heaven and an overcoming soldier of the cross, dead to self, alive to the Savior and alert to the devil. To experience this the devoted Christian must examine every doctrine blowing in the wind to see whether it is of the Spirit of God or of the god of this world, of the Spirit of truth or of the father of lies, For many so-called Christian leaders are merely blowing hot air, demonic doctrines of the prince of the power of the air. Fortunately, Christians can claim the promise: "Now we have received, not the spirit of the world but the Spirit who is from God, that we might know the things freely given to us by God" (1 Cor 2:12). "Things which eye has not seen and ear has not heard, and which have not entered the heart of man, all that God has prepared for those who love Him" (1 Cor 2:9).

FEBRUARY 28

When we fall down on our backs it is easier to look up. Then, when we rise up and face the Son, our shadows fall down and disappear behind us.

AVOIDING SPIRITUAL HEART FAILURE

Christians don't have to experience spiritual heart failure since God has put His unfailing laws upon our heart (Jer 31:33-34; Ezek 36:26-27; Heb 8:8-12; 10:15-18). The proper use and exercise of God's laws and wisdom brings health to the heart, renewal to the mind (Rom 12:1), refreshment to the bones, healing to the body (Prov 3:8) and life to the soul (Prov 3:22; 4:22). The one who stays in the Upper Room with the Great Physician will stay out of the emergency room of the world. The wisdom of God says: "Watch over your heart with all diligence; for from it flow the springs of life" (Prov 4:23). "A joyful heart is good medicine, but a broken spirit dries up the bones" (Prov 17:22).

FEBRUARY 29

Don't be so overly concerned about being raptured
out of the coming great tribulation that you fail
to be conformed by your present tribulations.

DOWN WITH DISCOURAGEMENT

Quench the devil's accusations, your forgiven.
Intercede for others.
Set your mind on Christ and heavenly things.
Count your blessings, He has given.
Overwhelmingly conquer as a citizen of heaven.
Understand the purpose of trials.
Revive your soul by the Scriptures.

Ask in faith for deliverance, cleansed of all leaven.

Give yourself to others.

Exult in God and in your salvation.

Claim His magnificent promises.

Meditate on His wonders.

Experience God's presence.

Sing a new song of praise.

Possess thankfulness of heart.

Release Christ's fragrance.

It is uplifting to be reminded that God desires that we not be downcast. Jesus said: "Come to Me, all who are weary and heavy-laded, and I will give you rest" (Mt 11:28). The apostle Paul wrote: "In everything give thanks; for this is God's will for you in Christ Jesus" (1 Thess 5:18). Being thankful is the will of God for such an attitude reveals a trust in God. The author of Hebrews even describes giving thanks as a sacrifice and act of worship: "Through Him then, let us continually offer up a sacrifice of praise to God, that is, the fruit of lips that give thanks to His name." (Heb 13:15).

MARCH 1

When we come to our senses and repent, He comes to our aid and rescues. When we are weakest, He is strongest. When we are humbled, we are exalted. When we die, we live.

INWARD WHOLENESS OR HIS HOLINESS: WHICH ARE YOU SEEKING?

Too many today are seeking inner wholeness rather than His holiness. They fail to understand that only by abiding in Christ can they truly be whole and set free from sin's stronghold (Jn 8:31-32, 36). Sin always takes them farther than where they want to go, keeps them there longer that they want to stay, and gives them rotten fruit that they do not want to eat. Sin captures sinners and sin incarcerates them. As it is written in proverbs: "His own iniquities will capture the wicked, and he will be held with the cords of sin" (Prov 5:22). Jesus said: "Truly, truly, I say to you everyone who commits sin is the slave of sin" (Jn 8:34).

But the good news is that Jesus came to set you free (Jn 8:36), to proclaim release to captives and to set free those who are downtrodden (Lk 4:18). The Son of God appeared in order to take away sins, and that He might destroy the works of the devil who has sinned from the beginning and whose children practice sin (1 Jn 3:5, 8, 10). Jesus is the Way, the Truth and the Life and by abiding in Him who is the truth one is free indeed from sin and from servitude to the devil, the father of lies (Jn 8:36, 44; 14:6; 2 Tim 2:25-26).

One can be completely free from enslavement to sin, knowing that he has been made complete in Him. For only in Him have we been made complete (Col 2:10) and Jesus only is the resurrection and the life (Jn 11:25). In Him are hidden all the treasures of wisdom and knowledge (Col 2:3). In Him we have been blessed with every spiritual blessing, including the blessings of righteousness, sanctification and redemption (Eph 1:3; 1 Cor 1:30). We have been made rich in Him because He became poor for us (2 Cor 8:9).

Whether it is a prayer closet at home or an altar call in a church, either one can be a good place where holiness begins, if one dies there. In a prayer closet hidden skeletons can be buried. Those who have been baptized into Christ's death to sin can be clothed and walk in resurrection life (Gal 3:27; Rom 6:3-11, 13:14). Likewise, true altar ministry can also alter one's spiritual walk. Fruitful ministry can often occur at church altars when trained believer priests are allowed to operate, rather than remain in the pew only to spectate. Those who truly die to self on the altar are more likely to return to the pew dead to sin.   But those who leave the altar with their old self still alive usually crawl to their pew with their old sinful self still alive and well.

MARCH 2

"Grace and peace be multiplied to you in the knowledge of God and of Jesus our Lord."

BECAUSE GOD IS.....

Because He is faithful, His lovingkindnesses indeed never cease (Lam 3:22a).

Because He is compassionate, His compassions never fail me (Lam 3:22).

Because He is immutable, He is the same yesterday and today and forever (Heb 13:8).

Because He is giving, I are not deprived (Jn 3:16; Rom 8:32).

Because He is truthful, it is impossible for Him to lie to me (Heb 6:18.)

Because He is omnipotent His promises are true and powerful (2 Pet 1:3-4).

Because He is holy, I can be holy (1 Pet 1:15-16).

Because He is omniscient, He knows my unspoken words, understands my thoughts and scrutinizes my paths (Ps 139:2-4; Heb 4:13).

Because He is omnipresent, His presence leads and guides me (Ps 139:7-10).

Because He is Light, darkness does not overwhelm me (Ps 139:11-12).

Because He is just, the wicked will be judged (Acts 17:30-31) and I can be justified (Rom 3:24-26).

Because He is love, I are loved and I can love (1 Jn 4:8; Jn 3:16; 1 Jn 3:16).

Because He is forgiving, I am cleansed (1 Jn 1:9).

Because He is merciful, He is slow to anger (Ps 86:15).

Because He is sovereign, He is ruler over all (Ps 103:19).

Because He is the only True God, all men are to fear and tremble before Him only (Dan 6:26-27; 1 Cor 8:6).

Because He is personal, how precious are His thoughts toward me (Ps 139:17).

Because He is the Creater I exist (Ps 33:6; Ps 139:13-16; 1 Pet 4:19).

MARCH 3

Turn your face to the Son of Righteousness and the
Light will dispel the darkness behind you.

GIVE ME HIS PRESENCE: THE BEST PRESENT TO HAVE.

"One thing I have asked from the LORD, that I shall seek; that I may dwell in the house of the LORD all the days of my life, to behold the beauty of the LORD and to meditate in His temple" (Ps 27:4). We practice God's presence, when we walk and fellowship with God's Spirit (2

Cor 13:14), rather than just giving lip service to God's existence. We experience God's holy presence when we are Holy Spirit enabled to claim God's magnificent promises, experience His awesome power, witness His loving providence, engage in prevailing prayer and proclaim His life giving Gospel.

The devil resists those who have such a godly pursuit and appreciation for God's magnificent presence and manifold blessings. The world surely doesn't understand it. Often even the believer may forget the benefits of entering God's presence because the wicked of Satan's world seem to be at ease, gay or wealthy; those who are ever trying to hinder others entering into God's joyful presence to enjoy being spiritually healthy. As the psalmist wrote long ago: "Behold, these are the wicked; and always at ease, they have increased in wealth. Surely in vain I have kept my heart pure, and washed my hands in innocence. For I have been striken all day long, and chastened every morning. If I had said, 'I will speak thus', Behold, I should have betrayed the generation of Thy children. When I pondered to understand this, it was troublesome in my sight until I came into the sanctuary of God; then I perceived their end. Surely Thou dost set them in slippery places; Thou dost cast the down to destruction" (Ps 73:12-18).

MARCH 4

Every Christian preacher who belittles sin is
speaking for the devil, the father of lies (Jn 8:44)
who has sinned from the beginning (1 Jn 3:8).

A CHRISTIAN IS A "WORK IN PROGRESS"

God is fully capable to weave our forgiven and forsaken sin ridden past as well as our mistakes into a tapestry of a God pleasing and fruitful life, if we let Him do the weaving and submit to His purposes. "And we know that God causes all things to work together for good to those who love God, to those who are called according to His purpose" (Rom 8:28). Christians have been saved from the penalty of sin, and so are blessed not cursed. They can be rescued from the power of sin as overcomers, and not be overcome.

Sin less living, not sinless perfection is a major theme in the New Testament. The believer can rest assured that he does not have to remain in bondage to sin. Freedom from sin's power and bondage is taught in many places in the New Testament (Rom 6:11-22; 8:13; 1 Jn 1:8,10, 3:10; Gal 5:16, 24; Jn 8:34-36). By the power of the Spirit of God and by practicing the Word of God Christians can be progressively sanctified or set apart from the presence of sin. Thus the Bible calls them saints, not sinners.

Though the word "progressively" is not in the Bible, Paul made mention of the fact that "we are being saved" (1 Cor 1:18) and that we are all on the road to greater godliness, until Christ be formed in us, until we become filled up with the fullness of Christ. The author of Hebrews speaks of those who are being sanctified (Phil 3:13-14; Col 1:28-29; Eph 4:13; Heb 10:14). So the saved, whom the Bible calls saints, make a conscious effort to be sanctified, as the apostle Paul and other New Testament writers taught and practiced: (1 Thess 4:3; Heb 12:14; 1 Cor 9:27; 1 Tim 4:7-8).

MARCH 5

We must be content with where God has placed
us if we are to enjoy what God has for us.

DON'T ABUSE YOURSELF; THERE'S NO EXCUSE FOR BONDAGE

Jesus came to set captives free, not keep them in mental and emotional bondage (Lk 4:18). Jesus sent the Holy Spirit, the Living Water, so we don't have to suffer spiritual dehydration (Jn 4:10, 14, 7:38-39). Jesus is the living bread out of heaven so we don't have to face starvation (Jn 6:51). Jesus has forgiven our past sins so we don't have to wallow in them in the present (Acts 2:38). We have been given full divine armor so we don't have to be taken captive by a conquered foe (Eph 6:11; Col 2:15). We have been promised a glorious future so we don't have to be plagued by doubt and gloom (1 Pet 1:3-5; Phil 3:21).

We can be assured that God causes all things to work together for our good, so we don't have to wonder when things appear to be working for the bad (Rom 8:28; Gen 50:20). We can be confident that God is able keep it all under control, even when we mess up and can't keep it together (Col 1:17). We don't have to worry and be anxious for tomorrow, for Jesus commands us to live by faith today (Mt 6:25-34).

So I will no longer abuse myself. Instead, "I will meditate on all Your work and muse on Your deeds. Your way O God, is holy. What god is great like our God? You are the God who works wonders; You have made known Your strength among the people. You have by Your power redeemed Your people" (Ps 77:12-15). So I excuse myself from remaining in bondage.

MARCH 6

*He who is filled with the indwelling Spirit of God knows that
everything else residing within the temple is but emptiness and
vanity, self-complacency and self-love, because the old man
still lives there as well. And though crucified, he often arises.*

IF GOD IS FOR US...

If God is for us, who can be against us (Rom 8:31)? If God is at work in us, what circumstance can work against us (Phil 2:13)? If the Spirit of God empowers us, what force can overpower us (Acts 1:8; 1 Jn 4:4)? If the victorious Son of God lives in us, why live in defeat (Gal 2:20)? If we are citizens of heaven, why live as captives of the world (Phil 3:20)? If Jesus has bruised the serpent on the head (Gen 3:15), and the God of peace wishes to crush Satan under our feet (Rom 16:20), why allow the devil to hold us under his thumb? If Christians are called saints, why walk as sinners (Rom 1:7)? If God wants to father us, why walk as prodigals (Rom 8:15; 2 Thess 2:16-17)? If the Spirit wants to walk in fellowship with us, why walk without Him (2 Cor 13:14; Rom 8:14)? If Christ, the hope of glory is in us, why be gloomy (Col 1:27)?

Maybe it is because we do not allow the Spirit to give us newness of life by teaching us how abide in Jesus, the Word of Life (Jn 6:31; 1 Jn 2:27; Rom 6:4). Or maybe it is because Jesus is Lord of little rather than Lord of all, or no Lord at all. Or maybe it is because we only ran to the altar but have never died on the altar, so as to live in resurrection life with Him. For "unless a grain of wheat falls into the earth and dies, it remains alone; but if it dies, it bears much fruit" (Jn 12:24). Or maybe it is because we are more concerned with living "the best life now" rather than dying to self and taking hold of the eternal life to which we were called (1 Tim 6:12). Maybe we are more in love with self than with the Savior, more interested in being happy and holy. Why settle for so little when we have been blessed with so much (Eph 1:3; Rom 8:32; Phil 4:19)?

MARCH 7

If the Word of God is not the Textbook and the Spirit of God is not the Teacher and the Son of God is not the Template, then it is only a matter of time before the tempter will come in like a flood with compromise and deception.

WHY THE DEVIL HATES FAITH

Faith saves. It overcomes the world. It quenches all the fiery darts of the wicked one. Faith walks on water. It pleases God. It refuses to believe the lies of the devil. Faith moves onward, not backward; upward not downward. Faith is active, not passive; fruitful, not fruitless. Faith works, not worries. Faith lays hold of divine promises, not man's problems. Faith receives divine approval. Faith sees the invisible, does the impossible and conquers the invincible. Faith pierces the devil's darkness with heavenly Light. Faith comes by reading, studying, and practicing the Word of God. It's time to walk in faith and let God who increases faith crush the enemy of faith under our feet.

MARCH 8

*Repentance removes towering mountains; faith bridges raging
rivers, so we can enjoy His peaceful rest even in the valleys.*

WHY NOT HASTEN HIS RETURN?

In times past God-appointed, Spirit-anointed, Kingdom-seeking preachers hit the nail on the head when they boldly preached the true Gospel of God in demonstration of the Spirit and of power (1 Cor 2:4; Rom 15:18-19). Today's self-appointed, flesh-anointed, pleasure-seeking preachers are hammering the last nail into the coffin of the Laodicean church. The contemporary church must arise from the dead and BE the church and become triumphant. As Paul said: "Awake, sleeper, and arise from the dead, and Christ will shine on you" (Eph 5:14). Why should the church walk in the world's darkness and revel in sin when we have been called to be lights in the world and reverence Him? Again Paul said: "If we are beside ourselves, it is for God; if we are of sound mind, it is for you" (2 Cor 5:13). "For to me, to live is Christ and to die is gain" (Phil 1:21).

The sooner we die to self and sin, the sooner we live for Him. If we have the mind and devotion of Christ, we will demonstrate His resurrection victory, His heavenly wisdom, His infinite power and His fullness of joy by being Spirit led as He was (1 Cor 2:16; Lk 10:21; Mt 4;1,4; Heb 9:14; Col 2:15). After all, Christ lives in the obedient, sanctified, Kingdom seeking Christian, having become to such ones "wisdom from God, and righteousness and sanctification, and redemption" (1 Cor 1:30). And, as if this is not enough, the true apostle Paul revealed even more heavenly provisions offered by our Heavenly Father: "He who did not spare His own Son, but delivered Him over for us all, how will He not also with Him freely give us all things" (Rom 8:32).

So if we have been made complete, why feel so incompetent (Col 2:10; 2 Cor 3:6)? If we have received Holy Spirit power why be so helpless (Acts 1:8)? If we are so securely saved why appear so lost? If God is at work in us accomplishing what is pleasing in His sight (Heb 13:20), why go on working ourselves to death to please self? If we are supposed to over-whelmingly conquer in all things (Rom 8:37), why be defeated in every-thing? If we are called to reign in life, why moan (Rom 5:17)? If we are called to persevere why throw in the towel? Maybe it is because so many are more in touch with institutional religion that they are in touch with the living Savior. Maybe they are not really for Him, but against Him. It's self-examination time (2 Cor 13:5). It's time to get real and get radi-cal for Him, "looking for and hastening the coming of the day of God" (2 Pet 3:12a).

MARCH 9

The institutional church is a great place to pretend.
Being religious, shaking a few hands with your favorite
strangers, watching people sing "just as I am" before
they exist in the same condition as they came in.

Those who bask in the Son, who are watered by the Spirit and are rooted in good soil, not hardened clay, will bear fruit. Our heavenly Father prunes such ones to bear more fruit (Jn 15:2). He also disciplines those whom He loves (Heb 12:6), rescues those in whom He delights

(Ps 18:19) and intimately abides in those who obey (Jn 14:23). God is personally known by those who love Him (1 Cor 8:3), delivers and sets securely on high those who know and trust in His name (Ps 91:1,2,14) and seeks those who truly worship Him (Jn 4:23). "O LORD, the God of Israel, there is no god like You in heaven or on earth, keeping covenant and showing lovingkindness to Your servants who walk before You with all their heart" (2 Chron 6:14). "For I know the plans that I have for you, declares the LORD, plans for welfare and not for calamity to give you a future and a hope" (Jer 29:13).

MARCH 10

How is it that one will quickly open a letter from his earthly employer and boss and yet leave closed the letter (Bible) from his Heavenly Father and His Lord and Master?

BE SET FREE

B elieve the Lord's statement that He came to set captives free (Lk 4:18). We can be free from sinful bondage, emotional turmoil, mental madness, soulish depression and fleshly struggles. Otherwise you make the statement that God is not willing, His Spirit is not capable, His Scriptures are not adequate, His promises are not invalid, His Son's intercession is not effective, and His Good News Gospel is not so really good after all. Don't live in fear over your past failures, but trust in God's future victories. Don't be paralyzed by your sense of inadequacy, but be energized by His divine adequacy (2 Cor 3:4-6). Hope in God's ability and commitment to work everything out for your good as you continue to love Him and fulfill His purpose (Rom 8:28). After all, we serve an awesome God.

MARCH 11

The devil won't leave you alone just because you go to church or have a religious bumper sticker on your car. You will have to resist him, before he will go very far!

BELIEVE IT OR NOT: SATAN IS A DEFEATED FOE.

It is a shame and inexcusable that so many so-called shepherds of churches fail to inform, instruct and equip their sheep to be overcomers of Satan's world and to destroy his works. The Good Shepherd and Son of God appeared for this purpose, to destroy the works of the devil (1 Jn 3:8). And He said: "as the Father has sent Me, so I also send you" (Jn 20:21). He told Peter if he loved Him, he was to tend to His lambs and shepherd His sheep (Jn 21:15, 16). We see many contemporary Christians sitting famished in the pews and malnourished in the world. Even in the "growing and successful" mega-churches, we often see the mesmerized masses mega-dosed on pastoral pastries and the world's finest fast food religion. Such a diet cannot produce strong solders of the Cross.

Thus, many of God's own die for of the lack of knowledge because they have rejected knowledge (Hosea 4:6), and truth by which they are sanctified (Jn 17:17). They refuse to be good servants of Jesus Christ, nourished on the words of faith and of sound doctrine (1 Tim 4:6). So we see God's people "go into exile for their lack of knowledge; and their honorable men are famished, and their multitude is parched with thirst. Therefore, Sheol has enlarged its throat and opened its mouth without measure; and Jerusalem's splendor, [a picture of the Church] her multitude, her din of revelry and the jubilant within her, descend into it" (Isaiah 5:13-14).

But not so with the militant, persevering and overcoming people of God. They will feed on every word that proceeds out of the mouth of God (Mt 4:4). Their diet is the inspired Word of God which makes them adequate and equipped for every good work (2 Tim 3:16-17). They overcome the devil, their accuser and deceiver. They do not love the world, their former residence. They are now citizens of heaven, seated in the heavenlies (Phil 3:20; Eph 2:6). They overcome because of the blood of the Lamb and because of the word of their testimony, and they do not love their life even to death (Rev 12:11). They are fully convinced that those who suffer with Christ will also be glorified with Him (Rom 8:17). They know that those who endure shall also reign with Him (2 Tim 2:12a). They claim the promise that momentary light affliction is producing for them an eternal weight of glory far beyond all comparison (2 Cor 5:17). This is a promise to be claimed in this life, (Rom 5:17; 2 Pet 1:3-4) and a hope to be realized in the next, when He returns to be glorified in His saints on that day (2 Thess 1:10).

MARCH 12

It is better to have our hearts pierced by the Dove from above than have our ears tickled by the devil from below.

DOWN AND DIRTY WITH THE DEVIL OR UP IN ETERNITY WITH THE DIVINE

When you keep eternity in yours eyes, you will keep the devil's dirt out of them. You will labor for that which endures and not for what disappears. You will reap heavenly rewards at the end of your life and walk on streets of gold, rather than vainly seek false treasures at the end of Satan's rainbow and walk on streets of gloom below.

In Scripture we read many exhortations. Even after Peter's first sermon we read that "with many other words he solemnly testified and kept on exhorting them, saving, 'Be saved from this perverse generation'" (Acts 2:40). And we learn that such apostolic exhortations recorded in Scripture "did not come from error or impurity or by way of deceit" (1 Thess 2:3). So the apostle Paul said: "Work out your salvation with fear and trembling" (Phil 2:12). "Test yourselves to see if you are in the faith" (2 Cor 13:5). "Pay close attention to yourself and to your teaching" (1 Tim 4:16). Likewise, Peter: "Make certain about His calling and choosing you" (2 Pet 1:10) and John: "Let no one deceive you" (1 Jn 2:26, 3:7). And finally Jesus: "Repent….he who has ears to hear, let him hear" (Rev 2:5-7).

Yet today we are "emerging", and so prosperous that even the devil is envious; experiencing our "Best Life Now", along with the Harlem shake, gold dust and angel feathers, even angels awaiting our beckoning. We can even become a "super apostle or super prophet", well oiled with "super anointings and adorned with super mantles". And no need for repentance because hyper grace white washes all our sins quite well. Are we missing something or is a distorted gospel being preached and another bible being read?

MARCH 13

*The ultimate goal of evangelical, biblical prayer is
not solitary contemplation but voluntary expansion
of the kingdom of God; not aiming at union with
God but maintaining communion with Him.*

JESUS' STATE OF THE CHURCH ADDRESS

It's time for all saints who understand the times to be sure they are BEING the Church, not merely GOING to church nor PLAYING church. Time is short, the devil is busy, the lost are dying, false religions are growing, religious fads are never ending and the world is laughing and mocking at contemporary Christianity. The devil is a master at division, diversion and derision. Jesus prayed for unity among His true followers (Jn 17). Paul warned about devilish diversions away from simplicity and purity of devotion to Christ (2 Cor 11:3).

If the Lord Jesus were present today, and allowed by the political establishment to speak to the Americanized church, I could see Him giving a State of the Church address, as He did to the seven churches in Revelation chapters two and three. Only to the faithful would He say: "well done, good and faithful slave…enter into the joy of your Master" (Mt 25:23). The author of Hebrews also commended the believing and obedient saints of former times who desired a better country than the world, that is, a heavenly one, saying that God was not ashamed to be called their God and had prepared a city for them (Heb 11:16). Jesus, likewise, assured those who had served and followed Him (Jn 12:26) that in His Father's house there would be a dwelling place which He would prepare for them to receive when He returned (Jn 14:2-3).

However, those who talk cheaply rather than walk costly may very well hear Him say: "I never knew you" (Mt 7:21-23). Don't let the ear-tickling, money grabbing, progressive, contemplative, emergent, purpose-drunken popular preachers deceive you with their Bible malpractice and pastoral pastries. Don't be diverted from the Lord's high calling nor be consumed with trivial doctrinal debates nor lured to jump onto the next religious band-wagon. Don't be deceived by those who "revile the things which they do not understand" (Jude 10) and who love "what is worthless and aim at deception" (Ps 4:2). Know this for sure, that the LORD has set apart the godly for Himself and will hear when they call out to Him in the difficult days ahead (Ps 4:3).

MARCH 14

The guidance of God is ever so clear when
we desire Him to be ever so near.

TRUE REVIVAL OR DEVILISH ARCADE?

True, lasting revival occurs where God is worshipped in Spirit and truth, the Son is followed in word and deed, the Spirit is relied on for power and instruction, the devil is resisted and defeated, sin is exposed and destroyed, love is practiced in deed and truth, and the world is forsaken and despised.

So how will one make it through the thorns and briars of this fallen world, to win the battle against wicked principalities and powers and to overwhelmingly conquer the constant uprising of the warring flesh? How will one endure politically correct politics, spiritually corrupt religion, and contemporary compromising Christianity? One must be clothed with the righteousness of Christ, armed with the full armor of God, devoted to prayer, obedient to their heavenly call, nourished on the Word of God and empowered by the Spirit of God. One must be aware of the deceptive schemes and games the devil loves for Christians to play. These would include easy believism that proposes that what one believes, rather than what one does is what matters and that saving faith need not be demonstrated by works that occur subsequent to salvation.

Then there is the increasingly popular sinner-friendly hyper grace which extols an "effortless" Christianity and which undermines holiness, sees little necessity for repentance and views sin lightly. There is the increasing occurrence of false signs, miracles and wonders and the emphasis on subjective feelings and experience more than the objective Word of God. There is also New Age contemplative prayer and mysticism. And last but not least there is the modern variety of the great commission which is more committed to securing decisions than making disciples.

MARCH 15

*The sooner we experience HOLINESS, the
sooner we will enjoy WHOLENESS.*

ISN'T IT TIME.....

Not to fear death but to die daily; not be followers of men but seekers of God; not wasting time but hastening His return (Mt 10:28; 1 Cor 15:31;

2 Pet 3:12). It will profit little if we oppose political correctness but allow spiritual compromise. We must not be lulled asleep by smooth talking clergy, but be awaken and sober to exercise our holy and royal priesthood (1 Thess 5:5-8; Eph 5:14; 1 Pet 2:5, 9). We must cease talking the game and begin winning the game; not be educated to death but empowered for life; not merely being church goers but Christ followers; not ashamed of truth but ambassadors of the Truth; not sinners but saints; not living for the almighty dollar but for the Almighty God; not burned out on hollow religion but fired up for holy living.

IT'S TIME to stop playing and start working; stop being entertained and start being equipped; stop ignoring the devil and begin resisting him, who prowls about as a roaring lion, cloaked in religious garb, seeking to steal, kill and destroy. It's time for the militant triumphant Church to assume her rightful place as the heavenly army trained for battle, equipped for victory, empowered from above, enlightened with heavenly wisdom and prayed up, no longer preyed upon.

MARCH 16

The Lord and His New Covenant have come to stay. He is waiting for His children to go and be.

A LITTLE IRONY AND A LOT OF TRUTH

We simply can't let Jesus be the Head of the Church and allow it to function by His Spirit. Jesus didn't go to seminary and get a degree. He never wrote a book on church growth. He was too caught up in casting out demons rather than on collecting tithes. He insisted on ministering to the outcasts rather than inviting them into a comfortable church. He didn't win friends and influence people. Rather, He ministered to the rejects and even suggested to His most loyal followers to hit the road if His Way was too rough for them (Jn 6:66-69). He was concerned with dead religious rituals and taboos, not wearing religious labels and tattoos. He kept telling people that they had to bear their cross, rather than merely wear one. He was too Spirit led to be purpose driven. He kept speaking about the eternal life hereafter, rather selling the best life now. The biblical Jesus just didn't fit it and He doesn't now. We need a new kind of Jesus.

Consequently, today we see religious idols emerging, preaching another Jesus and the contemporary Christian masses loving it so. The apostle Paul had to address such madness: "For if one comes and preaches another Jesus whom we have not preached, or you receive a different spirit which you have not received, or a different gospel which you have not accepted, you bear this beautifully" (2 Cor 11:4). We have popular religious "experts" building a decapitated Church, disconnected from her Head, Jesus Christ and devoid of His Holy Spirit and of power. A contemporary, popular, churchianity that is unaware that much of contemporary Christianity is mindlessly walking about in utter deception and moral depravity. The devil is so proud of his accomplishments. However, the True Church is arising and the evil one is paranoid that the Holy Spirit is moving and true Church is overcoming.

MARCH 17

You will walk triumphantly only when
you walk with Him who won.

WHY BE OVERCOME WHEN YOU ARE CALLED
TO BE AN OVERCOMER?

As believers in Christ, we alone have been made complete (Col 2:10), so there is no reason to feel all alone. We have been blessed with every spiritual blessing in the heavenlies in Christ, so we should not feel spiritually bankrupt (Eph 1:3). God's inspired and living word equips us for every good work, so we should not feel useless and expired (2 Tim 3:16-17). We have been chosen to be holy and blameless, and so we should not be trapped in sin (Eph 1:4; 2 Tim 1:9). We are called, commissioned and sent out to be ambassadors for Christ the King, therefore should not stay back as pacifists (2 Cor 5:20; Rev 17:14).

All believers are priviledged to participate in an active, holy and royal priesthood and thus are not confined into being mere spectators watching clergy performers (1 Pet 2:5, 9). We can overwhelmingly conquer as citizens of heaven and not be overwhelmed by the world's circumstances (Phil 3:20; Jn 16:33; Rom 8:37). Believers can joyfully serve Christ, the Head of the Church, being assured that He will crush Satan under their feet (Eph 5:23; Rom 16:20).

God always leads those who are Spirit led in His triumph in Christ (2 Cor 2:14; Rom 8:14). Those who are Spirit led will triumph in Christ, for the Spirit of God came to glorify the Son in us, the Son who overcame for us (Jn 16:14). The Spirit of truth was sent to teach us how to abide in the Son (Jn 14:26; 1 Jn 2:27). By abiding in Him who is truth one is truly set free (Jn 8:31, 32, 36). We also bear much fruit by abiding in Him and He in us (Jn 15:5). So we are not to be trapped in the devil's snares or deceived by his lies, for we have been set free from being his captives, no loner to walk in his darkness, but in newness of life (2 Tim 2:26; 1 Jn 2:10-11; Rom 6:4; Lk 1:78-79, 4:18). And Christ abiding in us is the hope of glory (Col 1:17), for from glory to glory the Holy Spirit continues to transform us by renewing our mind and creating the mind of Christ in us (2 Cor 3:17; Rom 12:1-2; 1 Cor 2:16).

MARCH 18

Many go the long way and in the wrong direction because they chose the easy comfortable road, not the path of hard knocks. They choose the high road of popularity and prosperity rather than the low road of humility and poverty.

Those who are Spirit led, rather than purpose drunken; Spirit-taught rather than man taught; who are seeking after the miracle working God rather than seeking after signs and wonders...Those who know, walk and abide in the God's eternal truth and heart piercing Word, rather than run after fables, esoteric wisdom, New Ages ideas and pseudo-spirituality and ear-tickling words...Such ones will run the race and win, rather than fall on their face in shame. Man's dull religious butter knife will not cut it against the devil's pitchfork of lies. The mighty Sword of the Lord is the only weapon of combat that can cut through the last day global deception (Eph 6:17). Proven soldiers of the cross will hear the words: "Good and well done, my faithful servant". These are God's Special Forces who will rescue victims from dead religion and superficial spirituality and introduce them to the true supernatural life. Then they can experience the true kingdom of God which is righteousness, peace, and joy in the Holy Spirit (Rom 14:17).

MARCH 19

It seems so foolish to please men who are dead in
sin and who care less for me, rather than to live
for Him who conquered sin and died for me.

A RECITAL OF THANKSGIVING BY THE PEOPLE OF GOD

This is the day which the LORD has made; let us rejoice and be glad in it (Ps 118:24). To You I shall offer a sacrifice of thanksgiving (Ps 116:17a), and proclaim with the voice of thanksgiving and declare all Your wonders (Ps 26:7). Give thanks to Him who alone does great wonders (Ps 136:4a). We give thanks to You, O God, for your name is near (Ps 75:1a) and we glory in your holy name (Ps 105:3a). Let the heart of those who seek the Lord be glad (Ps 105:3b).

For the righteous man will be glad in the LORD…all the upright in heart will glory" (Ps 64:10). Be glad in the LORD and rejoice, you righteous ones; and shout for joy, all you who are upright in heart (Ps 32:11). You heal the brokenhearted and bind up their wounds (Ps 147:3). You change a wilderness into a pool of water and a dry land into springs of water (Ps 107:35). You lead me beside quite waters (Ps 23:3b). You preserve the souls of your godly ones and deliver them from the hand of the wicked (Ps 97:10b). You favor those who fear You, those who wait for your lovingkindness (Ps 147:11). You preserve the souls of your godly ones (Ps 97:10a).

The LORD raises up those who are bowed down and loves the righteous (Ps 146:8b). You set the prisoners free (Ps 146:7c). You surround your people as the mountains surround Jerusalem, from this time forth and forever (Ps 125:2). How blessed is the nation whose God is the LORD; the people whom He has chosen for His own inheritance (Ps 33:12). The LORD takes pleasure in His people and will beautify the afflicted ones with salvation (Ps 149:4). No good thing do You withhold from those who walk uprightly (Ps 84:11b).

O God the Lord, the strength of my salvation. You cover my head in the day of battle (Ps 140:7). You have given food to those who fear You (Ps 111:5a). You have led forth Your own people like sheep and guided them in the wilderness like a flock (Ps 78:52). Whom have I in heaven but You? And besides You, I desire nothing on earth…For, behold, those who are far from You will perish; You have destroyed all those who are unfaithful to You (Ps 73:25, 27). But those who know Your name will put their trust in You, for You, O LORD, have not forsaken those who seek You (Ps 9:10). You lead your people through the wilderness, for Your lovingkindness is everlasting (Ps 136:16); everlasting …to those who fear You, and Your righteousness to children's children to those who keep Your covenant and remember Your precepts to do them" (Ps 103:17-18). You have made known to your people the power of your works (Ps 111:6a). You have made me glad by what you have done (Ps 92:4a). You have rescued my soul from death, my eyes from tears and my feet from stumbling. I shall walk before the LORD in the land of the living (Ps 116:8-9). Read this and be thankful. Recite this and be triumphant.

MARCH 20

Set your sail to the Spirit or get shipwrecked by the devil.

GET OUT OF THE BOAT

Jesus says, "Get out of the boat". Satan says: "Stay on the pleasure boat". In perilous times, the fearful jump off the boat, to tread water toward a life boat. The faithful jump off the boat to walk on the water, with eyes fixed on Him, toward their Life Saver. The fearful get their eyes off the Lord and get all wet. The fearless keep their eyes on Jesus and get wild. As the apostle Paul said: "If we are beside ourselves, it is for God; if we are of sound mind, it is for you" (2 Cor 5:13). The fearful fail to enter God's offered Promised Land because they see themselves as grasshoppers, overcome by strong enemies (Num 13:30-33). The fearless enter the Promised Land because they are God's giant killers. The fearful say: "It is hell with my soul". The faithful says: "It is well with my soul".

The time is now to become an overcomer. The time is now to put the devil, the roaring lion and undertaker in his place, under our feet, by taking every thought captive and destroying every speculation and lofty thing raised up against the true knowledge of God (2 Cor 10:3-5). "You will tread upon the lion and cobra, the young lion and the serpent you will trample down" (Ps 91:13).

MARCH 21

God's sovereignty over our life will be supernaturally displayed in our life when we allow Jesus to be Lord of our life.

CHRISTIANITY'S "LULL" AND "DECLINE" BEFORE THE STORM

Let the modern day "believers" sleep on in their soft pews, adorned by powerless religion, christless Christianity, fruitless faith and lack of repentance, rather than being clothed with the Lord Jesus Christ

(Rom 13:14; Gal 3:27). They have been lulled to sleep by pleasant preaching only to be awakened to religious entertainment. But the Lord Jesus Christ, the Chief Shepherd, Head Pastor, Divine Carpenter and heaven's Bridegroom continues to build His Church, His holy and blameless Bride (Eph 5:27). He builds His Church with living stones; those who have been raised from the dead (1 Pet 2:5). He sends out His messenges to contend for the faith and to proclaim the full message of eternal life and the whole purpose of God to those who are still dead in their trespasses and sins (Jude 3, Acts 5:20; 20:27, 24:25; Eph 2:1); to those still enslaved to and energized by the god of this world (2 Tim 2:26; Eph 2:2).

The gates of Hades shall not overpower His Church, nor can the statistics of man deny her (Mt 16:18) nor the Christ hating culture silence her. Besides, the Lord is not looking for numbers but for disciples, not for quantity but for quality. Any study, question or research having anything to do with Christianity is seriously flawed in that the term "Christian" and "Christianity" often is redefined to mean anything that seems right in the eyes of depraved man. And the devil has done a masterful job in blinding the minds of modern man as to the nature of biblical Christianity and the marks of a true Christian.

In recent times many have declined to describe themselves as Christians and for many reasons. At the same time others are inclined to call themselves Christians, but Christians of quite bizarre forms. Some who decline to be described as Christians do so because much of mainline popular televised Christianity which has become a laughingstock. It may entertain many and bring laughter, but it brings mourning to God fearing true Christians who refuse to join the circus or watch the side shows. Also, professing Christians fall away, no longer wanting to be identified with Christianity because of increased persecution of Christians and continual assault by a Christ-hating media and godless culture.

Then there are those who are inclined to call themselves Christians while at the same time denying foundational Christian values and teachings. Many belong to the popular emergent, redefined, progressive or "effortless" Christian variety. Many claim to be born gain, even those who don't embrace the person, work and gospel of the Lord Jesus Christ. Many bear their cross to the altar to recite "The Sinner's Prayer" only return to the pew, not becoming new creatures as they thought, but remaining the old sinners that they were. They remain doing what they want, living for the world and seeking their Best Life Now. Many contend for the prosperity gospel, waiting for the great heavenly snatch to gain their heavenly prize and grab their reserved seat in the heavenly Kingdom.

On the contrary, Jesus' true followers never win a popularity contest nor will His true Gospel appear on the best sellers list. He didn't come to win friends and influence people, but to win souls and enlist an army. He didn't come to build a mega church, but a mighty Church. Jesus constantly was downsizing His Church with such hard preaching and difficult statements that even many of His disciples would not listen and withdrew. He even asked His twelve disciples: "You do not want to go away also, do you?" (Jn 6:67). So today, we see many falling by the wayside rather than staying on the Way because there is increasing pressure to compromise and conform to the world rather than to keep the faith and be transformed.

As Christians continue to become increasingly compromised, spiritually paralyzed, morally bankrupt, void of the Spirit, less relevant to man's true needs and less able to address and heal society's sin disease, we will continue to see more "nones" and "dones" and thus "Christianity" "fall" in the polls. The "nones" are those who choose not to affiliate with Christianity and the "dones" are those who are "done" with dead, institutional Christian religion. The "dones" have jumped off the religious band wagon, leaving behind its wood, hay and straw. It doesn't mean they have given up on Christianity as the poll numbers may suggest. On the contrary, many are joining New Testament style churches which still preach Jesus, holiness, and sermons that pierce hearts rather than tickle ears, where members participate rather than spectate. Others join in on the growing home church movement, returning to the "way it used to be" during the first two hundred years of Christianity, when the Church upset the world, rather than being turned upside down by the world (Acts 17:6). Other "dones" are joining para-church ministries which take the Church to the highways and byways, where it belongs; BEING the Church, rather than just going to church; to the marketplace to wins souls rather than market religion to gain fame.

So be excited, expectant and assured that God's true Church continues to grow, is being refined, purged of dross and chaff, focused, empowered and fruitful. In the future, more not less, will give attention to God's only solution when the world continues to suffer greater and more intense pains of childbirth, until the final adoption of God's true children is accomplished (Rom 8:22-23). While God's shaking storms of judgment continue to arrive, His church will thrive (Heb 12:26-20). The Lord's Bride will arise and shine, not dressed for success, but clothed in fine linen, not lulled to sleep, but filled with the Spirit, not on the decline, but will recline in the kingdom of God (Rev 19:8; Eph 5:13-14; Lk 13:29). While the kingdom of heaven suffers violence, they will take it by force (Mt 11:12).

MARCH 22

There is a way which seems right for fallen man, but it only seems right because he sees wrong. But when the Son of Man who is the Truth is sought, the true way becomes clear, and His followers stand strong.

HYPER GRACE ISN'T SO GREAT

Hyper grace, as some call 'modern grace' is the idea that a true Christian is one who can continually live in sin because Jesus died for all sins for all time for the saved. Real repentance is not required since all sins have been paid for. Only lost rewards will be the result of sin, if that. But in reality the person who advocates such a view does not understand or acknowledge that the true grace of God that brings salvation also instructs believers to deny ungodliness and worldly desires and to live sensibly, righteously and godly in this present age (Tit 2:11-12). The Bible teaches: "Now those who belong to Christ Jesus have crucified the flesh with its passions and desires" (Gal 5:24). And we must remember what Jesus said: "For whoever does the will of My Father who is in heaven, he is My brother and sister and mother" (Mt 12:50). And concerning living in sin, one of Jesus' inner circle disciples said it this way: "By this the children of God and the children of the devil are obvious: anyone who does not practice righteousness is not of God, nor the one who does not love his brother" (1 Jn 3:10).

Hyper grace takes sins lightly because it teaches that one need not repent of sin, because after all, God does not see the sin of a saved one, but only their imputed righteousness. However, such an idea tramples underfoot the Son of God, and regards as unclean the blood of the covenant by which he was sanctified and insults the Spirit of grace (Heb 10:26-29). Those who teach such a sinner-friendly grace turn the grace of our God into licentious and deny our only Master and Lord, Jesus Christ (Jude 4). This same Jesus who warned the churches in Revelation to repent (Rev 2,3) also bore our sins in His body on the cross, so that we might die to sin and live to righteousness (1 Pet 2:24). For by His wounds we were healed from our death in trespasses and sins and were given spiritual life as new creatures (Jn 3:3,5; Eph 2:1-5; 2 Cor 5:17). We are seated in the heavenlies with Him no longer to love the world, but as citizens of heaven, to be aliens and strangers to the world (Eph 2:6; Phil 3:20; 1 Jn 2:15-17; 1 Pet 2:12). No longer sinners, but called saints, the Lord's own are being transformed as the Holy Spirit renews their minds and sanctifies their lives (Rom 12:1-2; 1 Thess 4:7-8; 2 Cor 6:14-18). It is time to stand against this new "hyper grace" and stand on God's saving and sanctifying grace (1 Pet 5:12).

MARCH 23

*Christians who do not sincerely press into Him
will eventually become stressed out.*

WHAT IS EASY BELIEVISM?

Easy believism is the false idea that one is saved and kept by a faith that consists of, and requires nothing more than, an intellectual acknowledge of Jesus as Savior or even a sincere "Sinner's Prayer" to receive Jesus as Savior. There doesn't need to be any acknowledgement of Jesus as Lord, nor any present or subsequent intention of submitting to Him as Lord. That is, saving and persevering faith need not be demonstrated by or be accompanied with any present or future works of Spirit-empowered righteousness or Spirit-born fruit of true repentance.

The apostle Paul really didn't mean what he said in verses such as: "Work out you're your salvation with fear and trembling" (Phil 2:12b) or "not the hearers of the Law are just before God, but the doers of the Law will be justified" (Rom 2:13). Proponents of easy believism also see repentance as only being a change in mind and not a change in behavior either present or subsequent to salvation. These proponents have created a false category of saved Christians who merely receive Jesus as Savior, but in life can deny Him as Lord. However, the apostle Paul said: "For we do not preach ourselves but Christ Jesus as Lord, and ourselves as your bond-servants for Jesus sake" (2 Cor 4:5) and again: "As you therefore have received Christ Jesus the Lord, so walk in Him" (Col 2:6). The truth of the matter is that the same faith that saves, that is, a faith exercised by God's grace and with Holy Spirit power, is also the same faith which heaven bound believers will keep to the end (James 2; 1 Pet 2:5,9, etc).

MARCH 24

The writing is on the wall. Now is the time for Christians to take off their 50 shades of gray sunglasses and see what is going on and fix their eyes on the Son.

WHY SETTLE FOR A BREAKDOWN WHEN YOU CAN EXPERI-ENCE A BREAK THROUGH?

The emergent church, contemplative spirituality, laughing "revivals", the Harlem Shake, the hyper-grace, the "purpose driven" and "best life now" spiritual fads and many others will continue to blow through the church. These and other novel ideas will continue to wash in like tsunamis hitting spiritually dry beaches. But instead of carrying God-pleasing servants to His watered promised land to bear edible fruit, their currents will continue to take self-pleasing victims out to sea, becoming food for shysters and sharks. These fads arise and deceive the masses not because of new proclaimed spiritual breakthroughs, but because of contemporary Christianity's religious breakdown, powerlessness and refusal to address and correct her spiritual deficiencies. But things are changing for the better, that is, for those who choose to have their minds renewed by the Bible, rather than their ears tickled by religious babble.

Spiritual breakthrough often comes when our faith is proven by trials (1 Pet 1:7), our life is cleansed of sin (2 Cor 7:1) and our soul is nourished on the words of life (Ps 107:20; Rom 15:4; Jn 6:63; 1 Tim 4:6). Christians who are prayed up (Eph 6:18) and powered by the Spirit (Acts 1:8) will prevail and persevere amidst coming persecution and societal breakdown. When believers continually assemble to provoke one another to love and good deeds (Heb 10:24), "devoting themselves to the apostles' teaching and to fellowship, to the breaking of bread and to prayer" (Acts 2:42), when they produce the fruit of the Spirit (Gal 5:22-23), and put on the full armor of God (Eph 6:11) they will walk in newness of life (Rom 6:4). When they prepare themselves for service by personal cleansing (2 Tim 2:21) and profitable Scripture (2 Tim 3:16-17) and pursue peace with all men and sanctification (Heb 12:14), they will experience spiritual breakthrough. When pastors teach sound doctrine (Tit 2:1) and proclaim Jesus, admonishing and teaching every man with all wisdom (Col 1:28) and equip the saints for effective service (Eph 4:11f) and make disciples, they too will experience spiritual breakthrough.

MARCH 25

If the Holy Spirit is in your prayer life there will be victory in your walk life, and increase in your praise life.

The coming last revival will be one consisting of revived, overcoming saints. These will be believers separated from the world who understand the times, who put on the full armor of God, who make the most of their time, fight the good fight, keep the faith and finish the course. They are unstained by the world and sustained by the Lord; not conformed to the world, but transformed by the Word; not drunk with the world but filled with the Spirit. They proclaim the Good News in bad times, rather than complain how bad it is in these last days. For they are convinced that God is still in control, for He has "established His throne in the heavens, and His sovereignty rules over all" (Ps 103:19).

And this spiritual outpouring and revival is not reserved for some class of super saints, super apostles or super prophets, but for all of God's called children, who are described as living stones in His spiritual house, called out of darkness to become a holy and royal priesthood (1 Pet 2:5, 9). The last great work of God will not be spear headed by a class of super professional clergy, but by a Spirit filled army, who understand the times and who have put on the full armor of God (1 Chron 12:32; Eph 6:11). As good soldiers of Christ Jesus they suffer hardship and the sufferings of Christ (2 Tim 2:3) and thus will experience His comfort (2 Cor 1:3-6). They do not embrace the god of this world and are not entangled in the affairs of everyday life, so that they may please the one who enlisted them as soldiers (2 Tim 2:4). They will be properly functioning members of the body of God (Eph 4:16, 5:23) and submitted to the Lordship of their Head, the Lord Jesus Christ (1 Pet 3:15).

The last great work of God is not reserved for those who have received some so-called last days special anointing or religious mantle, but for all those overcoming saints who have already received the anointing from the Holy One, and are filled with the Holy Spirit (1 Jn 2:20, 27; Eph 5:18). Such ones are subject to one another in the fear of Christ, rather than lord it over others in pride and disobedience to Christ (Eph 5:21; Mt 20:25-28). They have put on the Lord Jesus Christ and the breastplate of righteousness, not of religion; a breastplate of faith and love, not of doubt and hate (Rom 13:14; Eph 6:14). They wear the helmet of hope and salvation, not of fear and desperation (1 Thess 5:8; Eph 6:17a). It is for those who have faith to believe and do and who have a will to listen and obey. So the last great work of God will be accomplished by those separated and cleansed from sin, vessels "for honor, sanctified, useful to the Master, prepared for every good work" (2 Tim 2:21); by those nourished on Scripture and made adequate and equipped for every good work (2 Tim 3:16-17).

MARCH 26

"The Word of God is a looking glass, to show us our spots; and the blood of Christ is a fountain to wash them away." Thomas Watson

Happy Coming Resurrection Day to all Christians. I pray that the "Easter Religious Service" will become a Resurrection daily lifestyle for those who truly seek to live the resurrected life (Rom 6:4-5; Phil 3:10-11; Col 3:1-2). Jesus Christ who was resurrected almost 2,000 years ago is worthy to be the Resurrected Lord of our lives daily, since He is our life (Col 3:4). Like the apostle Paul, Bible practicing Christians are to count all things loss in view of the surpassing value of knowing Christ Jesus as the Resurrected Lord and live by His resurrection and imparted Holy Spirit power (Phil 3:8,10; Eph 3:16). Jesus must come before all worldly desires, earthly relationships, political affiliations, economic worries and emotional concerns.

When Jesus, His kingdom and His will are given first place, all else will follow in proper place. If He is for us, who can be against us? If His resurrection power resides in us, who can overcome us? If He reigns in us, no power can rule over us. If our Heavenly Father gives us all things with His Son, then we need never feel deprived of anything (Rom 8:32). If the resurrected Lord lives in us, we need never feel handicapped. If Jesus, the

Way leads us, we need not fear of getting lost. If Jesus, the Truth, guides us by His Holy Spirit (Jn 14:26; 1 Jn 2:27; Rom 8:14), we don't have to worry about being deceived by the evil one and his disguised servants of "righteousness".

MARCH 27

Jesus said: Go and make disciples. He didn't say stay and make excuses.

THE EASTER BUNNY OR THE RISEN LION OF JUDAH?

Victimized by the roaring lion or victorious with the Risen Lion of Judah?

It's an easy choice which is mine.
Though the lost and depraved revile and bring derision,
The saved and redeemed rejoice because of Him who has risen.
Mockers laugh now but will mourn then,
When the King returns and all acknowledge Him.
Some think they stand now safe and secure,
Wait till the Savior returns, they won't be so sure.
Some settle for the "Best Life Now" and live it up,
It's better to take hold of eternal life and drink from His cup.
Many play now, forever demanding "Give me more",
Wait till He who gave His all returns and settles the score.

The purpose drunken can continue being driven,
But let the Spirit-led will keep on truly living.
While most covet worldly riches which will rot,
It is better to prefer heavenly treasures which will not.
The foolish are married to sinful self and pride,
The wise are married to the Holy One as His spotless bride.
I don't care what the mocking and spiritually dead may say.
The Rocking and Risen One is on His way.

MARCH 28

"Hell is larger today than it was yesterday, because many of us have failed to pray." David Smithers

Every day should be a Resurrection Day for those who have been born again and raised up from being dead in trespasses and sins to walk in newness of life with Him (Eph 2:1; Rom 6:4). As new creations in Christ, old things have passed away; behold, new things have come (2 Cor 5:17). We forget past mistakes, confess present sins and run toward a hopeful future. When we claim His precious promises laid before us in His Word that fully prepares us, we will surely overcome all enemies rising up against us (2 Pet 1:3-4; 2 Tim 3:17; Rom 8:37). Since we have been blessed with every spiritual blessing in the heavenly places in Christ and are seated with Him as citizens of heaven (Eph 1:3, 2:6; Phil 3:20), we need not sit around, pouting, in bondage to the world's sin or leaven. As overcomers of the world and spoilers of the evil one, we are spokesmen of the Righteous One and soldiers of the Victorious

One. Having been anointed by the Holy One, we crush under our feet the defeated demonic serpents and scorpions of the evil one. Though the devil may roam and roar, seeking to destroy the Church, we serve the risen Savior, the Lion of Judah who prevailed, who reigns, and who continues to build His Church.

MARCH 29

One's label means nothing. One's life means everything.

SPIRITUAL WARFARE IS DAILY. THE BATTLEFIELD IS THE MIND.

Remember Peter's response to Jesus' foretelling of His death: "Peter took Him aside and began to rebuke Him, saying, 'God forbid it, Lord! This shall never happen to You'" (Mt 16:22). Because Peter set his mind on man's interests rather than on God's, he was a stumbling block to Jesus, rather than being the living stone he would become (Mt 16:23; Jn 20:22; 1 Pet 2:5). In these last days when we are called to die to self and sin and live for Him, our adversary the devil will come in like a flood to drown our mind with his lies, evil thoughts and religious disguises (2 Cor 11:13-15). The battlefield is the mind. We must remain alert and destroy every speculation and every lofty thing raise up against the knowledge of God and take every thought captive to the obedience of Christ" (2 Cor 10:5). Every temptation heeded is a prior evil thought unattended.

MARCH 30

Bearing the cross of Christ will often
bring us to a cross of our own.

BEWARE: THE DEVIL IS ON THE PROWL.

The devil loves to ensnare people to love his world so they will miss out on eternal life (1 Jn 2:15-17). The devil wants to befriend the children of God so they might become His enemies (Jam 4:4). But Jesus said that one cannot serve two masters. Too many contemporary Christians claim Jesus as Savior but fail to realize that He "gave Himself for us that He might redeem us from every lawless deed and purify for Himself a people for His own possession, zealous for good deeds" (Tit 2:14). They fail to sanctify Christ as Lord of their hearts (1 Pet 3:15), and to serve Him in whom are hidden all the treasures of wisdom and knowledge (Col 2:3), as well as the treasure of eternal life (Jn 17:3). They yield to the devil's temptations to grasp after the world's treasures and serve its gods, living for the best life now. The devil prowls about enticing the Lord's servants to disregard their obligations to their Master. He prefers that they not feast on Jesus, Living Manna from heaven, but rather indulge in pastoral pastries and deadly devil's food cake covered with religious icing and smoking candles.

MARCH 31

*A gentle blowing whisper from God is all it
takes to dispel the devil's stormy lies.*

REDEEMING RELIGION IS NOT CHEAP GRACE.

Obeying His heavenly Father costs Jesus all He had, and following Him will costs you all you have. He laid aside His heavenly glory to become the Son of Man, so that you could lay down your worldly glory and become a child of God (Phil 2:6-8). Paul reminded the Corinthian believers: "For you know the grace of our Lord Jesus Christ, that though He was rich, yet for you sake He became poor that you through His poverty might become rich" (2 Cor 8:9). He laid down His life so you could live, if only you will die to self and live for Him. He left His throne to take the cross, so we would leave the world and carry His cross. He surrendered His life and paid for our sin, so we would surrender our life in service to Him. God's costly and redeeming grace that saves repentant sinners from the depths of hell (Tit 2:11; Eph 1:8; 1 Pet 1:18-19), also was sent to disciple them how to overcome the dominion of sin and to "deny ungodliness and worldly desires and to live sensibly, righteously and godly in the present age" (Tit 2:12). Such grace is not cheap but was costly so that you might become rich; you who were formerly "separate from Christ, excluded from the commonwealth of Israel, and strangers to the covenants of promise, having no hope and without God in the world" (Eph 2:12). "For you know the grace of our Lord Jesus Christ, that though He was rich, yet for your sake He became poor, that you through His poverty might become rich" (2 Cor 8:9).

APRIL 1

*The more closely the sheep follow their Shepherd, the
more easily they will recognize and hear His voice.*

GUARD AGAINST TRUTH DECAY

If only the Bible were read, properly preached and devoutly practiced today, we would see less truth decay. Bible illiteracy and pastoral malpractice are perhaps the greatest sins today by those sitting in pews and those
standing behind pulpits. How can the promised Helper and Spirit of Truth
sanctify the believer who attributes little value to reading the Word of God
and less value to devout practice of the Word? Yet, there seems to be ample
time for malpractice of the Word of God, by clergy professionals who adulterate and peddle the Word (2 Cor 2:17, 4:2).

Consequently, although "Thy Word is Truth" we see much "Truth
Decay" in believers who prefer pastoral pastries over the solid food of sound
doctrine. Yet the blame also falls on contemporary believers who choose not
to read, hear and heed the written Word of God. Such are not blessed so
says Jesus in His final words to His churches (Rev 1:3). This was in keeping
with His earlier teaching: "If you know these things, you are blessed if you
do them" (Jn 13:17). And Jacob (James), the oldest half-brother of Jesus said:
"the one who looks intently at the perfect law, the law of liberty, and abides
by it, not having become a forgetful hearer but an effectual doer, this man
shall be blessed in what he does" (Jam 1:25). So we see that moral decay as
well as truth decay can be prevented when proper heart health is maintained.
For in the Old Testament it is written: "Watch over your heart with all diligence, for from it flow the springs of life" (Prov 4:23) and again, "Thy word
I have treasured in my heart, that I many not sin against Thee" (Ps 119:11).

APRIL 2

The hidden life of devotion must be balanced
with an outer life of demonstration.

WHAT THEN SHALL WE DO? PART 1

Evil men and imposters will proceed from bad to worse, deceiving and being deceived (2 Tim 3:13). False christs, false apostles and false prophets will arise who will deceive by their false signs, wonders and miracles all who are not abiding in the true Christ who is the only Way, the Light and the Truth (Mt 24:4, 5, 24, 25; Jn 8:12, 14:6). They will profess to be wise but are fools, will pretend to be spiritual but have no Holy Spirit. They will boast of having power but are only empowered by the god of this world. Though they may have a popular name and clout with the underworld, they are profane and without the God of heaven. While they proclaim with their mouth Christian jargon, they deny sound doctrine. Let them play their games. Wise Christian soldiers will run the race that matters: preaching the good news about the kingdom of God and the name of Jesus Christ (Acts 8:12), testifying solemnly of the gospel of the grace of God effective in those exercising genuine repentance toward God and true biblical faith in our Lord Jesus Christ (Acts 20:21, 24) not content with merely making converts but disciples of the Lord Jesus Christ (Mt 28:18-20) and not consumed with building a church but passionate about BEING the Church.

APRIL 3

Life has no problems that the Word of Life cannot solve.
Earth has no questions that heaven cannot answer. Creation
may groan and suffer, but the Creator is coming to deliver.

WHAT THEN SHALL WE, THE CHURCH, THE PILLAR AND SUPPORT OF THE TRUTH, DO? PART 2

Since God is pro-life and is a God of justice...Since He is True and is a defender of widows and protector of orphans...Since He is the Creator of marriage and family and is concerned about children and the elderly.... Since God abhors men of bloodshed and deceit (Ps 5:6) and hates all who do iniquity and violence (Ps 5:5, 11:5)...Since He desires that none perish but for all come to repentance (2 Pet 3:9)....Since the Lord has instructed that His followers pray for His kingdom to come and His will to be done on earth as it is in heaven (Mt 6:10)....Since His kingdom is righteous, peace and joy in the Holy Spirit, accomplished by the power of the Holy Spirit (Rom 14:17)... Since believers have been given divine authority to tread upon serpents and scorpions and over all the power of the enemy (Lk 10:19) .....Since they are urged to make "entreaties and prayers, petitions and thanksgivings on behalf of all men, for kings and all who are in authority in order that we may lead a tranquil and quite life in all godliness and dignity" (1 Tim 2:2)....

It is incumbent that we, the true Church, engage the wicked principalities and powers (Eph 6:12), having put on the full spiritual armor of God (Eph 6:11, 13) and the Lord Jesus Christ (Rom 13:14). Since all of those who have been baptized into Christ have clothed themselves with Christ (Gal 3:27), it is time to have the mind and attitude of Christ (1 Cor 2:16; Phil 2:5). Since we wrestle not against flesh and flood but against demonically energized sons of disobedience (Eph 2:2), we must be filled with the Holy Spirit in order to blind, confuse, bind and defeat their sinister agendas against the Holy purposes of God. As set apart (1 Cor 1:2; 2 Cor 6:14-18; Heb 12:14), Kingdom seeking (Mt 6:33), Bible believing (Rom 15:4), disciple making (Mt 28:19), truth proclaiming ambassadors (Jn 17:17; 2 Tim 4:2; 2 Cor 5:20) and enlisted heavenly soldiers, we must not become entangled with worldly affairs, but expose and oppose the enemies of the Gospel and the unfruitful deeds of darkness (2 Tim 2:3-4; Tit 1:10-11; Eph 5:11).

APRIL 4

There is a famine of hearing the words of God,
and a failure at heeding His words, because there
are too many feasting on words of men.

The Lord has already warned His people to come out from the wicked last day harlot religious system, lest they suffer from her coming and just plagues (Rev 18:4, 8). Those intoxicated with the world, deceived by the lies of its god, and held captive by his demons because they foolishly worship his false shepherds will continue to party on their sinking ark. Meanwhile, those praising God, trusting in Him, walking by faith, led by the Spirit, prayed up and armed up and instructed by His Word will ride out the flood in the life saving ark. They will walk on water, stand strong against blowing winds, and perform great exploits because they intimately know their King of kings and Lord of lords who is able to do exceeding abundantly beyond all that they ask or think.

APRIL 5

Blessed are those who expect what God promises,
who do what God commands, who believe what God
says, who shun what God forbids, who don't read
between the lines, but read what is on the lines.

HOW CAN THE CHRISTIAN BE DEPRESSED WHEN SO BLESSED?

Be encouraged because:

EVERY spiritual blessing in Christ is available, (Eph 1:3).

The Christian is a NEW creature in Christ, old things passed away; behold, new things have come, (2 Cor 5:17).

The Christian CAN do all things through Him who strengthens, (Phil 4:13).

The Christian OVERCOMES Satan the accuser and adversary by the blood of the Lamb, word of testimony and death to self, (Rev 12:11).

The Christian is UNITED and seated in the heavenlies with the resurrected and ascended Lord, (Rom 6:4; Eph 2:6).

The Christian can RESIST the devil and he will flee, (James 4:8).

The Christian is ANOINTED with the Holy Spirit and power, to do good and heal those oppressed by the devil, having been sent by the Father just as He sent His Son from heaven, (Acts 10:38 Jn 20:21).

GOD is able to do exceeding abundantly beyond all that we ask or think, (Eph 3:20).

Things IMPOSSIBLE with men are possible with God, (Lk 18:27).

NO temptation comes without God's provided way of escape, (1 Cor 10:13).

The GRACE of God is sufficient for our every weakness, (2 Cor 12:9).

APRIL 6

God is still on the throne and the future is still in His hands.

Many Christians today are being tempted to go the path of least resistance, to forsake the narrow way, to embrace an "effortless" Christianity, to lay down the cross, to embrace demonic doctrines and distorted gospels and to read the best sellers of men rather than the living and inspired Word of God. On the contrary, much blessing and true spiritual enlightenment comes from reading about true past and current revival works of God as well as biographies of former revivalists. They experienced loving intimacy with God, enjoyed fellowship with Holy Spirit, and the sustaining grace of the Lord Jesus Christ which was also on the heart of the apostle Paul (2 Cor 13:14). Otherwise, disappointed God-seekers will continue being disillusioned with their absentee God, religious rituals, institutional church, theological dogma and cultural irrelevancy.

The problem is not that biblical Christianity has been tried and found wanting. The problem is that biblical Christianity if often not tried at all, when found to be challenging, demanding and costly. But when Christianity is understood properly and practiced devoutly, it will be found to be abundantly providing and to be eternally rewarding.

APRIL 7

*"I never was fit to say a word to a sinner, except when
I had a broken heart myself; when I was subdued and
melted into penitence, and felt as though I had just
received pardon for my own soul, and when my heart
was full of tenderness and piety". Edward Payson*

OH, LORD, GIVE ME THE PROMISES. YOU CAN KEEP THEIR CONDITIONS.

As tribulation and persecution increase in the last days, many passages in Hebrews will become even more relevant such as: "Consider Him who has endured such hostility by sinners against Himself, so that you may not grow weary and lose heart. You have not yet resisted to the point of shedding blood in your striving against sin" (Heb 12:3-4). "Therefore, do not throw away your confidence, which has a great reward. For you have need of endurance, so that when you have done the will of God, you may receive what was promised" (Heb 10:35-36). John speaks of this promise: "And this is the promise which He Himself made to us: eternal life" (1 Jn 2:25). But today, many want the promises, but not their conditions, ear tickling smooth words, not heart piercing sermons. Thus, in contemporary Christianity we hear little preaching on repentance, but much on tolerance; little on endurance but much on indulgence; little on being poor in spirit, but much on prosperity; little on holiness, but much on happiness.

Peter reminds his Christian audience concerning another promise: the Lord's promised return: "Therefore, beloved, since you look for these things, be diligent to be found by Him in peace, spotless and blameless...The Lord is not slow about His promise, as some count slowness, but is patient toward you not wishing for any to perish but for all to come to repentance...Therefore, brethren, be all the more diligent to make certain about His calling and choosing you; for as long as you practice these things, you will never stumble, for in this way the entrance into the eternal kingdom of our Lord and Savior Jesus Christ will be abundantly supplied to you. Therefore, I shall always be ready to remind you of these things" (2 Pet 3:9, 13, 14, 1:10-12a). Peter would not have thought highly of today's hyper grace, "effortless" Christianity.

And John would not have taken lightly today's teaching that Christians may still take the mark of the beast and be fine. In Revelation we read how blessed and holy are those who maintain their testimony of Jesus and the word of God and who refuse to worship the beast or his image or receive his mark. They will take part in the first resurrection and over them the second death has no power (Rev 20:4-6). Their garments are not soiled with sin. They walk with Him in white, overcoming and clothed in white garments, whose names are not erased from the book of life (Rev 3:4-5). The promise is: "If we endure, we shall also reign with Him" but the warning is: "If we deny Him, He also will deny us" (2 Tim 2:12).

Oh, how we love the promises but loath their conditions. But for the one who overcomes, Jesus says: "I will confess his name before My Father and before His angels" (Rev 3:5). "I will grant to him to sit down with Me on My throne, as I also overcame and sat down with My Father on His throne" (Rev 3:21). For the Scripture says we are children of God and "fellow heirs with Christ, if indeed we suffer with Him so that we may also be glorified with Him" (Rom 8:17). And "through many tribulations we must enter the kingdom of God" (Acts 14:22). "For to you it has been granted for Christ's sake, not only to believe in Him, but also to suffer for His sake" (Phil 1:29). So we see again, that with this condition of believing in Jesus who is eternal life comes the assurance of possessing eternal life: "These things I have written to you who believe in the name of the Son of God, in order that you may know that you have eternal life" (1 Jn 5:13, 20).

APRIL 8

"Not for ourselves, but for others, is the grand law inscribed on every part of creation." Edward Payson

It's great to be on the winning side, overcoming with the Jesus the King who overcame. Even in trying times, God always leads His faithful ones in triumph in Christ (2 Cor 2:13-14). As we are led by the Spirit of God, we overcome the enemies of God by faith (1 Jn 5:4; Eph 6:16), because of the blood of the Lamb and word of our testimony, not loving our life even when faced with death (Rev 12:12). As King David said: "God trains my hands for battle, so that my arms can bend a bow of bronze...And I silenced those who hated me" (Ps 18:34, 40).

Our "bow of bronze" today is the living and active Word of God, sharper than any two-edged sword of man (Eph 6:17; Heb 4:12). It is the truth that sends the devil and father of lies fleeing (Jn 8:44); and even shuts up the tempter when quoted (Mt. 4:4, 7, 10).

David continues: "I pursued my enemies and overtook them, and I did not turn back until they were consumed. I shattered them, so that they were not able to rise, they fell under my feet" (Ps 18:37-38). So Jesus has given His sent out saints power and authority to crush demons under their feet (Lk 9:1, 10:1, 17-19). Yet all too often these defeated spiritual enemies, whom Jesus defeated and disarmed on the cross, are allowed to roam freely on the street (Col 2:15).

Yet the God of peace continues to crush Satan under the feet of faithful remnant who are obedient (Rom 16:19-20). As we destroy speculations and every lofty thing raised up against the knowledge of God and take every thought captive to the obedience of Christ (2 Cor 10:5), and continue in His truthful word, we will walk in true freedom and victory (Jn 8:31-32, 36). As we are taught and led by the Holy Spirit of Truth we will abide in the Truth, walk in liberty, and cast out the demons who seek to disrupt and imprison our lives (Jn 16:13; 1 Jn 2:27; Mt 12:28). Where the Spirit of the Lord is there is liberty (2 Cor 3:17). Christians who are seated in the heavenlies (Eph 1:20, 2:6; Col 3:1) with Christ, need never sit in the gutters of the world, despondent and defeated, in despair and ensnared by its god (2 Tim 2:25-26; 2 Cor 4:4; 1 Jn 4:4, 5:4, 5:19)

"Therefore, do not throw away your confidence, which has a great reward. For you have need of endurance, so that when you have done the will of God, you may receive what was promised" (Heb 10:35-36). "We are not of those who shrink back to destruction, but of those who have faith to the preserving of the soul" (Heb 10:39). Jesus forewarned: "You will be hated by all because of My name, but it is the one who has endured to the end who will be saved" (Mt 10:22, 24:13). "For whoever wishes to saved his life will lose it; but whoever loses his life for My sake will find it" (Mt 16:25). So don't lose out in inheriting eternal life by listening to those deceived religious ones who claim to have it.

APRIL 9

"The most of my sufferings and sorrows were occasioned by my own unwillingness to be nothing, which I am, and by struggling to be something." Edward Payson

The devil was defeated 2000 years ago. Isn't it time that the true Church claim the victory (1 Cor 15:57)? The devil was disarmed by Jesus on the cross (Col 2:15). Isn't it time for the spiritually armed Church to take up the Cross (Eph 6:11f)? The fear of death was conquered by His resurrection (Heb 2:14-15). Isn't it time that the triumphant Church rise up and stop fearing what the devil can't do (Mt 10:28; Rom 8:33-34, 38-39)? The Lord made proclamation to the spirits in prison (1 Pet 3:19). Isn't it time that we proclaim the Good News to those still in prison (Lk 4:18; Acts 8:12)?

The devil loves to parade about in churches as an angel of light, deceiving those who love to walk in darkness. He entertains those addicted to pleasure, passionate for the world and living for the present, those doing what is right in their own eyes and despising what is right in God's eyes, receiving whatever tickles their ears but rejecting that which pierces their heart. But God's true remnant will parade in victory throughout the world as beacons of light, salt preservers of good, and the only proclaimers of Good News.

They will proclaim liberty to those held in bondage in doing the devil's will (2 Tim 2:26), for they are filled with the Spirit, and where the Spirit of the Lord is there is victory (Eph 5:18; 2 Cor 3:17). As proclaimers of the Gospel of Truth, they invite sinners to turn from darkness to light and from the dominion of Satan to God (Acts 26:18a), knowing that God desires that none perish but for all to come to repentance (2 Pet 3:9). They proclaim Jesus as Savior and Lord (Lk 2:11; 2 Cor 4:5) and the Light of the world (Jn 8:12) who shines upon those who sit in darkness and the shadow of death (Lk 1:79) in order that they may receive forgiveness of sins and an inheritance among those who have been sanctified by faith in Him (Acts 26:18b). And that being delivered from the hand of the enemies of God those who receive heaven's gift of salvation by grace through faith may seek the face of God and serve Him without fear, in holiness and righteousness before Him all their days (Lk 1:74-75; Eph 2:8, 2 Cor 9:15; Jn 3:16).

The Savior's born again and delivered saints serve the risen King, who continues to rule over His household and whose kingdom will have no end (Lk 1:33). Meanwhile Satan's deceived sons of disobedience, dead in trespasses and sins, continue to serve their depraved self and dead prophets buried below the ground (Eph 2:1). However, God's children serve the King and True Prophet who sits victorious and exalted above the heavens at the right hand of God (Lk 7:16; Eph 1:20), having gone into heaven after angels and authorities and powers had been subjected to Him (1 Pet 3:22). So the devil was defeated 2,000 years ago and has continued facing defeat ever since by the Lord's risen and victorious army.

APRIL 10

"We may judge the state of our hearts by the earnestness of our prayers" Edward Payson

BEATEN DOWN IN DEPRESSION? BEGIN GIVING THANKS AND YOU WILL BE LIFTED UP.

Long ago God said: "If you do well, will not your countenance be lifted up?" (Gen 4:7a). It is written in the Psalms: "It is good to give thanks to the LORD, and to sing praises to Thy name, O Most High" (92:1). In the New Testament it is written: "In everything give thanks; for this is God's will for you in Christ Jesus" (1 Thess 5:18). Through Christ we are to continually offer up a sacrifice of praise to God that is, the fruit of lips that give thanks to His name (Heb 13:15). After all, "a joyful heart is good medicine, but a broken spirit dries up the bones (Prov 17:22).

The devil wants to stress out. The Lord wants to bless out. "Bless the LORD, O my soul, and forget none of His benefits" (Ps 103:2). God desires to redeem our life from the pit (Ps 103:4a). Through thanksgiving we can rise from Satan's pit and claim our position at God's right hand (Eph 2:6). We accomplish this by focusing our eyes and mind on Christ and our many spiritual blessings in the heavenly places in Christ, with whom we are seated (Heb 12:2; Eph 1:3, 2:6; Col 3:1-4). King David, a man after God's own heart, knew well the secret of spiritual victory and mental health: "I will give thanks to the LORD with all my heart; I will tell of all Thy wonders... When my enemies turn back, they stumble and perish before Thee...The LORD also will be a stronghold for the oppressed, a stronghold in times of trouble" (Ps 9:1, 3, 9). David knew the depressed soul is lifted when the Spirit renewed mind admonishes the soul saying: "Bless the LORD, O my soul, and all that is within me, bless His holy name. Bless the LORD, O my soul and forget none of His benefits" (Ps 103:1, 2; cp. Rom 12:2, Eph 3:16; 2 Cor 4:16).

When we begin singing and praising the LORD, and giving thanks for His everlasting lovingkindness and blessings, the LORD set's ambushes against our enemies who seek to discourage and destroy. Through praise and thanksgiving the enemies of our soul are routed and we are established (2 Chron 20:20-22). David experienced this many times and offered this helpful advice to the LORD's godly ones: "I will extol Thee, O LORD, for Thou hast lifted me up, and hast not let my enemies rejoice over me... Sing praise to the LORD, you His godly ones, and give thanks to His holy name...Thou hast turned for me my mourning into dancing; Thou hast loosed my sackcloth and girded me with gladness" (Ps 30:1, 4, 11). Then the depressed, parched and weary soul will joyously draw water from the springs of salvation and be lifted on that day we give thanks to the LORD and remember that His name is exalted forever (Isa 12:2-4).

APRIL 11

*"We live in a day of itching ears but I have no commission
from God to scratch them."Leonard Ravenhill*

Beware of false teachers who peddle the word of God and those who walk in craftiness, adulterating the word of God (2 Cor 2:17 4:2). Their deceived followers likewise use their religious scissors to cut out of the Scripture teachings they do not like and the commandments of God they do not want to obey. God's saving and sanctifying grace, the Sermon on the Mount, many writings of Paul, biblical faith, genuine repentance, the denial of the flesh, confession of sin, necessity of repentance, the call to holiness and dedication to God's will, and other passages that do not comfort their itching ears are either denied as being relevant for today or else are reinterpreted to justify their effortless and self-centered Christianity. The Spirit of Truth is quenched, grieved and resisted in favor of the spirit of the age.

Most popular leaders of contemporary Christianity drunkenly worship a god of their own imagination. There needs to be a supernatural awakening from this worldly stupor and false worship. There must be a return to a reverent worship of the God of the Bible in Spirit and in truth (Jn 4:23-24). The book of Revelation clearly reveals what will soon take place. "Behold, I am coming quickly, and My reward is with Me, to render to every man according to what he has done" (Rev 22:12). The Lord will soon return to "bring to light the things hidden in the darkness and disclose the motives of men's hearts; and then each man's praise will come to him from God" (1 Cor 4:5). Those who are selfishly ambitious and to not obey the truth, but obey unrighteousness, will receive God's wrath and indignation (Rom 2:8). But to those who by perseverance in doing good, seek for glory and honor and immortality, they will receive eternal life (Rom 2:7). "For God will render to every man according to his deeds" (Rom 2:6). Remember, Jesus said, "So then, you will know them by their fruits" (Mt 7:19). Of course this fruit is not produced by man's ability, for it is "not by might or by power, but by My Spirit, says the LORD of hosts" (Zech 4:6). The Holy Spirit is the power source for godly fruit (Gal 5:22-23).

"Therefore having overlooked the times of ignorance, God is now declaring to men that all everywhere should repent, because He has fixed a day in which He will judge the world in righteousness through a Man whom He has appointed, having furnished proof to all men by raising Him from the dead" (Acts 17:30-31). The good, faithful and fruitful servants of the Lord will hear Him say: "Well done, good and faithful slave...enter into the joy of your master" (Mt 25:23). But those who choose to remain spiritually asleep, lazy, unfaithful, unfruitful, unrepentant desiring rather to serve the god of this world will also be awakened. But they will hear the devil say something like this to them: "Well done, my wicked and faithful servant. Enter into the eternal torment with your master".

APRIL 12

"It costs something to be a true Christian. It will cost us our sins, our self-righteousness, our ease and our worldliness." J.C. Ryle

IT'S TIME TO RUN AFTER, NOT TURN BACK.

The sons of Ephraim were archers equipped with bows, yet they turned back in the day of battle (Ps 78:9). And God also "rejected the tent of Joseph, and did not choose the tribe of Ephraim" (Ps 78:67), but chose the tribe of Judah…and David His servant" (Ps 78:67-68a, 70a). So God does to the "stubborn and rebellious generation that does not prepare its heart and whose spirit is not faithful to God" (Ps 78:8). The generation that disdains the truth and knowledge of God flees in fear of man and away from spiritual battle. God has warned: "My people are destroyed for lack of knowledge. Because you have rejected knowledge, I also will reject you from being My priest" (Hosea 4:6). The living God has no delight in dead religion, vain worship, doctrines, precepts and the tradition of men (Mk 7:7-8) and feigned obedience by His enemies (Ps 66:3). "For I delight in loyalty rather than sacrifice and in the knowledge of God rather than burn offerings" (Hosea 6:6). God prefers obedience over religious show.

Woe to the generation that questions God's ability and provision during trying and testing times; the generation that speaks against Him saying: "Can God prepare a table in the wilderness…Can He give bread also? Will He provide meat for His people?" (Ps 78:19-20). Such put God to the test by asking for fast food according to their desire, rather than for spiritual food for God's mission (Ps 78:18). Such a generation often deceives God with their mouth and lies to Him with their tongue, possessing a heart that is not steadfast toward Him, neither are they faithful in His covenant (Ps 78:36-37).

Not so with David, a man after God's own heart, committed to doing God's will (Acts 13:22). His heart was steadfast toward God (Ps 57:7) and caring toward God's people. "He shepherded them according to the integrity of his heart, and guided them with his skilled hands" (Ps 78:72). The warrior King David displayed a confident heart toward God in the midst of his desert experience while he was warring against his enemies: "Even though I walk through the valley of the shadow of death, I fear no evil, for You are with me; Your rod and Your staff, they comfort me. You prepare a table before me in the presence of my enemies; You have anointed my head with oil; my cup overflows" (Ps 23:4-5).

So the Lord would say to those who enter their desert and face their adversary the devil, not to whine before this roaring lion, but to dine with the reigning King and Lion of Judah. Those who labor in His vineyard will never lack His favor. Jesus said: "My food is to do the will of Him who sent Me and to accomplish His work" (Jn 4:34). John spoke of the Lord's victorious search and rescue mission: "You know that He appeared in order to take away sins....the Son of God appeared for this purpose, to destroy the works of the devil"(1 Jn 3:5,8). The God of peace will soon crush Satan under the feet of those who continue to run after Him (Rom 16:20; Ps 18:29-33).

It is time for serious spiritual warfare against all evil as well as all false and dead religion. It is time to deliver deceived sheep from the jaws of religious wolves and divert their attention off their beloved idols long enough to look on their beloved Savior, who died for them, so they could live and die for Him. It is not by repeated trips to the altar and sitting before buffet pulpits of pastoral pastries and ear tickling sermons, that we enter the kingdom of God. It is by dying on the altar, by persevering in faith (2 Tim 4:7-8) through many tribulations (Acts 14:22; Heb 10:32-39; Mt 24:13) and by being nourished on sound doctrine (Tit 2:2).

APRIL 13

*"We are not diplomats but prophets, and our message
is not a compromise but an ultimatum." A.W. Tozer*

God is busy drafting an army of Christian soldiers and ambassadors of the King of Kings who understand the times (1 Chron 12:32; 2 Tim 2:3-4). They know who the real enemies are and what they are doing and how to use their spiritual weapons effectively against them (1 Chron 12:33;

Eph 6:12; 2 Cor 6:7). God is looking for those who are wisely redeeming the time in fighting the good fight, rather than passing time playing church with the devil. God most effectively uses those whose eyes are fixed on Christ above, having His mind, rather than having their eyes fixed on the world, and emptying and opening their minds to find some 'god' within (1 Cor 2:16; Col 3:1-4).

Too many Christians are being caught up in the New Age contemplative spiritual formation movement, when they should be sold out to the Author and Perfecter of our faith, the Lord Jesus Christ and exercised in biblical spiritual disciplines (Heb 12:2; 1 Tim 4:6-11; Acts 2:42). It's time to quit going AWOL from the good fight and show up for duty. The deceptive devil, the uncrucified self, and those entangled by the world love to grant leave of absence from our Christian duty. However, the true "best life now" or that abundant life Jesus came to give, is experienced in the battle field, not in the devil's playground; having hands trained for war, not ears tickled by man.

APRIL 14

"Christians don't tell lies they just go to
church and sing them". A.W. Tozer

EFFORTLESS CHRISTIANITY OR A WORK IN PROGRESS?

A close and honest study of Scripture proves that Christianity is not an effortless walk with God, but is a diligent working together with God as He works within us and with us. Paul urged the Corinthian believers saying: "And working together with Him, we also urge you not to receive the grace of God in vain" (2 Cor 6:1). Paul knew that the grace of God that brought salvation to all men also instructed those saved to deny ungodliness and worldly desires and to live sensibly, righteously and godly in the present age (Tit 2:11-12). The apostle Paul thought it necessary to exhort the Philippian believers who had demonstrated a life of obedience, saying: "work out your salvation with fear and trembling; for it is God who is at work in you, both to will and to work for His good pleasure" (Phil 2:12b-13). He knew that a healthy fear or reverence of the Holy God is necessary in pursuing holiness that pleases God.

So Paul exhorted believers to separate themselves from anything having to do with lawlessness, darkness, idolatry, uncleanness and unbelief. Then they could rest in the promise that God would dwell in them and walk among them as His own sons and daughters (2 Cor 6:14-18). Without sanctification no one will see the Lord (Heb 12:14). For 'the one who practices sin is of the devil...and no one who is born of God practices sin" (1 Jn 3:8-9).

Regarding such promises, Paul went on exhorting them saying, "Therefore, having these promises, beloved, let us cleanse ourselves from all defilement of flesh and spirit, perfecting holiness in the fear of God" (2 Cor 7:1). By claiming such promises and meeting their conditions, such as having escaped the corruption that is in the world by lust, believers can become partakers of divine nature (2 Pet 1:4).

Paul practiced what he preached, for he told the Corinthian believers "Therefore knowing the fear of the Lord, we persuade men" (2 Cor 5:11). Paul wanted them to understand how important and how necessary it was to have an ambition to walk in a manner that pleased God, both in life and in death (2 Cor 5:9). And he revealed one motivation that would help motivate one to such an ambition. He said: "For we must all appear before the judgment seat of Christ, that each one many be recompensed for his deeds in the body, according to what he has done, whether good or bad" (2 Cor 5:10). And such a walk is not accomplished by human labor and ability but by relying on God's available favor and laboring grace. Paul revealed his secret: "But by the grace of God I am what I am, and His grace toward me did not prove vain; but I labored even more than all of them, yet not I, but the grace of God with me" (1 Cor 15:10).

One who is really controlled by a love for Christ, will live for Him, because He died for him (2 Cor 5:14). He will love God because God first loved him (1 Jn 4:19). John showed his appreciation for divine love in saying: "See how great a love the Father has bestowed upon us, that we should be called children of God" (1 Jn 3:1a)…we know love by this, that He laid down His life for us; and we ought to lay down our lives for the brethren" (1 Jn 3:16). Paul said it this way: "He died for all, that they who live should no longer live for themselves, but for Him who died and rose again on their behalf" (2 Cor 5:15).

This "work in progress" in which we work out our salvation, or walk in newness of life, or die to self, in becoming slaves to God and to righteousness, having been freed from enslaving power of sin, does not come automatically and with no effort. It often requires distressing trials (1 Pet 1:6-7), testing of faith (Jam 1:2-4), Fatherly discipline (Heb 12:4-11), temporary suffering (1 Pet 5:10), steadfast endurance (Heb 10:35-39), self discipline (1 Cor 9:24-27), and cleansing of sin (2 Tim 2:21). Since this is a spiritual conquest, it also involves putting on the full armor of God (Eph 6:11f), resisting the devil (Jam 4:7) and destroying evil thoughts (2 Cor 10:3-5), and putting to death the deeds of our warring flesh (Rom 8:13; Gal 5:16; 1 Pet 2:11) by the power of the Holy Spirit. Thus, Paul was assured of the crown of righteousness that would be awarded to him by the Lord on that day because he fought the good fight, finished the course and kept the faith (2 Tim 4:7-8). "For momentary, light affliction is producing for us an eternal weight of glory far beyond all comparison" to all who eagerly await His appearing (2 Cor 4:17; Heb 9:28; 1 Thess 1:10).

APRIL 15

"I might have entered the ministry if certain
clergymen I knew had they not looked and acted
so much like undertakers." Source unknown

A NORMAL CHRISTIAN IS NOT NOMINAL BUT
PHENOMENAL

Why settle for being a normal and nominal religious person when one can be a born again Christian, indwelt by the Spirit of God (1 Cor 3:16), raised up with the Son of God (Eph 2:6) adopted by the Father of glory (Rom 8:15; Eph 1:17) to walk in the supernatural? After all, Christians are citizens of heaven (Phil 3:20) and aliens and strangers to this world which is under the influence of the evil one (1 Pet 2:11; Jn 17:16; 1 Jn 5:19). We are new creations waiting eagerly for our adoption as sons, the redemption of our body, no longer to be part of a fallen creation which groans and suffers (Gal 6:15; 2 Cor 5:17; Rom 8:22-23). We are a chosen race, a royal priesthood and a holy nation (1 Pet 2:9). We have been delivered from the domain of darkness (Col 1:13) and saved to walk in newness of life with Him who is the Light (Rom 6:4; Jn 8:12). We can experience the Kingdom of God which is righteousness and peace and joy in the Holy Spirit (Rom 14:17), who dwells in us and who is greater than the devil and god of this world (1 Jn 4:4; 2 Cor 4:4).

We are God's workmanship, created in Christ Jesus for good works, which God prepared beforehand that we would walk in them (Eph 2:10). If only we work with God, not receiving His grace in vain, but labor by His power and depend on His grace (2 Cor 6:1; Col 1:28-29; 1 Cor 15:10). Just as the heavenly Father sent His only begotten Son into the world, so the victorious Son has sent His own into the world (Jn 17:18). Both anointed with the Holy Spirit and with power (Acts 10:38; Acts 1:8; 1 Jn 1:20), to preach the Good News in demonstration of the Spirit and of power (1 Cor 2:4). Just as the Son was baptized by the Spirit of God (Mt 3:13f) to fulfill all righteousness (Mt 3:13-15), so God's born again children have been baptized by the Spirit to walk in righteousness as Spirit-led (Rom 8:14), Spirit empowered (Mt 3:11; Acts 1:8; Gal 5:16; 1 Cor 12:13) and Spirit taught disciples (1 Jn 2:27; Tit 2:11-12).

As with the apostle Paul, Christ wants to accomplish great things through us as He lives in us, resulting in obedience to the gospel by word and deed (Acts 26:16-19; Rom 1:5, 15:18, 16:26; Gal 2:20; Rom 8:10). The normal Christian walk should be phenomenal since God desires to work in us that which is pleasing in His sight (Heb 13:21). The God who created the world is more than able to accomplish this. God is able to do far more abundantly beyond all that we ask or think, according to the power of His Spirit who works within us (Eph 3:20).

The divine commission has not changed. We are to proclaim everywhere the kingdom of God, even though unrepentant sinners and God haters may ignore us and continue living in spiritual death, being more concerned with worldly matters (Lk 9:60). Such kingdom business is phenomenal since it is accomplished by the Spirit of God (Rom 14:17; Mt 12:28). One can become a supernatural, phenomenal Christian equipped for every divine work by being nourished on the Word of God (2 Tim 3:16-17), cleansed from sin (2 Tim 2:21) and full of faith in the gospel of God and His faithful promises (Rom 1:16; 1 Thes 2:13; 2 Cor 6:18-7:1; 2 Pet 1:3-4; Acts 20:24; 24:24-25). This is really the normal Christian, though to many, is may appear abnormal. Today, there is nothing special nor attractive to the lost about being a nominal Christian or religious person, but something unique, exciting and inviting about being a phenomenal and spiritual Christian.

APRIL 16

"Lord grant that the FIRE of my heart may
melt the lead in my feet." Unknown

"He has granted to us His precious and magnificent promises, so that by them you may become partakers of the divine nature, having escaped the corruption that is in the world by lust" (2 Pet 1:4). So we see three steps in the pursuit of holiness and partaking of divine nature. First, we must escape the world's corrupting lusts. This is accomplished by the power of the Holy Spirit (Rom 8:13) who teaches us to abide in the truth which brings freedom from sin's dominion (1 Jn 2:27; Ps 119:9, 11; Jn 8:31-36).

This first act of getting rid of sin before receiving from God is a common theme in the New Testament. When it comes to Christian service the apostle Paul taught: "Therefore, if a man cleanses himself from these things, he will be a vessel for honor, sanctified, useful to the Master, prepared for every good work" (2 Tim 2:21). Jacob (James) taught the same in regard to receiving from the life saving word of God: "Therefore putting aside all filthiness and all that remains of wickedness, in humility receive the word implanted, which is able to save your souls" (Jam 1:22). The author of Hebrews taught the same thing in regard to approaching God: "let us draw near with a sincere heart in full assurance of faith, having our hearts sprinkled clean from an evil conscience and our bodies washed with pure water" (10:22).

Second, to realize the blessings and promises we have received in Christ (cf. Eph 1:3) is one thing, but to be entitled to appropriate them by complying with their conditions is quite another. Take for example this popular promise: "And we know that God causes all things to work together for good" (Rom 8:28a). Yet notice the conditions: "to those who love God, to those who are called according to His purpose" (8:28b). Likewise many love the promise made by Jesus to His sheep: "I give eternal life to them, and they shall never perish" (Jn 10:28a). Yet the promise is for His sheep whom He describes as those who "hear My voice, and I know them, and they follow Me" (10:27).

Third, after understanding the promises and fulfilling their conditions, we must claim them, walking by faith, not by sight (2 Cor 5;7). For by trusting in them, one becomes a partaker of divine nature, becoming righteous and growing in faith. One progresses in holiness by claiming God's promises and exercising a faith that believes that God can even call into being that which does not exist (Rom 4:17). This overcoming faith believes that God is able to perform what He promised (Rom 4:21). It is the faith that overcomes the world and removes mountains.

APRIL 17

"This much, however, I know: that I am herein promised all salvation, from all sin, into all purity, to the highest degree of which my nature is capable." Richard Treffry Jr.

SAVING FAITH AND HOLINESS GO TOGETHER

Saving and persevering faith cannot be disconnected from works of righteousness. Faith without works is dead. "What use is it, my brethren, if someone says he has faith but he has no works? Can that faith save him...

even so, faith, if it has no works, is dead, being by itself. You see that a man is justified by works and not by faith alone [ie, faith without works]" (James 2:14, 17, 24). Paul commended the Thessalonian believers for their "work of faith, labor of love and steadfastness of hope" (1 Thess 1:3). And he reminded the Galatian believers that "in Christ Jesus neither circumcision nor uncircumcision means anything, but faith working through love" (Gal 5:6).

Salvation from sin's damnation is demonstrated by deliverance from sin's dominion. This results in a freedom to walk in newness of life, dead to sin and no longer a slave to sin. Paul, in describing how the believer has died with Christ, says "For the death that He died, he died to sin, once for all; but the life that He lives, He lives to God. Even so consider yourselves to be dead to sin, but alive to God in Christ Jesus" (Rom 6:10-11).

This is not so say that the Christian will ever be sinless, for "if we say that we have no sin, we are deceiving ourselves and the truth is not in us" (1 Jn 1:9). Yet, we are to pursue sanctification, a state of progressive holiness, without which no one will see the Lord (Heb 12:14). That sanctification is the holiness and separation that marks true believers; a walk accomplished by the power of the Spirit of God as one renews his mind with the Word of God (Gal 5:16; Rom 12:1-2). After all, John says to Christians: "My little children, I am writing these things to you so that you may not sin (1 Jn 2:1a). As new creatures, born of God's Spirit, we are to walk as new creatures, to walk in newness of life, considering ourselves as dead to sin, but alive to God (2 Cor 5:17; Rom 6:4, 11). We have supporting promises to help in this adventure such as "No temptation has overtaken you but such as is common to man; and God is faithful, who will not allow you to be tempted beyond what you are able, but with the temptation will provide the way of escape also, that you may be able to endure it" (1 Cor 10:13).

APRIL 18

*"How can you pull down strongholds of Satan
if you don't even have the strength to turn
off your TV?" Leonard Ravenhill*

Beware of any religious movement that exalts drama over doctrine, hype over hope, doubt over certainty, pleasuring the present over preparing for the future. Though young people may give their lives for an exclamation point, they will surely not lose their lives for a question mark. Biblical Christianity is the real deal. There is no point in receiving a raw deal from another faddish religious movement. Emergent younger generations are not impressed by a sterile religion without power, offered by preachers without credibility, to aimless people following after passing religious fads.

Because truth is lacking in the pulpit we have entertainment on the stage and paralysis in the pews. Since few die at the altar and most sleep in the pew, no wonder the youth of today who engage true Christianity are few. When God's truth is not known, His person is not feared and His great and magnificent promises are not claimed, the biblically ignorant are left to worship a god of their own making and to live a life of their own choosing.

Discerning Christians quickly learn that the devil prowls about like a roaring lion seeking someone to devour (1 Pet 5:8). Evil shepherds come into flocks to steal, kill and destroy (Jn 10:10a). The religious persecute and murder (Jn 15:20, 16:2), and wild beasts and dogs attack (1 Cor 15:32; Phil 3:2). Yet believers can wait for the LORD to gain new strength. They can mount up with wings like eagles. They can run and not get tired, and walk and not become weary (Is 40:28-31). They can soar as eagles over all opponents because they are seated with Christ in the heavenly places (Eph 2:6).

They are not captives of the world but are citizens of heaven (Phil 3:20). They are led by the Holy Spirit not by the evil spirit of the age (Rom 8:14; 1 Cor 12:2). They are loved by the God of heaven and not at the mercy of the god of this world. They are united with Christ who overcame the world.

For the time being, Satan is alive and well, emerging as a roaring lion, running fast and furious, devouring truth and deceiving masses. Yet discerning and bold Christian soldiers of God know that the devil is really a defeated and upset kitten. For Satan knows his time is short and the Reigning Lion of Judah is rapidly approaching to put an end to his play time and to cast him into the infernal litter box called hell.

APRIL 19

"The Azusa revival began where every revival should rightly begin – in repentant tears. It began in tears, it lived in tears, and when the tears ended the Azusa revival ended." A. G. Osterberg

THE SINNER'S PRAYER OR THE SAINT'S PROCLAMATION

The "Sinners Prayer" more often than not turns out to be nothing more than a "prayer of sinners". This often occurs when there is no passionate confession of Jesus as Lord, but only a verbal acknowledgement of Jesus as Savior. There is no subsequent changed life, but merely a return to life as usual, not a Holy Spirit-empowered supernatural walk in newness of life (Gal 5:16; Rom 6:4, 8:13). There is no sincere intent of submission to Jesus as Master of one's life (1 Pet 3:15; Col 2:6; 2 Cor 4:5), nor any conscience effort to turn away from sin and its strongholds by displaying a genuine repentance toward God and an active faith Jesus and pursuit of sanctification (Acts 20:21; Heb 12:14).

Rather, there is merely a commitment to a sin-friendly and cheap invitation. Instead of carrying the cross and dying to self, most prefer to wear the cross of a convenient, popular and effortless Christianity with its easy believism and cheap grace. But the Lord of Glory desires every saint who has been truly born again by the Spirit and made into a new creation, and who is no longer dead in trespasses and sins, to work out their salvation with fear and trembling (Phil 2:12) and walk out the Gospel in demonstration of the Spirit and of power (1 Cor 2:4). Only then will the abundant life be experienced rather than the ho-hum "Best Life Now". Only then will one cash in on the unfathomable riches of Christ (Eph 3:8) and every spiritual blessing in Christ (Eph 1:3) and the great and magnificent promises of God, rather than become spiritually bankrupt by a prosperity gospel and left holding a bag full of empty promises.

APRIL 20

The games the devil loves to play

A favorite game of the devil is to get Christians distracted and consumed with fighting bad fights rather than fighting the good fight, arguing over the faith rather than keeping the faith. The devil often succeeds in preventing many from finishing the course by having them focus on vain discourse. The devil opposes Christians running the race with perseverance by enticing them to cheapen God's grace with perversion.

The devil also loves to gets the saved and forgiven to fret over their past and to condemn themselves over previous failures. But the forgiving God of mercy, the God of the second change and of mercy would say, "confess, forsake and forget". It is water under the bridge. The Lord is now saying it is time to walk on the water. Jesus told His disciples: "Follow Me and I will make you fishers of men". It makes more sense as Jonah would say, to obey and go fishing for the lost, rather than to disobey and be swallowed by a whale.

Another game of the devil is to indulge his victims with games, toys and idols that leave no time for God and spiritual things of eternal value. Judgment day will reveal that "he who dies with the most toys will be found to have played with the devil the most time". Earthly trinkets cannot be carried to heaven, only heavenly treasures. The former satisfies for a season, the later endures forever.

APRIL 21

If hollow religion has left you, don't sweat it; you miss nothing. If holiness religion has left you, you better sweat blood and tears, for you have missed it all.

The last will be first and the first last. Often times in the Christian life we are reminded of what God told Isaiah long ago: "For My thoughts are not your thoughts, neither are your ways My ways, declares the LORD.

For as the heavens are higher than the earth, so are My ways higher than your ways, and My thoughts than your thoughts" (55:8-9).

In the New Testament it is written: "God is opposed to the proud but gives grace to the humble" (Jam 4:6). God often uses the poor and foolish and weak to shame the rich, wise and strong (1 Cor 1:25-31). Often those who are not professionally educated, seminary trained and seminar instructed demonstrate great wisdom to the educated religious class.

Those who are Spirit-filled, Spirit-taught and who spend time with the Lord and experience the supernatural working of God, often silence their religious wise opponents with a testimony they cannot refute, with answers they cannot question and with a power they cannot oppose (Acts 4:12-13; cp. Ps 119:42). Philip, one of the first deacons of God's new assembly, being full of wisdom and faith and the Spirit (Acts 6:3, 5), cast out demons, healed the sick and performed signs and great miracles. And he did this by preaching the good news about the kingdom of God and the name of Jesus (Acts 8:7, 12-13). It was not by relying on his education, degrees, wisdom, power or experience (Acts 8). After all, Philip had recently become a GED, a God Empowered Disciple, not a card-carrying Ph.D (Acts 1:8).

APRIL 22

"Study the history of revival. God has always sent revival in the darkest days." Adrian Rogers

Many today believe America is in the balance of God's wrath and is found wanting. Satan is enjoying his last party in his unholy sanctuaries, having thoroughly infiltrated society, before the Lord comes for the final house cleaning. The remaining remnant will be saved as the Gospel spreads throughout the world (Mt 24:14), in demonstration of the Spirit and of power (1 Cor 2:4), with Holy fire burning hotter by the fires of persecution. Then the end will come. While a national revival is unlikely, we will see a true work of God coming when Christians who fear the holy God and are jealous for the kingdom of God will rise up to BE the Church, to make certain their calling and to make clear their message (2 Pet 1:10-11).

APRIL 23

"Revival is a renewed conviction of sin and repentance, followed by an intense desire to live in obedience to God. It is giving up one's will to God in deep humility." Charles Finney

It is time to get off the pew, come out of the closet, and get on the battle-field. The common religious invitation to "Come as you are, Sing: Just as I am; Now go as you were" or the common "Sinner's Prayer", will not be adequate to fight against the tide of evil sweeping through the country and deception coming against God's people. Today, there is too much preaching without passion, teaching without action, religion without power, "salvation" without repentance, "conversion" without conviction, sin without godly sorrow, faith without works and prayer without faith. It is time for Christians to wake up, stand up, suit up and step out into the world and gather up fruit for eternal life in the Lord's harvest fields. This is not the time for Christians who are seated in the heavenlies to be sitting in the gutters of the world.   To live the victorious, overcoming resurrection life doesn't require a Ph.D. in church growth or expertise in "Quantum

Spirituality". Rather, it requires being instructed by the Holy Spirit in the school of hard knocks (1 Jn 2:27; 1 Pet 5:10).

Being on fire as a God Empowered Disciple, having earned that GED will prove to be more effective than possessing 32 degrees from seminaries, graduated and yet still frozen, professing to be wise while being foolish, not understanding the times and not knowing what to do (1 Chron 12:32). It is time to focus on BEING the Church, rather than just GOING to church, on building strong disciples, rather than soliciting quick decisions. We don't need to 'Reinvent Christianity" but to "Re-ignite" contemporary Christianity with Holy Spirit fire and the fear of God.

APRIL 24

"Preacher, keep your knees on the ground & your eyes on the throne." Leonard Ravenhill

OFF WITH THE GRAVE CLOTHES, ON WITH THE RISEN LORD.

The Bible commands believers to "Put on the Lord Jesus Christ, and make no provision for the flesh in regard to its lusts" (Rom 13:14). Lord, I rejoice that I have been born again (Jn 3:3, 5), no longer dead in trespasses and sins (Eph 2:1). My "Best Life Now" is knowing that my past life is gone and buried. I am a new creature in Christ, the old things passed away; behold, new things have come (2 Cor 5:17). Why should I live in the gutters with the devil when I am seated with Christ in the heavenlies (Eph 1:20, 2:6)?

I have been crucified and raised up with Christ, so why have my hands and feet still in grave wrappings (Rom 6:3f; Eph 2:5-6; Jn 11:44a). I have been freed from Satan's shackles and chains (Mk 5:5,15) to walk in newness of life (Rom 6:4), no longer tormented by his hassles and pains. I am now clothed with Christ' righteousness (1 Cor 1:30; Phil 3:9), not with religious fig leaves. So I will head to the Kingdom rather than hide in the garden. The next time I am tempted by the devil, I will say to him "It is written" just as the Lord did, when He triumphed (Mt 4:4,7,10). I will submit to God and resist the devil and he will flee (Jam 4:7).

I will have a right mind, the mind of Christ (Mk 5:15; 1 Cor 2:16), no longer out of my right mind, doing the devil's will (2 Tim 2:26). I will be thankful for and benefit from my spiritual blessings in Christ (Eph 1:3), while denouncing the prosperity gospel which bankrupts the soul. I have made complete in Christ (Col 2:10), in whom are hidden all the treasures of wisdom and knowledge (Col 2:3). My ambition is not to be purpose driven but be Spirit led as Jesus was so led (Mt 4:4). I will rejoice in the Lord always, experiencing the fruit of the Spirit (Phil 4:4; Gal 5:22), just as Jesus rejoiced in the Spirit (Lk 10:21). Having been anointed with the Holy Spirit (1 Jn 2:20), I will cast out demons by the Spirit (Mt 12:28), just as Jesus was anointed by the Holy Spirit and healed all who were oppressed by the devil (Acts 10:38). By the power of the Spirit I will present my body as a living and holy sacrifice acceptable to God (Rom 12:1, 8:13), just as Jesus offered Himself up as an offering and a sacrifice to God as a fragrant aroma (Eph 5:2; Heb 9:14).

What is needed today is not "A New Kind of Christian" but a biblical sort of Christian. Lord, help me become such a true disciple who takes up the cross and dies daily to my old ways (Lk 14:27; Eph 2:3; 1 Pet 4:1-3), rather than wear a cross and live for self. Having received the Pentecostal mandate to go out into the world to be a witness and martyr (Acts 1:8), let my story not be found written in the devil's book of deserters. After all, Jesus said: "Truly, truly, I say to you, unless a grain of wheat falls into the earth and dies, it remains alone; but if it dies, it bears much fruit" (Jn

12:24). "For whoever wishes to save his life will lose it, but whoever loses his life for My sake, he is the one who will save it" (Lk 9:24).

APRIL 25

"I want to help you decide that, by the power of God, you will not be ordinary." Smith Wigglesworth

CHRISTIAN CONQUERORS

As believers in the Lord Jesus Christ we have been washed, sanctified and justified in the name of the Lord Jesus Christ and in the Spirit of our God (1 Cor 6:11). Being washed by the blood, we should not be stained by sin. Being sanctified or set apart from the world, we should not live like the world. Being justified and acquitted of the sin's condemnation, we don't have to listen to the devil's accusations and walk in self condemnation. And being seated in heavenly places at the right hand of God with Christ, we do not have to wallow in the gutters of the world under the devil's thumb (Eph 2:6; Col 3:1-4). In Christ, we can overwhelmingly conquer in life through our death and surrender, because He overwhelmingly conquered the devil through His death and resurrection (Rom 8:37).

Only Jesus following, Spirit filled, prayed up, Sword wielding Christians will overcome in these last days of great demonic deception and opposition. The devil loves it when Christians wrestle against their own flesh and blood, against the truly saved and God pleasing members of the body of Christ. The devil fights hard to promote disunity in the Body of Christ, making it harder to preserve the unity of the Spirit in the bond of peace in His one body (Eph 4:3-4). He loves it even more that when we wrestle against the lost flesh and blood sons of disobedience (Eph 2:2) and ignore the fact that they are being energized by the god of this world and his fallen principalities and powers (Eph 6:12). Victorious Christian soldiers choose their battles wisely and discern their enemies carefully. They wisely engage in spiritual warfare against the demons that control them, by effectual prayer (Rom 15:30-31), by a wise walk (2 Tim 2:24-26), and spiritual armor (Eph 6:10-18) and by proclaiming the gospel in demonstration of the Spirit and of power (1 Cor 2:4; Rom 15:18-20). The apostle Paul did that very thing as he evangelized (Acts 13:6-12), engaged in prayer (Acts 16:16-18) and fought the good fight of faith (Eph 6:12, 13, 16; 2 Tim 4:7).

APRIL 26

*"Beware of the dogs, beware of the evil workers,
beware of the false circumcision". Paul*

False and deceived professing Christians are ever so prone to sneak into churches to bring true Christians into bondage (Gal 2:4), to promote unrighteousness, denying our only Master and Lord, Jesus Christ (Jude 4), and introduce destructive heresies, denying the master who bought them (2 Pet 2:2). Amazingly, in "Christian" America, the land of the free and home of the brave, we see religious bondage of many kinds: bondage to demonic doctrines, worldly idols, religious rituals and pop-theology. We are even blessed to have Christianity of many flavors to choose from: "re-defined", "progressive" and "effortless" Christianity and powerless. We have materialistic shepherds peddling the word, passing offering plates and preaching prosperity gospels. We have smooth talking pastors offering up pastoral pastries hot off the pulpits. We have puffed up theologians selling their private interpretations. We have many empty talkers, few faith walkers; more false apostles and prophets and hireling pastors than true apostles and prophets and Christ serving shepherds (Jn 21:15-17).

Many are followers of men rather than God, nourished on traditions of men rather than God's truth (Mk 7:8), consumed with today rather than living for tomorrow, having dollars signs in their eyes rather than eternity on their mind (1 Tim 6:17-19). Many will wear a cross, but few will bear the cross (Lk 9:23). Many run to church, but few run the race. Many leaders seek to control, yet have little self-control (Mt 20:25-28; Gal 5:23; Acts 24:25; 1 Cor 9:24-27). Many are improperly adorned with the worldly attire rather than properly clothed with spiritual armor. They seek entertainment rather than equipping, are pleasure seeking rather than kingdom seeking. Though preachers may invite many to the altar, they seldom expect them to die there. Often they are more concerned with people making decisions, than they are about being obedient in making disciples. They appear to be more interested in having people experience the "best life now" than helping them to inherit eternal life in the hereafter.

APRIL 27

Only FINDERS of God's truth and KEEPERS of the Christian faith will avoid becoming LOSERS in Satan's world and WEEPERS in his hell.

GET YOUR "GET OUT OF HELL CARD"

Lord, thank You for my Get Out of Hell Card, the Gospel of Good News. Though I was formerly a prisoner to the world and held captive by the devil to do his will (2 Tim 2:26), I have been redeemed from my incarceration because of your Incarnation. For You partook of flesh and flood, so that through your death You might render powerless him who had the power of death, that is, the devil (Heb 2:14). Heavenly Father, I realize that by your Son's incarnation He became the merciful and faithful high priest to make propitiation for the sins of your people (Heb 2:17). For You satisfied your righteous requirements by doing for me what I could not do for myself, "for it is impossible for the blood of bulls and goats to take away sins" (Heb 10:4). Religious works cannot make one right with You.

"For all of us have become like one who is unclean, and all our righteous deeds are like a filthy garment" (Is 64:6). For who can say, "I have cleansed my heart, I am pure from my sin"? (Prov 20:9). "For in Your sight no man living is righteous" (Ps 143:2). "If we say that we have not sinned, we make Him a liar and His word is not in us" (1 Jn 1:10). "For whatever is not from faith is sin" (Rom 14:23). "And to one who knows the right thing to do and does not do it, to him it is sin" (Jam 4:17). And "whoever keeps the whole law and yet stumbles in one point, he has become guilty of all" (Jam 2:10). How vain and foolish it is for anyone to claim he never sins and has no need for the Savior. For there is no one who can justify himself before God (Lk 16:15).

God, I realize now that You can be just and the justifier of only the one who has faith in Jesus (Rom 3:26). Heavenly Father, You sent forth your Son, born of a woman, born under the Law, so that I could be adopted into your family (Gal 4:4-5) and be baptized into Christ who fulfilled the Law (Mt 5:17; Lk 24:26-27; Rom 1:1-2; 10:4). So I am no longer in bondage to a spirit of slavery and fear, but have received the Spirit who gave me a new spiritual birth and heavenly adoption into your family (Rom 8:15; Jn 3:3, 5).

For my jail bond was paid, not with silver or gold of fallen man, but with the precious blood of the Lamb unblemished and spotless, the Son of Man (1 Pet 1:18-19).

LORD, may your people sing to You a new song, and your praise in the congregations of the godly ones. For You take pleasure in your people and will beautify the afflicted ones with salvation. With the high praises of God in their mouth and with the two-edged sword, the Word of God, in their hand they will "execute vengeance on the nations, and punishment on the peoples; to bind their kings with chains and their nobles with fetters of iron; to execute on them the judgment written; This is an honor for all Your godly ones (Ps 149:1, 4, 6-9). "Those who know Your name will put their trust in You, for You, O LORD, have not forsaken those who seek You" (Ps 9:10). Your Get Out Of Hell Card never expires.

APRIL 28

"Men's hearts are being searched...it is a tremendous sifting time, not only of actions but of inner motives. Nothing can escape the all-searching eye of God."
Frank Bartleman, AZUSA STREET

It is common for demons, working through unbelievers, to mock Christians who have so quenched the Holy Spirit that they have no power and who are so ignorant of spiritual warfare that they cannot battle. The demons didn't have it so good with Paul and Philip. They knew them well (Acts 19:15; 8:7). But today, demons mock saying to many Christians: "Who are you?"

In these last days, the most important thing we can do is to wisely and boldly proclaim the Gospel of God and offer true liberation and God's invitation to all to receive Jesus Christ as Lord and Savior. Deal with whatever opposition arises, while making the most of your time (Eph 5:16). It is wise to ignore complacency, to resist religious and doctrinal entanglements. Seek out those whom the Lord is drawing (Jn 12:32) and the Spirit is convicting (Jn 16:8) and who have heard and learned from the Father (Jn 6:45). The vast majority will choose the broad and easy path, rather than the narrow way that lead to Jesus, who is the Way.

We don't have time to cast pearls before swine or cast demons into sea, especially before those who are dead set in being unrepentant sinners. If one is not willing to wholeheartedly obey and sincerely repentant from sin and turn to God and receive Jesus as Lord and Savior, little spiritual progress can be achieved in bringing about salvation and deliverance (Acts 20:21; Rom 10:9; Jn 1:12). Plant the seed and move on, letting others water the seed and trusting God to cause the growth (1 Cor 3:6). However, demonic trouble makers and distractors often need to be dwelt with as Paul often had to do (Acts 13:9-12; 16:16-18).

APRIL 29

"If the Lord tarries, there may yet be a grass-roots awakening that will overflow all sectarian barriers. There are a host of good people... who long for a visitation from heaven in old-time power. The kindling wood is scattered all round in all the churches. May God help us to rake off the ashes, uncover the live coals and may He blow upon us with the breath of His Spirit!" Vance Havner

The Lord of Heaven is soon returning to expose the moral corruptness of political correctness and religious compromise which is being expounded by Satan, the god of this world from the White House to the church house. God's message at the Temple Gate of Jerusalem was: "Behold, you are trusting in deceptive words to no avail" (Jer 7:8). Today, people are trusting in politicians, religious fads and movements rather than reading and obeying the Word of God and listening to those few chosen leaders of God through whom God is warning as He did in times past: "I spoke to you, rising up early and speaking, but you did not hear, and I called you but you did not answer" (Jer 7:13). Concerning the sin and treachery of His people, God said: "Why then has this people, Jerusalem, turned away in continual apostasy? They hold fast to deceit, they refuse to return. They have spoken what is not right; no man repented of this wickedness. My people do not know the ordinance of God" (Jer 8:5-6,7b).

God spoke through other prophets in similar manner: "Therefore My people go into exile for their lack of knowledge; and their honorable men are famished, and their multitude is parched with thirst" (Is 5:13). "My people are destroyed for lack of knowledge. Because you have rejected knowledge, I also will reject you from being My priest. Since you have forgotten the law of your God, I also will forget our children" (Hos 4:6). And in the New Testament we read: "For it is time for judgment to begin with the household of God; and it is begins with us first, what will be the outcome for those who do not obey the gospel of God" (1 Pet 4:17).

But it's comforting to know that God always preserves His faithful remnant, for He is ever building up His Church and "the gates of Hades shall not overpower it" (Mt 16:18). "Jesus Christ is the same yesterday and today, yes and forever" (Heb 13:8). "The eyes of the LORD move to and fro throughout the earth that He may strongly support those whose heart is completely His" (2 Chron 16:9a). "Those who know their God will display strength and take action" (Dan 11:32b).

Likewise, today those who fear God and count all things to be loss in view of the surpassing value of knowing Christ Jesus as Lord, those who desire to know Him intimately and the power of His resurrection and the fellowship of His sufferings, they will walk in newness of life. They will be overcomers, not overcome, hopeful, not hopeless, will be bright lights in a dark world and not be overcome by the hour and power of darkness that is fast approaching. They will overcome "because of the blood of the Lamb and because of the word of their testimony, because they did not love their life even unto death (Rev 12:11).

APRIL 30

"I would say without any hesitation that the most urgent need in the Christian Church today is true preaching." Dr. Martyn Lloyd Jones

You, as a believer in the Lord Jesus Christ, are part of the holy assembly of God, which today is commonly called the Church. The Bible describes it as being the household of God, the pillar and support of truth, composed of God's called out ones, children of the living God (1 Tim 3:15; Jn 1:12). It is up to you, whom Jesus calls the light of the world (Mt 5:14), to expose the unfruitful deeds of darkness (Eph 5:11), and to bring to light things hidden in darkness (Eph 5:13), as well as to pray for kings and for all who are in authority (1 Tim 2:2). You belong to a nation of holy and royal priests appointed by God as His ambassadors and His new creations. You have been entrusted with the ministry of reconciliation and Gospel of God whereby those hostile and alienated from God can be reconciled to Him in order to escape the coming wrath of God (1 Pet 2;5,9; 2 Cor 5:17-21).

The word of God performs its work in those who believe, which also means to obey (1 Thes 2:13, cf. Jn 3:36). But the word has to be spoken and the speakers have to believe and obey. If God's people do not repent and open their door and let the Lord take charge of His household divine judgment will continue to sweep over the nation.

God's promise long ago still holds true but the conditions are clear: if "My people who are called by My name humble themselves and pray, and seek My face and turn from their wicked ways, then I will hear from heaven, will forgive their sin, and will heal their land" (2 Chron 7:14). The Lord has been standing outside, knocking on the church door, slammed shut and locked up by an unrepentant church. The Son stands to judge her proud parades, pathetic and powerless religion, plentiful idolatries and pastoral pastries. Judgment begins with the household of God. For Peter writes: "For it is time for judgment to begin with the household of God; and if it begins with us first, what will be the outcome for those who do not obey the gospel of God" (1 Pet 4:17).

There is hope for a move of God. The spiritual, faithful, true remnant and holy nation of God always exists (1 Pet 2:9; 1 Tim 4:10). God desires for all to come to repentance (2 Pet 3:9). "Those who wait for the LORD will gain new strength; they will mount up with wings like eagles" (Is 40:31a). Those who know their God will display strength and take action (Dan 11:32). "Those who have insight will understand" (Dan 12:11).

MAY 1

To exit and leave earth with its dirt is no dread for those who are prepared to enter heaven with its glory.

WHEN THE STORM COMES

"For the eyes of the LORD move to and fro throughout the earth that He may strongly support those whose heart is COMPLETELY His" (2 Chron 16:9a). "You shall love the LORD your God with all your HEART, and with all your SOUL, and with all your MIND, and with all your STRENGTH" (Mk 12:30). "But sanctify Christ as Lord in your HEARTS, always being ready to make a defense to everyone who asks you to give an account for the hope that is in you, yet with gentleness and reverence" (1 Pet 3:15). "If anyone wishes to come after Me, he must deny himself, and take up his cross and follow Me. For whoever wishes to save his life will lose it; but whoever loses his life for My sake will find it. For what will it profit a man if he gains the whole world and forfeits his SOUL? Or what will a man give in exchange for his SOUL?" (Mt 16:24-26). "For who has known the mind of the LORD, that he will instruct Him? But we have the MIND of Christ" (1 Cor 2:16). "For this purpose also I labor, striving according to His POWER, which mightily works within me" (Col 1:29).

And what is that purpose: not churchianity, but proclaiming Christ and making true disciples: "We proclaim Him, admonishing every man and teaching every man with all wisdom, so that we may present every man complete in Christ" (Col 1:28). Only such ones will be sustained in these lasts days when the world is falling apart. When the wind and shaking of persecution hits our shores, some will ride the mighty waves, but the great tide will take most away. It all depends on whether you have your eyes fixed on the Savior or on the storm.

MAY 2

"The evangelist who preaches for eternity is never great on numbers. He is not apt to count hundreds of converts where there is no restitution, no confession..."E.M. Bounds.

SANCTIFICATION THAT MATTERS

"Now those who belong to Christ Jesus have crucified the flesh with its passions and desires" (Gal 5:24). As a life principle, we will experience victory in this struggle with the lusts of the flesh. In this lifelong journey in sanctification, we find the principle that evil is ever present tempting us, because of the law of sin in the members of our body of flesh with its evil practices and corruption (Eph 4:22; Col 3:9; Rom 7:21-23). Therefore to experience victory over sin, we must walk according to the Spirit, relying on His power to put on the new man which has been created in righteousness and holiness of the truth by renewing the mind with truth (Gal 5:16-17; Rom 12:1-3; Eph 4:23-24; Col 3:10-11). And by the Spirit's power we also put to death the deeds of the body (Rom 8:13; Eph 4:22), laying aside the old self with its evil practices (Col 3:9). Therefore, we can be set free from this law of sin and death and walk in newness of life (Rom 8:1-4, 6:4), as the new creatures we are in Christ (2 Cor 5:17a). We forget what was, the old things passed away, and reach forward to what lies ahead, for behold new things have come (2 Cor 5:17b, Phil 3:13).

After all, there will be an observable change in our life if we have been truly baptized, buried, raised up and united with Christ, (Rom 6:1-5). It is surely a unique Americanized gospel invitation, whose meek appeal to holiness is often merely the unspoken mantra: "Come as you are, sing 'just as I am', now go as you were". Many go to the altar and return to the pew unchanged, because they never died at the altar.

MAY 3

*"When the Gospel was preached in these first ages
of the Church, it was revealed to the hearts and
consciences of sinners with great power. They deferred
not their repentance one day." Thomas Reade*

BRAVEHEARTS WIN, TIMID SOULS WHINE

To be a braveheart soldier of the cross takes more courage than boldly slipping up the hand while every head is bowed and every eye is closed and no one is looking around. As true soldiers of the cross we learn quickly that we have a new class of enemies to battle. We now struggle "against rulers, against the powers, against the world forces of this darkness, against the spiritual forces of wickedness in the heavenly places" (Eph 6:12). We are no longer dead in trespasses and sins, and thus no threat to the devil (Eph 2:2). But we have been spiritually raised from the dead with Christ and seated with Him in the heavenly places (Eph 2:6), to fight the good fight, to finish the course and to keep the faith (2 Tim 4:7).

We have been given a new mission to destroy the works of the devil who comes to steal, kill and destroy (1 Jn 3:8b; Jn 10:10a). For just as the Father sent His Son into the world, so His Son has sent us into the world (Jn 17:18; 20:21). Just as the Son came to call out and make disciples (Mt 4:19), we have been commanded to go and make disciples, teaching them to observe all that Jesus commanded (Mt 28:18-20), which is the spiritual discipline the devil most despises.

Fortunately, to accomplish this we were not given a spirit of timidity, but of power, love and sound mind (2 Tim 1:7). We are no longer out of our senses and in the devil's snare, held captive by him to do his will (2 Tim 2:26). We have the mind of Christ (1 Cor 2:16), in whom are hidden all the treasures of wisdom and knowledge (Col 2:3), and in Him have been blessed with every spiritual blessing (Eph 1:3), so we can accomplish His will.

And for further assistance, Jesus also sent the promised Holy Spirit as our Helper, Teacher and Power source (Jn 14:26; Acts 1:8). This Holy Spirit who was sent to glorify the Christ who lives in us (Jn 16:14), is greater than the antichrist spirit and god of this world who fights against us (1 Jn 4:4). So we have been well outfitted for victory. The only thing lacking is deciding to become bravehearts, much like Joshua and Caleb in times past or like David's mighty men of valor, who understood the times, who went out to war, in proper battle formation, and skilled in the use of all kinds of weapons (1 Chron 12:21,22, 32,33).

And we have better weapons, spiritual weapons perfectly suited to defeat our spiritual enemies. For our weapons are not of the flesh, for we war not according to the flesh (2 Cor 10:3-4; Eph 6:12). But they are spiritual weapons, the sword of the Spirit (Eh 6:17), praying in the Spirit (Eph 6:18), and being armed with evangelistic zeal (Eph 6:15; 1 Cor 2:4), overcoming faith (1 Jn 5:4), the breastplate of righteousness (Eph 6:14b) and truth (Eph 6:14a), all of which are produced by the Spirit of God, creating the Lord's heavenly army of bravehearts, not timid spirits.

MAY 4

"Destitute of the Fire of God, nothing else counts;
possessing Fire, nothing else matters." Samuel Chadwick

NAME AND CLAIM THE CONDITIONS, AND YOU WILL GET THE PROMISES.

There is promise for the "Name and Claim It" ones who claim their promises as well as their conditions. God is the great Promise Keeper to all who take His conditions seriously. Such ones can confidently proclaim: "And we know that God causes all things to work together for good to those who love God, to those who are called according to His purpose" (Rom 8:28). "Things which eye has not seen and ear has not heard, and which have not entered the heart of man, all that God has prepared for those who love Him" (1 Cor 2:9). "If anyone loves God, he is known by Him" (1 Cor 8:3). "I will welcome you. And I will be a father to you, and you shall be sons and daughters to Me,' says the Lord Almighty" (2 Cor 6:16b-17), to those who obey His command to "come out from their midst and be separate and who do not touch what is unclean" (2 Cor 6:17a).

"Therefore He is able to save forever those who draw near to God through Him, since He always lives to make intercession for them" (Heb 7:25). "Draw near to God and He will draw near to you" (Jam 4:8a). "If we endure, we will also reign with Him" (2 Tim 2:12a). "The Spirit Himself testifies with our spirit that we are children of God, and if children, heirs also, heirs of God and fellow heirs with Christ, if indeed we suffer with Him so that we may also be glorified with Him" (Rom 8:16-17). "If we walk in the Light as He Himself is in the Light, we have fellowship with one another, and the blood of Jesus His Son cleanses us from all sin" (1 Jn 1:7). So it is written: "And we desire that each one of you show the same diligence so as to realize the full assurance of hope until the end, so that you will not be sluggish, but imitators of those who through faith and patience inherit the promises" (Heb 6:11-12). "And this is the promise which He Himself made to us, eternal life" (1 Jn 2:25).

Thus the apostle Paul himself claiming such promises and fulfilling their conditions often made declarations such as this: "For this reason I endure all things for the sake of those who are chosen, that they also may obtain the salvation which is in Christ Jesus and with it eternal glory" (2 Tim 2:10). To name and claim God's promises and experience their blessings, one must know and keep their conditions. "For not the hearers of the Law are just before God, but the doers of the law will be justified" (Rom 2:13). This is in harmony with what Jesus taught: "For whoever does the will of My Father who is in heaven, he is My brother and sister and mother" (Mt 12:50).

Of course this is all accomplished by the grace of God which labors with us and instructs us: "But by the grace of God I am what I am, and His grace toward me did not prove vain; but I labored even more than all of them, yet not I, but the grace of God with me" (1 Cor 15:10). "For the grace of God has appeared, bringing salvation to all men, instructing us to deny ungodliness and worldly desires and to live sensibly, righteously and godly in the present age" (Tit 2:11-12). Notice Paul said "the grace of God with me". For we must work together with Him, not receiving the grace of God in vain but standing on His true grace. "And wording together with Him, we also urge you not to receive the grace of God in vain" (2 Cor 6:1). This is not a stroll in the park enjoying an "effortless" Christianity, falling for the modern day hyper grace. Peter knew better and said: "And after you have suffered for a little while, the God of all grace who called you to His eternal glory in Christ, will Himself perfect, confirm, strengthen and establish you.....this is the true Grace of God. Stand firm in it!" (1 Pet 5:10, 12).

MAY 5

"Whatsoever we have over-loved, idolized, and leaned upon, God has from time to time broken it, and made us to see the vanity." John Flavel

GOD'S CHOSEN ASSEMBLY

The New Testament clearly profiles a true assembly of God, as one composed of believers in the Lord Jesus Christ who are committed to effectual prayer, Biblical teaching, purposeful discipleship, progressive sanctification and aggressive outreach to the lost. In the early church days it often was a home assembly committed to teaching, fellowship, breaking of bread and prayer (Acts 2:42; Rom 16:3-5; 1 Cor 16:15-16). They were Spirit led rather than purpose driven, Christ-following rather than self-serving; a place to be equipped not entertained. They were committed to holiness rather than happiness, a church that cast out demons rather than courted them (Acts 8:12; 10:38; 16:16-18).

They were involved in "one another" ministry as holy and royal believer priests rather than only sitting and receiving from a professional clergy cast (1 Pet 2:5,9; 1 Cor 12:27, 14:26; Eph 4:16; Col 3:15-16). That is real the Church, made up of living stones, not a building of dust, brick and mortar.

We are ALL to go, live out and preach the gospel of salvation, of peace, of liberation and of hope, being shining lights, preserving salt and living epistles (Mt 28:18-19; 1 Pet 3:15; Mt 5:13-14; 2 Cor 3:2-3). To whom much is given much is required (Lk 12:48). Pew dusters seldom venture out to get their feet dirty. Instead of shaking the dust off their feet before poor and protesting unbelievers, most residing in today's prosperous institutional churches would rather buy new shoes to impress the imprisoned crowds who gather for their weekly religious show and pastoral pastry.

MAY 6

"He makes His ministers a flame of fire.' Am I ignitible?...
make me thy fuel, flame of God.'" Jim Elliot

JESUS IS AN EQUAL OPPORTUNITY EMPLOYER

Jesus will employ all without discrimination who are willing to work out their salvation with fear and trembling (Phil 2:12). But remember, He is the boss, not us. We work according to His rules not our own. We need no additional entitlements since we have already been blessed with every spiritual blessing in the heavenlies in Christ (Eph 1:3). If anyone is not willing to work, he will not eat of the Tree of Life; for we have not been hired to do nothing but to be fruitful (Jn 15:2,6, 8,16; Mt 7:20; Lk 6:46). After all, His employees are His property having been bought with a price and redeemed out of the slave market of sin, and out of the domin-ion, domain and authority of the slave driver, the devil (Acts 26:18; Col 1:13; 1 Cor 6:20). We are now His workmanship, created in Christ Jesus for good works that God prepared beforehand that we should walk in them (Eph 2:10). We have been chosen according to the foreknowledge of

God the Father, by the sanctifying work of the Spirit to obey Jesus Christ and be sprinkled with His blood (1 Pet 1:2). That is the divine "Labor Union" working on our behalf.

MAY 7

"A Crucified Lord must have a Crucified Bride." W.B. Dunkum

Christians are commanded in the Bible to be active soldiers of the cross, and to expect suffering and not to be entangled in the affairs of everyday life (2 Tim 2:3-4). They are to be Spirit-filled, prayed up and nourished on sound doctrine so they can fight the good fight, keep the faith, run the race and finish the course (1 Cor 9:24-27; 2 Tim 4:7). The Lord expects His followers to be overcomers, not overcome. We are privileged to walk in triumph in Christ; being anxious for nothing and trusting God in everything (2 Cor 2:15; Phil 4:6).

Peter assured those scattered saints and chosen ones of God and aliens to this world saying: "God's divine power has granted to us everything pertaining to life and godliness through the true knowledge of Him who called us by His own glory and excellence" (1 Pet 1:1, 2:11, 2 Pet 1:3). By His precious and magnificent promises we can become partakers of divine nature, having escaped the corruption that is in the world by lust, by obeying His commands to be holy as He is holy (2 Pet 1:4; 1 Pet 1:15-16). Being aliens and strangers to this world, we are to live as citizens of heaven, pursing His kingdom rather than doing our thing (1 Pet 2:11; Phil 3:20; Mt 6:33).

Christians making up the true Church are described as a chosen race and a holy and royal priesthood and living stones in His temple (1 Pet 2:5, 9). We are not to be a congregation of passive, sickly, needy, sheep overly dependent on a local shepherd for protection and instruction. The Lord Jesus Christ, the Shepherd and Guardian of our souls, has healed us completely, causing us to be born again, so that we are no longer are dead in trespasses and sins (Eph 2:1). We are no longer ungodly, helpless, sinners, enemies and alienated from God (Rom 4:5, 5:6, 8, 10), but have been reconciled to Him to be His saints. Jesus "Himself bore our sins in His body on the cross, that we might die to sin and live to righteousness" (1 Pet 2:24).

The Holy Spirit desires to be active in God's true Temple, sanctifying us, renewing our minds with the Word of God, filling us, guiding us, comforting us and empowering us to overcome the world, the flesh and the devil, and today's false religion. And if the Son of God was anointed with the Holy Spirit and with power so He could do His supernatural ministry and demonstrate the kingdom of God (Acts 10:38; Mt 12:28), how much more must the children of God depend on the Holy Spirit. No wonder Paul wished that the fellowship of the Holy Spirit would be mightily present with his Corinthian believers along with the grace of the Lord Jesus Christ and the love of God (2 Cor 13:14).

MAY 8

"The highway of Christian living is strewn with has-beens." Leonard Ravenhill

S tand on the grace of God. Don't be disgraced and fall. The bad news is that "just as through one man sin entered into the world, and death through sin, and so death spread to all men, because all sinned" (Rom 5:12). However, the Good News is: "For the grace of God has appeared, bringing salvation to all men, instructing us to deny ungodliness and worldly desires and to live sensibly, righteously and godly in the present age" (Tit 2:11-12). Jesus "died for all, so that they who live might no longer live for themselves, but for Him who died and rose again on their behalf" (2 Cor 5:15). "For the death that He died, He died to sin once for all; but the life that He lives, He lives to God. Even so consider yourselves to be dead to sin, but alive to God in Christ Jesus" (Rom 6:10-11). "Therefore do not let sin reign in your mortal body so that you obey its lusts" (Rom 6:12). "For sin shall not be master over you, for you are not under law but under grace" (Rom 6:14). "For the law of the Spirit of life in Christ Jesus has set you free from the law of sin and of death" (Rom 8:2). The new birth and indwelling Holy Spirit of God have made you a new creature; the old things passed away; behold, new things have come (Jn 3:3,5; 2 Cor 5:17). You never have to become a has-been stranded beside the road, if you let the grace of God labor with you keeping you on the Way. Paul said it like this: "But by the grace of God I am what I am, and His grace toward me did not prove vain; but I labored even more than all of them, yet not I, but the grace of God with me" (1 Cor 15:10).

MAY 9

"As long as we are content to live without revival, we will." Leonard Ravenhill

THE FIVE-FOLD AND "ONE-ANOTHER" MINISTRIES

The five-fold ministry is sorely needed today to equip the body of Christ for service (Eph 4:11f). This five-fold ministry, when correctly understood, addresses the ministry of apostles, prophets, evangelists, pastors and teachers, more particularly in the Church universal. It's unlikely that the local assemblies meeting in homes for the first two hundred years of Christianity would have been so blessed to have all five ministries operating in one localized gathering. This is not to say that this five-fold ministry was not operative in the city churches. It probably was to the extent that believers followed the biblical pattern of a plurality of spiritual leadership (Tit 1:5) and a properly functioning believer priesthood (1 Pet 2:5, 9).

The nature of the more multifaceted ministry in the local house church level is described by the many "one another" mandates in the New Testament. And this "one-another" ministry is one which every believer is equipped and expected to practice. This is clearly taught in passages teaching on interactive ministry: "Now you are Christ's body, and individually members of it" (1 Cor 12:27). "When you assemble, each one has a psalm, has a teaching, has a revelation, has a tongue, has an interpretation. Let all things be done for edification" (1 Cor 14:26). The New Testament is full of such passages: 1 Cor 14:26; 1 Pet 4:10; 1 Cor 12:7; Rom 12:6; Eph 4:16; 5:19, 21; Col 3:16; 2 Cor 4:5.

A properly functioning "one another" believer priesthood ministry greatly facilitates a fruitful and sustaining ministry, especially in these last difficult and trying days: "And let us consider how to stimulate one another to love and good deeds, not forsaking our own assembling together, as is the habit of some, but encouraging one another; and all the more, as you see the day drawing near" (Heb 10:24-25). Christian ministry marked more by personal interactive participation rather than mere passive observation is the New Testament model of "church" (Eph 4:11f; 1 Cor 12:27, 14:26; 1 Pet 2:5, 9, 4:10).

The early and powerful church assembled for teaching, fellowship, breaking of bread and prayer (Acts 2:42). They went out boldly proclaiming the gospel with signs and wonders following, sinners repenting and believing, and demons fleeing (Acts 4:12, 8:12). In contemporary Churchianity we see little that is truly supernatural within and outside the walls of the church. Instead, we see many distorted gospels, false conversions, an "effortless and christless Christianity. We see more fleecing of the flock than feeding them, by shepherds who seem to be concerned with making a name than proclaiming the Name. Many are led by the spirit of the age rather than by the Spirit of God. We need True Revival not more "church as usual".

MAY 10

"If you will let God clean you up on the inside, you will not be long cleaning up the outside." W.B. Dunkum

POWER PREACHING TRULY PROFITS

The Gospel of the Kingdom is powerfully demonstrated by those who believe (1 Cor 2:4-5, 4:20). Paul said: "For I am not ashamed of the gospel, for it is the power of God for salvation to everyone who believes; to the Jew first and also to the Greek" (Rom 1:16). "For the word of the cross is foolishness to those who are perishing, but to us who are being saved, it is the power of God" (1 Cor 1:18). The living and active word of God is not imprisoned (2 Tim 2:9b; Heb 4:12). When one hears, accepts and believes the Word as being from God rather than from men, it will perform its work. Paul said: "For this reason we also constantly thank God that when you received the word of God which you heard from us, you accepted it not as the word of men, but for what is really is, the word of God, which also performs its work in who believe" (1 Thess 2:13).

Who can be impressed with a gospel that has no power that is often proclaimed by preachers who have no anointing? Biblical preaching that is anointed by the Spirit of God will glorify the Son of God, promote repentance, call for obedience, supernatural living and abstinence from sin (Jn 16:14; Acts 20:21; 1 Pet 1:1-2, 2:24; Acts 24:24-25; Gal 3:5; Rom 6:4). Paul said: "For I will not presume to speak of anything except what Christ has accomplished through me, resulting in the obedience of the Gentiles by word and deed, in the power of signs and wonders, in the power of the Spirit..." and such is the fully preached gospel of Christ (Rom 15:18-19). "My message and my preaching were not in persuasive words of wisdom, but in demonstration of the Spirit and of power, so that your faith would not rest on the wisdom of men, but on the power of God" (1 Cor 2:5). Those who repudiate the Gospel and thus judge themselves unworthy of eternal life will not experience its supernatural power, but rather God's divine judgment (Acts 13:46; 2 Thess 1:8-9).

Though the Lord "is not wishing for any to perish but for all to come to repentance" (2 Pet 3:9b); yet most will perish, because they are unwilling to come to Jesus and have eternal life (Jn 5:40). Because of their stubbornness and unrepentant heart they are storing up wrath for themselves in the day of wrath and revelation of the righteous judgment of God (Rom 2:5). We live in the last days of increasing religious deception, demonic doctrines and devilish schemes operating through his disguised apostles and servants of false righteousness, deceiving many by their false signs and false wonders. "But realize this, that in the last days difficult times will come. But evil men and impostors will proceed from bad to worse, deceiving and being deceived" (2 Tim 3:1,13). They will be judged because they will refuse to "receive the love of the truth so as to be saved". They choose not to" believe the truth, but take pleasure in wickedness (2 Thess 2:9-13). They pursue happiness rather than holiness, believe in human myth rather than divine truth, living for today rather than for tomorrow, with eyes fixed on the world rather than on eternity. Power preaching brings true and eternal profit.

MAY 11

"There was a day when I died, utterly died-died to George Mueller, his opinions, preferences, tastes, and will; died to the world, its approval or censure; died to the approval or blame even of my brethren and friends-and since then I have only to show myself approved to God." George Mueller.

THE MYTH OF NEUTRALITY

The wise one will say: "How foolish it is to please the lost who are dead in trespasses and sins and who care less for me, rather than live for Him who conquered sin and died for me" (Eph 2:1; Gal 2:20). And why love the world and the lustful things in the world which are passing away rather than live for the Kingdom of Heaven which cannot be shaken (1 Jn 2:17; Heb 12:28)? Why be concerned for the earth and its works which will be burned up (2 Pet 3:10), rather than prepare for heaven which will last forever? And why be worried about anything, since the Lord said to be anxious for nothing (Matt 6:25-34)? Besides, if God is for me, who can be against me (Rom 8:31)?

Friendship with the world is hostility toward God...whoever wishes to be a friend of the devil's depraved world makes himself an enemy of God and deprived of the blessings of heaven (Jam 4:3-4). Those who don't flee from idolatry and (1 Cor 10:14) guard themselves from idols (1 Jn 5:21), are in danger of becoming sharers in demons (1 Cor 10:20; 12:2). Instead of resisting the devil so that he will flee (Jam 4:7), many accommodate him (2 Cor 2:11; Eph 4:27; 1 Tim 3:7). Instead of being fully suited with the armor of God and standing firm against the devil, they stand unprepared to resist his schemes (Eph 6:11). Not having their loins girded with the truth of God (Eph 6:14a) nor their heads protected with the helmet of salvation, their minds become targets for his lies (Eph 6:17a). Jesus, when tempted by the devil, three times resisted him by saying "It is written" (Mt 4:4, 7, 10). Instead of being prayed up, many are preyed upon (Eph 6:18; 1 Pet 5:6-8).

Thus, instead of overwhelmingly conquering through Christ and His victory, many are overwhelmingly conquered by His defeated foe and live in fear and defeat (Rom 8:37; Col 2:15; Heb 2:14-15). From all these passages it is clear that there is no neutrality in the Christian life. One is either for God or against Him. Jesus said: "He who is not with Me is against" (Mt 12:30a).

MAY 12

Don't be fooled. Jesus was a friend to sinners so they would listen and repent. He was not a friend of sin allowing it to continue (Heb 7:26, 10:26). He came to take away sin and to destroy the works of the devil who sinned from the beginning.

CASTING STONES OR ENCOURAGING LIVING STONES?

In such a time as this it is necessary to preach the true grace of God which "has appeared, bringing salvation to all men, instructing us to deny ungodliness and worldly desires and to live sensibly, righteously and godly in the present age" (Tit 2:11-12) It is time to consider seriously the mercy of God and stop "thinking lightly of the riches of His kindness and tolerance and patience" knowing that the "kindness of God leads to repentance" (Rom 2:4). It is time to preach repentance because this Laodicean church age is marked by stubbornness of will and unrepentance of heart. And because of such the wrath of God is being stored up in the day of wrath and revelation of the righteous judgment of God, who render to each person according to his deeds" (Rom 2:5-6).

For God is not only a God of love but also a holy and just God. He will not tolerate the rebellious and cannot justify the unholy. But by His grace every Christian can and is expected to walk in obedience, pursue sanctification and practice holiness to which we have been called and without which no one will see the Lord (Eph 1:4; 2 Tim 1:9; 1 Pet 1:15-16, 2:1; Heb 5:9; 12:15).

Those who advocate genuine repentance and holiness are not casting stones and causing division as some may claim, but are gathering living stones into His Temple (1 Pet 2:5). They are encouraging the saints of God to be properly functioning members of His body, His Church, which He is building (Mt 16:18; Eph 4:4; Col 3:15).

MAY 13

"The reason why men do not look to the Church today is that she has destroyed her own influence by compromise." G Campbell Morgan

WITHOUT THE GRACE OF GOD YOU HAVE NOTHING TO STAND ON.

Grace is often seen as a license to sin and salvation as only a free get out of hell card, available to those who only have to sincerely say a little prayer or verbally confess a little doctrine, and then live as they please. How foolish and deceived such people are to think that God's grace is so cheap and His salvation so easy. "For by grace you have been saved through faith....As you therefore have received Christ Jesus the Lord, so walk in Him" (Eph 2:8; Col 2:6). There you have it: sanctifying grace and active faith, the two essentials for salvation and sanctification.

Yet they are most often misunderstood, misused, and ignored by modern day religionists. Those rightly related to God's grace will finish the race and those who aren't will fall in disgrace. The God of all grace (1 Pet 5:10) has clearly revealed what we need to know about His grace (2 Pet 1:2). All that is left is that we grow in the knowledge and practice of that grace (2 Pet 3:18). The purpose of God's grace is seen in Tit 2:12-13; 2 Cor 8:9. The expression of God's grace is seen in the person and work of the Lord Jesus Christ and His spiritual blessings, (Jn 1:14; 2 Cor 8:9; Eph 1:3; Rom 12:6). The necessity of God's grace is seen in passages such as 1 Cor 15:10; 1 Pet 5:12; 2 Cor 13:14; Eph 2:8, Col 2:6. The dangerous sins against God's grace are discussed in passages like Jude 4; Heb 10:29; Gal 5:4. Peter warns and encourages all: "This is the true grace of God. Stand firm in it" (1 Pet 5:12)!

MAY 14

"An empty Christian talks out of his head, but a Spirit-filled Christian talks out of his heart. The Holy Spirit does not live in our brains but in our heart. A head religion will talk anything, but a heart religion talks Jesus and the Holy Spirit." John T. Hatfield

Work out your salvation with fear and trembling (Phil 2:12). Examine yourself (2 Cor 13:5). Pay close attention to yourself (1 Tim 4:16). Make certain about His calling and choosing you (2 Pet 1:10). Let no one deceive you (Mt 24:4; 1 Jn 2:26, 3:7). "Repent....he who has ears to hear, let him hear" (Rev 2:5-7). Such exhortations are rarely heard in the contemporary, "Effortless", "New", "Progressive", "Redefined", "Politically Correct" Christianity.

Yes, today we are "emerging", so they say. The Church has become so rich from the Prosperity Gossip that even the devil is envious. With envy he sits back in agony, watching the Church experience her "Best Life Now", along with the shakes, gold dust and angel feathers. Assisting angels even await her beckoning as she cruises on in happy hyper grace. We even have "super apostles" and "super prophets", well oiled with "super anointings" and adorned with "super mantles" to equip the Church to finally bring in that long awaited Kingdom of God. Then the Lord will return and send the devil back where he belongs, so they think. And meanwhile, there is no need for repentance because hyper grace white washes away all sins past, as well as present and future, quite well. Can it get any better than this? Are we missing something or is another gospel being preached and another bible being read?

MAY 15

"Before God uses the man, God breaks the man." C.H. Spurgeon

Don't spend too much time arguing and debating religious "ism's". One can waste much time trying to convince minds already made up or trying to explain to the unteachable the Gospel of God and sound doctrine. Speak the truth to those whom the Lord is drawing (Jn 12:32), whom the Holy Spirit is convicting (Jn 16:8), and those who are responsive, having heard and learned from the Father (Jn 6:45). In these last days Satan seeks to divert the Lord's soldiers away from the battle field unto the sidelines, to fight theological skirmishes and disputes about words, while he kills or captures more prisoners of war on the battlefield.

The gospel is the power of God unto salvation to everyone who believes (Rom 1:16). The word of God performs its work in those who believe (1 Thess 2:13). Without faith one can't please God (Heb 11:6). Blessed are those who see the Lord by faith rather than insist on seeing Him with their minds (Jn 20:29). We walk by faith not by sight (2 Cor 5:7). The wisdom and truth of God is foolishness to the lost until they are divinely enabled to understand the things of God (1 Cor 2:14). And such saving faith will be confirmed by subsequent signs of the new birth and the new creation (Mk 16:20; Jn 3:3; 2 Cor 5:17). The authenticity of Christianity will be proven beyond doubt by those who exercise sincere faith. It's one thing to warn and protect vulnerable sheep from dangerous teachings of wolves. It is quite another thing to try to win to the truth those who remain hostile to truth.

MAY 16

"We want his power more than his purity." David Wilkerson

THE CARETAKER OF YOUR SOUL CAN TAKE CARE OF YOUR
DAY.

Bible believing Christians need not be condemned by the past, nor discouraged over the present nor dismayed about the future. The Lord has taken care of our past in His substitutionary death, for there is no condemnation for those who are in Christ Jesus (Rom 8:1). And He is more than able to carry us in the present by His intercessory life. "For Christ did not enter a holy place made with hands, a mere copy of the true one, but into heaven itself, now to appear in the presence of God for us" (Heb 9:24). And He will even to carry us to His Father's mansion at His glorious return. "So Christ also, having been offered once to bear the sins of many, will appear a second time for salvation without reference to sin, to those who eagerly await Him" (Heb 9:28). "I go to prepare a place for you. If I go and prepare a place for you, I will come again and receive you to Myself, that where I am, there you may be also" (Jn 14:2b-3).

MAY 17

"I cannot agree with those who say that they have 'new truth' to teach. The two words seem to me to contradict each other; that which is new is not true. It is the old that is true, for truth is as old as God himself." Charles Spurgeon

WHY LET THE DEVIL RAIN ON YOUR PARADE, WHEN YOU CAN REIGN OVER HIM IN PRAISE?

There is no reason for Christians to feel deprived, depressed, incomplete, lacking or ill equipped for Christian service. After all, we have already been blessed with every spiritual blessing in the heavenlies in Christ (Eph 1:3).

We are seated with Him, the Victorious One, in heavenlies places (Eph 2:6). We have been made complete in Christ (Col 2:10), in whom are hidden all the treasures of wisdom and knowledge (Col 2:3). We have been made new creatures in Christ to reign with Him in life (2 Cor 5:17; Rom 5:17). And besides, "He who did not spare His own Son, but delivered Him up for us all, how will He not also with Him freely give us all things (Rom 8:32)?

The apostle Paul revealed a few keys to unlocking these treasures in order to enjoy and "practice His presence". First, he considered the knowledge of and participation in the sufferings of Christ as being most important. He said: "I count all things to be loss in view of the surpassing value of knowing Christ Jesus my Lord, for whom I have suffered the loss of all things, and count them but rubbish in order that I may gain Christ...that I may know Him, and the power of His resurrection and the fellowship of His sufferings...in order that I may attain to the resurrection from the dead" (Phil 3:8,10-11), that is, to walk in newness of resurrection life (Rom 6:4). For Paul had learned that "just as the sufferings of Christ are ours in abundance, so also our comfort is abundant through Christ" (2 Cor 1:5). Paul remembered well Jesus' statement to him: "My grace is sufficient for you, for power is perfect in weakness." (2 Cor 12:9). Therefore in spite of having a persistent thorn in his flesh he could say: "Therefore I am well content with weaknesses, with insults, with distresses, with persecutions, with difficulties for Christ's sake; for when I am weak, then I am strong" (2 Cor 12:10). No "effortless" and "worthless" Christianity for Paul.

Second, he died to his self and his own ambitions. He said: "I have been crucified with Christ, and it is no longer I who live, but Christ lives in me; and the life which I now live in the flesh I live by faith in the Son of God who loved me, and delivered Himself up for me" (Gal 2:20). Cross bearers and Christ followers are biblically purpose driven: "Therefore also we have as our ambition, whether at home or absent, to be pleasing to Him" (2 Cor 5:9).

There are other spiritual disciplines that will help Christians overcome depression and feelings of inadequacy and deprivation and so achieve God's purposes. These include relying on adequacy that is from God (2 Cor 3:5), being filled with the Spirit of God (Eph 5:18), being nourished by the Word of God (2 Tim 3:16-17) and being cleansed from all defilement of flesh and spirit, perfecting holiness in the fear of God (2 Cor 7:1; 2 Tim 2:21). Then they will take their seat with Him on His throne (Rev 3:21) and reign with Him in their life (Rom 5:17; Rev 1:5, 5:10).

MAY 18

The more we pay for God's truth, the better is our bargain.
The more we play with Satan's lies the greater is our loss.

WHAT'S ON YOUR PLATE: PASTORAL PASTRIES OR SOUND DOCTRINE?

False teachers and wayward shepherds have set up camp in the sanctuary to roast marshmallows and bake pastoral pastries; to tickle ears and entertain lukewarm souls. "An appalling and horrible thing has happened in the land: the prophets prophesy falsely, and the priests rule on their own authority; and My people love it so! But what will you do at the end of it?" (Jeremiah 5:30-31). Just as Jeremiah lamented the siege of Jerusalem so we see the Church under siege today: "The kings of the earth did not believe, nor did any of the inhabitants of the world, that the adversary and the enemy could enter the gates of Jerusalem" (Lam 4:12).

Until God's people become obedient to the Lord's commandment to read and obey the Word of God (Mt 4:4; 2 Tim 3:16; Joshua 1:8) and become nourished on sound doctrine (1 Tim 4:6; Tit 2:1; 1 Pet 2:1-2), and skilled in its use

(2 Tim 2:15; Heb 5:14; Eph 6:17) rather than malnourished on popular spiritual fast food and pastoral pastries, they will continue to be deceived by the devil (1 Tim 4:1; Col 2:8), devoured by the lion (1 Pet 5:8), destroyed for lack of knowledge (Hosea 4:6), and taken captive by the powers of darkness (Isaiah 5:13).

It's interesting that the true children of God against whom the dragon and antichrist will wage war are called "those who keep the commandments of God and hold to the testimony of Jesus and keep their faith in Him (Rev 12:17; 14:12). The devil and his demons know well such ones who overcome him (Acts 19:15). They are those who overcome because of the blood of the Lamb, because of the word of their testimony and because they do not love their life even to death (Rev 12:11).

Just because Jesus fulfilled the Law, it doesn't mean we can ignore His commandments. Jesus said, "He who has My commandments and keeps them, he is it who loves Me" (Jn 14:21a) and "You are My friends, if you do what I command you" (Jn 15:14). Sin is lawlessness (1 Jn 3:4) and the wages of sin is death (Rom 6:23). And Peter wrote: "and He Himself bore our sins in His body on the cross, that we might die to sin and live to righteousness; for by His wounds you were healed" (1 Pet 2:24).

Paul said "for it is not the hearers of the Law who are just before God, but the doers of Law will be justified" (Rom 2:13). But the ability to obey does come from within, from some New Age inner guide, or latent divinity. It is not necessary for a "New" Christian to emerge. Rather, it is by the power of indwelling Holy Spirit that we put to death the deeds of the body and walk in the Spirit (Rom 8:13; Gal 5:16). It is by the Spirit's power, not by powerless religion, that one is able to obey the law of the Spirit of life, having been set free from the law of sin and of death (Rom 8:1-4, 13). Then we can obey Jesus' great commission to His called out holy nation to go out and make disciples of all the nations, teaching them to observe all that He commanded (1 Pet 2:9; Mt 28:18-20).

MAY 19

"The early church was married to poverty, prisons and persecutions. Today, the church is married to prosperity, personality, and popularity." Leonard Ravenhill

The will of God and the commandment of the Lord Jesus Christ is for God's own to be holy and separated (1 Pet 1:15-16; 2 Tim 1:9; Eph 1:4; 2 Cor 6:14-18). Jesus taught and commanded His disciples to make converts into holy disciples and followers of Him (Mt 4:19; 28:18-20). Salvation through the Lord Jesus Christ which provides deliverance from the penalty of sin (Acts 4:12; Rom 6:23; Rom 8:1) must continue with sanctification which brings deliverance from the power of sin (Heb 10:10; 1 Cor 1:18). For without sanctification no one will see the Lord (Heb 12:14).

Children of God are to persevere through trials and continue to walk in the light, rather than hide in the dark (Rom 15:4; Heb 10:39; 1 Jn 1:7). They should not merely "go to church" but should be consumed with "being" the Church. They are to be imitators of the Lord Jesus Christ, who came to destroy the works of the devil and to take away sin (1 Jn 3:5,8). Instead we see many becoming imitators of Christian celebrities who enjoy the works of darkness and take sin lightly.

Much of contemporary Christianity employs religious experts and deploys human strategies to build worldly churches. They accommodate sin and accumulate riches rather than deplore sin and store up heavenly treasures. We have many a Judas today, who are more concerned with saving silver than with saving souls. Too many contemporary churches and Christian leaders are not exhorting and equipping believers to be the preserving salt and shining lights they were called to be (Mt 5:13-14; Eph 4:13-14). Many prefer stale religious crumbs falling from worldly pulpits rather than heaven's Living Manna.

MAY 20

*When flames of true revival burn, the devil
is resisted, demons are expelled, doubts are
removed and God's promises are claimed.*

GOD WHO IS PATIENT WITH YOU ALSO HAS A PATENT ON YOU.

The God of heaven not only is patient with you, but also has His own patent on you. You were specially created for a special mission, a holy vocation, a supernatural existence, and an eternally promising future. King David acknowledged this, saying: "For You formed my inward parts; You wove me in my mother's womb. I will give thanks to You, for I am fearfully and wonderfully made. Wonderful are Your works, and my soul knows it very well. My frame was not hidden from You, when I was made in secret, and skillfully wrought in the depths of the earth" (Ps 139:13-15). And now He is patiently working in your, both to will and to work for His good pleasure (Phil 2:13). He is co-laboring with you, making you a showcase of His handiwork, a letter of Christ written by His Spirit, and a vessel through whom He is demonstrating His wisdom and workmanship (2 Cor 3:3; Phil 2:12; Eph 2:10, 3:10). Since God doesn't create junk, don't settle for being a piece of ordinary junk mail, tossed aside, useless and abused by the god of this world. And though you may at times feel completely alone, remember, you alone have been made complete (Col 2:10).

MAY 21

Between the many "bone yards" of dead bones
and "barn yards" of wishbones, we often
find the fertile fields of living stones.

CONFESSIONS OF AN OVERCOMER

I will seek fellowship with the Holy Spirit (2 Cor 13:14) who was sent to be my Helper and to glorify the Lord Jesus Christ (Jn 14:26, 16:14). Help me to get out of myself and to get into Him, and to be pro-Him, because He is pro-me. As Paul said: "I have been crucified with Christ; and it is no longer I who live, but Christ lives in me; and the life which I now live in the flesh I live by faith in the Son of God, who loved me, and delivered Himself up for me" (Gal 2:20).

I will not be preoccupied with going within; nor worried about going without, but dedicated to going on with Him, forgetting myself and focusing on Him; dying to self and living for Him. I know I will experience my best life now when my whole life is in Him.

Why be overcome and downcast in sin, rather than an overcomer, raised up with Him?

I will resist and overcome the devil who roams about like a roaring lion, by the blood of the Lamb and great Deliverer who reigns victoriously from above

(1 Pet 5:8-9; Jam 4:7; Heb 10:12-13; Ps 2:12; 110:1-3). His redeeming blood washed away my sins so that the accusing one will not win (1 Pet 1:18-19; Jn 1:29; Rom 8:33-34). By His precious blood I was redeemed, bought and rescued out of Satan's domain of darkness and dominion of sin (1 Pet 1:18-19; Acts 26:18; Col 1:13). By His wounds I was healed (1 Pet 2:24), no longer dead in trespasses and sins, but made alive to live holy for Him (Eph 1:4, 2:1,5).

I overcome the evil one because of the word of my testimony which I maintain (Rev 12:11; 6:9), testifying to His Name which is above every name (Phil 2:9). His Name has delivering power to torment demons (Mk 5:7), healing power to cause the lame to walk (Acts 3:16) and saving power to rescue lost sinners (Acts 4:12).

I will overcome the evil one by not loving my life even when faced with death. I fix my eyes on Him who partook of flesh and blood so that "through death He might render powerless him who had the power of death, that is, the devil (Heb 2:14). And thus I am delivered from the fear of death and slavery to sin (Heb 2:15).

I will fix my eyes on Him who is seated in the heavenlies, (Heb 12:2; Eph 2:5-6), the last Adam who became a life-giving spirit (1 Cor 15:45), rather than on my old self which is crucified, dead and buried (Rom 6:3-4). I am convinced that He is able to guard what I have entrusted to Him until that day when He rescues me from every evil deed and brings me safely to His heavenly kingdom (2 Tim 1:23, 4:18). For to be absent from the body is to be at home with the Lord (2 Cor 5:8).

The heavenly minded are prone to ask: "Is your 'Best Life Now' tomb proof? Is your religion fire proof?" For in these last days many professing believers are entombed by deception and doctrines of demons. They are not taught by the Spirit of truth. They do not extinguish strange fire with Holy Spirit water. They are in danger of being engulfed by fire along with their coveted prosperity gossip, pastoral pastries, worldly treasures, sinner-friendly hyper grace and easy-believing workless faith.

MAY 22

"We are in danger of forgetting that we cannot do what God does, and that God will not do what we can do." Oswald Chambers

Christians are all ministers in the sense that they are all servants. Even the apostle Paul with all his great religious training (Phil 3:5-7) and having been divinely appointed as a preacher and an apostle and a teacher (2 Tim 1:11), still saw himself as a fellow-bondservant (2 Cor 4:5), along with Peter and John (Acts 4:29). He also said, "let a man regard us in this manner, as servants of Christ" (1 Cor 4:1).

Christians are equipped individually as gifted ministers to do the work of ministry for mutual and corporate edification (Eph 4:11-12; 1 Cor 12:7,11, 27; 1 Pet 4:10; Rom 12:5-6). While each one has his or her own calling and gifting as members of the body of Christ, all are equally regarded as servants and ministers of the Great Shepherd and Lord Jesus Christ, the Head of the body (Eph 5:23; 1 Cor 12:12,20; Eph 1:22-23). The Bible teaches that we are to "be subject to one another in the fear of Christ" (Eph 5:22).

There is no clergy and laity class distinction being that every Christian is part of the royal and holy priesthood (1 Pet 2:5, 9). Distinctions in biblical Christian ministry is made according to function, spirituality, gifting and calling rather than by a clergy and laity class distinction. In the early church, even leaders of ministry like elders and deacons were selected on the basis spiritual qualities, not based on artificial class distinction or professional training (Acts 6:3-5, 4:12-13; 1 Tim 3; Titus 1:5-9). Such practice would reduce the common tendency for some to lord over and control others in an unbiblical manner.

There is a great difference between laboring among others and lording it over others. Jesus condemned the latter. "You know that the rulers of the Gentiles lord it over them, and their great men exercise authority over them. It is not so among you, but whoever wishes to become great among you shall be your servant, and whoever wishes to be first among you shall be your slave; just as the Son of Man did not come to be served, but to serve, and to give His life a ransom for many." (Mt 20:25-28). The apostle commended the former. "But we request of you, brethren, that you appreciate those who diligently labor among you, and have charge over you in the Lord and give you instruction, and that you esteem them very highly in love because of their work. Live in peace with one another." (1 Thess 5:12-13).

To "have charge over in the Lord" is beautifully described in another passage that describes the proper duties and relationships between leaders and those whom they serve: "Remember those who led you, who spoke the word of God to you; and considering the result of their conduct, imitate their faith. Obey your leaders, and submit to them; for they keep watch over your souls, as those who will give an account. Let them do this with joy and not with grief, for this would be unprofitable for you" (Heb 13:7, 17). The apostle Paul describes such biblical leadership this way: "For our exhortation does not come from error or impurity or by way of deceit; but just as we have been approved by God to be entrusted with the gospel, so we speak, not as pleasing men but God, who examines our hearts. For we never came with flattering speech as you know, nor with a pretext for greed—God is witness—nor did we seek glory from men, either from you or from others, even though as apostles of Christ we might have asserted our authority. But we proved to be gentle among you, as a nursing mother, tenderly cares for her own children. Having thus a fond affection for you, we were well-pleased to impart to you not only the gospel of God but also our own lives, because you had become very dear to us" (1 Thess 2:3-8).

Though ministry distinctions are determined by one's gifting and calling rather than one's classification, one's effectiveness is dependent on one's spirituality not on one's position or office, every ministering servant should be a cleansed and prepared vessel for God's use (2 Tim 2:21). But even in the case of elders and deacons, it is not an appointment to an office or position, being that the word "office" in not in the original text. Rather, it is a calling to a type of ministry, to conduct the "work" of an elder or deacon.

There are varieties of ministries, but the same Lord to whom we serve, using the gifts of the Holy Spirit, allowing God to work all things in all people (1 Cor 12:4-6). Such ministry will manifest the power, leading and presence of the Holy Spirit working toward the unity, edification and common good of the body of Christ (1 Cor 12:7; 14:12; Jn 17; Eph 4:3f). If a minister seeks to be in the spot light, then he is following the wrong light, not the Light of the world, but the false light of the evil one.

MAY 23

"Only those who will risk going too far can possibly find out how far one can go." T.S. Eliot

DON'T THINK FOR A SECOND THAT GOD IS NOT IN CONTROL OF EVERY MINUTE...

God rules the angels of heaven and the kings of the earth. "The LORD has established His throne in the heavens; and His sovereignty rules over all. Bless the LORD, you His angels, mighty in strength, who perform His word, obeying the voice of His word. Bless the LORD, all you His hosts, you who serve Him, doing His will." (Ps 103:19-21). Though world leaders may boast and brag of their control and flaunt their authority against God and His people, they are merely energized puppets in the hands of the evil god of this world (Eph 2:1; 2 Tim 2:26; 1 Cor 12:1), who is on a leash held by the Holy One of Heaven.

Concerning the control and fulfillment of future events it is written: "the four angels, who had been prepared for the hour and day and month and year, were released, so that they would kill a third of mankind" (Rev 9:15). Even the defiant kings of the earth will fulfill God's purposes. Concerning the future the ten kings who receive authority as kings with the beast, having one purpose and giving their power and authority to the beast, it is written: "God has put it in their hearts to execute His purpose by having a common purpose, and by giving their kingdom to the beast until the words of God will be fulfilled" (Rev 17:13,17). So it is written: "the king's heart is like channels of water in the hand of the LORD; he turns it wherever He wishes" (Prov 21:2).

So rest assured that God is in control who works all things after the counsel of His will (Eph 1:11b). His Church still stands (Mt 16:18). There is no end to the increase of His government or of peace (Is 9:7) and no overthrow of His Kingdom. "Thy kingdom is an everlasting kingdom, and Thy dominion endures throughout all generations" (Ps 145:13).

Though "the kings of the earth take their stand and the rulers take counsel together against the LORD and against His Anointed, saying, 'Let us tear their fetters apart and cast away their cords from us!' He who sits in the heavens laughs, the Lord scoffs at them" (Ps 2:2-4). The sovereign King of kings is soon to return and the overcoming Christians will rejoice and reign with Him (Rom 8:16-17; 2 Tim 2:12a) just as they had reigned in life through Him (Rom 5:17).

MAY 24

The Christian ideal has not been tried and found wanting. It has been found difficult and left untried." G.K. Chesterton

THREE ESSENTIALS FOR THE ABUNDANT CHRISTIAN LIFE

Paul desired that the Corinthian believers possess three essentials of the Christian life: the grace of the Lord Jesus Christ, the love of God, and the fellowship of the Holy Spirit (2 Cor 13:14). When we stand firm in the true grace of God during our life (1 Pet 5:12), we will look back on our life having fought the good fight, having finished the course and having kept the faith (2 Tim 4:7). We can look forward to hearing our Lord and Savior say, "Well done, good and faithful slave" (Mt 25:21).

The second great essential is practicing and experiencing the love of God, rather than being consumed with loving the world and self. This is the love of God, that we keep His commandments and His commandments are not burdensome (1 Jn 5:3). The more we walk in the Spirit and bear the fruit of the Spirit (Gal 5:22), the more the love of God is poured out within our hearts through the Holy Spirit who was given to us (Rom 5:5). This objective love toward God and the subjective experience of being loved by God protects us from the devil's hostility, the world's hatred and the allurement of self-love. All this is made possible by the third great essential: fellowship with the Holy Spirit.

Jesus was led by the Spirit (Mt 4:1), rejoiced greatly in the Holy Spirit (Lk 10:21), cast out demons by the Holy Spirit (Mt 12:28), and offered Himself up through the eternal Spirit (Heb 9:14). Since believers are to follow Christ and possess the mind and attitude of Christ, it is reasonable to likewise walk with total dependency on the power, leading, teaching and transforming fellowship of the Holy Spirit (Rom 12:1-2; Mt 4:19; 1 Cor 2:16; Phil 2:5). Christians walking in the baptism of the Holy Spirit and of fire from above will burn up all obstructions below, originating from the world, the flesh and the devil. They will enjoy the fruit of the Spirit which is love, joy, peace, patience, kindness, goodness, faithfulness, gentleness and self-control (Gal 5:22-23). They will have a composed and quieted soul, walking by faith that overcomes the world and persevering in hope that anchors the soul (Ps 131:2; 1 Jn 5:4; Heb 6:19).

One may ask: "What about prayer, discipleship, obedience, holiness and other spiritual disciplines? Are they not also necessary to experience the abundant life?" As one fellowships with the Holy Spirit who sanctifies (1 Thess 4:7-8) and receives the grace of the Lord Jesus Christ which enriches (2 Cor 8:9) and experiences the love of God which encourages (Rom 5:5), these other necessary spiritual disciplines will be developed.

MAY 25

"No sort of defense is needed for preaching outdoors, but it would take a very strong argument to prove that a man who has never preached beyond the walls of his meetinghouse has done his duty. A defense is required for services within buildings rather than for worship outside of them." William Booth

EASY STREET RELIGION

Too many modern day Christians covet "Easy Street Religion". They want to stroll effortlessly downhill on an easy, smooth, broad, popular road. They refuse to toil uphill on a hard, narrow, less familiar road which is often rough and forces one to rely on God's strength and direction. They want to travel in this life on a well populated road. A road adorned on both sides with sights and sounds of happiness that please the eye and pleasure the soul; with flashing signs which cry out "come this way", "rest area ahead", "shopping mall ahead". They avoid the road less traveled. They despise road signs that say, "Wrong Way" or "One Way" or "Don't Enter Here". They are too busy enjoying their ride to stop and minister to the poor, needy and suffering, lost alongside the road. Such happy-go-lucky worldly travelers may well miss out on walking on streets of gold in Paradise, with saints of old, who read and obeyed heaven's road signs, the Bible. They may miss heaven's beauty at the end of the road, because they failed to fear God and follow His Word.

MAY 26

*"Solid, lasting missionary work is done
on our knees." J.O. Fraser*

GOOD MORNING AMERICA...THE SON HAS RISEN

It is "Good Morning" again to all born again Christians for the Son has risen. "This is the day which the LORD has made; let us rejoice and be glad in it" (Ps 118:24). The bright and morning star has risen (Rev 22:16). The devil no longer has to rain on your parade, but you can reign over him. Since you are in Christ, who conquered death, you can defeat the devil who seeks to devour. Whenever the devil arises to remind you of yesterday's mistakes and sins, remind him of his future misery and condemnation.

If we have died with Christ, we believe that we shall also live with Him (Rom 6:8). "If we endure, we will also reign with Him" (2 Tim 2:12a). This is not only a future promise but a present reality. For "those who receive the abundance of grace and of the gift of righteousness will reign in life through the One, Jesus Christ" (Rom 5:17).

For the apostle Paul, whom we are to imitate, said: "I have been crucified with Christ; and it is no longer I who live, but Christ lives in me; and the life which I now live in the flesh I live by faith in the Son of God, who loved me and gave Himself up for me" (Gal 2:20). And "when Christ, who is our life, is revealed, then you also will be revealed with Him in glory" (Col 3:4). We know that "momentary light affliction is producing for us an eternal weight of glory far beyond all comparison" (2 Cor 4:17).

MAY 27

"A preacher who preaches the truth uncompromisingly will be asked, 'Does your preaching always have to be so pointy? Does it always have to be so sharp?' And of course the answer is no. He can blunt his message if he'd like, and become just as dull as the average preacher." Jesse Morrell

Jesus who came from heaven, died and rose again, will appear a second time, for His own to take them to heaven. He said: "In My Father's house are many dwelling places; if it were not so, I would have told you; for I go to prepare a place for you. If I go and prepare a place for you, I will come again and receive you to Myself, that where I am, there you may also be" (Jn 14:2-3). Thank the Lord there will be no foreclosures in heaven. And no landlord will be there evicting, for the Lord of Heaven will be there inviting. He will be inviting His faithful servants who have not loved the world, nor the things in the world, nor their life to come home and live forever (1 Jn 2:15-17). Jesus promised: "He who loves his life loses it, and he who hates his life in this world will keep it to life eternal. If anyone serve Me, he must follow Me; and where I am there my servant will be also; if anyone serves Me, the Father will honor him" (Jn 12:25-26).

MAY 28

"No flesh shall glory in His presence, and the religious flesh is no more acceptable than the irreligious." T. Austin-Sparks

We must beware of the serpent's craftiness in leading our minds astray from the simplicity and purity of devotion to Christ (2 Cor 11:3). Some labor to fully understand complex things of theology such as God's sovereignty and man's free will or the nature of the Trinity. So what is the most biblical and sensible way to view such statements like "God has shut up all in disobedience so that He may show mercy to all" (Rom 11:32)? How about following Paul's example: "Oh, the depths of the riches both of the wisdom and knowledge of God! How unsearchable are His judgments and unfathomable His ways" (Rom 11:33)!

In the Old Testament Moses wisely said: "The secret things belong to the LORD our God, but the things revealed belong to us and to our sons forever, that we may observe all the words of this law" (Deut 29:29). King David humbly said it this way: "O LORD, my heart is not proud, not my eyes haughty; nor do I involve myself in great matters, or in things too difficult for me" (Ps 131:1).

There is also the temptation when discussing less lofty subject matters, to acquire a morbid interest in controversial questions and disputes about words (1 Tim 6:4), to become entangled in foolish and ignorant speculations which produce quarrels (2 Tim 2:23). Beware of pop theologians, religious experts, self-promoting apostles and prophets who are preoccupied with "worldly chatter and opposing arguments of what is falsely called knowledge" (1 Tim 6:20). I am speaking of prosperity preachers and many of the emergent, contemplative and New Age types, as well as hyper grace and hyper-Calvinistic brands of Christianity and the popular ear-tickling, live-for- now preachers. They are always learning and never able to come to the full knowledge of the truth nor abide in it (2 Tim 3:7; Jn 8:31-32, 36). Often they hold to a form of godliness, although they have denied its power (2 Tim 3:5), paying attention to "deceitful spirits and doctrines of demons" (1 Tim 4:1), rather than being taught by the Spirit of truth. As Jesus said: "Rightly did Isaiah prophesy…This people honors Me with their lips, but their heart is far from Me….teaching as doctrines the precepts of men. Neglecting the commandment of God such hold onto the tradition of men" (Mk 7:7-8).

Instead, we should give undue attention to "testifying to both Jews and Greeks of repentance toward God and faith in our Lord Jesus Christ" (Acts 20:21). After all, we have been called to evangelize boldly and make disciples, not to debate endlessly and reason vainly (Mt 28:18-20).

MAY 29

"Worry is a cycle of inefficient thoughts whirling around a center of fear." Corrie ten Boom

ONLY TRUE CONVERSION CAN CONTEND WITH THE LAST DAY PERVERSION.

The practice of first century believers consisted of frequent assembling and sincere devotion to the apostles' teaching, and to fellowship, to the breaking of bread and to prayer (Acts 2:42). Early on, the Christian faith invited and provided for participation of all present in the exercise of spiritual gifts (1 Cor 14:26; 1 Pet 4:10) for the common good (1 Cor 12:7) and for the edification of the body (1 Cor 14:12). Each believer was seen as part of a holy and royal priesthood whose duty was to offer up spiritual sacrifices acceptable to God (1 Pet 2:5, 9; Rom 12:1-2; Heb 13:15). Each believer was to proclaim the excellencies of God who called him out of the devil's dark world into the kingdom of His Son, the Light of the world (1 Pet 2:5,9; Col 1:13; Jn 8:12).

The local assemblies, being thus edified, would also be equipped by gifted leaders, not religious talkers, GED's (God empowered disciples), not religious Ph.D's, for the work of service, to the building up of the body of Christ through evangelizing the lost and discipling the saved. Having been empowered from on high (Acts 1:8) they were commissioned to go out into the world as Christ's ambassadors preaching the good news of the kingdom of God (Mt 28:18-20; Acts 8:12a; 2 Cor 5:20-21) in demonstration in the Spirit and of power (1 Cor 2:4).

Deceitful spirits and doctrines of demons, deception and heresy will spread more and more in the last days to vigorously oppose the preaching of the Gospel of God and His truth (1 Tim 4:1; Mt 24:4; 2 Pet 2:1,15,21; 2 Tim 4:3-4). However, proper spiritual immunization against such diseased teaching consists of being taught and empowered by the Spirit of God in the Word of God. Approved servants and soldiers of the cross will not feast on religious fast food and poisonous religious doctrines of disguised angels or wolves in sheep's clothing.

MAY 30

Crucify the three T's: contrary thoughts, corrupting temptations and the careless tongue, and you will carry the cross well. Come out from the world and you will overcome it well.

The devil knows his days are numbered. So he is trying to abort the ministry of the Holy Spirit so that no spiritual life is conceived and born and no spiritual fruit is produced but only weeds and tares. Like a master chef he mixes them up and dresses them up to look like wheat, deceiving naive observers.

Too many Christians today are woefully ignorant of the schemes of the devil. They foolishly think that he is only hiding out in some far away country among witch doctors and the like. In reality, he is prowling about and standing behind many contemporary Christian pulpits, whispering to preachers and exalting their doctors of religion, performing on their stages, inspiring their books, and dishing out pastoral pastries to those who can't stomach the solid meat of the Word.

When the prince of the power of the air comes whispering lies and fear into your ear, don't complain "woe is me" but wait on God and proclaim "awesome is He". Don't run like a chicken but mount up with wings and fly as an eagle. Be lifted up by God's Truth, soaring high by His Spirit, upward to His Son with whom you are seated, above wicked principalities and powers.

MAY 31

"He looks today, as He has ever looked, not for crowds drifting aimlessly in His track, but for individual men and women whose undying allegiance will spring from their having recognized that He wants those who are prepared to follow the path of self-renunciation which He trod before them." H. A. Evan Hopkin

The assembling of believers is for the equipping, participation and encouragement of the body (Eph 4:11f). Believers will learn how to stimulate one another to love and good deeds (Heb 10:24). They will worship God in spirit and in truth (Jn 4:23-24). They will love in deed and in truth because they were first loved by Him who is love and truth (1 Jn 3:18, 4:8,19; Jn 14:6).

If the Lord's presence is evident in the "service" and lost sinners happen to show up, they would see a powerful and relevant faith demonstrated, agape love practiced and the true gospel preached. This is the Good News the lost needs to hear, and the saved need to hear again and again. Unfortunately, most believers assemble and seek happiness rather than holiness, and expect to receive rather than to give, to be entertained rather than equipped, to have itching ears scratched rather than prepared hearts pierced. They leave unchanged because they didn't encounter the God who brings change.

When the Lord is given His proper place, one doesn't have to fear what might take place. For all things will work together for good, though some things may appear bad. The Bright Morning Star will rise daily, to them who die daily. Darkness will be cast aside, when Jesus the Light, is standing at your side.

JUNE 1

"Your life is like a coin - you can spend it any way you wish, but you can spend it only once." Unknown

WHAT IS A TRUE CHRISTIAN?

Just as Jesus was asking His disciples "Who do people say that the Son of Man is?" (Mt 16:13), so today one could ask: "How does the Bible describe a true son of God"? The New Testament describes one who is saved in many ways: one who is led by the Spirit of God (Rom 8:14), who is born again rather than dead in sin (Jn 3:3,5; Eph 2:1), who is baptized into Christ (Rom 6:3; 1 Cor 12:13), who is a new creature (2 Cor 5:17), who is called a "saint", not a sinner (1 Cor 1:2), who is a friend of Jesus by doing what He commands (Jn 15:14) as one who doesn't just talk the talk but walks the talk (Mt 7:21). He is clothed with Christ (Gal 3:27), is an overcomer of the world rather than a lover the world (1 Jn 2:15-17; 5:4) and has crucified the flesh with its passions and desires (Gal 5:24).

A true believer is described as one who is sanctified and is being sanctified (Heb 10:10; 12:14), who is not perishing but saved and is being saved (1 Cor 1:18), who confesses with his mouth that Jesus as Lord, and believes in his heart that God raised Him from the dead (Rom 10:9). He perseveres to the end (Heb 10:36-39; Mt 24:13) and practices righteousness and not sin (1 Jn 3:8-10; Gal 5:21). A true Christian loves his brother rather than hates him (1 Jn 3:15, 4:7), believes (Jn 3:16; 1 Jn 5:13; 1 Pet 1:4-5, 9) and obeys (Jn 3:36; 1 Pet 1:2; Heb 5:9). And the list goes on.

One quickly notices that most of these passages address the subject of sin or walking according to the flesh. And this is not surprising considering that Jesus appeared as the sacrificial Lamb of God to take away sins (Jn 1:29; 1 Jn 3:5). God made Him who knew no sin to be sin, so that we who were dead in sin could die to sin (2 Cor 5:21; Eph 2:1; 1 Pet 2:24; Rom 6:11). Jesus came to destroy the works of the devil who sinned from the beginning (1 Jn 3:8). Besides, salvation has everything to do with sin. It delivers one from past condemnation of sin, the present power of sin and the future presence of sin.

On the contrary, modern day Christianity chooses to redefine a Christian in any way that contradicts God's truth and that is politically correct; using any conjured up description that pleases lost souls, entertains depraved minds and tickles itching ears.

JUNE 2

"The vague and tenuous hope that God is too kind
to punish the ungodly has become a deadly opiate
for the consciences of millions." A.W.Tozer

THE FAMILY OF GOD IS SAFE AND SECURE

"God is in the midst of her, she will not be moved" (Ps 46:5a). We will not fear, though the earth should change and though the mountains slip into the heart of the sea (Ps 46:2). When the storms come we will walk on the sea by fixing our eyes on the Lord who reigns from above, not on our foes below, for we receive a kingdom which cannot be shaken (Heb 12:28). For even in martyrdom, Christians are not killed, but merely have their physical address changed. The LORD of hosts is with us for who can be against us? (Ps 46:7; Rom 8:31).

God is our refuge and strength, a very present help in time of trouble. Even when we walk through the valley of the shadow of death we are safe and secure (Ps 46:1-2; 23:4). Therefore we are not tossed about by winds of postmodern uncertainty, political corruptness, man's private religious and vain interpretations and media's railing judgments. We sail smoothly on by God's eternal promises, biblical correctness and divine revelation. (Eph 4:14; Jude 1:9). For Jesus who is the way, the truth and the life is waiting on the other side.

JUNE 3

"We are plainly told in the Scriptures that in the last days men will not endure sound doctrine and will depart from the faith and heap to themselves teachers to tickle their ears. We live in an epidemic of this itch, and popular preachers have developed "ear-tickling" into a fine art." Vance Havner

SHEPHERD OR WOLF: WHO WILL YOU LET IN?

Jesus is standing at the door knocking to enter and live in you, if He has not yet been invited to reside in and reign over your life (Jn 1:12, 14:21, 23; Rev 3:20; 1 Pet 3:15). Beware! Sin, as well as the devil who sinned from the beginning, may be crouching at the door to entice, ensnare, enter and kill you (Gen 4:7; Jam 1:13-15; 1 Pet 5:8; 1 Jn 3:8). To whom will you yield: the Holy and Righteous One, the Good Shepherd who seeks to snuggle and care or the evil one, the wolf, who seeks snatch and scatter (Jn 10:10-12)?

Resist the devil and he will flee (Jam 4:7). Crack the door open and he will have you for lunch. Open the door for the Great Shepherd and He will prepare a table before you in the presence of your enemies (Ps 23:4-5). The choice is yours to dine who the Light of the world or dwell in darkness with the devil, the god of this world.

Will you be embraced by the Savior's love or be captured in Satan's claws? Be wise and taste and see that the Lord is good (Ps 34:8). Don't be foolish, taste of forbidden fruit and experience that the devil is evil.

JUNE 4

"A popular evangelist reaches your emotions. A true prophet reaches your conscience." Leonard Ravenhill

CHRIST MINDED SAINTS HEAR THE SPIRIT OF GOD CLEARLY

Christians who have the mind of Christ have ears to hear what the Spirit says (1 Cor 2:12,13,16). The Spirit of God was sent to glorify the Son and to teach believers how to abide in Him (Jn 14:26; 1 Jn 2:27), in whom are hidden all the treasures of wisdom and knowledge (Col 2:3). On Christ the Solid Rock they stand, not blown about by every wind of doctrine and shifting sand.

Jesus is the Cornerstone and His own are the living stones of His Temple (Eph 2:20 1 Pet 2:5). Jesus, as the Head His Church, is building it upon the sure foundation of God's holy apostles and prophets (Eph 2:20) and making it strong by the properly functioning members of His body (1 Pet 2:5; Eph 4:16). These members are holy and royal priests and sent out ambassadors of the great King, High Priest, and Commander (1 Pet 2:5,9; 2 Cor 5:20). Christian ministers don't lord it over others as worldly masters do but serve others as their heavenly Master did (Mt 20:25-28; 1 Pet 5:1-4). When He returns with His reward, they will rejoice in glory with Him, whom they served and with whom they suffered.

JUNE 5

"There are no crown-wearers in heaven who were not cross-bearers here below." Unknown

Believers are commanded to resist the father of lies and reverence the Father of lights, with whom there is no variation or shifting shadow (Jn 8:44; Jam 1:17, 4:7; Prov 8:13-14; 2 Cor 5:10-11). You can't trust a word the devil whispers to you, but you can surely trust in every inspired word that God has spoken and preserved for you (Mt 4:4; 2 Tim 3:16-17). "As for God, His way is blameless; the word of the LORD is tried; He is a shield to all who take refuge in Him" (Ps 18:30). "Forever, O LORD, Thy word is settled in heaven" (Ps 119:89). We overcome Satan who disguises himself as an angel of light (2 Cor 11:14-15) as well as his servants of righteousness by destroying devilish speculations and every lofty thing raised up against the true knowledge of God (2 Cor 10:5a).

"Bless the LORD, O my soul; and all that is within me, bless His holy name" (Ps 103:1). By the knowledge of the Holy One, we overcome the evil one. One who knows His name will not be put to shame. "The people who know their God will display strength and take action" (Dan 11:32b). God turns to and is gracious to those who love His name (Ps 119:132). "It is good to give thanks to the LORD and to sing praises to Your name, O Most High, to declare Your lovingkindness in the morning and Your faithfulness by night" (Ps 92:1-2). I will not be afraid of the terror by night, or of the arrow that flies by day (Ps 91:5). "For You light my lamp; the LORD my God illumines my darkness" (Ps 18:28).

JUNE 6

"Is this really the church of Christ, or are we just calling it the church because of our traditions and history?" K.P. Yohannan

SEEK HIS PRESENCE FIRST AND HIS PRESENTS WILL FOLLOW

Let us be like David who said: "One thing have I desired of the LORD, that will I seek after; that I may dwell in the house of the LORD all the days of my life, to behold the beauty of the LORD, and to inquire in His temple" (Ps 27:4). There is no want for those who reverence Him (Ps 34:7). Those who adore God for what He eternally is will not be anxious concerning what they may temporarily lack. For God withholds no good thing from them who walk uprightly (Ps 84:11b). Even in times of severe difficulty and personal affliction, because of God's all sufficient grace, the apostle Paul could say: "Therefore I am well content with weaknesses, with insults, with distresses, with persecutions, with difficulties, for Christ's sake; for when I am weak, then I am strong" (2 Cor 12:10). And it has also been promised: "He who did not spare His own Son, but delivered Him over for us all, how will He not also with Him freely give us all things" (Rom 8:32)?

Those chosen in Christ have it all, for in Him they have already been blessed with every spiritual blessing (Eph 1:3). Though they may feel completely alone in the world, yet they alone have been made complete in Christ (Col 2:10). Though they were formerly without God in the world, now they are the adopted sons of God and overcomers of the world (Eph 2:12; Rom 8:14-15; 1 Jn 5:4). They have been made alive together with Christ, raised up and seated with Him in the heavenly places (Eph 2:5-6), in whom are hidden all the treasures of wisdom and knowledge (Col 2:3).

The apostle Paul spoke of the surpassing value of knowing Christ Jesus as his Lord (Phil 3:8). And when Jesus is Lord over everything, we will not lack for anything. When we seek first His presence, we will enjoy His presents. As King David said: "in Your presence is fullness of joy; in Your right hand there are pleasures forever" (Ps 16:11).

JUNE 7

*"The kingdom of God is not going to advance by our
churches becoming filled with men, but by men in our
churches becoming filled with God." Howard Spring*

God's sovereignty over our life will be supernaturally displayed in our
life when we invite Jesus to be Lord of our life (1 Pet 3:15). That is
the abundant life which Jesus came to give, which is much better than the
"best life" which so many seek to have. God's sovereign care in working out
all things for our good is observed when we love Him, walk worthy of the
Christian call and desire to accomplish His purpose for our life and please
Him (Rom 8:28-29; 14:7-8).

Of course, the knowledge of such a worthy walk that pleases the
Father of glory and Father of light comes from reading His holy Word
which is the only trustworthy and all sufficient lamp to our feet and light
to our path (Ps 119:105; 2 Tim 3:16-17; Ps 19:7-11). "How can a young
man keep his way pure? By keeping it according to Thy word" (Ps 119:9).
This applies to every Christian. "Thy word I have treasured in my heart,
that I may not sin against Thee" (Ps 119:11). Yet today most hide the
Word from their sight and store up worldly treasures in their heart, rather
than seeking first the kingdom of God and His righteousness, and making Jesus the Lord of the heart (Mt 6:33; 1 Pet 3:15). And we see the
fallout: Christians stumbling in the dark, falling into the ditches of life,

hitchhiking through life and often picked up by the devil's chauffeurs and couriers of demonic doctrines playing devilish music as they travel down the road to destruction, ignoring all of God's road signs warning of dangers and giving directions.

JUNE 8

"I would rather teach one man to pray than ten men to preach." J. H. Jowett

Satan knows his time is short. He is working ever so diligently in and through his sons of disobedience (Eph 2:2), preventing them from coming to their senses so they will remain in his snare and remain captive to do his will (2 Tim 2:26). Yet God's arm is fully capable of delivering His servants out of the devil's grasp if they will do their part in resisting his advances. Discerning solders of God know they struggle "not against flesh and blood, but against the rulers, against the powers, against the world forces of this darkness, against the spiritual forces of wickedness in the heavenly places" (Eph 6:12). They take seriously spiritual warfare principles found in Scripture: "For though we walk in the flesh, we do not war according to the flesh, for the weapons of our warfare are not of the flesh, but divinely powerful for the destruction of fortresses" (2 Cor 10:3-4).

Those who have the mind of Christ will put on the helmet of salvation so they can guard their minds from Satan's mental attacks against the knowledge of God (1 Cor 2:16; 2 Cor 10:5; Eph 6:17a). They know they have to resist the devil before he will flee (Jam 4:7b). Peter learned the lesson well when he foolishly pulled Jesus aside to rebuke Him for speaking of His coming suffering, death and resurrection. Jesus said to him: "Get behind Me, Satan! You are a stumbling block to Me; for you are not setting your mind on God's interests, but man's" (Mt 16:23).

Wise soldiers of the cross know that they have to put on the full armor of God before they can stand firm against the schemes of the devil (Eph 6:11). They know that they have to take up the full armor of God in order to be able to resist in the evil day (Eph 6:13a). They know that even after submitting themselves to God and relying totally on His power and putting on the full armor of God, they must continually stand firm (Jam 4:7a; Eph 6:10,13b).

They know they must remain separated from the world which lies in the sphere of the god of this world and remain submitted to the Lordship of the Great Shepherd if they are to expect to benefit from His shepherding care. If Jesus' Lordship is denied, progress in sanctification and separation from the world is hindered. Unfortunately, too many contemporary Christians are not aware of the devil's presence, power and progress in the world and in the professing Church. The devil will continue expanding his playground in areas where the Church fails to expose his unfruitful deeds of darkness and take back their lost ground (Eph 5:11).

JUNE 9

"Some people become tired at the end of ten minutes or half an hour of prayer. What will they do when they have to spend Eternity in the presence of God? We must begin the habit here and become used to being with God." Sadhu Sundar Singh

Many Christians start off their Christian life excited to live God's way, in newness of life, as new creatures in Christ (Rev 2:4-5; Rom 6:4; 2 Cor 5:17). Yet, they often see their fire going out, and slowly begin to deviate from the Way and live their own way. They may even stumble, get angry, become impatient over perceived unanswered prayers and be tempted to tell the Lord to hit the highway. Then they wonder why they are led off the road into the ditch.

Jesus warned many churches in Revelation 2 and 3 of the need to repent, return to their first love, and not be lukewarm. Paul warned of the dangers of deception and of returning to the slavery of sin (Eph 5:1-6; Rom 6; Gal 4:9, 5:1, 13). Peter exhorted believers to continue progressing in godliness and to make certain their calling (2 Pet 1). Paul even exhorted the Corinthian believers saying: "test yourselves to see if you are in the faith" (2 Cor 13:5a).

The Christian life is a lifelong battle in sanctification; the process by which a believer becomes more separated from the world and holy before God (2 Cor 6:14-18). It is not uncommon for new believers who are not discipled to become prey to the devil and his tricks, for they are not told and trained to be alert to his schemes (2 Cor 2:11; Eph 6:11). Also, when believers fail to submit to Jesus as Lord of their heart, as prescribed in 1 Pet 3:15, there will be many occasions when one will stumble and backslide because one fails to watch over the heart with all diligence, for from it flow the springs of life (Prov 4:23). And the unguarded heart is more deceitful than all else and is desperately sick; who can understand it? (Jer 17:9). But those who have an honest and good heart hear God's word, and hold it fast, and bear fruit with perseverance (Lk 8:14). Those whose heart is steadfast, will sing praises with their soul (Ps 108:1), for God saves the upright in heart (Ps 7:10).

JUNE 10

"My main ambition in life is to be on the devil's most wanted list." Leonard Ravenhill

W-eapons of our warfare are not of the flesh but are divinely powerful for the destruction of fortresses of the mind and spiritual enemies on the battlefield (2 Cor 10:4-5; Eph 6:12). Overcoming Christian soldiers will be strong in the Lord (Eph 6:10), will put on the full armor of God (Eph 6:11), will be clothed with the righteousness of Christ (Eph 6:14b; Rom 13:14; 1 Cor 1:30) and will effectively wield the sword, the Word of God, under the direction of the Holy Spirit (Eph 6:17b). They will be mentally prepared to suffer (2 Tim 2:3) and not be entangled in the affairs of everyday life (2 Tim 2:3-4).

A-lertness in battle is crucial because our adversary the devil prowls around like a roaring lion, seeking someone to devour (1 Pet 5:8). Those who are intoxicated with the world rather than sober minded and Spirit filled will be prey to the devil, the ravenous wolf and angel of light who comes to steal, kill, destroy and deceive (Jam 4:4; 1 Jn 2:15-17; Eph 5:18; Jn 10:10a; 2 Cor 11:13-15).

R-esist the devil or he will not flee (James 4:7; 1 Pet 5:9; Eph 6:13). Satan's demons will not leave except by force. Even Jesus had to cast out his demons by the Spirit of God (Mt 12:28). "The kingdom of heaven suffers violence, and violent men take it by force" (Mt 11:12). Let the high praises of God be in your mouth, and His word, the two-edged sword be in your hand (Ps 149:6; Heb 4:12).

F-aith. The shield of faith is the weapon that extinguishes all the flaming missiles of the evil one (Eph 6:16). This is not a faith in ourselves, but biblical faith in God "who gives life to the dead and calls into being that which does not exist" (Rom 4:17); the faith that sustains (Heb 10:35-39). It is an active faith in the living God of all grace who called you to His eternal glory in Christ; a faith that is confident that He will perfect, confirm, strengthen and establish you after encountering fiery attacks of the devil (1 Pet 5:9-10). Faith is essential if one is to be an overcomer in these last days, for without faith God is not pleased nor is the world overcome (Heb 11:6; 1 Jn 5:5).

A-rmor up with the full armor of God. You must put on the full armor of God. We must not be like so many today: nudist soldiers in Satan's camp, covered at best with religious fig leaves from the garden rather than with the full armor of God. We ought not to be clothed in shame and timidity when given a spirit of power, love and discipline (2 Tim 1:7).

R-ecognize the real enemy and discern the proper battles to fight. Satan delights to see Christian soldiers fighting among themselves, bickering over trivial matters and diverted off the battlefield while his demonized troops advance his kingdom. We are to fight the good fight of faith along with all who proclaim the true gospel, who exalt Jesus and proclaim Him as Lord and Savior, who walk by the Spirit and fear the Father. "If you address as Father the One who impartially judges according to each one's work, conduct ourselves in fear during the time of your stay on earth" (1 Pet 1:17). Be more concerned with giving the devil a black eye rather than with plucking splinters out of another Christian's eye.

E-ngage the enemy. We are at war. The time is short, the battles are many, the warfare is fierce and the devil is determined. If you are following Christ the devil is after you. "Beloved, do not be surprised at the fiery ordeal among you, which comes upon you for your testing, as though some strange thing were happening" (1 Pet 5:12). Jesus said: "A slave is not greater than his master. If they persecuted Me, they will also persecute you" (Jn 15:20). "As the Father has sent Me, I also send you" (Jn 20:21). The Son of God appeared to destroy the works of the devil (1 Jn 3:8). Likewise, Christians are to be lights in Satan's world, piercing its darkness with the light of the Gospel, walking in the Light of His presence (Jn 8:12; Gal 2:20; Gal 5:25).

JUNE 11

"There is no power like that of prevailing prayer, of Abraham pleading for Sodom, Jacob wrestling in the stillness of the night, Moses standing in the breach, Hannah intoxicated with sorrow, David heartbroken with remorse and grief, Jesus in sweat of blood… Such prayer prevails. It turns ordinary mortals into men of power. It brings power. It brings fire. It brings rain. It brings life. It brings God." Samuel Chadwick

THE THREE D'S OF THE DEVIL

Beware of the devil's deceptions, divisions and diversions. This is the day for undivided attention, undiluted devotion and uncompromised commitment to the things of God.

We will see more and more religious celebrity idols appearing on the horizon as rising stars. In reality they are wondering and fallen stars (Jude 13) promising freedom while they have become slaves of corruption (2 Pet 2:19). Forsaking the right way they have gone astray (2 Pet 2:15), speaking out arrogant words of vanity they have denied God's Word of truth (2 Pet 2:18), having invented a sinner friendly hyper grace, they have insulted God's sanctifying Spirit of Grace (Heb 10:29; Jude 4; 1 Thess 4:3,8).

Satan is blinding the minds of everyone who refuses to believe and practice the Word of God and walk in the light of the Gospel (2 Cor 4:4). A great shaking is occurring and that which is not built on the Rock but on sand, will be blown away by deceitful spirits and demonic doctrines (Heb 12:25-29; Mt 8:24-26; 16:16-18; 1 Tim 4:1).

Good soldiers of the Cross who understand the times, who know how to use their spiritual weapons and who serve the King of Kings will overcome (1 Chron 12:32-33; Rev 12:11). "Those who know their God will display strength and take action" (Dan 11:32). Those preaching and practicing sound doctrine will have the discernment needed to avoid being taken captive by philosophy and empty deception (Heb 5:14; Col 2:8).

On judgment day it won't matter how big the churches were or how famous or successful preachers became or how prosperous Christians were. What will matter is how faithful and sensible each was as a steward of God's grace, Gospel and household (Eph 3:2, 7; 1 Cor 9:17-18; Mt 24:45). The Chief Shepherd rewards shepherds who feed and care for His sheep, but will judge those who build religious cathedrals, who fleece and don't feed. The Lord will receive and bless those who bless and serve others rather than serve self. He will bless those who read and practiced heaven's Best Seller, not those who only read the world's best sellers.

JUNE 12

"Nothing is too big for my God to accomplish, and nothing is too little for Him to use in accomplishing it!" Unknown

LIVING STONES ARE DEAD ROCKS?

"The grace of God has appeared bringing salvation to all men, instructing us to deny ungodliness and worldly desires and to live sensibly, righteously and godly in the present age" (Tit 2:11-12). We must not turn God's grace into licentiousness (Jude 4) nor insult the Spirit of grace (Heb 10:29). Working together with God we are not to receive the grace of God in vain, (2 Cor 6:1), but allow the grace of God to labor within us (1 Cor 15:10). In this way we work out our salvation with fear and trembling, knowing that God is at work in us, both to will and to work for His good pleasure (Phil 2:12-13).

We must forever remind ourselves that "we are HIS workmanship, created in Christ Jesus for good works, which God prepared beforehand so that we would walk in them" (Eph 2:10). It is not about being 'purpose driven' but Spirit led and Kingdom seeking. We are not called to be "church builders" but "church BE-ers". When we let the Lord Jesus Christ build His Church as He promised, it will be built properly and victoriously, comprised of living stones, not dead bricks and mortar (Mt 16:15-18; 1 Pet 2:5).

JUNE 13

"The Bible is either absolute, or it's obsolete." Leonard Ravenhill

HOARD NOT THE MIGHTY DOLLAR BUT THE ALMIGHTY WORD

King David said: "Your word I have treasured in my heart, that I may not sin against You" (Ps 119:11). "How sweet are Thy words to my taste! Yes, sweeter than honey to my mouth!" (Ps 119:103). "Therefore I love Thy commandments above gold yes, above find gold" (Ps 119:127). "The words of the LORD are pure words, as silver tried in a furnace on the earth, refined seven times" (Ps 12:6). "The law of Thy mouth is better to me than thousands of gold and silver pieces" (Ps 119:72). "Thy word is very pure, therefore Thy servant loves it" (Ps 119:140). "Seven times a day I praise Thee, because of Thy righteous ordinances" (Ps 119:164). "My eyes anticipate the night watches, that I many meditate on Thy word" (Ps 119:147). "If Thy law had not been my delight, then I would have perished in my affliction" (Ps 119:92). "This is my comfort in my affliction, that Thy word has revived me" (Ps 119:50).

Prophet Jeremiah also highly valued God's Word: "Your words were found and I ate them, and Your words became for me a joy and the delight of my heart" (Jer 15:16). Persevering Job said: "I have not departed from the command of His lips; I have treasured the words of His mouth more than my necessary food" (23:12). Tested Jesus said: "Man shall not live on bread alone, but on every word that proceeds out of the mouth of God" (Mt 4:4). Wise Solomon said: "Wise men store up knowledge" (Prov 10:14a). And lastly, the good hand of God was upon Ezra because "Ezra had set his heart to study the law of the LORD, and to practice it, and to teach His statutes and ordinances in Israel" (Ezra 7:10).

JUNE 14

"Revival can be brought to this generation by prayer, by faith, by cleansing, and by obedience to the will of God." Leonard Ravenhill

When we are afflicted by the devil, we persevere by the Word, the Sword of the Spirit, resisting him firm in the faith (1 Pet 5:8; Rom 10:17). This faith comes from hearing and practicing the Word of God. (Eph 6:17). The apostle Paul understood the connection between the Scriptures and perseverance and encouragement. He said: "For whatever was written in earlier times was written for our instruction, that through perseverance and the encouragement of the Scriptures we might have hope" (Rom 15:4). Those who do not persevere often end up in a world of hurt and on the verge of destruction. For God said: "My people are destroyed for lack of knowledge" (Hosea 4:6a). God's inspired Scripture makes His servants fully adequate and equipped for every good work, even in very bad times (2 Tim 3:16-17).

Those who are too busy to read and meditate on God's Word, are too BUSY: Too "Being Under Satan's Yoke", laboring for that which has no eternal value. This reminds me of the epitaph on Leonard Ravenhill's tombstone: "Are the things you are living for worth Christ dying for?" The serpent loves to lead believers astray from the simplicity and purity of devotion to Christ by various deceptive means (2 Cor 11:3). The one who is not musing on the things of God is most likely being amused by the things of the world, which is under the influence of the evil one (1 Jn 5:19). The devil intoxicates everyone he can with the world and entices them to love the world, so they will not be filled with the Spirit of Truth nor bear His fruit nor abide forever with God (Eph 5:18; Jn 14:17; Gal 5:22-23; Jn 15:8; 1 Jn 2:15-17).

God's saints of old knew better. So Asaph said: "I shall remember the deeds of the LORD; surely I will remember Thy wonders of old. I will meditate on all Thy work, and muse on Thy deeds" (Ps 77:11-12). David also practiced this devotion to God and His word: "Tremble and do not sin; meditate in your heart upon your bed and be still" (Ps 4:4).

"I rise before dawn and cry for help; I wait for Thy words" (Ps 119:147). "Seven times a day I praise Thee, because of Thy righteous ordinances" (Ps 119:164). Ezra likewise knew how to experience God's

"Best Life Now", that is "His Good Hand: "The good hand of his God was upon him. For Ezra had set his heart to study the law of the LORD, and to practice it, and to teach His statutes and ordinances in Israel' (Ezra 7:9b-10).

JUNE 15

"The nature of Christ's salvation is woefully misrepresented by the present-day evangelist. He announces a Savior from Hell rather than a Savior from sin. And that is why so many are fatally deceived, for there are multitudes who wish to escape the Lake of fire who have no desire to be delivered from their carnality and worldliness." A.W. Pink

Who says being holy, upright, godly, obedient and loving God is of little profit? Not the God of heaven, but the god of this world, the devil. He advised disobedience to God in the garden and tempted the innocent one saying: "Eat this fruit and you will be like God, knowing good and evil" (Gen 3:5). And later, he tempted the Holy One in the wilderness saying: "all the kingdoms of the world and their glory I will give if You fall down and worship me" (Mt 4:9). But the Word of God said: "It is written" (Mt 4:4,7,10). But the word of God continues to say: "Godliness is profitable for all things, since it holds promise for the PRESENT LIFE and also for the life to come" (1 Tim 4:8).

So quit listening to the godless one, but to holy ones like David who acknowledged to the LORD saying: "It is You who blesses the righteous man, O LORD, you surround him with favor as with a shield" (Ps 5:12).

The LORD keeps all who love Him, but all the wicked He will destroy" (Ps 145:20). Being righteous brings great profit for it is written: "Hate evil, you who love the LORD, who preserves the souls of His godly ones; He delivers them from the hand of the wicked. Light is sown like seed for the righteous and gladness for the upright in heart. Be glad in the LORD, you righteous ones, and give thanks to His holy name." (Ps 97:10-12). True happiness comes from holiness. So don't listen to the devil's tempting advice to the contrary.

It is only by the power of the Holy Spirit that can we crucify the flesh and die to the old man, and its deeds (Rom 8:13; Gal 5:16). But such labor of God's grace within us brings joy as well as holiness, spiritual profit as well as emotional peace (1 Cor 15:10; Gal 5:22-23; 2 Cor 12:9-20). It is necessary to be nourished on the words of the faith and of the sound doctrine (1 Tim 4:6) and on the word of God (Ps 119:9,11) and to have minds renewed by the Word (Rom 12:2). Those who are taught by the Holy Spirit of Truth to abide in Christ who is the truth, they are set free indeed and will profit eternally (Jn 8:31,32; 14:16-17, 26; 1 Jn 2:27; Jn 17:3).

JUNE 16

Those unchurched need to see spiritual Christians BEING
His Church rather than religious leaders building their own.

There are several spiritual disciplines, if practiced, would help usher in true revival in the land and biblical Christianity in the Church. When all the gifts of the Spirit are properly exercised (1 Pet 4:10; 1 Cor

12:7; Rom 12:6), along with the five-fold ministry properly understood (Eph 4:11f), combined with holiness preaching, full Gospel proclamation, true repentance and separation from the world (2 Cor 6:14-18), individual as well as corporate revival would be experienced. Other spiritual fruit would be produced such as obedience, evangelistic zeal, lay empowerment rather than clergy control, active faith rather than intellectual assent, genuine repentance rather than temporary sorrow, receiving Jesus as Lord, not merely trusting in Him as Savior, and making disciples not making decisions.

This would be a powerful witness to the unchurched who are not impressed by religious leaders consumed with building their own churches and counting noses and nickels. They need to witness Jesus building His true Church, using His true followers who are committed to BEING the Church, those who count the cost, who carry their cross, who preach and reach out to the poor (Lk 9:23-24; Mt 11:5; 25:31-46). This would also advance the kingdom of God which is righteous, peace and joy in the Holy Spirit (Rom 14:17). Being Holy Spirit filled, led and taught, rather than purpose driven, led astray and man taught would help carry this new work of God forward. It would expand God's work outside the four walls and into the market place. There the unchurched would see true believers, being the Church, rather than just attending one. Christians would act as holy and royal priests and living stones whom the Lord uses in building His Church rather than sit back and watch religious leaders build their own (1 Pet 2:5,9; Mt 16:17-18).

JUNE 17

"A man says to me, 'Can you explain the seven trumpets of the Revelation?' No, but I can blow one in your ear, and warn you to escape from the wrath to come." C.H. Spurgeon

Though hell's world leaders may push their executive orders for temporary global government, the Lord of heaven is on His way to execute His last order. And there will be no end to the increase of His government (Is 9:6-7). Though the bad news of the New World Order is around the corner, the saved can joyfully and boldly hit the streets with the Good News of the Gospel on every corner. We continue fighting the good fight, keeping the faith and taking hold of eternal life, until we finish the course knowing that prophesy is being fulfilled before our eyes (1 Tim 6:12; 2 Tim 4:7). Though men may faint from fear and the expectations of the things which are coming upon the world, the Lord's soldiers enter on the battlefield, standing straight with heads lifted up knowing that their Redeemer and King is returning soon, and their full redemption is drawing near (Lk 21:25-28).

As sons of God, we eagerly await our final adoption, the redemption of our body (Rom 8:23; Heb 9:28), when this perishable must put on the imperishable, and this mortal must put on immorality (1 Cor 15:53). For the Son of Man will come in a cloud with power and great glory (Lk 21:27), and we shall be like Him, because we shall see Him just as He is, not as a crucified Lamb led to slaughter but as the Lion of Judah returning in glory (1 Jn 3:2; Is 53:7 Jn 1:29; Rev 5:5).

As overcoming true Christians, we continue to engage our spiritual enemies being clad with the full armor of God (Eph 6:11), preaching the full gospel, and exalting name of Jesus Christ (Acts 8:12), the name that is above every name (Phil 2:9). By exercising His authority, relying on His power, and standing on His true grace (1 Pet 5:12) we seek first His kingdom and His righteousness. As God fearing citizens and soldiers of heaven and not as world embracing enemies of God and captives of the devil, we will see His enemies crushed under our feet. We will experience true happiness from holiness and total adequacy from His intimacy.

JUNE 18

"Lock yourself in a room; throw the key away; do something! Seek God and be found of Him. That is His promise: "If you will seek for Me with all your heart and all your soul, you shall be found of Me" (Deut. 4:29). When you do obtain that knowledge, maintain it, or else you will lose it." Art Katz

God does not dwell in buildings made of hands but in His temples created and constructed by His Holy Spirit (Acts 17:24; 1 Cor 3:16, 6:19). This is God's true Temple founded upon the sure and perfect Rock, the Lord Jesus Christ, not on shifting sand. God's Temple is comprised of living and breathing spiritual believers, living stones, not dead religious brick and mortar (1 Pet 2:5; 2 Tim 3:5). Christians have been delivered from the domain of darkness and dominion of Satan to proclaim His name, not to seek fame (Col 1:13; Acts 8:12, 26:18; Col 1:28). We are commanded to go and BE the church, not to build a church; exhorting believers to take hold of eternal life, not the "Best Life Now".

We are to be Spirit-led, not purpose driven. Christians have been blessed with every spiritual blessing in Christ and thus don't need today's Prosperity Gossip. The household of God does not a "new" and "improved" Christianity or a "New" definition of Christianity, but a genuine demonstration of Biblical Christianity. The spiritual need today is not to embrace a new "emergent" Christianity, but the old and proven Cross. The sooner we stop relying on man's ideas, strength and approbation, and start resorting to God's blueprint, power and presence, the sooner we will begin to experience true revival.

JUNE 19

"Instead of preaching the good news that sinners can be made righteous in Christ and escape the wrath to come, the gospel has degenerated into the pretext that we can be happy in Christ and escape the hassles of life." Ray Comfort

Blessed be the God and Father of our Lord Jesus Christ who has blessed us with every spiritual blessing in the heavenly places in Christ (Eph 1:3). Blessed be the Father of mercies and God of all comfort who comforts us in all our affliction (2 Cor 1:3-4a). After we have suffered for a little while, living in the devil's world and experiencing his afflictions, (1 Pet 5:8,10a; 1 Jn 5:19), the God of all grace, who called us to His eternal glory in Christ, will Himself perfect, confirm, strengthen and establish us (1 Pet 5:10b).

Our heavenly Father is the Father of glory (Eph 1:17). The LORD's lovingkindnesses indeed never cease, for His compassions never fail. They are new every morning. Great is Your faithfulness (Lam 3:22-23). He is the Father of lights with whom there is no variation or shifting shadow (Jam 1:17). You are my heavenly Father who impartially judges according to each one's work, and thus I will conduct myself in fear during the time of my stay on earth (1 Pet 1:17).

I know that just as a father has compassion on his children, so You have compassion on those who fear You (Ps 103:13). How blessed is the man who fears the LORD, who greatly delights in His commandments (Ps 112:1). Light arises in darkness for the upright (Ps 112:4). Surely the righteous will give thanks to Your name; the upright will dwell in Your presence (Ps 140:13). If anyone loves You, they are known by You (1 Cor 8:3). The LORD is near to all who call upon Him, to all who call upon Him in truth" (Ps 145:18).

The LORD keeps all who love Him (Ps 145:20a). The LORD sustains all who fall and raises up all who are bowed down (Ps 145:14). The LORD favors those who fear Him, those who wait for His lovingkindness (Ps 147:11). Oh, how blessed it is to put things in the hand of our heavenly Father, whose hand is mighty and whose right hand is exalted, rather than to take things into our own hands (Ps 89:13). Our heavenly Father regards the lowly, but the haughty He knows from afar (Ps 138:6). He takes pleasure in His people; He will beautify the afflicted ones with salvation (Ps 149:4). He dwells on a high and holy place, and also with the contrite and lowly of spirit in order to revive the spirit of the lowly and to revive the heart of the contrite (Is 57:15).

The heavenly Father welcomes and walks among those who come out of from darkness and separate from Satan's world (2 Cor 6:16-18). Concerning those who seek and desire His heavenly kingdom, "God is not ashamed to be called their God; for He has prepared a city for them" (Heb 13:16). For there will be a place prepared for each faithful believer in the Father's house where we will reside with Jesus our Savior, (John 14:1-3).

All those who have served Him and have followed Him will be honored by His Father (Jn 12:26). For we know that God, our Heavenly Father, causes all things to work together for good to those who love Him and are called according to His purpose (Rom 8:28). No one can snatch out of the Father's hand anyone who hears the voice of His Son and follows Him (Jn 10:27-29). If our heavenly Father is far us, who can be against us? "He who did not spare His own Son, but delivered Him over for us all, how will He not also with Him freely give us all things?" (Rom 8:32). Worshipping our heavenly Father in Spirit and truth is our proper duty today, Father's Day, and every day.

JUNE 20

"Praise Christ for everything. He is the foundation of every good thought, desire and affection. It should be our aim to draw all we can from him by prayer, and return him all we can by praise." Edward Payson

PRAISE ALL DAY KEEPS THE DEVIL AWAY.

When we begin singing to the Lord and praising Him in holy attire, the Lord sets ambushes against our enemies and they are routed (2 Chron 20:20-22). When we worship God in spirit and in truth (Jn 4:24), when we worship Him in holy array (Ps 29:2), and volunteer freely to serve Him in the day of His power, we will see the Lord take dominion over our enemies, crushing them under our feet (Ps 110:1-3; Rom 16:20). As King David said: "My heart is steadfast, O God; I will sing, I will sing praises, even with my soul…Through God we will do valiantly, and it is He who will tread down our adversaries" (Ps 108:1,13).

As the psalmist says: "In God we have boasted all day long, and we will give thanks to Your name forever" (Ps 44:8). "My mouth is filled with Your praise and with Your glory all day long" (Ps 71:8). "From the rising of the sun to its setting the name of the LORD is to be praised" (Ps 113:3). In Your name I rejoice all day and by Your righteousness I am exalted (Ps 89:16). David advised: "Sing to God, sing praises to His name; lift up a song for Him who rides through the deserts, whose name is the LORD, and exult before Him" (Ps 68:4). "It is good to give thanks to the LORD and to sing praises to Your name, O Most High; to declare Your lovingkindness in the morning and Your faithfulness by night" (Ps 92:1-2).

"For His name alone is exalted; His glory is above earth and heaven and He has lifted up a horn for His people, praise for all His godly ones" (Ps 148:13-14). I will "sing the glory of His name and make His praise glorious" (Ps 66:2). "Our help is in the name of the LORD, who made heaven and earth" (Ps 124:8). So, Lord, I will praise You for I am certain that You can make my day. "My tongue shall declare Your righteousness and Your praise all day long (Ps 35:28). And in so doing today, I know that the devil stays away.

JUNE 21

"The modern church has gone right around the globe preaching the Sinner's Prayer. But what if it is simply another product of our instant "drive-thru" culture? A kind of McSalvation to get people into our modern McChurch?" Andrew Strom

CHRISTIAN SOLDIERS: IT GOES WELL WITH YOUR SOUL WHEN YOU WAR AGAINST YOUR FOES

The world hates us, the devil prowls about to devour us, demons seek to deceive us, God-haters mock us, liberals blaspheme us, prosperity preachers rob us, the institutional church incarcerates us, the uncrucified flesh opposes us, fear paralyzes us, doubt restrains us and this present evil age entices us. Yet, many naïve Christians go on living life as if there were no real spiritual warfare. However, the spiritually wise know otherwise. They don't live in a dream world, but in the battlefield. The devil knows who they are, because they know how he works (Acts 19:14-15).

The Spiritual Battleground is being laid out. The sons of disobedience who are promoting their hedonistic and sinful lifestyles are gathering, being energized by spiritual forces of wickedness (Eph 2:2). They are promoting a lifestyle and worldview that is in contradiction to the Word of God. It doesn't matter what scoffers and mockers may say. God is still alive and well and is in charge. "The LORD has established His throne in the heavens and His sovereignty rules over all" (Ps 103:19). For God "who made heaven and earth, the sea and all that is in them" and "in whose hand are the depths of the earth and His hands formed the dry land" has not lost His grip. (Ps 146:6; 95:4-5). His Word is forever settled in heaven (Ps 119:89) and His purpose is unchangeable (Heb 6:17).

We are in a war, a war fundamentally not of bullets and bombs, but a spiritual war against demonic doctrines (1 Tim 4:1) and lies of the evil one (Jn 8:44). This war is fought with the spiritual sword, the Word of God, with prevailing prayer and with the true Gospel of God. It is a war where the souls of men, biblical marriage, strong families and the destiny of a country are at stake. So Christian soldiers must march onward: not to their local religious pub for another pastoral pastry and stale milk, but on to the battlefield, to the byways and highways, nourished on sound doctrine and filled with the Spirit.

JUNE 22

"My greatest thought is my accountability to God." Daniel Webster

BLESSED ARE WHO?

Blessed are the Christian nobodies, for they are His Body (2 Cor 12:11; 1 Cor 12:27).

Blessed are those whose Lord is Him, who are not lorded over by men (Rom 14:9; 2 Cor 1:24).

Blessed are those who covet communion with God, not consumption with the world (Ps 27:4; Jam 4:4).

Blessed are those who are reconciled to the living God, not to dead religion (Rom 5:10; 1 Tim 4:10; 2 Tim 3:5).

Blessed are those whose eyes are fixed on eternity, not on prosperity (2 Cor 4:18; Prov 23:4-5; 1 Tim 6:17).

Blessed are the citizens of heaven, no longer captives of the world (Phil 3:20; 1 Jn 4:5, 5:19).

Blessed are the aliens of this world, no longer friends of the world (1 Pet 2:11; Jam 4:4).

Blessed are those who are called names, for they will be given a new name (1 Pet 4:14; Rev 2:17).

Blessed are those who boast in their inadequacy, and trust in His adequacy (1 Cor 1:31; 2 Cor 3:4-5; Gal 6:14).

Blessed are those who take refuge in the LORD, rather than to trust in man (Ps 118:8).

Blessed are those who see life's disappointments as His divine appointments (2 Cor 2:12-14).

Blessed are God's own whom He chastens, in order to partake of His holiness (Heb 12:7, 11; Ps 119:67, 71).

Blessed is the branch which is pruned, that it may bear more fruit for His name (Jn 15:2).

Blessed are those who are last now, for they shall be first then (Mt 19:29-30).

Blessed are the humbled, for they shall be exalted (Pet 5:6).

Blessed are the weak, for in them God's power is great (2 Cor 12:9).

Blessed are the poor in spirit, yet filled with His Spirit (Mt 5:3; Eph 5:18; Rom 14:17).

Blessed are those who have a Heavenly Father, who can be called Abba Father (Rom 8:14-16).

Blessed are those who are empty of self, but full of Himself (Eph 4:22; 3:19).

Blessed are the pure in heart, for they shall see Him who in invisible (Mt 5:8; Heb 11:27).

Blessed are the disinherited, for they possess an eternal inheritance (Mk 10:29-30).

Blessed are those who have exchanged earthly trinkets for heavenly treasures (1 Tim 6:9-10, 19).

Blessed are those who are tested and prevail, yet are triumphant and rejoice (1 Pet 1:6-7).

Blessed are those who are disowned by man, yet owned by Him (Acts 7:35; Heb 11:24-26).

Blessed are the unknown among men, yet well known by Him (2 Cor 6:9; 1 Cor 8:3).

Blessed are those who know God intimately and passionately, not intellectually and causally (2 Tim 1:12; Phil 3:8-10; Gal 1:13-14; Phil 3:4-7).

Blessed are those despised by men, yet prized by the Lamb (Mt 12:50; 1 Cor 4:13; Jam 2:5).

Blessed are those who have died to sin, and live for Him (Rom 6:11; 1 Pet 2:24).

Blessed are the poor of the world, yet are rich in heavenly blessings (Jam 2:5; 2 Cor 6:10).

Blessed are those disgraced by sinners, yet graced by the Savior (Jn 1:16; 2 Cor 8:9).

Blessed are those tested by fire and purified by trials (1 Pet 1:6-7).

Blessed are those who take up His mantle, rather than throw in their towel (2 Kg 2:8 Heb 10:35-36).

Blessed are those who do not wallow in sorrow, but hope in tomorrow (2 Cor 6:10; Heb 6:19; 2 Tim 4:7-8).

Blessed are the hated in the eyes of the world, yet are the apple of His eye (Mt 5:11-12; Ps 17:8).

Blessed are the foolish to the world, yet who shame the wise of the world (1 Cor 1:27).

Blessed are those who have the mind of Christ, not a mind of their own (1 Cor 2:16).

Blessed are those who know that God's ways are not our ways (Is 55:8-9).

JUNE 23

"Prayer can do anything that God can do." E.M. Bounds

SIX THINGS WHICH THE LORD LOVES, YES, SEVEN IN WHICH HE DELIGHTS:

A faith that moves mountains
A mouth filled with praise and thanksgiving
A Christian led by the Spirit
A Christian devoted to prayer
A walk that is God-pleasing
A servant running with the Gospel
A mind occupied with Christ

JUNE 24

*"When we become too glib in prayer we are most
surely talking to ourselves." A. W. Tozer*

THE MIRACLE WORKING GOD IS NOT SO HIGH ON POWERLESS RELIGION AND CESSATIONISM.

The word of God states: "It is God who is at work in you, both to will and to work for His good pleasure" (Phil 2:13). And the surpassing greatness of God's power is evident toward those who believe in accordance with the working of the strength of His might (Eph 1:19). The reason many don't see the mighty works of God demonstrated in and through their lives is that they have no faith and nor expectation of them. Yet "we are His workmanship, created in Christ Jesus for good works, which God prepared beforehand so that we would walk in them" (Eph 2:10).

In the early church believers were not so intellectually incarcerated and religiously paralyzed, and so they walked supernaturally and ministered mightily. Though they often were uneducated and untrained, yet because they had been with Jesus and boldly proclaimed His name, they experienced God working supernaturally through them and silencing the nay-sayer religious crowds who opposed them (Acts 4:12-14; 3:16). They believed that God was able to do exceeding abundantly beyond all that they could ask or think, according the power that worked in them, the power of His Spirit (Eph 3:16, 20).

These Spirit filled servants of God upset the whole world (Acts 17:6). For God was working through them is such a way that lost sinners noticed them, rather than laughed at them; and demons recognized them and were cast out by them (Acts 19:15; 8:4-8; 16:16-18). Concerning Philip it is written: "Even Simon himself believed; and after being baptized, he continued on with Phillip, and as he observed signs and great miracles taking place, he was constantly amazed" (Acts 8:13). Paul also spoke of such supernatural power working through him as a minister of Christ Jesus: "For I will not presume to speak of anything except what Christ has accomplished through me, resulting in the obedience of the Gentiles by word and deed, in the power of signs and wonders, in the power of the Spirit" (Rom 15:18-19a). Even to the foolish and bewitched, and powerless and religious Galatians Paul stated: "Does He then, who provides you with the Spirit and works miracles among you, do it by the works of the Law, or by hearing with faith" (Gal 3:1, 5)?

And this should be no surprise for Jesus said: "Truly, truly, I say to you, he who believes in Me, the works that I do, he will do also; and greater works than these he will do; because I go to the Father" (Jn 14:12). Jesus would ascend to His Father and send the Holy Spirit to baptize, indwell and empower His followers (Mt 3:11; Jn 16:7; Lk 24:49; Acts 1:8) and to glorify the Son through them (Jn 16:14). Jesus said to His Father: "And the glory which You have given to Me I have given to them" (Jn 17:22a), for just "As Thou didst send Me into the world, I also have sent them into the world" (Jn 17:18). And that glory was first demonstrated by His first miracle at the wedding in Cana. John comments on Jesus' act of turning water into wine:

"This beginning of His signs Jesus did in Cana of Galilee, and manifested His glory, and His disciples believed in Him" (Jn 2:11). And God has not ceased to this day to demonstrate His glory. For this "Christ in you, the hope of glory" (Col 1:27), "is the same yesterday and today, yes and forever" (Heb 13:8). We do not need a new definition of Christianity, but that old time preaching and true "demonstration of the Spirit and of power" (1 Cor 2:4-5).

Believers understand that the supernatural acts of God build up their faith as John remind them at the end of his book "Therefore many other signs Jesus also performed in the presence of the disciples, which are not written in this book, but these have been written so that you may believe that Jesus is the Christ, the Son of God; and that believing you may have life in His name" (Jn 20:30-21). Of course we do not worship the miracles of God, but the God of miracles; not the gifts but the Giver; not signs and wonders, but the Son in wonder. Proper worship of God in Spirit and truth will not place Him inside a religious box with His hands tied, but outside the box free to work.

And just as the apostle Paul taught: "Now there are varieties of gifts, but the same Spirit. And there are varieties of ministries, and the same Lord. There are varieties of effects, but the same God who works all things in all persons" (1 Cor 12:4-6). And the exalted and glorified Jesus gave to His Church "some as apostles, and some as prophets, and some as evangelists, and some as pastors and teachers, for the equipping of the saints for the work of service, to the building up of the body of Christ; until we ALL ATTAIN TO THE UNITY OF THE FAITH, AND OF THE KNOWLEDGE OF THE SON OF GOD, TO A MATURE MAN..." (Eph 4:11-13). And the last time I looked, His Church has not yet obtained that state and there is still a need for the equipping of the saints.

JUNE 25

*"Don't be afraid of tomorrow -- God
is already there." Unknown*

If I should say, my foot is about to slip, Your lovingkindness, O LORD,
will hold me up. But when my mind is stayed on You, You make my feet
like hinds feet and I skip.

When my anxious thoughts multiply within me, Your consolations
delight my soul; when your magnificent promises are my food, demons
flee.

When the devil tries to pen me down in a neck hold, your faithfulness
raises my head, oh my stronghold.

Come, let us worship and bow down, put away every frown; let us
should joyfully to the rock of our salvation, knowing that from of old He
has established His throne.

Sing to the Lord a new song, teach us to number our days; give us a
psalm as our daily bread and make us to know your ways.

"You will make know to me the path of life. In Your presence is fullness
of joy; in Your right hand there are pleasures forever" (Ps 16:11). In His
presence is fullness of joy which motivates us to make know to others the
path of life.

The more one is shut in with Him the more inspired one is to shout
out about Him. One is more inclined to serve Him, who has first reclined
with Him. The Lord is closest and most dear to the one who has entered his
closet and shut the door.

JUNE 26

"God sends no one away empty, except those who
are full of themselves." (Dwight L. Moody)

WHEN THE BODY OF CHRIST RISES UP AND BEGINS TO WALK...

When the Body of Christ rises up and begins to walk in the Way rather than stand by the wayside; when the Body begins walking the talk outside the church as well as properly conducting itself inside the four walls, each member contributing and functioning correctly (Eph 4:16); when each member is being empowered by the Spirit of God (Eph 3:16) rather than by the spirit of the age; when the Lordship of Jesus Christ rather than the lordship of man is observed (Eph 5:23-24; 1 Pet 3:15; Rom 14:9); when we begin to seek first the Kingdom of God and His righteousness in this fallen world (Mt 6:33), rather than man's religious and worldly agendas; when the Lord's saints resume practicing holiness, making disciples, exercising strong faith and their royal priesthood, demonstrating agape love and seeking to preserve the unity of the Spirit in the bond of peace....

Then we will begin to see the Temple of the living God, the Church, prevail over the lukewarm, dysfunctional, prosperity drunken, entertainment addicted and self-seeking institutional church. Then the Lord's Spirit led, taught and empowered faithful stewards and bondservants will not be deceived by today's wayward, flesh-anointed, self-appointed and self-exalting religious caste. The Lord's wise disciples will not listen to nor follow after the untaught and unstable who promote their Prosperity Gossip nor the so-called Emergent Church nor the New Effortless Christianity and other novel last days religious deceptions. The Lord is soon coming back for such a bride who has made herself ready, being clothed in bright and fine linen, which is the righteous acts of the saints (Rev 19:7-8), even the works of God which He prepared beforehand that we should walk in them (Eph 2:10). Then we will see and experience true revival, not rehashed religion.

JUNE 27

When repentant sinners receive the Lord's Gospel
invitation and truly experience His visitation, the wise
without hesitation will follow Him without reservation.

AS ONE CRYING IN THE WILDERNESS...

A modern day true prophet would surely ask: Where are the assemblies of born again, Spirit-filled saints (Eph 5:18), properly fitted for spiritual warfare (Eph 6:11-18), scripturally equipped for every good work (2 Tim 3:16-17) and fully clothed with the Lord Jesus Christ (Rom 13:14)? Where are those who are treading upon serpents and scorpions and over all the power of the enemy (Lk 10:1,17-19), boldly and passionately preaching the good news about the kingdom of God and the name of Jesus Christ (Acts 4:12; 8:12, 13:9-12) and worshiping God in spirit and truth (Jn 4:23-24) in His House of Prayer (Mk 11:17)? Where are those who are reverently obeying Jesus' commands and thus enjoying His abiding presence (Jn 14:21, 23), humbly following Jesus' example and His command to make disciples (Mt 4:19; 28:18-20), dying to self daily and carrying His cross devoutly (Lk 9:23-24)? Where are those who are daily nourished on the words of the faith and of sound doctrine (1 Tim 4:6; Mt 4:4), being shrewd as serpents and innocent as doves (Mt 10:16), abiding in Him and bearing much fruit proving to be His disciples (Jn 15:4,5,8)? Where are those who are honestly calling Him Lord by doing what He said, proving to be His servants (Lk 6:46), having eyes looking upward, not inward (Heb 12:2, Col 3:1) and praying "Thy kingdom come, Thy will be done" (Matt 6:10)? Where are those who realize that it is more blessed to give than to receive (Acts 20:35) and more Christlike to serve than be served (Mk 10:45)? Where are those who are baptized with the Holy Spirit and with fire and remain on fire (Mt 3:11; Acts 1:8) rather than become paralyzed by the spirit of the age and with lukewarmness and being on the verge of burnout like a dying bonfire?

Wherever you find such assemblies you will see true revival. May it not only be in the book of Acts written long ago, but also in today's living and walking epistles, Christ following assemblies of saints gathered in His name, with hearts written upon by the Holy Spirit of truth and not by the false spirit of the age (2 Cor 3:2-3).

JUNE 28

"Learn to hold loosely all that is not eternal." A.M. Royden

You can walk in resurrection life, because the Resurrection and the Life lives in you (Gal 2:20; Jn 11:25). No longer fear death but enjoy His life, because the Prince of Life defeated the devil and murderer, as well as the fear of death (Acts 3:15; Jn 8:44; Heb 2:14-15). Though the devil may seek to kill, steal and destroy and prowl around like a roaring lion, seeking someone to devour, we serve the victorious and reigning Lion of Judah, who came that we may have eternal and victorious life (Jn 10:10; 1 Pet 5:8).

After all, God has not given us a spirit of timidity, but of power and love and sound mind (2 Tim 1:7). We possess the fruit of self-control of the Spirit and the mind of Christ (Gal 5:23; 1 Cor 2:16). We walk by faith in Jesus, the Giant Killer, and not in fearful sight of our little goliaths (2 Cor 5:7; 1 Sam 17:26). Such overcoming faith comes from hearing the Word of God and being taught by the Spirit of God (Rom 10:17; 1 Jn 2:27). It is living by faith and relying on the power of the Spirit that we overcome Satan's world, even to the casting out of his demons (Gal 5:25; 1 Jn 5:4-5; Mt 12:28) and the casting out of fear (1 Jn 4:18). As Jesus said: "And do not fear those who kill the body, but are unable to kill the soul; but rather fear Him who is able to destroy both soul and body in hell" (Mt 10:28).

JUNE 29

*"If Jesus preached the same message minister's preach today,
He would have never been crucified." Leonard Ravenhill*

THE LINE IS CLEARLY DRAWN AND IT'S TIME TO CROSS OVER.

The line is clearly drawn in the sand. Where will you stand? Being entertained by the enemy or engaging the enemy? Playing church or BEING the Church? Therefore, call this to mind true Christians in these difficult last days. The next time the devil is in your face, remember that

Jesus is at your side for He promised His disciple-makers: "lo, I am with you always, even to the end of the age" (Mt 28:20b). He "has your back" so don't look back, but keep looking forward and looking upward, because your redemption is drawing near (Lk 21:28).

And remember, we have received His authority to "tread on serpents and scorpions, and over all the power of the enemy" (Lk 10:19a). So don't go down without a fight, but go up fighting the good fight (2 Tim 4:7-8; 2 Cor 5:8; Phil 1:23). For nothing can injure those who are born again unto everlasting life. Nothing can enslave those whom Jesus has indeed set free (Lk 4:18). Nothing can separate those from the love of God who are united with Christ and share in His sufferings (Rom 6:5, 8:17, 35-39).

JUNE 30

"I wonder also how many Christians in our day have truly and completely abandoned themselves to Jesus Christ as their Lord. We are very busy telling people to "accept Christ"-and that seems to be the only word we are using. We arrange a painless acceptance."A.W.Tozer

"The name of the LORD is a strong tower; the righteous runs into it and is safe" (Prov 18:10). The more we know His name, that is, His character and attributes, the more He will become that strong tower. David wrote: "For You have been a refuge for me, a tower of strength against the enemy" (Ps 61:3). Notice, the righteous are those who can run into that tower for safety from their enemies. "The path of the upright is a highway" (Prov 15:19b). "Salvation is far from the wicked; for they do not seek Your statutes" (Ps 119:155). And "the sacrifice of the wicked is an abomination to the LORD, but the prayer of the upright is His delight" (Prov 15:8). "The way of the wicked is an abomination to the LORD, but He loves one who pursues righteousness" (Prov 15:9).

But "surely His salvation is near to those who fear Him: (Ps 85:9a). "Blessed be the LORD, my rock, who trains my hands for war, and my fingers for battle; my lovingkindness and my fortress, my stronghold and my deliverer, my shield and He in whom I take refuge....How blessed are the people who are so situated; how blessed are the people whose God is the LORD!" (Ps 144:1-2, 15).

"Therefore let us draw near with a sincere heart in full assurance of faith, having our hearts sprinkled clean from an evil conscience and our bodies washed with pure water (Heb 10:22)." Therefore let us draw near with confidence to the throne of grace, so that we may receive mercy and find grace to help in time of need" (Heb 4:16). For we know that when we draw near to God with clean hands and pure hearts, He will draw near to us and then we can resist the devil and he will flee from us (Jam 4:7-8).

JULY 1

The question isn't "Were you challenged"? The question is "Were you changed"?

CARRY THE VICTORY BANNER OR CRY "VICTIM"? THE FREE CHOICE IS YOURS

God has given a banner to them who fear Him, that it may be displayed because of the truth (Ps 60:4). After all, only by abiding in the truth, even Jesus who is the Truth, can one be set free (Jn 8:31.32.36; 14:6). For He came to proclaim release to the captives and to set free those who are oppressed (Lk 4:18). God anointed Him with the Holy Spirit and with power so that He went about doing good and healing all who were oppressed by the devil, for God was with Him (Acts 10:38). It is wise to recall the Lord's high priestly prayer to His Father concerning His disciples: "Sanctify them in the truth. As You sent Me into the world, I also have sent them into the world" (Jn 17:17-18).

So true Christians have also been sent to proclaim the Good News and to set captives free by going and making disciples of all the nations, baptizing them in the name of the Father and the Son and the Holy Spirit, teaching them to obey all that Jesus commanded (Mt 28:18-20). Jesus said GO and BE the church, penetrate the world. We are to walk supernaturally and in glory for Jesus said: "Peace be with you; as the Father has sent Me, I also send you" (Jn 20:21). We don't merely "GO" to church for WE ARE the Church. We have been anointed and baptized with the Holy Spirit and power, and have no reason to sit around pouting, powerless and paralyzed, for Jesus is with us always, even to the end of the age (Mt 3:11; Acts 1:8; Mt 28:20).

So we will sing for joy over our victory, and in the name of our God we will set up our victory banners (Ps 20:5). For in all things we overwhelmingly conquer through Him who loved us, even when we "are being put to death all day long and are considered as sheep to be slaughtered". For after all, who can kill one who has already died and has been raised up to everlasting life, united with Jesus who is the Resurrection and the Life? (Rom 8:36, 37; 6:1-5; Jn 11:25).

JULY 2

"The world lives in such a time of crisis. Christians alone are in a position to rescue the perishing. We dare not settle down to try to live as if things were normal." A.W. Tozer

The Lord of lords has provided the cure for complacency, timidity and carnality which has taken residence in too many churches today. The cure is called biblical Christianity, a full gospel demonstration of the Spirit and of power by bold Christians (1 Cor 2:4). "For God hath not given us a spirit of timidity but of power and love and sound mind" (2 Tim 1:7 KJV). We don't need a new definition of Christianity but a true demonstration of it. The so-called modern Effortless Christianity, Emergent Christianity, Progressive Christianity, Politically Correct Christianity, or New Christianity fleshed out by those who are deceived by darkness can't hold a candle to those living in the Light.

It is time for weak-kneed Christians to rise up off their pews and become brave souls in the battlefield. "The right hand of the LORD does valiantly" (Ps 118:15). And that is where true Christians are seated, with Christ at the right hand of God. Believe it or not, the faithful choose to believe it (Eph 2:6; 2 Cor 4:13). The good soldier of Jesus Christ will not expect to find ease in this evil world, for it is a battlefield (2 Tm 2:3; Phil 1:29; Acts 14:22) nor expect to find peace with this world, for it is a war zone, nor expect to receive friendly treatment from the world, because it is at enmity with God (Jn 15:18-19).

Complacent Christians who are satisfied with where they are will go nowhere, and those satisfied with what they have will continue in spiritual bankruptcy (Rev 3:17). But those who are compassionate for Him will go places and recount their spiritual blessings (Eph 1:3). They will run and not get tired and walk and not become weary. They will go the right Way and not become lost. They will see the Light at the end of the tunnel and not quit. They will walk through the valley of the shadow of death, fearing no evil (Ps 23:4). They will dine peacefully with their Great Shepherd in the presence of their enemies (Ps 23:5).

God will lead them in triumph in Christ who said "It is finished" (Jn 19:30), because He disarmed the rulers and authorities having triumphed over them (Col 2:14). By putting on the full divine armor that God has furnished and claiming the magnificent promises which God has granted (2

Pet 1:4) they too will finish the course they have started (2 Tim 4:7-8). God who impartially judges according to each man's work, the Father of glory and Father of lights, will manifest through His own the sweet aroma of the knowledge of Christ in every place (1 Pet 1:17; Eph 1:17; Jam 1:17; 2 Cor 2:14). Grace and peace will be multiplied to them in the full knowledge of God and of Jesus their Lord (2 Pet 1:2).

JULY 3

"In some circles, God has been abridged, reduced, modified, edited, changed and amended until He is no longer the God whom Isaiah saw, high and lifted up." A.W. Tozer

WHERE ARE THE PASTORS?

Where are the pastors who are committed to making disciples rather than being content with people only making decisions? Who produce brave hearts rather than timid souls? Who warn and teach his sheep to follow the Lion of Judah, rather than let them become food for the roaring lion? One reason the devil wins many spiritual battles is because Christians are laying down their spiritual armor. But the faithful remnant will continue to put him to flight, because they have him in their sights. When they pray and resist, the devil flees to the next church to play and infest. There will be no place found for the devil and his demons in churches where Jesus is Head, God is worshiped and the Spirit in invited.

JULY 4

*"No matter what the circumstances, we Christians
should keep our heads. God has not given us the spirit
of fear, but of power, of love and of a sound mind.
It is a dismal thing to see a son of heaven cringe in
terror before the sons of earth." A.W. Tozer*

Be hopeful in the coming days God which has for you to accomplish the works which He prepared beforehand (Eph 2:10). Our shortcomings are taken care of by our Advocate with the Father, Jesus Christ the righteous (1 Jn 2:1). Our overcoming is made possible by the Spirit of God who is greater in us than the spirit of antichrist who is in the world (1 Jn 4:4). All this is to prepare us for our great homecoming when we will reign with Christ for a thousand years and later see the holy city, new Jerusalem, coming down out of heaven from God, made ready as a bride adorned for her husband, the Lamb (Rev 20:6, 21:21,9).

We don't need a religious kook to sell us some Prosperity Gossip, when we have already been told in the great Book that we have been blessed with every spiritual blessing in the heavenlies (Eph 1:3). The Church does not need worldly hirelings on the prowl who seek to rob us of our heavenly heritage. After all, "He who did not spare His own Son, but delivered Him up for us all, how will He not also with Him freely give us all things?" (Rom 8:32). Whenever the hour and power of darkness arrives to accuse, attack and stumble, we know that "the LORD is a sun and shield; the LORD gives grace and glory; no good thing does He withhold from those who walk uprightly" (Ps 84:11).

JULY 5

"Some people read their Bible in Hebrew, some in Greek; I like to read mine in the Holy Ghost." Smith Wigglesworth

God desires to work supernaturally through His people. "For the eyes of the LORD move to and fro throughout the earth that He may strongly support those whose heart is completely His" (2 Chron 16:9). He is seeking and waiting for those who are willing to wait on Him and work with Him (2 Cor 6:1), those who allow the grace of God to labor in them, rather than receive the grace of God in vain (1 Cor 15:10; 2 Cor 6:1). God is pleased with those who have faith to believe that He "is able to do exceeding abundantly beyond all that we ask or think, according to the power that works within us" (Heb 11:6; Eph 3:20).

The Father of glory, of mercies and of all comfort (Eph 1:17;2 Cor 1:3) is looking for those who will work out their salvation with fear and trembling, in the power of the indwelling Holy Spirit who gives life to their mortal bodies (Phil 2:12-13; Gal 5:25; Acts 1:8; Rom 8:11) and who puts to death their morbid sins (Rom 8:13). The Lord has little use for those who are content to sit on their salvation, inside church buildings darkened by lamps lacking oil, listening to sermons which bring no conviction, crunching on pastoral pastries which give no nourishment and embracing a compromised and distorted gospel that has no power.

JULY 6

"God's choice acquaintances are humble men." Robert Leighton

SAVED FOR WHAT? TO MAKE HIS NAME KNOWN, NOT OURS.

The LORD has gazed upon the earth "to hear the groaning of the prisoner, to set free those who were doomed to death, that men may tell of the name of the LORD in Zion, and His praise in Jerusalem" (Ps 102:20-21). "Help us, O God of our salvation, for the glory of Your name; and deliver us and forgive our sins for Your name's sake" (Ps 79:9). "Not to us, O LORD, not to us, but to Your name give glory because of Your lovingkindness, because of Your truth" (Ps 115:1). "Sing the glory of His name; make His praise glorious" (Ps 66:2).

The LORD has saved and gathered us from among the nations "to give thanks to His holy name and to glory in His praise (Ps 106:47; Col 1:13; Eph 1:5-6). David said: "I will praise the name of God with song and magnify Him with thanksgiving" (Ps 69:30). "I will give thanks to You, O Lord my God, with all my heart, and will glorify Your name forever" (Ps 86:12). I will "Sing to God, sing praises to His name; and lift up a song for Him who rides through the deserts, whose name is the LORD and exult before Him" (Ps 68:4).

Other psalms exhort us to: "Glory in His holy name; let the heart of those who seek the LORD be glad" (Ps 105:3). In God I will boast all day long, and I will give thanks to Your name forever (Ps 44:8). In Your name I rejoice all the day and by Your righteousness I am exalted (Ps 89:16).

The early Church also practiced this and we see the results. "But when they believed Philip preaching the good news about the kingdom of God and the name of Jesus Christ, they were being baptized, men and women alike" (Acts 8:12). "And there is salvation in no one else; for there is no other name under heaven that has been given among men by which we must be saved" (Acts 4:12). "We proclaim Him, admonishing every man and teaching every man with all wisdom, so that we may present every man complete in Christ" (Col 1:28).

JULY 7

Decisional evangelism with its omission of intentional discipleship has produced the great omission in the Great Commission. Discipleship is the best way to keep new converts out of the hands of the devil.

"Let not a wise man boast of his wisdom, and let not the mighty man boast of his might, let not a rich man boast of his riches; but let him who boasts boast of this, that he understands and knows Me, that I am the LORD who exercises lovingkindness, justice and righteousness on earth; for I delight in these things, declares the LORD" (Jer 9:23-24).

Every Christian can earn the proper and necessary degree by graduating from God's school of hard knocks and receiving His GED confirmation. He can graduate from being an overcome sinner and be transformed into an overcoming saint, and become a "God Empowered Disciple" (Acts 1:8; Mt 4:19). This degree is far more terminal to the devil than man's mere

Ph.D, as useful as that may be. Let the religiously educated of this world
look upon Jesus' followers as uneducated and untrained (Acts 4:13), as up-
starts and misfits, as lay members rather than priestly ministers (1 Pet 2:5,
9). They will continue to just read, believe and heed the Bible, spending
quality time with Him who is the Truth and in whom are hidden all the
treasures of wisdom and knowledge (Jn 14:6; Col 2:3). They will witness
His miracles and follow the example of those who turned the world upside
down (Acts 17:6; 2 Tim 3:10-11).

Take Philip for example, a man full of wisdom and of the Holy Spirit
(Act 6:3-5). After waiting tables for widows and filling their plates, he continued waiting on God and later we find him cleaning the devil's plate. For
he went preaching the good news about the kingdom of God and the name
of Jesus Christ, casting out demons and performing signs and great miracles
(Acts 8:4-13). He was a God Empowered Disciple.

JULY 8

*Spiritual complacency in life reveals a
vacancy of Lordship of heart.*

EACH DAY IS A NEW DAY BECAUSE YOU ARE A NEW CREA-
TURE WALKING IN THE SUPERNATURAL.

I am a beautiful display case of His grace, nor a basket case in disgrace (Jn
1:16; Eph 1:7b-8).

I am a fruitful branch of the Tree of Life, not a dead branch of a fallen
tree (Jn 15:1f; Jn 14:6; Rom 11:17).

I am a liberated new creature in Christ, not bound up by old habits (Gal 5:1, 13, 6:15; Eph 2:2-3).

I am a living stone in God's Holy Temple, not a dirt clod in a church building (1 Pet 2:5; Mt 24:2).

I am blessed with eternal life that God prepared for His people, not cursed with eternal fire prepared for the devil and his angels (Mt 25:41; 1 Jn 5:13).

I am blessed with every spiritual blessing, no longer cursed by the fall (Eph 1:3).

I am confident that God works all things together for my good, so I don't anticipate the bad (Rom 8:28, 31; Gen 50:20).

I am no longer dead in trespasses and sins, but alive in Him who appeared to take away sin (Eph 2:1, 5; 1 Jn 3:5).

I am no longer led by the evil spirit of the world, but by the Holy Spirit sent from heaven (Rom 8:14; 1 Cor 12:2).

I am no longer under the thumb of the god of this world, but in the hands of the God of heaven (2 Tim 2:26; Jn 10:28-29).

I am no longer working for the devil, but living for Him who came to destroy the works of the devil (1 Jn 3:8).

I claim that old things have passed away, behold new things have come (2 Cor 5:17b).

I forget what lies behind and reach forward to what lies ahead (Phil 3:13b).

I know that God works in me and for me, because I am no longer without God or an enemy of God (Phil 2:12-13; Eph 2:12; Rom 5:10).

I lay aside the old self with its evil practices and put on the new self created for holiness (Col 3:10; Eph 4:24).

I no longer harbor a poor image of myself because I am a new creature in Christ who is the image of God (2 Cor 5:17; Heb 1:3)

I overwhelmingly conquer through Him rather than being conquered by circumstances (Rom 8:37).

I possess the mind of Christ in whom are hidden all the treasures of wisdom and knowledge, refusing worldly wisdom (1 Cor 2:16; Col 2:3;

Rom 1:22; Jam 3:15-17) and avoiding what is falsely called knowledge (1 Tim 6:20).

I reach forward to what lies ahead because I have forgotten what lies behind (Phil 3:13).

I will walk in the supernatural, because I am no longer natural.

JULY 9

Apostles and prophets have to go. They rock our boat and spoil our show. After all, what do they know? When we invite them to jump on our bandwagon they always say 'No'.

CESSATIONISM IS FOR THE BIRDS. SUPERNATURAL GIFTS ARE FOR EAGLES.

There is a growing number of "cessationists", those who believe that certain spiritual gifts such as speaking in tongues, word of knowledge, word of wisdom, healing, interpretation of tongues, apostles and prophets, ceased with the closing of the Canon of Scripture and/or the death of the last apostle. And there are many "arm chair" theologians who don't believe that God speaks and works signs, wonders and miracles today through His people and through supernatural spiritual gifts. They have more faith in their interpretations of the Bible than in the Author of the Bible. They claim God only spoke during the time the Canon of Scripture was being written, and since it's completion has decided to remain mute, no longer speaking, counseling or teaching apart from what is written in the Bible. It would appear that they must also deny that the Spirit speaks, teaches or leads apart from merely enlightening one's mind to understand only what is written on the printed page of the Bible.

Such ones and their admirers, have their eyes blinded by unbelief and ears closed or tickled by popular theology. They try to keep God shut up in their religious box or bound up by their theological straight jacket or keep the supernatural Jesus outside knocking on the church door. However, those who have eyes to see and ears to hear invite Him in to be Lord of their hearts knowing that God is at work in them both to will and to work according to His good pleasure (Phil 2:13). They expect to walk in the works which God prepared beforehand for them (Eph 2:10) and God, being supernatural, often works in the supernatural.

Though there are many God's pleasing churches, an apparent problem in the mainline institutional and powerless church today is that too many are too busy coming and going, buying and selling, building and rebuilding, debating and arguing, to stop long enough to hear and listen, to pray and practice, and to learn what the Spirit of truth is saying and what the Word of God plainly teaches.

This reminds me of the apostle Paul. Before he fell to the ground and heard the voice of Truth speaking to him (Acts 9:4), he was busy advancing his own religious thing "in Judaism" being extremely zealous for his ancestral traditions (Gal 1:13,15). Then he learned that being educated under Gamaliel was not so sufficient and valuable after all (Acts 22:3; Phil 3:5-7). He counted it all to be loss in view of the surpassing value of knowing Christ Jesus his Lord (Phil 3:8).

True apostles and prophets and their ministries and all the gifts continue on today as we read in (Rom 1:5; Eph 4:11; 1 Cor 12:28, 14:3, 31; Rom 12:7; 2 Cor 8:23; Rev 18:20; etc). They will be necessary "until we all attain to the unity of the faith, and of the knowledge of the Son of God, to a mature man, to the measure of the stature which belongs to the fullness of Christ" (Eph 4:13). Believe it or not, the church still needs these gifts and ministries to equip the saints for the work of service (Eph 4:12). Also remember, Jesus warned of false apostles and false prophets in these last days. Satan always counterfeits the real. Just because the vast majority today abuse these gifts and callings, it doesn't mean we deny their validity, any more than when we see many Christian teachers peddling and adulterating the word of God (2 Cor 2:17; 4:2), do we deny the gift and ministry of teaching.

JULY 10

In a day when god-haters laugh, the proud strut about, the liberals lie, the religious kill, the depraved pervert, judges malpractice, preachers entertain, and prophets deceive, it's nice to know that the day is soon coming when heaven's great Judge, King, Prophet, Shepherd and Ruler, the Lord Jesus Christ will return to earth to have the last laugh, declare the last verdict, set the record straight, exalt the humble, reward the holy and to be glorified amidst His saints.

DESTRUCTION OF FORTRESSES

"For the weapons of our warfare are not of the flesh, but divinely powerful for the destruction of fortresses" (2 Cor 10:4).   What are some of the devilish fortresses Christian soldiers are to destroy and how? They destroy the fortress of Satan's lies with God's Truth (Jn 8:44; Jn 17:17; Eph 6:17); the fortress of dead religion with a living relationship with God (1 Tim 4:10); the fortress of worldly happiness with the Spirit's joy (Gal 5:22); clergy lording over laity with Jesus' Lordship of His priesthood (Mt 20:25-28; 2 Cor 1:24; 1 Pet 2:5,9, 3:15); strange fire with Holy Spirit fire (Num 3:4; Mt 3:11); modern hyper grace with God's true grace (1 Pet 5:12; Tit 2:11); "effortless" Christianity with Cross Christianity (Lk 9:23; Phil

2:12-13). Other fortresses destroyed and replaced include false confessions with true conversions (2 Cor 5:17; Rom 10:9-10); worldly remorse over sin with true repentance from sin (2 Cor 7:9-10; Acts 20:21); demonic doctrines with sound doctrine (1 Tim 4:1; 1 Tim 4:6; Tit 2:1); private religious interpretations with scriptural proclamations (2 Pet 1:20-21; Col 1:28-29) and temporary worldly pleasures with eternal heavenly treasures (Mt 6:19-21; Jam 5:1-3; Tim 6:18-19).

JULY 11

*"The world out there is not waiting for a new
definition of Christianity; it's waiting for a new
demonstration of Christianity." Leonard Ravenhill*

DON'T JUST STAND THERE. USE YOUR KEYS!

God has given all His true children divine, master keys to open the doors of Satan's dark world. Lost sinners who are held captive by the devil are exhorted and invited by Christ's ambassadors and are spiritually enabled by God's grace to turn from the domain of darkness and step into God's marvelous Light, the Lord Jesus Christ, and to receive Him as their new Master (Jn 1:12; 2 Cor 5:18-20; Acts 2:40, 26:18; Col 1:13; 2 Tim 2:26). By saving faith in Him they are delivered from the dominion of Satan and transferred to the kingdom of His beloved Son, in order to receive forgiveness of sins, and an eternal inheritance by those who are sanctified (Eph 2:8-9; Col 1:13; Heb 10:14). They can be delivered from sin's power and sin's condemnation (Rom 6:18-23).

Only Christians are authorized and enabled to enter the strongman's house, Satan's territory, to bind him and recover his stolen possessions (Mt 12:29). Jesus cast out demons by the power of the Holy Spirit, demonstrating the superior power of the kingdom of God (Mt 12:28; 1 Jn 4:4). Those who follow Jesus and imitate Him will also become fishers of men (Mt 4:19). Like Him, they too have been anointed with the Holy Spirit and with power to do good and to heal all who are oppressed by the devil (Acts 10:38; Jn 17:18; Acts 1:8; 8:4-13). They seek first His kingdom and His righteousness (Mt 6:33), which often is accomplished when the works of the devil are destroyed (1 Jn 3:8) and his demons cast out (Mt 12:28). They snatch the perishing out of Satan's fire (Jude 23), those who are being taken away to death (Prov 24:11).

The Bible describes the kingdom of God as righteousness, peace and joy in the Holy Spirit (Rom 14:17), not eating and drinking with the god of this world. And advancing the kingdom of God is not accomplished by mere talk but by a powerful walk in the Spirit (Rom 14:17; 1 Cor 4:20). The soldiers of the Lord are to rescue those held captive by the devil to do his will. Such are ensnared by him, not in their right mind and are lured away by his idols (2 Tim 2:26; 1 Cor 12:2, 10:20). They often pay attention to doctrines of demons (1 Tim 4:1) and pay tribute to liberal doctors of divinity, who parade around as disguised servants of righteousness (2 Cor 11:13-15).

Christians have been given the unlocking keys. Speaking to His disciples, Jesus said: "I will give you the keys of the kingdom of heaven" (Mt 16:19a)…"Go therefore and make disciples…" (Mt 28:19a). Only those truly born of God, born from above possess the keys to unlock the doors below. They alone have been called, commissioned and spiritually armed to proclaim the good news of the Kingdom of God, to secure release to the captives and to set free those who are oppressed (Lk 4:18, 9:1-2, 10:2f).

The keys on God's golden keychain are many. One key is the true and full Gospel (Acts 20:21, 27; 24:24-25; 8:12). Another key is the authority Jesus gave to His Church (Mt 10:1; Mt 28:18f). Another key is the name of Jesus the exalted one (Acts 3:6, 16, 8:12), the name which is above every name (Phil 2:9), He who is both Savior and Lord and the only name under heaven that has been given among men by which we must be saved (Acts 4:12). Another key is the indwelling Holy Spirit of God sent from above who is greater than the evil, demon spirits below (Jn 14:26; 1 Jn 4:4).

And finally, there are the key promises of Jesus, the Head of the Church, such as: "I will build My church; and the gates of Hades will not overpower it" (Mt 16:18b)…"I am with you always, even to the end of the age" (Mt 28:20b); and the great and magnificent promises of God by which we can become partakers of divine nature (2 Pet 1:4).

JULY 12

In the early days of the Church many died for the faith as documented in the classic Fox's Book of Martyrs. In these last days of Churchianity and apostasy will your name be written down in the Lamb's Book of Life or in the Devil's Book of Deserters?

THERE IS NO TIME TO PLAY WHEN YOU'RE IN WAR.

Don't underestimate the importance of spiritual warfare with the spiritual rulers, powers and world forces of wickedness in the heavenly places (Eph 6:12). If you do, you may very well end up cruising along with them in the devil's world rather than seeing God crush him under your feet (Rom 16:20). A smart Christian soldier does not make a truce with his enemy the devil (Jam 4:7; 2 Cor 6:14-18), nor is he a friend of the devil's world (Jam 4:4). Though a good soldier of the Cross will suffer hardship, yet he enjoys victory (2 Tim 2:3; Rom 8:37). A victorious soldier does not entangle himself in the affairs of everyday life (2 Tim 2:4).

Be cautious that you are not diverted by the devil off the battlefield into his playground to play with his toys, or to jump onto his merry-go-round, fighting trivial religious doctrinal skirmishes and going nowhere. Take up the full armor of God, lay aside every encumbrance and the sin which so easily entangles and fight the good fight warring against the true enemies (Eph 6:13; Heb 12:1; 1 Tim 6:12). If the devil is not in your crosshairs, you may very well be in his. Only by resisting him will he flee. And that means extinguishing and destroying, by the shield of faith and the Word of God, all his flaming arrows of falsehood, deception and diversion coming into your mind contrary to the true knowledge God (Eph 6:16-17; 2 Cor 10:3-5). The battle is in the mind, the victory is in walk.

JULY 13

"Praise focuses our hearts on God. Praise cleanses our hearts of cares, fears, and earth-centered thoughts. Praise begets and increases faith. Praise invokes God's presence, God's power, and God's forces. Praise confounds, terrifies, restrains, and thwarts Satan". Wesley Duewel

FULL GOSPEL OR PROSPERITY GOSSIP

The almighty miracle working God desires to works mightily in us and through us. And this should not be surprising since the

Christian life begins with the supernatural new birth and continues by a supernatural walk, led and empowered by the supernatural Holy Spirit. Thus we expect to see miracles of various sorts (Phil 2:12-13; Phil 4:13; Eph 3:20-21; Gal 3:5). Having begun our Christian walk with the new birth of the Holy Spirit, we must not continue it by relying on carnal religious practices of men (Jn 3:3, 5; Gal 3:2-3). If we are working together with God (2 Cor 6:1), if we are being led by the Spirit of God (Rom 8:14), if the Son of God is living in us (Gal 2:20), if we believe in and proclaim Jesus' mighty name (Jn 1:12; Acts 3:16, 8:12), then the supernatural will happen. We don't have to seek signs and wonders. They will follow if they are needed for power evangelism (1 Cor 2:5, 4:20; Acts 8:5-6; Rom 15:28-20; Gal 3:5; 1 Thess 1:5; Jn 20:30-31). Don't let those who have never experienced such things deceive you into denying their existence. The full gospel of God will supernaturally satisfy the spiritual needs of men.

This whole purpose of God is detailed when the full gospel of God is preached. Paul did not shrink from declaring the whole purpose of God (Acts 20:27), testifying solemnly of the gospel of the grace of God (Acts 20:24), the true grace of God that brings salvation to sinners (Tit 2:11) and produces ongoing sanctification in saints (Tit 2:12), with the outcome, eternal life (Rom 6:22). The true gospel of God has nothing to do with easy believism and cheap grace, but everything to do with repentance toward God and faith in our Lord Jesus Christ (Acts 20:21, 24:24). And such saving faith addresses righteousness, self-control and the judgment to come (Acts 24:25), three salvation issues that a Spirit-filled evangelist will address (Jn 16:7-11). The devil loves to bewitch the deceived by preaching distorted gospels full of pleasant words (Gal 1:6,7; 3:10) that tickle the ears (Isa 30:10-11; 2 Tim 4:3). Beware of those who spew out prosperity gossip, false teaching and hot air. They promise freedom while yet are slaves to corruption (2 Pet 2:19). They preach distorted and false gospels that condemn and bankrupt the soul.

JULY 14

"Some women will spend thirty minutes to an hour preparing for church externally (putting on special clothes and makeup, etc.). What would happen if we all spent the same amount of time preparing internally for church - with prayer and meditation?" Leonard Ravenhill

HOW IS IT THAT ...

In America we have hundreds of thousands of churches, crystal cathedrals, mega-millions of dollars put in offering plates of mega-churches. We have more religious Ph.D's that a dog has fleas, countless liberal seminaries offering many degrees, yet graduating the dead and frozen. And the devil is having the time of his life. Sin is rampant, deception is widespread, mainline denominations are declining. More and more are becoming "dones" and "nones": "Done" with institutional religion and "none" in regard to claiming any Christian affiliation. And according to some theologians, God isn't in the miracle working business anymore!

Churchianity has become a stumbling block to the very lost souls we are called to win, offering a religion without power, pastoral pastries that are losing their sweetness and prosperity gossip that is bankrupting many. Even the popular "successful" Christian televangelists seem to be the biggest losers. Why has much of the Americanized church become the greatest circus littering the land with their freakish side shows and animal stunts, laughing when they should be mourning; living it up when they should be looking up, living for their "Best Life Now" with little regard to Eternal Life hereafter?

Yet, the religious masses are still searching for substance and the real thing, a relevant and authentic Christianity. So we have a "Progressive" Christianity, a "New" Christianity, a "Redefined" Christianity, an "Emergent Christianity" and even an "effortless" Christianity. Oh, the many shades of gray the devil invents to hide the true light of biblical Christianity. Is the institutional church missing something or Someone?

JULY 15

"A religion that costs nothing is worth nothing." W.B. Dunkum

Look up for your Redeemer, the Light of the world, is soon returning. When the Bright Morning Star appears there will no longer be any night to fear. For the Lord God will illuminate and the Son will forever shine. There will be no death and mourning but only eternal life and rejoicing. There will be no tears when God dries every eye and no despair because the devil will be bye and bye. No sickness because the Great Physician resides. No loneliness because the blessed Trinity abides. No sin to condemn and defile, but only the Savior's approval and smile. The worry of the world will be replaced by heaven's glory and earthly servitude by eternal gratitude. No wicked kings will rule because the Righteous King will reign. There will be no more evil thrones because the Lord God, the Almighty will forever be on His righteous throne. Who would be so foolish so as to reject the Savior's prize and accept

Satan's disguise? Only those who fall for lies of men rather than stand on the truth of God.

JULY 16

"Do not pray for easy lives, pray to be better men and women. Do not pray for tasks equal to your strength, pray for strength equal to your tasks." Phillips Brooks

This is the day the Lord has made. I will rejoice and be glad in it. In everything I will give thanks, for the LORD has established His throne in the heavens, and His sovereignty rules over all (Ps 103:18). I am on the winning side; the devil has already lost and is awaiting judgment. I am convinced that God causes all things to work together for good to those who love God, to those who are called according to His purpose (Rom 8:28). For the kingdom is the LORD's and He rules over all.

I will seek to redeem the time, being filled with the Holy Spirit, seeking first His kingdom which is righteousness, peace and joy in the Holy Spirit (Mt 6:33; Rom 14:17). I will persevere in faith for I know whom I have believed and I am convinced that He is able to guard what I have entrusted to Him (2 Tim 1:12). For He is able to do exceeding abundantly beyond all that I ask or think (Eph 3:21). According to the power of His Spirit who works in me, I will crucify the old man and put on the new man, the Lord Jesus Christ so that it is no longer I who lives, but Christ living in me (Rom 8:13; Gal 5:16; Eph 3:16; Gal 2:20).

JULY 17

"It is far better to drive men away by faithful preaching than to drive the Holy Spirit away by unfaithful preaching!" Al Whittinghill

THE SEVEN P'S OF THE OVERCOMER: POWER, PEACE, PRESENCE, PURPOSE, PROMISES, PRAYER, PERSEVERANCE

POWER of God: "But you shall receive power when the Holy Spirit has come upon you and you shall be My witnesses/martyrs both in Jerusalem, and in all Judea and Samaria, and even to the remotest part of the earth" (Acts 1:8). PEACE of God: "Be anxious for nothing, but in everything by prayer and supplication with thanksgiving let your requests be made known to God. And the peace of God, which surpasses all comprehension, will guard your hearts and your minds in Christ Jesus" (Phil 4:6-7). PRESENCE of God: "For where two or three have gathered together in My name, I am there in their midst" (Mt 18:20). PURPOSE of God: "He has saved us and called us with a holy calling, not according to our works, but according to His own purpose and grace which was granted us in Christ Jesus from all eternity" (2 Tim 1:9). PROMISES of God: "For by these He has granted to us His precious and magnificent promises, so that by them you may become partakers of the divine nature, having escaped the corruption that in the world by lust" (2 Pet 1:4). PRAYER to God: "With all prayer and petition pray at all times in the

Spirit" (Eph 6:18a). PERSEVERANCE of the saints: "Be on the alert with all perseverance and petition for all the saints" (Eph 6:18b). "Here is the perseverance of the saints who keep the commandments of God and their faith in Jesus" (Rev 14:12).

JULY 18

"We're not here to get to know the Word of God, but to get to know the God of the Word". Leonard Ravenhill

Walking in the power of the Holy Spirit, possessing the mind of Christ, being renewed by the Spirit, and by wielding the Sword of the Spirit, I will destroy speculations and every lofty thing the devil may raise up in my mind against the knowledge of God (2 Cor 10:3-5). I will meditate on the true knowledge of God. For I know that even God's people can be taken captive and destroyed for lack of such knowledge (Hosea 4:6; Isa 5:13). I will take every invading thought captive to the obedience of Christ, knowing that the fear of the Lord is the beginning of wisdom and of knowledge (Prov 1:7, 9:10). Like the apostle Paul, I will purpose to know Him, in whom are hidden all the treasures of wisdom and knowledge (Phil 3:7-10; Col 2:3). For those who have divine insight will shine brightly and understand the times (Dan 12:3, 10) and those who know their God will display strength and take action (Dan 11:32). Miracles will follow those who believe in

His name, the name which is above every name (Phil 2:9), the name in which the afflicted are healed (Acts 3:16), the name at which every knee will bow (Phil 2:10) and the name by whom demons are tormented (Mk 1:23-24, 5:7).

JULY 19

"It is not the thing on which we spend most time that molds us, but the thing that exerts the greatest power. Five minutes with God and His word is worth more than all the rest of the day." Oswald Chambers

DON'T LET THE DEVIL, THE THIEF, ROB YOU BLIND

Don't let the devil rob you blind when you have been so heavenly blessed. How does he accomplish this? The devil delights in planting seeds of deprivation, distraction, division and depression in God's people so they will become defeated and dysfunctional members of the Body of Christ. The devil greatly fears when God's own called out citizens of heaven learn to walk in the Light, coming out of his darkness, becoming free from his dominion and refusing to walk along his shadowy ways. He hates seeing Christians walking with single minded devotion and unity of purpose, with living hope, active faith, irreproachable character and inexpressible joy.

JULY 20

*"God wants His people to be ablaze with Holy
Ghost activity." Smith Wigglesworth*

IF THE SPIRIT OF GOD IS TRULY PRESENT, THE SON OF GOD WILL BE GLORIFIED.

Jesus promised to send the Holy Spirit to empower and teach His disciples to abide in Him and to empower them to put to death the deeds of the body (Jn 14:26; 16:7; 1 Jn 2:27; Rom 8:13). The Holy Spirit was sent also to glorify the Son (Jn 16:14). The Spirit accomplishes this when we "put on the Lord Jesus Christ" (Rom 13:14), have the mind of Christ (1 Cor 2:16) and imitate Him as the apostle Paul did (1 Cor 11:1). Jesus said His house is to be known as a house of prayer (Mt 21:13), occupied with those praying in the Spirit (Eph 6:18; Jude 20). It is also to be a lighthouse in the dark world, possessed by those filled with Holy Spirit oil, lit up and shining, exposing the world's unfruitful deeds of darkness (Mt 5:14; 25:1-13; Eph 5:11-15). And lastly, the church is called the pillar and support of the truth (1 Tim 3:15), proclaiming the name of Jesus who is the Truth (Acts 4:12, 8:12; Jn 14:6).

JULY 21

*Many contemporary Christians wear cloaks of dead
religion. Some wear wrist bands asking "What
Would Jesus Do". But few are the faithful who are
Christ's hands doing what Jesus commanded.*

IS OBEDIENCE OPTIONAL?

In Scripture we read that heaven bound, persevering saints are described as those who keep the commandments of God and their testimony and faith in Jesus (Rev 12:12; 14:12). Jesus is said to be the source of eternal salvation to them who obey Him (Heb 5:9). Jesus questioned the religious: "Why do you call Me Lord and do not do what I say?" (Lk 6:46). Paul repeatedly made statements similar to this: "For not the hearers of the Law are just before God, but the doers of the Law will be justified" (Rom 2:13). And don't forget John: "By this we know that we have come to know Him, if we keep His commandments" (1 Jn 2:4). John also said: "This is His commandment, that we believe in the name of His Son Jesus Christ, and love one another, just as He commanded us" (1 Jn 3:23). John understood "believing" and "obeying" as being two sides of the same coin. He said: "He who believes in the Son has eternal life; but he who does not obey the Son will not see life, but the wrath of God abides on him" (Jn 3:36). Notice that John used two different Greek verbs, so as to clarify biblical saving and persevering faith.

And finally in Revelation we read: "Blessed are they that do his commandments, that they may have right to the tree of life, and may enter in through the gates into the city" (Rev 22:14). So much for the new "effortless" Christianity being proposed by those who peddle hyper grace. So long to true saving faith by those promoting easy believism. Also deceiving are those who "sell" assurances of salvation to those who only say a "Sinner's Prayer" or make a fruitless confession or temporary decision or run to an altar over sorrow for sin, but with no mention of repentance from sin.

That form of "Christianity" has little value, no power and declining appeal to the lost who are seeking what is real. The spiritually wise will follow the apostle Paul's advice: "Present your bodies a living and holy sacrifice which is your reasonable service of worship" (Rom 12:1) or David who said: :"I will not offer a burnt offering which costs me nothing" (1 Chron 21:24). They take seriously what Jesus said: "If anyone wishes to come after Me, let him deny himself, and take up his cross daily, and follow Me. For whoever wishes to save his life shall lose it, but whoever loses his life for My sake, he is the one who will save it" (Lk 9:23-24). Those following biblical Christianity simply trust what the Word of God claims, obey what its commands (1 Thes 2:13) and thus enjoy what it promises (2 Pet 1:3-4; Rom 8:32; Jn 17:13; 2 Cor 1:20; Tit 1:1-2).

JULY 22

"If you're going to be a true Christian, I'll tell
you one thing amongst others: it'll be a lonely life.
It's a narrow way and it becomes narrower and
narrower and narrower." Leonard Ravenhill

The household of God is called the church of the living God (1 Tim 3:15), the body of Christ, submitted to Him as the Head (Eph 5:21-24). True believers are His members (1 Cor 12:27) and are to function properly as they were created, gifted and empowered to function by the Holy Spirit for the purpose of building up the body (Eph 4:16; 1 Cor 12:7, 11).

The Church is also called the temple of God, indwelt by the Holy Spirit (1 Cor 3:16). Contrary to many contemporary church growth experts, the Lord in His wisdom, not man with his marketing skills, is building His Church and Temple. And the Lord builds with living stones, not dead religious brick and mortar (1 Cor 3:16; 1 Pet 2:5; Mt 16:18). The apostle Paul describes all this as a work of the Holy Spirit who gives life to those who walk in the Spirit until "Christ be formed in you" (Rom 8:11, 9:14; Gal 4:19, 5:16, 25).

It's easy to see how involved the Holy Spirit desires to be in the household of God and in this ministry of bringing glory to the Lord Jesus Christ. "But when He, the Spirit of truth comes...He shall glorify Me" (Jn 16:13, 14). "But we all, with unveiled face beholding as in a mirror the glory of the Lord, are being transformed into the same mage from glory to glory, just as from the Lord, the Spirit" (2 Cor 3:18). "As each one has received a special gift, employ it in serving one another, as good stewards of the manifold grace of God. Whoever speaks, let him speak, as it were, the utterances of God; whoever serves, let him do so as by the strength which God supplies; so that in all things God may be glorified through Jesus Christ, to whom belongs the glory and dominion forever and ever, Amen" (1 Pet 4:10-11).

Rather than practice biblical Christianity, popular contemporary Christianity prefers the feel good, tribulation free, weekly hour of self-serving prosperity religion and self-help gospel. Cultural fast food religion and one's busy daily schedule often quench and grieve the sanctifying presence and delivering power of the Holy Spirit. There is the constant temptation to pursue God's "Best Life Now" and sacrifice themselves to television, sports, leisure, electronic toys and prosperity trinkets. Yet, a faithful remnant will arise, persevere and swim against the religious current. It will not throw in the towel when increasingly dangerous rapids arrive. The true Church longs for a true revival and a public show down of the false Baals; a heaven sent revival and spiritual awakening which will arouse the contemporary church out of her stupor.

JULY 23

The Bible becomes obsolete to the world when it is no longer absolute to the church! Leonard Ravenhill

Jesus said "It is written, 'Man shall not live on bread alone, but on every word that proceeds out of the mouth of God'" (Mt 4:4). But today, religious masses prefer pleasant pastoral pastries over sound doctrine, milk over solid food of the Word (2 Tim 4:3; Is 30:10; 1 Cor 3:1-2; Heb 5:12-14). Many prefer to have a good time rather than to "fight the good fight" (1 Tim 6:1; 2 Tim 4:7). They would rather play and be at peace with the world than pray and overcome the world. And we see the fruit of such Americanized Christianity. In spite of all the seminaries and conferences, church growth experts and Ph.D's, churches and books, and super prophets and world class apostles roaming the countryside, we see deception, false prophets, unruly priestly authority and debauchery continue to spread in the churchyard. And again God says: "My people love it so" (Jer 5:30-31). When God's laws become obsolete Satan's lies become absolute.

JULY 24

"God will not do, apart from prayer, what He has
promised to do in answer to prayer." Al Whittinghill

THE DEVIL IS HAPPY WHEN A CHRISTIAN ENJOYS SELF RATHER THAN CRUCIFIES IT.

It's far better to be prayed up than preyed upon, to be stirred up rather than stressed out; to BE the church, rather than play church; to preach repentance, rather than accept complacence; to perform the signs of a true apostle with godly fear, rather than to perform before an audience to tickle an ear.

Of course this requires loving the Creator, not the creation; serving Him, not self; being Christ-minded, not carnal minded; fighting the good fight, not giving up the fight; walking in the light and not sleeping in darkness.

Jesus stands knocking on the church door, but the contemporary Laodicean church invites wolves in to devour. The devil is wise and cunning, he knows his time is short; so he deceives the religious masses and has them seeking fun and sport. When Satan toot's his pulpit horn his followers abound, it is because few have ears to ear the Spirit's warning trumpet sound.

JULY 25

"Most Americans worship their work, work at their play, and play at their worship." Al Whittinghill

GOD SAYS TO HIS OWN:

I have blessed you with every spiritual blessing in the heavenly places in Christ (Eph 1:3). I have made you complete in My Son, who is your total adequacy, so you no longer have to walk in darkness, feeling incompetent (Col 2:10; 1 Cor 1:5,7; 2 Cor 3:4-5 8:9; Rom 8:32). I have given you the heavenly Helper, the Holy Spirit of truth, to renew your mind and teach you how to abide in Christ, the Truth (Jn 16:13; Eph 3:16; Rom 12:1-2; 1 Jn 2:27). Thus you can enjoy true liberty rather than endure pure misery (2 Cor 3:17). The Holy Spirit enables you to put to death the deeds of the flesh, gifts you to edify the church, and empowers you to be witnesses of the King of Kings and Lord of Lords (Rom 8:13; 1 Cor 2:4; Acts 1:8).

I have given you all authority to go and make disciples, to tread on serpents and scorpions and over all the power of the enemy (Lk 9:1; Mt 28:18-20). At salvation I provided you with the heavenly wardrobe so that having been baptized into Christ, you are no longer spiritual naked but clothed with Christ (Gal 3:27; 1 Cor 1:30, 12:13; Rom 13:14; Col 3:10; Gal 4:19). You are no longer incarcerated in Satan's world but have been delivered, called and drafted into My army as My soldiers and ambassadors (Col 1:13; Acts 26:18; 2 Tim 2:3; 2 Cor 5:20). I have provided you with the full armor of God, so you can advance My kingdom which is righteousness, peace and joy in the Holy Spirit (Eph 6:11f; Rom 14:17).

You can overwhelmingly conquer through Him who loves you and released you from you sins by His blood (Rom 8:37; Eph 1:7). You don't have to be a disgrace among men but can run the race and win (2 Cor 9:24-27). You no longer have to stumble in darkness but can walk in the Light, no longer a victim accused by the devil whom Jesus defeated, but rather can experience victory with Him who is seated (Eph 5:8; Rom 8:33-34,37; Eph 2:6; Col 3:1).

I made you to be a spiritual kingdom and royal priest to reign with Christ on the earth, buried with Him in death to your former self life, to rise up in resurrection life, your new self (1 Pet 2:5,9; Rev 1:5; Rom 5:17, 8:17; Col 3:1,10; Rom 6:4). You can be Spirit led in triumph in Christ in the world, because you are united with Him who overcame the world (2 Cor 2:14; Rom 8:14; 1 Jn 4:4; Rom 6:5; Jn 16:33). You have been born again by spiritual conception to serve and worship God in spirit and truth, no longer serving the father of lies and master of deception (Jn 3:3, 5; 4:24; Jn 8:44; 2 Tim 2:25-26; 1 Jn 3:10; 2 Cor 11:3). You were created in Christ for good works and commanded to be cleansed from religious dead works (Eph 2:10). You can be cleansed from all defilement of flesh and spirit, perfecting holiness in the fear of God and sanctified by His Spirit of Truth (2 Cor 7:1; Jn 17:17; 1 Thess 4:8; 1 Pet 1:1-2). By crucifying the flesh with its passions and desires, you are enabled to do all things that He desires (Eph 4:22; Col 3:9-10; Gal 5:24-25; Phil 2:12-13, 4:13).......

So that you no longer say to Him: But, But, But...

JULY 26

"We made a deal - we preached and they beat us. We were happy preaching and they were happy beating us, so everyone was happy." Richard Wumbrand

The plague of worldliness and preoccupation with worldly affairs is preventing more and more Christians from being effective and fruitful in doing the Father's business. Living in a world that is becoming more depraved and antichristian by the hour, many are finding it more difficult to keep focused on Christian duties and spiritual disciplines needed to be spiritually prepared for soon coming persecution and the Lord's return. Yet the Lord is always looking for good soldiers who are not compromised by sin or entangled in the world. Such ones are willing to become properly trained, skillfully proficient and spiritually bold in spiritual warfare and spiritual weaponry. In coming days, such ones will ultimately become overcomers, though the devil may temporarily overcome.

JULY 27

"Let me go out on a limb a little bit and prophecy. I see the time coming when all the Holy men whose eyes have been opened by the Holy Spirit will desert worldly evangelicalism one by one. The house will be left desolate and there will not be a man of God, a man in whom the Holy Spirit dwells, left among them......I would like to live long enough to see the time when the men and women of God---Holy, separated and spiritually enlightened---walk out of the evangelical church and form a group of their own; when they get off the sinking ship and let her go in the brackish waters of worldliness and form a new Ark to ride out the storm." A.W. Tozer

GOD IS LOVE BUT:

It's nice to know that "God is love" and that "God so loved"….but what about Jesus' statements concerning conditions for experiencing God's love? John records Jesus saying: "He who has My commandments and keeps them is the one who loves Me; and he who loves Me will be loved by My Father, and I will love him and will disclose Myself to him. If anyone loves Me, he will keep My word; and My Father will love him, and We will come in to him and make Our abode with him" (Jn 14:21, 23). "For the Father Himself loves you, because you have loved Me and have believed that I came forth from the Father" (Jn 16:27). And Jesus said: "For this reason the Father loves Me, because I lay down My life that I may take it again" (Jn 10:27). And Jesus again in His last words to that beloved disciple reiterates the necessity of keeping His words: "Blessed is he who reads and those who hear the words of the prophecy, and heed the things which are written in it; for the time is near" (Rev 1:3). And how much nearer is the day of His return.

JULY 28

*Before the Lord will move in power, our orthodoxy will have
to be stabbed, our conventions shattered, and
our stony hearts again know tears".*
Leornard Ravenhill

THE ADVERSITY GOSPEL GIVES YOU TRUE PROSPERITY

The ADVERSITY gospel promises true and everlasting prosperity. "For to you it has been granted for Christ's sake, not only to believe in Him, but also to suffer for His sake" (Phil 1:29). Christians will face adversity when they suffer for Jesus name, proclaim the Good News Gospel and live it out. "If you are reviled for the name of Christ, you are blessed, because the Spirit of glory and of God rests upon you" (1 Pet 4:14). "But to the degree that you share the sufferings of Christ, keep on rejoicing; so that also at the revelation of His glory, you may rejoice with exultation" (1 Pet 4:13).

"But even if you should suffer for the sake of righteousness, you are blessed" (1 Pet 3:13a). "And after you have suffered for a little while, the God of all grace, who called you to His eternal glory in Christ, will Himself perfect, confirm, strengthen and establish you" (1 Pet 5:10). "Do not fear what you are about to suffer. Behold, the devil is about to cast some of you into prison, so that you will be tested, and you will have tribulation for ten days. Be faithful until death, and I will give you the crown of life" (Rev 2:10). Paul said: "I have fought the good fight, I have finished the course, I have kept the faith; in the future there is laid up for me the crown of righteousness, which the Lord, the righteous Judge, will award to me on that day; and not only to me, but also to all who have loved His appearing" (2 Tim 4:7-8). "For momentary, light affliction is producing for us an eternal weight of glory" (2 Cor 4:17a).

For all who have been baptized into Christ have clothed themselves with Him (Gal 3:27). And it is that outer righteous attire that the world, the devil and his energized sons of disobedience, and even the religious ones hate so much. "Blessed are those who wash their robes, so that they may have the right to the tree of life; and may enter by the gates into the city [New Jerusalem]" (Rev 22:14).

The Holy and Righteous One said: "A slave is not greater than his master. If they persecuted Me, they will also persecute you; if they kept My word, they will keep yours also" (Jn 15:20). "To him who overcomes, I will grant to eat of the tree of life which is in the Paradise of God" (Rev 2:7). We have the promise that the children of God are "heirs also, heirs of God and fellow heirs with Christ, if indeed we suffer with Him in order that we may be glorified with Him" (Rom 8:17).

JULY 29

*"The greatest miracle that God can do today is to take
an unholy man out of an unholy world and make
him holy, then put him back into that unholy world
and keep him holy in it."Leonard Ravenhill*

Miracles still do happen! They occur whenever someone encounters a Bible believing, God worshiping, Spirit filled, Jesus following and full Gospel proclaiming church. We are talking about a real Christian fellowship not addicted to happiness over holiness, hype over hope, strange fire over holy fire, pleasure over persecution, prosperity over spiritual blessing and evil compromises over His magnificent promises.

Of course the devil is always roaming about to counterfeit the authentic. So we see a spirit of false humility, false signs and wonders, false prophesies, false anointings, false mantles, false dreams and false spiritual disciplines abound today. The devil and father of lies is up to no good with all his cleverly disguised servants of righteousness who so blindly serve him who is cleverly disguised as an angel of light (2 Cor 10:13-15). True humility brings blessing (Jam 4:10; 2 Cor 12:11; Gal 6:3; 1 Cor 8:2; 2 Cor 3:3-6; Gal

6:14; Gal 2:20; Jn 15:5; Zech 4:6; Ps 44:1-8).   Humility brings the Holy One close, and thus holiness. It casts away pride and the evil one (Jam 4:6-7).

JULY 30

"Do all the good you can, by all the means you can, in all the ways you can, in all the places you can, at all the times you can, to all the people you can, as long as ever you can." John Wesley

The Lord and Master has sent you to proclaim Good News of great joy to the poor and depressed in these in bad times (Lk 2:10); to proclaim release to Satan's captives (Lk 4:18; 2 Tim 2:26), the recovery of sight to those blinded by the devil (2 Cor 4:4; Lk 4:18); to set free those who are oppressed (Lk 4:18); to offer the new birth to those dead in trespasses and sin (Eph 2:1); to imitate Christ who came to destroy the works of the devil and to take away sin (1 Jn 3:5,8; 1 Cor 11:1); to do good and heal those oppressed by the devil (Acts 10:38) and even to do greater works than these by believing in Him (Jn 14:12). So what are we doing for God sitting in the pews casting dollars in the plate in order to receive our promised prosperity or with stretched out arms grasping for our Best Life Now ? Very little.

JULY 31

*Now I know why so many people confuse cemeteries with
seminaries. Everyone is dying to get into the former,
while many are dead when they get out of the latter.*

AVAILABILITY VS. ABILITY

God always looks for availability more than ability, for He is our adequacy, we are His vessels. He is the Master, we are the subjects; He is the Captain we are His soldiers; and He is the Truth, we are to be His truth bearers. Just as He won, we win, victorious over sin, reigning with Him. When we allow the Holy Spirit to empower us we will overwhelmingly conquer through Him who both loved us (Rom 8:37) and promised to send the Holy Spirit and Helper to assist us (Jn 16:7).

Though the Holy Spirit has been given to all believers, the challenge for every believer is to be controlled and filled with that power and to use it properly (Rom 8:9,11,13; Eph 5:18; Gal 5:16, 25). The same can be said of the Word of God. It is given to all Christians, but this spiritual sword must be used under the power of the Holy Spirit (Eph 6:17). Otherwise we may inflict spiritual harm to our fellow Christian soldiers.

Every believer has been clothed with Christ, having been baptized into Him (Gal 3:27; 1 Cor 12:13). The question is whether one is walking so divinely clothed, or keeps putting on the garments of old man who has been buried. Burial clothes are never attractive garments. Rather, we are to put on the resurrected Lord Jesus Christ and be a fragrance of Christ to God among those who are being saved and among those who are perishing (Rom 13:14; 2 Cor 2:15).

AUGUST 1

> *"Any objection to the carryings on of our present golden-calf Christianity is met with the triumphant reply, 'But we are winning them!' And winning them to what? To true discipleship? To cross-carrying? To self-denial? To separation from the world? To crucifixion of the flesh? To holy living? To nobility of character? To a despising of the world's treasures? To hard self-discipline? To love for God? To total committal to Christ? Of course the answer to all these questions is no." A.W. Tozer*

The New Testament clearly lays out what we are to believe and how we are to live. The problem is not that Christianity is difficult to understand, but that it is seldom seriously tried. If believers would truly believe and take God at His Word and step out in faith instead of putting His Word on the shelf, they would not stumble in doubt. They would expect and see miracles following their believing. They would not experience unnecessary misery and uncalled for setbacks. They would stand not fall, run not faint, and be overcomers, not overcome. Instead of groping in the fairy land of make-believe, they would continue hoping and believing in God who makes things happen.

AUGUST 2

*Most today do not want to repent and make the
necessary U-turn, but rather continue going the
wrong way on the one way road, going farther
and farther away from Him who is the Way.*

The PRIMARY reason we see unrestrained evil and the devil prevail throughout our American culture is that the professing church has ceased being the pillar and support of the truth (1 Tim 3:15), the salt and light to a dark and deteriorating culture (Mt 5:13-14; Eph 5:13-14). Too many are content just going to church rather than BEING the Church. Christians have become passivists in spiritual warfare and conformed to the world, relying on its welfare. They have become religious nudists (Rev 3:18), covered with religious fig leaves but devoid of Holy Spirit power, not being clothed with the Lord Jesus Christ (Rom 13:14) nor with the full armor of God (Eph 6:11). Too many professing Christians are too busy having a good time, to take the time to spread the Good News. They are too busy playing to engage in serious biblical praying. They are too busy chasing after religious American idols to crave God and His Kingdom.

Consequently, the faithful few who are still zealous for the things of God are viewed as the crazies by the lost who are not even in their right mind, but are held captive by the devil, doing his will (2 Cor 5:13; 2 Tim 2:25-26). But by the true grace of God the faithful and true remnant will prevail. For just as the world in the first century could not keep the Righteous One down, so the world in the 21st century will not succeed in keeping the true saints down.

AUGUST 3

"We need a baptism of clear seeing. We desperately
need seers who can see through the mist--Christian
leaders with prophetic vision. Unless they come soon
it will be too late for this generation. And if they do
come we will no doubt crucify a few of them in the
name of our worldly orthodoxy." A.W. Tozer

PROPHETIC MINISTRY AND PASTORAL AWOL

Unfortunately, many in contemporary Christianity have gone AWOL, because they listened to wayward pastors declare "peace, when there is no peace" and financial prosperity when there is spiritual poverty (Rev 3:17). They promise happiness without holiness. They hold out promises and withhold their conditions. We see many apostles not sent by God, but they go anyway; prophets who are not spokesmen for God, but they speak anyway (Jer 23:21). With pleasant words, pastoral pastries and purpose drunken dribble falling from their lips they lead the deceived sheep to slaughter and right into the devil's grips.

A true prophet proclaims His name, while profiteers seek fame. The former displeases the masses, the later, appeases them. The former calls down holy fire while the latter run from the fire. To the true prophet it is either black or white, to the latter it is neither. Many erroneously believe prophets ceased long ago. No wonder the church has fallen so low. Heaven would come. Leaven would go. If we had more Elijahs today, we could keep wicked rulers at bay. Righteousness would reign, that would be the day.

Why is it that when the Lord's prophets step on pastoral toes, they just kick them out, and resume tickling ears? Why are prosperity pastors more concerned about passing their plates than they are about filling the plates of the poor? Fleecing the flock rather than feeding them? What kind of shepherding is it that keeps the sheep as babes, content to see them crawling back to church week after week to be bottle fed? Did not Jesus tell Peter "If you love Me, feed My lambs, shepherd My sheep" (Jn 21:15-18)? But instead, popular prophets today have become like foxes among ruins (Eze 13:4). Pastors falsely shepherding have allowed wolves to steal, kill and destroy (Jn 10:10, 12).

AUGUST 4

"Revival will come only to a desperate church, not a contented one. He is ever the Rewarder of those who 'diligently seek Him.' not the mere casual inquirer." Al Whittinghill

FEAST NOT FAMINE FOR GOD SEEKERS

There are many who are longing for some god of their own making or some encounter with a paranormal god of the New Age. Because they are alienated from the supernatural God of the Bible, they long for a god of the contemplative, mystical and Eastern variety. They want to mystically encounter the "'god within" rather than have reverence for the majestic God above. They are under the spell of the father of lies and his false shepherds and the spirit of this religious and evil age. They are so busy hunting for the treasure at the end of the rainbow or chasing the mirage in the desert, that they fail to encounter the Father of lights and the Father of glory (Jam 1:17; Eph 1:17).

But there are also many who are looking for the true Shepherd, the Heavenly Father and true divine intimacy. These sincere God seekers and truth lovers desire to become what they were created to be, rather than follow just another somebody (Ps 139:13-17; Jer 29:11). They desire to BE the Church, rather than just GO to church; to be living stones in God's holy temple, rather than dead, dry bricks in a manmade church. The Holy Spirit is every so ready to rain upon them the unfathomable riches of Christ and the daily morning dew of God's unfailing lovingkindness and compassion. They will feast on God's true promises and rest in the Promised Land.

AUGUST 5

"Deliverance from believing lies must be by believing truth." Jessie Penn-Lewis

The prayer "Thy will be done on earth" is not accomplished by lip service. It is accomplished by feet and hand service. God's will is done by those who do, those who work out their salvation with fear and trembling, knowing that God is at work in them, both to will and to work for His good pleasure (Phil 2:12-13). After all, we are "His workmanship, created in Christ Jesus unto good works, which God hath before ordained that we should walk in them" (Eph 2:10). We are God's fellow-workers: "And working together with Him, we also urge you not to receive the grace of God in vain" (2 Cor 6:1).

We are not talking about whitewashed "effortless" modern sinner-friendly 'hyper-grace' but blood cleansing, sin-destroying divine grace. "For the grace of God has appeared bringing salvation to all men instructing us to deny ungodliness and worldly desires and to live sensibly, righteously and godly in the present age" (Tit 2:11-12). The author of Hebrews exhorts: "See to it that no one comes short of the grace of God "(Heb 12:15a). Peter wrote: "And after you have suffered for a little while the God of all grace, who called you to His eternal glory in Christ, will Himself perfect, confirm, strengthen and establish you....This is the true grace of God. Stand firm in it" (1 Pet 5:10, 12). Likewise Paul stated: "For by grace you have been saved through faith; and that not of yourselves, it is the gift of God...As you therefore have received Christ Jesus the Lord, so walk in Him" (Eph 2:8a; Col 2:7a).

Everyone who merely talks about and refuses to walk by His grace today will be disgraced tomorrow when "all will appear before the judgment seat of Christ, that each one may be recompensed for his deeds in the body, according to what he has done, whether good or bad" (2 Cor 5:10). Jesus warns: "And behold, I come quickly and my reward is with me, to give every man according as his work shall be" (Rev 22:12). For is it written: "Pure religion and undefiled before God and the Father is this, to visit the fatherless and widows in their affliction and to keep himself unspotted from the world" (Jam 1:27).

AUGUST 6

"Preaching is God's great institution for the planting and maturing of spiritual life. When properly executed, its benefits are untold. When wrongly executed, no evil can exceed its damaging results." E.M. Bounds

If someone were to ask what a "pleasing-to-God" church service would look like, how would you respond? How about something like this: A house of prayer and place of service where Jesus is exalted, God is worshiped in Spirit and truth; the Spirit is allowed to minister; the saints are equipped and allowed to be holy and royal priests inside the church. The service would be a place where the Word is taught without compromise, love is practiced without partiality; demons are cast out without mercy; the lost are evangelized without condemnation, sin is exposed without shades of gray and repentance is preached without hesitation....and one could go on.

AUGUST 7

"One of these days some simple soul will pick up the Book of God, read it and believe it. Then the rest of us will be embarrassed". Leonard Ravenhill

MEDITATING, STUDYING AND PRACTICING THE WORD OF GOD IS NOT OPTIONAL.

In these days of increasing deception, demonic doctrines, compromise and lies many will forsake proper devotion to the Word of God, the source of our faith and saving knowledge of God. Consequently, they will stumble in doubt like drunkards, crawl like babes, become preoccupied with the world's bad news and often defeated on the spiritual battle field. Last days falsehoods are becoming as numerous as the sand on the seashore. It will become more important than ever that the serpent's craftiness does not lead our minds astray from the simplicity and purity of devotion to Christ (2 Cor 11:3).

The apostle Paul exhorted believers not to wrangle about words, to refuse foolish and ignorant speculations and to avoid the opposing arguments which some profess and yet go astray from the faith (2 Tim 2:14, 23; 1 Tim 6:20-21). We must not waste time building intellectual sand castles on the beach only to be washed away by another rising tide of demonic doctrine.

If you know the Truth, the lies of the devil will roll off like water on a duck's back. "The people that do know their God shall be strong, and do exploits" (Dan 11:32). God is known through His written word as well as by the spoken word taught by the Holy Spirit of Truth who teaches us how to abide in Christ (1 Cor 2:13; 1 Jn 2:27, 3:24, 4:13). Jesus said" "Man shall not lie by bread alone, but by every word that proceeds out of the mouth of God" (Mt 4:4). Paul said: "All scripture is given by inspiration of God, and is profitable for doctrine, for reproof, for correction, for instruction in righteousness; that the man of God may be perfect, thoroughly furnished unto all good works" (2 Tim 3:16-17, KJV). The psalmist wrote: "How can a young man keep his way pure? By keeping it according to Thy word. Thy word I have treasured in my heart, that I may not sin against Thee" (Ps 119:9, 11).

Ezra demonstrated the proper balance: "For Ezra had set his heart to seek the law of the LORD, and to practice it, and to teach His statutes and ordinances in Israel" (Ezra 7:10). Since believers are confronted with spiritual warfare constantly in this evil world as aliens and citizens of heaven, it is imperative that they follow Paul's instruction: "you will be a good servant of Christ Jesus, constantly nourished on the words of the faith and of the sound doctrine which you have been following (1 Tim 4:6). "No soldier in active service entangles himself in the affairs of everyday life, so that he may please the one who enlisted him as a soldier" (2 Tim 2:4). Pick your battles wisely. Contend for the faith which was once for all delivered to the saints, lest you waste your time foolishly arguing over opinions and traditions of men (Jude 3).

AUGUST 8

"Today's church wants to be raptured from responsibility." Leonard Ravenhill

LEGO CHURCHES OR THE LIVING TEMPLE

Much of contemporary Christianity is more concerned about constructing cookie cutter happy lego churches rather than instructing Christians to be God's uniquely created and properly functioning living stones and royal priests in His holy Temple which Jesus is building (Ps 139:13-14; Eph 4:16; 1 Pet 2:5, 9). Though one may claim to hold fast Jesus' name and not deny the faith, yet Jesus rebukes the religious who tolerate and associate with those who place stumbling blocks before the children of God (Rev 2:13-14). Titus spoke of those who "profess to know God, but by their deeds they deny Him, being detestable and disobedient, and worthless for any good deed" (Tit 1:16). Jesus said: "Many will say to Me on that day, 'Lord, Lord, did we not prophesy in Your name, and in Your name cast out demons, and in Your name perform many miracles?' And then I will declare to them, 'I never knew you; depart from Me, you who practice lawlessness" (Mt 7:22-23). Sin is lawlessness (1 Jn 3:4b). No one who is born of God practices sin, but rather is of the devil (1 Jn 3:8,9a). Many will think they will enter the kingdom of God and will begin to say "We ate and drank in Your presence, and You taught in our streets; and He will say, 'I tell you, I do not know where you are from; depart from Me, all you evildoers'" (Lk 13:20, 26-27)

Many preachers are stumbling blocks today, building entertainment houses out of lego believers rather than building up believer priests as living stones in God's holy temple (1 Pet 2:5). They tickle ears with pleasant words to build up self-esteem, rather than deliver heart piercing sermons that crucify the self. Are you nourished on sound doctrine and on the True Manna and Living Bread descended out of heaven? Does your spiritual diet consist of fast food religion or solid food spirituality? Are you dining on pleasant words (Is 30:10) and drinking from broken cisterns that can hold no water (Jer 2:13) or feeding on sound doctrine and drinking from the well of Holy Spirit living water (Ps 34:8; Jn 4:14, 7:37-38; Eph 5:18; Jn 4:14)?

How many Christians endorse acts of immorality because they listen to and believe devilish and Jezebel false teaching that leads astray Jesus' bond-servants (Rev 2:14, 20)? Scripture describes believers as holy temples not made with hands, created for His purposes, vessels for honor, sanctified, useful to the Master, prepared for every good work (Rev 2:14, 20; 2 Tim 2:21; 1 Cor 3:6; 6:15-20; Eph 4:30). However, many choose to be defiled and rendered incapable of being such vessels.

How many will be rejected from being God's priests (Hosea 4:6), though called to be a royal priesthood (1 Pet 2:9), because they are not warned and exhorted to follow Him who is the Way, the Truth, and the Life (Jn 14:6)? Instead they are enticed to follow the god of this world, down the path of deception, worldliness, compromise and dead religion. They fill churches having a name appearing to be alive, but are dead (Rev 3:1). Today religious cathedrals, megachurches and American religious idols claim to be rich and wealthy, in need of nothing, and yet are bankrupt of true spiritual riches (Rev 3:17). They are in need of repenting from love of self and worldly things and returning to their first love and devotion to first things (Rev 2:4-5).

Though many may go to church, be religious and be lavishly clothed, yet they are spiritually naked and clad with soiled unrighteous garments (Rev 3:4, 17). The Lord is calling His own to BE the Church and be clothed with Him (Rom 13:14), in the fine linen of righteous acts, bright and clean (Rev 19:8), having His mind (1 Cor 2:16) and being led by His Spirit (Rom

8:14). His coming judgment fires will soon purge churches of their thorns and briars, but will refine His true Church, the pillar and support of the truth (1 Pet 4:16-18; Heb 12:25-28; 1 Tim 3:15).

AUGUST 9

Entertainment is the devil's substitute for joy.
The more joy you have in the Lord the less
entertainment you need."Leonard Ravenhill

TRUST AND OBEY FOR THERE IS NO OTHER WAY TO FOLLOW THE TRUE WAY.

Faith and obedience are the keys and conditions to being blessed by God, to being fruitful and useful. The kingdom of God is advanced by those who walk the walk, not those who just talk the talk. Christ minded doers move mountains. Double minded doubters stumble over ant hills.

Jesus' Lordship essentially involves obedience: "Why do you call Me, 'Lord, Lord,' and do not do what I say?" (Lk 6:46). And the Christian life is one of ongoing and increasing obedience. Saving and persevering faith can't be separated from ongoing obedience: "He who believes in the Son has eternal life; but he who does not obey the Son will not see life, but the wrath of God abides on Him" (Jn 3:36). Christians reside in this world as its aliens (1 Pet 1:1), having their citizenship in heaven (Phil 3:20). They love not the world nor the things in the world, in order to experience the love and intimate presence of God (1 Jn 2:15; Jn 14:21, 23). They freely choose not to be a friend of the world, lest they make themselves an enemy of God (Jam 4:4).

Of course this is made possible by the indwelling Holy Spirit who renews the mind (Rom 12:2; Eph 3:16). The Holy Spirit leads and empowers God's own to walk righteously and put to death the deeds of the body (Rom 8:9, 13-14; Gal 5:16). The Spirit gives life to our mortal bodies so we can walk in newness of life (Rom 8:11, 6:4). Christians are chosen to obey Jesus Christ and be sprinkled with His blood (1 Pet 1:2) as they walk in the light the blood of Jesus His Son cleanses them from all sin (1 Jn 1:7). They are chosen to be holy and blameless before Him (Eph 1:4), becoming holy in all behavior (1 Pet 1:14-16). Peter exhorts believers to make certain about God's calling and choosing them so they will be supplied the entrance into the eternal kingdom of their Lord and Savior Jesus Christ (2 Pet 1:8-11).

Jesus said: "Not everyone who says to Me, 'Lord, Lord,' will enter the kingdom of heaven; but he who does the will of My Father who is in heaven" (Mt 7:21). Jesus said those who do not soil their garments will walk with Him in white, for they are worthy (Rev 3:5). Such overcomers will be clothed in white garments and not have their name erased from the book of life (Rev 3:5). Jesus will give white robes to those who will be slain because of the word of God and because of the testimony which they will maintain (Rev 6:9).

Those who remain faithful until death during increased tribulation will receive the crown of life rather than be hurt by the second death, which is the lake of fire (Rev 2:10-12, 21:8). "If we endure, we will also reign with Him; if we deny Him, he also will deny us" (2 Tim 2:12). Jesus said: "He who overcomes, and he who keeps My deeds until the end, to him I will give authority over the nations" (Rev 2:26). Paul wrote: "We are heirs of God and fellow heirs with Christ, if indeed we suffer with Him so that we may also be glorified with Him" (Rom 8:17). "For yet in a very little while, He who is coming will come, and will not delay. But My righteous one shall live by faith; and if he shrinks back, My soul has no pleasure in Him. But we are not of those who shrink back to destruction, but of those who have faith to the preserving of the soul" (Heb 10:37-39). The time is soon approaching when many of the unprepared, unrepentant, pew warming, easy believing, cheap grace and fast food eating, sin loving, "Christians" will not resist taking the mark of the beast and worshiping his image. Many will not be prepared nor willing to exchange their "Best Life Now" for eternal life hereafter.

AUGUST 10

"Our Faith must be tested. God builds no ships
but what He sends to sea." D.L. Moody

FIVE PRINCIPLES FOR SPIRITUAL VICTORY

Reverently praying daily the Lord's prayer with understanding (Mt 6:9-13). Jesus expressed the importance to His disciples in praying daily for deliverance from "the evil" (one). This includes deliverance from the devil who seeks to kill, steal and destroy (Jn 10:10a). He prowls about like a roaring lion seeking someone to devour (1 Pet 5:8). He must be resisted if he is to flee (1 Pet 5:9; James 4:7; Eph 6:11-13). This also means deliverance from "the sin which so easily entangles us" so we can run with endurance the race that is set before us (Heb 12:1).

Claiming daily God's precious and magnificent promises. In this manner believers become partakers of the divine nature, walking holy as He is holy (2 Pet 1:4; 1 Pet 1:15-16).

Relying daily on the Spirit's power. It is only by walking by the power of the Holy Spirit that we are able to put to death the deeds of the body and experience the abundant and overcoming life. Those walking without His power often live a defeated life with its repeated failures and disappointments, carrying out the desire of the flesh (Rom 8:13; Gal 5:16). The horsepower of the Spirit is dependent on the willpower of the person: whether he or she is willing to be strengthened with power through God's Spirit in the inner man (Eph 3:16).

In this way one is transformed into Christlikeness by the renewing of the mind (Rom 12:2) and possessing the mind of Christ (1 Cor 2:16). It is important that Christians skillfully wield the Sword of the Spirit, the word of God (Eph 6:17). Those who immerse themselves in the Word are less likely to be ambushed by the devil. An unguarded mind is the devil's playground. The devil disdains a mind guarded against his incoming lies.

Standing firm in the true grace of God (1 Pet 5:12b). The grace of God has appeared bringing salvation to all men (Tit 2:11), including salvation from the penalty of sin and eternal punishment or the second death (Rom 6:23; Mt 25:46; Rev 2:11, 21:14). The grace of God also instructs one how to experience deliverance from the power of sin in order to enjoy the kingdom of God (Rom 14:17; Mt 19:16,23). Paul wrote much about grace: "But by the grace of God I am what I am, and His grace toward me did not prove vain; but I labored even more than all of them, yet not I, but the grace of God with me" (1 Cor 15:10). "For by grace you have been saved through faith" (Eph 2:8a)... "do not receive the grace of God in vain" (2 Cor 6:1), but "as you therefore have received Christ Jesus the Lord, so walk in Him" (Col 2:6). For "those who receive the abundance of grace and of the gift of righteousness will reign in life through the One, Jesus Christ" (Rom 5:17).

AUGUST 11

*"No man is greater than his prayer life. The pastor
who is not praying is playing; the people who are not
praying are straying. We have many organizers, but
few agonizers; many players and payers, few pray-ers;
many singers, few clingers; lots of pastors, few wrestlers;
many fears, few tears; much fashion, little passion; many
interferers, few intercessors; many writers, but few fighters.
Failing here, we fail everywhere." Leonard Ravenhill*

G reat wisdom is needed to engage in effective evangelism in this post-modern, post-Christian society which disdains truth, despises biblical Christianity, is depraved in behavior and delights in deception. Paul often sought for prayer support as he spoke forth the mystery of Christ. He solicited prayer support so he would know how he ought to speak (Col 4:4) and that he would speak with boldness (Eph 6:19-20) and with grace (Col 4:6).

As a proclaimer of the gospel, Paul knew that he had to conduct himself with wisdom toward outsiders (Col 4:5). Often he had to correct with gentleness those who were in opposition, relying on God's grace to grant repentance leading the lost and captives of the devil to a saving knowledge of the truth (2 Tim 2:25-26). He taught that one must make the most of the opportunity as well as making the most of one's time because of evil days (Col 4:5b; Eph 5:16).

In environments hostile to the Gospel street evangelists are often more fruitful if they can identify those would whom the Lord is drawing, whom the Spirit is convicting and who are listening and responding to God's grace; those willing to exercise repentance toward God and faith in the Lord Jesus Christ (Acts 20:21). For those who have only itching ears, hardened hearts, closed minds and blinded eyes are not interested in God's truth that liberates but only in the devil's falsehoods which incarcerate, for the god of this world blinds the minds of the unbelieving to the light of the gospel (2 Cor 4:4).

AUGUST 12

"You will never please everybody. Some men will say you have gone too far. Other men will say you haven't gone far enough. I just compromise and say I won't please anybody." A.W. Tozer

HOW TO TAP INTO THE WELL RATHER THAN DIE OF THIRST IN THE DESERT.

If we confess our sins, God is faithful and righteous to forgive us our sins and to cleanse us from all unrighteousness. (1 Jn 1:9). Only after laying aside all malice, and all guile and hypocrisies, and envies, and all evil speaking, will the born again child of God be more inclined to desire and take in the sincere milk of the word (1 Pet 2:1-2). Only after the Christian has purged himself from iniquity and dishonorable things, can he become a vessel for honor, sanctified, useful to the Master, prepared for every good work (2 Tim 2:21). It is only after we lay aside every encumbrance and the sin which so easily entangles us, that we can run with endurance the race that is set before us (Heb 12:1). Only after our hearts are sprinkled clean from an evil conscience and our bodies washed with pure water, can we draw near to God's throne of grace in full assurance of faith to receive mercy and find grace to help in time of need (Heb 10:22, 4:16). It is only after we have laid aside the old self with its evil practices that we can put on the new self who is being renewed to a true knowledge (Col 3:8-10; Eph 4:22-24). The heavenly seated, spiritually born again Christian, only after escaping the corruption that is in the world through lust, can live consistently as a citizen of heaven in love, and increasingly become a partaker of divine nature in life (Jn 3:3, 5; 2 Cor 5:17; 2 Pet 1:4; Eph 2:6; Phil 3:20; 2 Pet 1:4).

When such a one is filled with the Spirit of God, possesses the mind of Christ and worships God in spirit and truth, he will drink from the well of living water and not die of thirst in the desert (Eph 2:6; 5:18-19; Phil 3:20). When we view ourselves as aliens and strangers to this world, we will no longer think of and love the world from which we have been delivered (1 Pet 2:11; Heb 11:15; 1 Jn 2:15; Jam 4:4). Then we will begin to minister as priests of a holy and royal priesthood and experience the Kingdom of God and conduct ourselves as citizens of heaven (1 Pet 2:5, 9; Rev 1:6; Col 1:13; Phil 3:20). Instead of being conformed to this world, we will be transformed. Instead of being tempted in a devilish dry desert, we will tap into the bottomless well of living water (Jn 4:14). Forgetting what lies behind, we reach forward to what lies ahead (Phil 3:13). So let's start drinking from the well rather than dying of thirst in the desert. Let's stay hydrated by the Spirit.

AUGUST 13

"What else will do except faith in such a cynical, corrupt time? When the country goes temporarily to the dogs, cats must learn to be circumspect, walk on fences, sleep in trees, and have faith that all this woofing is not the last word." Garrison Keillor

WHAT CONTEMPORARY CHURCHIANITY NEEDS IS...

Sin-denouncing repentance, fruitful faith, meaningful participation, authentic fellowship, genuine worship, sanctifying grace, intentional discipleship, effective prayer, bold evangelism, heart piercing preaching, love demonstrated, Holy Spirit empowerment and Christ preeminence. Too many churches today would rather download these essentials or downright deny them. Yet the faithful and persevering remnant will not be weak in faith, give up the fight nor lose hope that the Laodicean church will eventually rise from the dead to acquire gold refined by fire rather than covet earthly riches destined for fire (Eph 5:14; 1 Jn 2:15-17; Rev 3:14-18; James 5:2-3). After all the Bridegroom is returning "to present to Himself the church in all her glory, having no spot or wrinkle or any such thing, but that she should be holy and blameless" (Eph 5:27).

God's faithful remnant will get dressed in proper heavenly attire (Rom 13:14) and be prepared for the heavenly wedding which the depraved cannot defile or will their court redefine (Rev 19:7f). Such faithful ones will put on the full armor of God (Eph 6:11f) and get to work, doing the Father's business in the world while remaining unstained by the world (Lk 12:42-44; Rev 19:7-8; Jam 1:27). They will practice the true and living religion not a false and dead one (Jam 1:27; Tit 1:16). They will experience the abundant life now (Jn 10:10b) and taste of the eternal life to come. That is to say, they will truly know the heavenly Father and Jesus Christ whom He has sent and who is exalted in glory (Jn 17:3; Phil 2:9-11, 3:8), rather than settle for the "Best Life Now" with all its passing glitter, glamor and glory. There is hope. After all, "God has chosen the foolish things of the world to shame the wise, and God has chosen the weak things of the world to shame the things which are strong, and the base things of the world and the despised, God has chosen, the things that are not, that He might nullify the things that are" (1 Cor 1:27-28).

AUGUST 14

*"Why do so many Christians pray such tiny prayers
when their God is so big?" Watchman Nee*

Since Jesus can heal the emotionally depressed and deliver the spiritu-ally oppressed, why are so many unchurched observers not impressed? Maybe because much of the church is abscessed, being impacted with truth decay and not experiencing real freedom from bondage of various kinds. In the psalms we read that God sent His word and healed them (Ps 107:20). Jesus said: "Thy Word is Truth" and that by abiding in the Word one is set free indeed (Jn 8:31, 32, 36; 17:17). Jesus promised to send the divine Helper, the Holy Spirit, to remind His disciples what He said (Jn 14:26). He would send the Holy Spirit of truth to guide them into all the truth (Jn

16:13). That Holy Spirit anointing would teach them to abide in Jesus who is the Truth (Jn 1:20, 27; Jn14:6). Where the Spirit of the Lord is there is liberty (2 Cor 3:17).

AUGUST 15

"The shortest distance between a problem and the solution is the distance between your knees and the floor." Anonymous

TRUE FIRE-POWER EVANGELISM BEATS STRANGE FIRE ENTERTAINMENT.

Why do so many believe charlatans who peddle demonic magical potions that cure nothing when one can believe and experience the real thing? It's because they prefer to have their ears ticked by the father of lies, rather than be convicted by the Holy Spirit of truth. "For I am not ashamed of the gospel, for it is the power of God for salvation to everyone who believes, to the Jew first and also to the Greek" (Rom 1:16). When we engage in power evangelism the lost will take notice. When Philip went down to the city of Samaria to proclaim Christ to them, "the multitudes with one accord were giving attention to what was said by Philip, as they heard and saw the signs which he was performing" (Acts 8:5-6). For after all, his preaching the good news about the kingdom of God and the name of Jesus Christ (Acts 8:12), was like that of the apostle Paul, "not in persuasive words of human wisdom, but in demonstration of the Spirit and of power" (1 Cor 2:4). This was how Paul evangelized: "in mighty signs and wonders, by the power of the Spirit of God...I have fully preached the gospel of Christ" (Rom 15:19).

By such evangelism the early church upset the world (Acts 17:6). Even "unclean spirits, crying with a loud voice, came out of many who were possessed; and many who were paralyzed and lame were healed" (Acts 8:7). And this should not be so strange since "if anyone is in Christ, he is a new creation; old things have passed away; behold, all things have become new" (2 Cor 5:17). True fire evangelism is perceived strange by those who prefer to be entertained by strange fire.

AUGUST 16

"When we grow careless of keeping our souls,
then God recovers our taste of good things
again by sharp crosses." Richard Sibbes

DON'T SEARCH FOR THE "GOD" WITHIN, OR YOU WILL GO WITHOUT

Searching for and trying to connect with some New Age god within or inner guide is a very subtle ploy of the evil one. It is a form of self-love and self-worship rather than expressing love for and awesome worship of the true God in spirit and truth (Jn 4:23-24; Phil 3:3). It is also a carnal perversion of the Christian's rightful duty and blessed privilege to fellowship with the God sent, equally divine Helper, Teacher and Holy Spirit who dwells within (2 Cor 13:14). Likewise, it is a devilish diversion from enjoying intimacy with the Lord Jesus Christ who desires to be Lord of our heart (1 Pet 3:15) and whose manifest presence is dependent on individual obedience (Jn 14:21, 23) and corporate assembly in His name, to do His will (Mt 18:20).

AUGUST 17

"Many of us are hunting mice - while lions devour the land." Leonard Ravenhill

ARE YOU IN THE LORD'S BATTLEFIELD OR IN THE DEVIL'S ARCADE?

Too many are playing Church today, seeking happiness not holiness. They are lovers of self rather than lovers of God; idolizing creation rather than worshiping their Creator. Jesus said: If you love Me you will keep My commandments (Jn 14:15). Most would rather follow men's suggestions. Though drafted into the Lord's army, many have gone AWOL away from the battlefield to play in the devil's arcade, giving and sacrificing to him their energy, time and money. Only those who fight the good fight, who finish the course and keep the faith will wear the crown of righteousness and obtain the inheritance reserved for them which is imperishable and undefiled and will not fade away, the salvation of their souls (2 Tim 4:8; 1 Pet 1:4, 9).

The devil often sets up his arcade in religious establishments we call "churches" and he is not partial to any denomination. Even Catholics don't have a monopoly on spiritual depravity. It falls on Protestants as well. Spiritual depravity and deception is coddled by popes as it is by Protestant proud priests, by some Pentecostals as well as by some Evangelicals, by followers of all denominations and followers of no denominations. The devil does not discriminate. He obliges all who open their minds to believe his teachings, all who extend their arms to embrace his world, and all who compromise their temples to accommodate and worship his demons (1 Cor 10:14, 20).

AUGUST 18

*"Christ always identified Himself with the
least, the last, and the lost." Unknown*

WITHOUT THE RESURRECTION YOU DON'T HAVE A FAITH, BUT ONLY A FROWN.

For "if Christ has not been raised, your faith is worthless, you are still in your sins...If we have hoped in Christ in this life only, we are of all men most to be pitied" (1 Cor 15:17, 19). Only Christianity offers a real faith and living hope. The founders of all other religions are nothing more than a pile of dead bones buried beneath the earth. But Jesus Christ, the Founder of Christianity, is raised and ascended far above all the heavens (Eph 4:10).

It should be proclaimed from the north to the south, from the east to the west, that only Jesus is the Resurrection and the Life (Jn 11:25). This should cause all sinners to get saved and all saints to rise up and BE the Church and walk in newness of life (Rom 6:4), not with a religious frown, no longer without hope (Eph 2:12). Those born again walk in the light as shining new creatures in Christ (2 Cor 5:17; Eph 5:8, 13; 1 Thes 5:5), having no fear of man nor of death nor of condemnation for sin, but possessing so great a salvation and appreciation for Him (Mt 10:28; Heb 2:15; Rom 8:1, 33-34). As the apostle Paul said: "For this reason it says, Awake, sleeper, and arise from the dead, and Christ will shine on you" (Eph 5:14).

So Jesus after saying to the frowning and despondent Martha, "I am the resurrection and the life" (Jn 11:25a)… "everyone who lives and believes in Me will never die" (Jn 11:26a), He then asked: "Do you believe this" (Jn 11:26b)? And today, He asks the same question. His desired answer is "Yes" and the only appropriate response is: rise up and BE the living Church.

AUGUST 19

"I too have found a secret and I hope it will prove
the defining point of my life. It is not so much
where I am, or what I am doing, rather it is all
about WHO is with me." Alan Martin

When all the gifts of the Spirit are properly used, along with the five-fold ministry, combined with holiness and separation from the world, we will see biblical Christianity in the church. When we observe obedience rather than compromise, evangelistic zeal instead of timidity of spirit, lay empowerment rather than clergy control, active faith rather than intellectual assent, genuine repentance rather than temporary sorrow we will see true revival come to the land. When true spirituality promotes receiving Jesus as Lord, not merely as Savior, making disciples not faking decisions, being Holy Spirit led, not purpose driven, Spirit taught, not man taught, seeking out the lost and poor, not seeking to be rich and famous, then churchianity will be replaced by biblical Christianity.

All this is Christianity 101 and is apparently too difficult for many religious PH.D's, Church growth "experts" and the clergy caste to understand. Leave it to the GED's, (God's Empowered Disciples) to demonstrate it. And often it is too much to ask of the admirers of such intellectual and religious celebrities. For they are often too BUSY (Being Under Satan's Yoke), being encumbered with Satan's world, enamored with his novel religious experiences, nourished on pastoral pastries, bound by religious rituals and programmed by man-made doctrine to break free and BE the Church and true disciples.

Thank the living God that Christianity is not a dead religion, but a living relationship. Jesus said: "This is eternal life, that they may know You, the only true God, and Jesus Christ whom You have sent" (Jn 17:3). The liberated Christian isn't concerned about keeping a set of rules or arguing over popular religious opinion, but with keeping in step with the Ruler and Lord of his heart (1 Pet 3:15), and the Shepherd and Guardian of his soul (1 Pet 2:25).

AUGUST 20

"Action without prayer is arrogance, prayer without action is hypocrisy." Jose Zayas

"Test yourselves to see if you are in the faith; examine ourselves! Or do you not recognize this about yourselves, that Jesus Christ is in you--unless indeed you fail the test?" (2 Cor 13:5). One becomes disqualified or as the Greek says, apostate or a cast away (1 Cor 9:27), when one stops running the Christian race, stops fighting the good fight, and never finishes the chosen course. Not so with the apostle Paul (2 Tim 4:7-8) who exercised self control over his body in his pursuit of holiness (1 Cor 9:24-27). Peter also exhorted believers to make certain God's calling and choosing them (2

Pet 1:10-11). Christians are expected to be holy and blameless as called (Eph 1:4; 1 Pet 1:15-16), not deny Jesus (2 Tim 2:12) and nor cease pursuing sanctification (Heb 12:14). Such ones God calls His own (2 Cor 6:14-18). Jesus said: "For whoever does the will of My Father who is in heaven, he is My brother and sister and mother" (Mt 12:50).

One cannot claim Jesus as Lord who does not obey Him (Lk 6:46). The author of Hebrews writes that Jesus is the source of eternal salvation to all who obey Him (Heb 5:9). Confessing Jesus as Lord (Rom 10:9) as well as believing with obedience (Jn 3:36) are both seen as conditions for salvation. This was preached by the apostle Paul (2 Cor 4:5), was practiced by the triumphant early church (Col 2:6) but now is denounced by the easy believing, hyper grace, ear tickling preachers who peddle and adulterate the Word of God (2 Cor 2:17, 4:1, 2 Cor 6:1; 2 Tim 4:3).

AUGUST 21

"Paul never glamorized the gospel! It is not success, but sacrifice! It's not a glamorous gospel, but a bloody gospel, a gory gospel, and a sacrificial gospel! 5 minutes inside eternity and we will wish that we had sacrificed more!!! Wept more, bled more, grieved more, loved more, prayed more, given more!!!" Leonard Ravenhill

SPIRITUAL WARFARE VS. MATERIAL WELFARE

Spiritual warfare is more important than material welfare. The devil will gladly give you physical treasures of the world's fading glory to turn you away from enjoying your eternal spiritual riches of Christ and eternal glory. The devil desires that you worship and serve him instead, as you once did (Eph 1:3; Mt 4:8-9; 1 Cor 10:14, 20; 12:2; 2 Tim 2:26). The evil one will even give you false emotional happiness, so you will not pursue the true joy of the Holy Spirit (Gal 5:22).

For the tempter knows well that if you recount your spiritual blessings in Christ (Eph 1:3) and if your soul forgets none of the LORD'S benefits (Ps 103), he will have a greater challenge courting you away from divine blessing into his deception. For you would be more prone to wage spiritual warfare on behalf of God's kingdom, loving Him through obedience, loving Him because He first loved you (Jn 14:23; 1 Jn 5:3; 4:19). You may even become convinced that God, who did not spare His own Son, but delivered Him over for us all, will also freely give you all things (Rom 8:32).

So why search for Satan's treasure of fools gold when your Savior has already granted you His precious and magnificent promises enabling you to become a partaker of divine nature (2 Pet 1:3-4) and qualifying you to walk on streets of gold (Rev 21:21)? For the God of peace is faithful to sanctify you entirely so that your spirit and soul and body may be preserved complete, without blame at the coming of our Lord Jesus Christ (1 Thes 5:23-24).

AUGUST 22

"You can go with emotions. You can go with experiences. I'm going to stay with the Word." Michael L. Brown

To repent AND overcome seems quite important. In the book of Revelation we read that they overcame "because of the blood of the Lamb and because of the word of their testimony, and they did not love their life even when faced with death" (12:11). To such repentant overcomers Jesus promises:

I will confess his name before My Father and before His angels, (Rev 3:5).
  I will give him the bright morning star, (Rev 2:28, 22:16).
  I will grant to him to sit down with Me on My throne, (Rev 3:21).
  I will grant him to eat of the tree of life, (Rev 2:7).
  I will write on him the name of My God, (Rev 3:12).
  I will not erase his name form the book of life, (Rev 3:5).
  Such will be clothed in white garments, (Rev 3:5).

AUGUST 23

"Great sermons lead the people to praise the preacher. Good preaching leads the people to praise the Savior." Charles Finney

IT'S IMPORTANT TO DISTINGUISH HERETICAL FAITH FROM ERRING FAITH.

Heretical faith must be exposed and destroyed. Erring faith must be lovingly corrected with patience and great instruction (Acts

18:24-25; 2 Tim 4:2-4; Jam 5:19-20). We are to destroy speculations and every lofty thing raised up against the knowledge of God and take every thought captive to the obedience of Christ (2 Cor 10:5). Sometimes these mind invading thoughts come from heretical false believers. Other times they come from deceived yet sincere believers or from young believers not being taught by the Spirit of truth. If such fortresses are allowed to remain in the mind, the devil will have a greater chance to influence that person's life. We should resist such thoughts that do not further one's true knowledge of God nor lead to greater obedience to Christ. We should take them captive rather than be taken captive by them, in obedience to Jesus who is the Truth.

AUGUST 24

"If I profess with the loudest voice and clearest exposition
every portion of the truth of God except precisely that
point which the world and the devil are at that moment
attacking, I am not confessing Christ, however boldly
I may be professing Christ. Where the battle rages,
there the loyalty of the soldier is proved, and to be
steady on all the battlefield besides, is mere flight and
disgrace if he flinches at that point." Martin Luther

The spiritual enemies of God shake in fear when they see or hear of the resurrection life of God entering almost dead but repenting Christians, waking them up from sleep (Rev 3:1-4,15-20; Eph 5:14; 1 Thes 5:6-11) and raising them upon their feet. For those enemies whom the Lord disarmed and defeated through His victorious death (Col 2:15) will see His followers turning from former deadness to walk in newness of life (Rom 6:4), no longer lukewarm but baptized with fire (Lk 3:16; Acts 1:5). Complacency of spirit becomes fervency of prayer (Acts 12:5; Rom 12:12) and the spirit of timidity becomes Holy Spirit boldness (2 Tim 1:7; Acts 4:29-31, 9:27, 13:46; 2 Cor 3:12; Eph 6:19-20). They are no longer sinners in the hands of an angry God, but are saints in the hands of their mighty God. They have been washed, sanctified and justified in the name of the Lord Jesus Christ (1 Cor 6:11). They no longer walk in worry and defeat being overcome, but rise up and become overcomers for Him who overcame.

AUGUST 25

"They have sold the truth for popularity!" Derek Prince

THE PRESCRIBED WAY TO DEAL WITH THE DEVIL'S LIES IS TO KNOW AND OBEY GOD'S TRUTH.

After the devil had quoted and misused the Word of God to Jesus, He stopped him dead in his tracks by correctly quoting and using Scripture. His first and effective rebuttal to the devil's tactics was: "It is written, man shall not live on bread alone, but on every word that proceeds out of the mouth of God" (Mt 4:4). Peter, who often put his foot into his mouth, because he got his mind off the Word (Mt 16:23), later said this: "like newborn babes long for the pure milk of the word, that by it you may grow in respect to salvation" (1 Pet 2:2).

The apostle Paul taught that the Christian soldier's weapon of mass destruction against the devil was the sword of the Spirit, the word of God (Eph 6:17). It is by the inspired Word of God, not by private interpretations of men, that Christian servants and soldiers are made adequate and equipped for every good work (2 Tim 3:17; 2 Pet 1:20-21). Only when we decide to grow up into mighty men and women of valor, adorned with full spiritual armor and cease being babes in church nurseries, will we see the kingdom of darkness invaded by the Kingdom of God (1 Chron 12:21-22; Mt 11:12). Then the enemies of God will be put in their proper place, crushed under the feet of those proclaiming the Gospel of peace (Rom 10:15; 1 Cor 15:24-25; Heb 1:13).

AUGUST 26

"We put men into pulpits because they have degrees. But you can have 32 of them and still be frozen!" Leonard Ravenhill

Christians must respond to modern day's challenges to biblical Christianity with biblical clarity, strong conviction and bravehearted courage. Christians are called to be the light of the world, the city on a hill and the people of the Word. They are the salt and the light. They are prophetic and not pathetic, overcomers, not overcome. They follow after Jesus, not follow from afar. They are loyal walkers and keepers of the faith, not empty talkers and lacking faith. They are saints and true apostles, prophets, evangelists and pastors and teachers, not false ones. They are children who bear the cross, not merely wear a cross. They are the fruit of the tomb and the product of the upper room. They give no room to the devil nor produce fruit of the flesh. They are the redeemed of the Lord, the sheep of His pasture. They are forgiven, free and favored by the Savior, not to be condemned, enslaved and devoured by the devil. They are the called and the chosen. They are warriors and worshippers of God, not worriers and worshippers of self. They are world changers and history makers, not world conformers and history repeaters. They are not Hollywood, Microsoft or Starbucks, but holy, a mighty army and heavenly treasures. They are the Church of the Lord Jesus Christ. And the gates of hell can not, may not and will never prevail against the Church. They are the Church, the bride of Christ, who is, who was and who is to come.

AUGUST 27

"One reason the church has so little influence over the world is because the world has so much influence over the Church"..."No wonder the unconverted think hell is fiction when we live as if it were so." Spurgeon

A true move of God is evident in many ways: by biblical evangelism and intentional discipleship as well as by effectual prayer and intercession modeled in the New Testament. Bible believing Christians die to self and sin and live in humility and total non-conformity to both the religious and secular world. They preach true reconciliation of the lost to God and practice unity within the Body of Christ. They exercise biblical discernment regarding this world's angel of light, the devil and his false ministers of righteousness, including false apostles and prophets and their deceptions. They express an increasing desire to be nourished on sound doctrine and the words of faith. They possess greater commitment to the pursuit of holiness and compassion for the poor and afflicted. They demonstrate a supernatural walk with God as He continues to work mightily in and through them. They exercise dependence on the grace of God and the empowering presence of His Spirit. Glory and preeminence is given to the Son of God and is evidenced by submission to His Lordship. God is worshiped in Spirit and truth and loved with their whole heart, soul, mind and strength. They even joyfully embrace, fully anticipate and effectively prepare for the great persecution coming in these last days.

AUGUST 28

*"The backslider likes the preaching that wouldn't hit
the side of a house, while the real disciple is delighted
when the truth brings him to his knees." Billy Sunday*

WHAT THE SPIRIT IS SAYING TO THE CHURCH?

In Revelation 2-3 Jesus gave some very important exhortations through the Spirit of God to the churches concerning what they should do, what to repent of and what to expect and practice. It is high time that churches wake up, rise up, repent and start being the overcomers, pillars and supporters of truth, the salt and light and temples of the Living God that they are called to be. Twice the Spirit talks about those who claim to be Jews (true spiritual ones) but weren't (Rev 1:9, 2:9), who loved doing deeds but had left their first love (2:4); who had a name that suggested life, yet were dead (3:1); who claimed to be wealthy and adorned, yet were spiritually bankrupt and naked (3:17-18). Thank the Lord that His will and desire is for those whom He loves, reproves and disciplines to respond properly and become overcomers of all that threatens to overcome, and become true partakers of Him who overcame.

Those who overcome will soon find their adversary the devil coming against them to bring them back down to his fallen world. When the devil and his demons have you in their sights, put on the full armor of God (Eph 6:11-18) and put them all to flight. Begin meditating on praise psalms (92, 93, 98, 99), psalms of thanksgiving (103, 136), warfare psalms (18, 20, 34, 91) and psalms and songs of ascents as you ascend to your heavenly exalted place as citizens of heaven (120-134).

AUGUST 29

"If you look at the world, you'll be distressed. If you look within, you'll be depressed. If you look at God you'll be at rest." Corrie Ten Boom

When you see man's sin-friendly hyper grace preferred over God's sanctifying grace; when Scripture is rewritten or rendered not applicable because it conflicts with one's desires and private interpretations; when forbidden and rotten fruit of the flesh is desired over godly fruit of the Spirit; what do you see? You see those who may know God intellectually, but not intimately; those who profess to be wise yet exalt their foolishness. Their nourishment does not come from the Tree of Life but from a poison oak. They are not in love with the Great Shepherd but are in a love affair with the world. They make themselves enemies of the God of heaven (Jam 4:4) and will not abide forever in His presence (1 Jn 2:15-17).

As long as the Christian population continues to watch the American idol we call TV, support the educational retraining camps we call public schools, be entertained by a religious establishment we call the church house and be nourished on pastoral pastries rather than solid food...As long as the brainwashed media and entitlement addicted populace continue to elect liberal political hirelings in the White House or those who change their colors by the hour, Satan will continue to strengthen his hold on the family and maintain his strongholds in the church. God's judgment will continue to increase in the land and His professing Church will continue its descent into greater irrelevance and further diminish in power. Responsibility falls not only on pastoral accountability to God's calling, but also on the congregational stewardship of the Gospel, gifts and blessings of God.

AUGUST 30

"One hundred religious persons knit into a unity by careful organization do not constitute a church any more than eleven dead men make a football team." A.W. Tozer

Much can be learned by reading Paul's last verse and benediction to the Corinthian church: "The grace of the Lord Jesus Christ, and the love of God, and the fellowship of the Holy Spirit be with you all" (2 Cor 13:14). Paul saw the importance of possessing these three spiritual treasures available to every child of God. And it is this biblical FELLOWSHIP with the Holy Spirit that is often poorly understood, not appreciated and seldom experienced by most contemporary Christians. This is quite surprising since Jesus promised to send the Holy Spirit to believers to provide help (Lk 24:49; Jn 14:26; 16:7), comfort (Acts 8:31), instruction (Jn 16:13; 1 Jn 2:27), worship (Jn 4:24; Phil 3:3), spiritual development (Gal 5:22-23) and gifts (1 Cor 12:7,11) as well as empowerment for Christian living (Lk 24:49; Acts 1:8; Rom 8:11,13, Eph 3:16).

It is essential that believers participate in this ministry of the Holy Spirit. Having a mind renewed and strengthened by the Spirit (Rom 12:2; Eph 3:16), they can possess the mind of Christ (1 Cor 2:16), whom the Spirit came to glorify (Jn 16:14). They can walk in newness of life (Rom 8:13-14, 6:4), no longer demonically led astray to idols (1 Cor 12:2), nor controlled by the desire of the flesh (Gal 5:16). The Spirit helps them progress in sanctification (1 Thes 4:7-8; Heb 10:14; Rom 8:13; 2 Cor 7:1; 2 Pet 1:8) as well as in prayer (Rom 8:26, Jude 20). By the Holy Spirit demons are cast out and the kingdom of God is experienced (Mt 12:28; Rom 14:17). By becoming a good steward of the gifts of the Spirit (1 Cor 12:7,11; 1 Pet 4:10), by living by the Spirit (Gal 5:25), and by being taught by the Spirit of truth (Jn 14:26; 1 Jn 2:27), one increases in the knowledge of Him who is the Way, the Truth and the Life (Jn 14:6, 26; 1 Pet 1:1-2; 2 Pet 3:18)

Jesus, thank You for sending the Holy Spirit to be my Helper (Jn 14:16) and my true Inner Guide to teach me how to abide in You (1 Jn 2:27). Help me to exercise faith and proclaim the testimony of God by relying on Your presence and power (1 Cor 2:1-5). Teach me and assure me when I am abiding in the true Vine (1 Jn 3:24; 4:13) so that I can bear much Holy Spirit fruit (Jn 15:4-5; Gal 5:22-23) and experience your abundant life which my Lord came to give (Jn 6:63, 10:10b). Convict me of faulty living (Phil 3:15; Ro 8:16, 9:1) so that I will not be guilty of quenching and grieving You (Eph 4:30; 1 Thess 5:19). Instead, I choose to be obedient and filled with You (Eph 5:18) and to drink from Your living well (Jn 7:37-38), rather than from the world's broken cisterns which can hold no water (Jer 2:13).

AUGUST 31

"A true love of God must begin with a delight in his holiness." Jonathan Edwards

The final reformation or spiritual revolution will be the restoration of the first century style overcoming Church. And this may very well be a qualitative rather than a quantative revolution. Like the early church, the last move of God may involve the committed few sitting at the feet of Jesus in living rooms rather than the masses running to religious buildings. The early Church was not conformed to the world but upset the world. It did not preach to tickle ears but to pierce hearts. This spiritual revolution may well be experienced and expanded in areas where two or three are gathered in Jesus' name, not in man's name, to advance the Kingdom of God, not some religious agenda. It will be a restoration of righteous, peace and joy accomplished by the empowering presence of God and intimate fellowship of the Spirit of God (Rom 14:17; 2 Cor 13:14).

This spiritual revolution will not eradicate all evil nor snatch the world that is sinking in sin out of the hands of the devil as some religious dominionists may claim. Rather it will warn sinners not to fall into the hands of an angry God and encourage saints be received and embraced by the hands of their loving Father. Christ-minded, Spirit-led, God-fearing and Bible believing Christians will be the lights that expose evil, by having Jesus who is the Light of the world, shine through them. They will shine before the world by being separated from the world. They will not be conformed to the world but will be overcomers of the world, for they will not be of the world though they are in the world.

SEPTEMBER 1

Don't be fooled. Jesus was a friend to sinners so they would
listen and repent. He was not a friend of sin allowing
it to continue. He came to take away sin and to destroy
the works of the devil who sinned from the beginning.

SIN OR NOT TO SIN?

Since believers are called saints and are commanded to cleanse them-selves from all defilement of flesh and spirit, perfecting holiness in the fear of God, (2 Cor 7:1), how can many claim they don't have to stop liv-ing in sin? How can they embrace the new sinner-sensitive "hyper grace" that belittles sin and repentance? Since the fear of the LORD is to hate and to turn away from evil (Prov 3:7b, 8:13a), why do many walk in sin and compromise? Since the Spirit of God was given to deliver one from the power of sin (Rom 8:13) and the Word of God was given to cleanse one from defilement of sin (Ps 119:9, 11; Eph 5:26) how is it that many undermine the seriousness of sin? Since believers are commanded to be holy in all their behavior (1 Pet 1:15), to consider themselves to be dead to sin (Rom 6:11), why do they listen to those who turn the grace of our God into licentiousness (Jude 4) and deny His grace that brings salvation from sin's power and condemnation (Rom 6:1, 15; 1 Jn 3:9-10; Rom 6:22-23; 8:1; Tit 2:11)?

Believers are commanded to resist every temptation (1 Cor 10:13), to walk by the Spirit and not carry out the desire of the flesh (Gal 5:16), to take every thought captive to the obedience of Christ (2 Cor 10:5), and to walk in the light and be cleansed from all sin (1 Jn 1:7, 9). Yet many continue in their old ways, excusing themselves from pursuing holiness and sanctification.

This behavior results from reading bibles rewritten by men or listening to the lies of the evil one who has sinned from the beginning (1 Jn 3:8). Rather than being taught by the Holy Spirit to abide in the truth which sanctifies (1 Jn 2:27; Jn 17:17), they are being brainwashed by the evil spirit of the age. The devil prefers that we take holiness lightly, rather than pursue holiness devoutly. He desires for people to remain unrepentant and held captive by him to do his will (2 Tim 2:25-26), rather than become sorrowful over sin to the point of repentance leading to salvation and deliverance from sin (2 Cor 7:9-10). The devil prefers that his children remain bound by the cords of sin (Prov 5:22; 1 Jn 3:8, 10) rather than be set free and serve the Lord in freedom (Lk 4:18; Jn 8:31-36; Gal 5:1, 13).

God has granted us everything pertaining to life and godliness (2 Pet 2:3). We are being built up as spiritual house for a holy priesthood (1 Pet 2:5), to present our bodies a living and holy sacrifice, acceptable to God, which is our reasonable service of worship (Rom 12:1). Dying to sin is both a daily and a lifelong discipline, we call sanctification, without which no one will see the Lord (Heb 12:14).

SEPTEMBER 2

"Religion today is not transforming people; rather it is being transformed by the people. It is not raising the moral level of society; it is descending to society's own level, and congratulating itself that it has scored a victory because society is smilingly accepting its surrender." A. W. Tozer

*H*ow wonderful it would be to hear the Lord saying: I stand at the door and knock; not to knock it down, but to be invited in, for with Me is eternal security. Without Me is pure misery. I am the Promise Keeper, not the keeper of lies. Those who serve Me as Lord will not be incarcerated by the god of this world. I am the Lion of Judah coming to reign, delivering vulnerable victims from the jaws of roaring lion coming to devour. This is the day I have made and this year can be prosperous for all who properly fear. I will render powerless him who has the power of death, and will overcome and reign in life with believers who love not their life when faced with death, and who fear nothing but the Giver of life.

So "the conclusion, when all has been heard is: fear God and keep His commandments, because this applies to every person. For God will bring every act to judgment, everything which is hidden whether it is good or evil" (Eccl 12:13-14). "I am He who searches the minds and hearts; and I will give to each one of you according to your deeds" (Rev 2:23b).

SEPTEMBER 3

"Can we follow the Savior far, who have no wound or scar?" Amy Carmichael

Jesus alone has the keys of death and Hades (Rev 1:18). And He has given His followers keys to open up the kingdom of heaven (Matt 16:18-19), which is righteousness, peace and joy in the Holy Spirit (Rom 14:17) to those willing to enter by God's enabling grace (Tit 2:11; Eph 2:8). Jesus, who opens doors which no one can shut, will open doors to those who are Holy Spirit empowered, who keep His word, and who do not deny His name. He is the Lord and Savior of all who call upon His name and receive Him as Lord and Savior in sincere repentance and with intended obedience. God makes former sinners into saints, the has been's and dirt clods into new creations and living stones. They are holy and royal priests to His Temple, the true Church (Rev 1:6; 2 Cor 5:17; 1 Pet 2:5, 9).

They advance His kingdom and proclaim the unfathomable riches of Christ their King and the excellencies of God who called and delivered them from the domain of darkness into His kingdom and marvelous light (Eph 3:8; Col 1:13; Acts 26:18; 1 Pet 2:9). Just as God anointed Jesus of Nazareth with the Holy Spirit and with power to do good and heal all who were oppressed by the devil (Acts 10:38), Jesus has sent out His own to do likewise, anointed with the Holy Spirit and with power (Lk 24:49; Acts 1:8; 1 Jn 2:20; Jn 17:18).

SEPTEMBER 4

"God, who foresaw your tribulation, has
specially armed you to go through it, not without
pain but without stain." C.S. Lewis

IN THESE TRAVAILING TIMES, ONLY THE JESUS-BUILT CHURCH WILL PREVAIL.

How can Christians be most prepared, abundantly fruitful and bold overcomers in these last evil and trying days? It will be accomplished by being biblically nourished (1 Tim 4:6; Mt 4:4), Scripturally equipped (2 Tim 3:16-17), Spirit taught (Jn 14:26; 1 Jn 2:27), Jesus exalting (Acts 4:12, 8:12); disciple trained (Mt 28:18-20; Acts 14:21-22; 2 Tim 3:10-11), mentally prepared (2 Cor 10:3-5; Pet 5:8), spiritually alert (1 Pet 5:8), devoted in prayer (Col 4:2; Eph 6:18; 1 Thes 5:17) and committed to holiness (2 Cor 7:1; 1 Tim 4:7).

They will be fully and spiritually armed to fight the good fight (Eph 6:11; 1 Tim 6:12; 2 Tim 4:7), determined to keep the true faith (2 Tim 4:7), and disciplined to finish the divine course (2 Tim 4:7; 1 Cor 9:24-27). They will be innocent as doves and shrewd as serpents (Mt 10:16), understanding the times (1 Chron 12:32), making the most of their time (Eph 5:16), choosing their battles carefully (Eph 6:12), trusting the Lord completely (Prov 3:5; 2 Tim 1:12), resisting the devil persistently (Eph 6:13; Jam 4:7; 1 Pet 5:9), and filled with the Spirit continually (Eph 5:18; Lk 4:1).

They will claim His cleansing blood, be bold in their testimony and dead to themselves (Rev 12:11). They will seek to maintain a loving and unified testimony before the world (Jn 17). In humility they will preserve the unity of the Spirit in the bond of peace (Eph 4:3-4). They will avoid creating strife and division over religious traditions of men and opposing arguments (Mk 7:8; Gal 1:14; 1 Tim 6:20). They will contend earnestly and corporately for the faith and sound doctrine (Jude 3; Tit 2:1). For they know that all things are possible to them who believe (Mk 9:23), knowing that they can do all things by Him who strengthens (Phil 4:13).

SEPTEMBER 5

"We want to be saved, but insist that Christ do all the dying. No cross for us, no dethronement, no dying. We remain king within the little kingdom of Mansoul and wear our tinsel crowns with all the pride of a Caesar; but we doom ourselves to shadows and weakness and spiritual sterility." A.W. Tozer.

IN CHRIST, WE HAVE IT ALL...

True Christians, those in living relationship with the Lord Jesus Christ are not bound up in legalism and dead religion. Rather, they have been blessed with every spiritual blessing in the heavenlies in Christ (Eph 1:3). They have been made new creatures in Christ (2 Cor 5:17). They are buried and raised up with Him to walk in newness of life (Rom 6:3-12). They are seated with Him in the heavenlies (Eph 2:6), to reign in life with Him who conquered death (Rom 5:17), with Him who is the ruler of the kings of the earth (Rev 1:5), who upholds all things by the word of His power (Col 1:17), in whom are hidden all the treasures of wisdom and knowledge (Col 2:3), who became to us wisdom from God, righteousness, sanctification and redemption (1 Cor 1:30), in whom we have been made complete (Col 2:10).

Heaven bound Christians have been delivered from the corrupting presence, controlling power and condemning penalty of sin. They proclaim Him, admonishing every man and teaching every man with all wisdom, so they may present every man complete in Christ (Col 1:28). They do not leave the hopeless of the world without Christ (Eph 2:12). They warn those groping in the dark after a prosperity gospel full of empty presents (1 Tim 6:17) and those seeking an emergent religion submerged in New Age deception. They do not live for the Best Life Now, but for Jesus who offers the abundant life now and eternal life hereafter.

SEPTEMBER 6

*"Some want to live within the sound of church
or chapel bell; I want to run a rescue shop
within a yard of hell." C. T. Studd*

Christ in you, the hope of glory, the author and perfecter of faith, is the only sure Foundation, solid Rock and true Anchor of the soul in the midst of increasing persecution, spreading abomination, religious deception, political corruption and pulpit compromise (Col 1:27; Heb 12:2, 6:19-20; 1 Cor 3:11; Mt 16:16-18). The true "Best Life Now" and only life worth living, is the one lived by depending on the grace of our Lord Jesus Christ; the one experiencing the love of God and walking in fellowship with the Holy Spirit (Jn 10:10b; 2 Cor 13:14). Don't be robbed of heaven's eternal blessings by relying on the world's temporal enjoyments. Only by God's resurrection power, Jesus' rewarding presence and the Spirit's renewing fellowship can we truly live, move forward, be fruitful and purposely exist (Rom 8:11; Jn 15:4; 2 Cor 13:14; Acts 17:28). For apart from abiding in the Lord Jesus Christ we can do nothing (Jn 15:5), hope for nothing, and accomplish nothing. But by believing, obeying and loving Him we can do all things, endure all things, hope all things and overwhelmingly conquer all things (Rom 8:37; 1 Cor 13:6).

SEPTEMBER 7

"Our murmuring is the devil's music." Thomas Watson

It only takes a little pain to give great thanks. Rejoice in the Lord and make the devil depressed. Wait upon the Lord and fly like an eagle for your citizenship is in heaven. Don't flounder in the world and stay in the chicken coup. Don't be downtrodden seeing your enemies as giants and yourself as a grasshopper, hopeless abound and hopping around to escape your circumstances (Num 13:33). Rather, be upbeat like King David who confessed to His LORD: "For by You I can crush a troop and by my God I can leap over a wall" (Ps 18:29). "Be strong in the Lord and in the strength of His might and put on the full armor of God (Eph 6:10-11). Be convinced that God's grace is all sufficient in all difficulties, His power is perfected in all weaknesses, His praise is uplifting in discouragement, making your soul well content at all times (Phil 4:4; 2 Cor 9:8, 12:9-10).

SEPTEMBER 8

*"We fear men so much because we fear God so little.
One fear cures another." William Gurnall*

When you find the front door closed to your hopes, dreams and pursuits don't try to sneak out through the back door or climb out through the window. You may very well fall down outside into a thorn bush. And when you find yourself behind closed doors because of unrepentance or dead religion, run to Him who is the Way and through Him who is the Door, to a living relationship with Him who is the Life (Jn 14:6). It is more pleasant walking through a door God has opened, even with a little Holy Spirit power, than trying to bust through a door in your own strength; a door often closed by rebellion and pad locked by religion. And maintaining a repentant heart, keeping His word and claiming His promises, is much preferred to being locked up behind any closed door, only to hear Him knocking (Rev 3:8, 20).

SEPTEMBER 9

*"To be right with God, has often meant to
be in trouble with men." A.W. Tozer*

The 23rd Channel
The TV is my shepherd, I shall not want.
It makes me like down on the sofa.
It leads me away from the scriptures.
It destroys my soul.
It leads me in the path of sex and
violence for the sponsor's sake.
Yea, though I walk in the shadow of
my Christians responsibilities, there will be
no interruption for the TV is with me.
It's cable and remote control, they comfort me.
It prepares a commercial before me
in the presence of my worldliness.
It anoints my head with humanism.
My coveting runneth over.
Surely laziness and ignorance shall follow me all
the days of my life;
And I shall dwell in the house watching
TV forever.

Author unknown

SEPTEMBER 10

"If you are under the dominion of sin, you are yet an utter stranger to the salvation of God." Catherine Booth

Christians are loved by the Father, sought by the Son and empowered by the Spirit. With the Triune Godhead on your side, who cares if wicked man is "in your face". When we have the face of God smiling at us, we don't have to fear our foes, tremble at their threats nor be shaken by their schemes. Those without God have always been at enmity with those who walk with God. As Citizens of Heaven and aliens of this world, Bible believing Christians view such hostility, opposition and trial as an opportunity to share their earthly testimony and store up heavenly treasure (Mt 6:20; 1 Tim 6:18-19). For we overcome our accuser the devil and his energized sons of disobedience because of the blood of the Lamb and because of the word of our testimony, not loving our life even to death (Rev 12:10-11; Eph 2:2). Jesus' followers overcome Satan's puppets on a string, for they are secure in God's hands, are kept by the Lord's prayers (Jn 17; 1 Jn 2:1-2) and are overcomers by the Spirit's power (1 Jn 4:4; Rom 8:11).

SEPTEMBER 11

"Purity is vital to faith." Smith Wigglesworth

F aith comes from studying the Word of God (Rom 10:17). Discernment comes from practicing the Word of God (Heb 5:14). Knowledge of the truth comes from doing the will of God (Jn 7:17). The beginning of wisdom is the fear of God and a good understanding have all those who do His commandments (Ps 111:10). We see a severe deficiency in overcoming faith, spiritual discernment, knowledge of God and practical wisdom because few are sincerely devoted to the study and practice of the Word of God. Where are the Ezra's? "The good hand of his God was upon him. For Ezra had set his heart to study the law of the LORD, and to practice it, and to teach His statutes and ordinances in Israel" (Ezra 7:9b-10).

SEPTEMBER 12

"There are a lot of Christians who are halfway fellows. They stand in the door, holding on to the Church with one hand while they play with the toys of the world with the other. They are in the doorway and we can't bring sinners in." Mordecai Ham

C hurch attending religious folk can sometimes be a great hindrance to new Christians when it comes to advancing the kingdom of God. Often when sinners get truly saved and therefore become enemies of the devil they fail to take seriously his schemes to steal, kill and destroy (2 Cor 2:11; Eph 6:11; Jn 10:10a; 1 Pet 5:8-9). They join an institutional church where the self is improved, ears are tickled, compromise is applauded, spiritual warfare is ignored and religious rituals are followed. The more spiritual may even get baptized, run to the altar, direct traffic and serve cappuccino. Yet they remain unchanged for the most part, seldom read the Bible or pray, are slack in evangelism and slow in pursuing holiness. They go with the religious flow and are swept away in the deceptive flood. They stroll through life along with others who are unchanged, unrepentant and unprepared to suffer persecution as called and are untrained soldiers to persevere and overcome as required (Phil 1:29; 2 Tim 2:2-3; 1 Pet 4:12-16; Rev 2-3).

And with all the evil in society, insanity in government, vain religion in church, dysfunction in the family, disease in the body and lack of funds in the bank, no wonder the devil has been so successful in casting a spirit of sadness, depression, oppression, loneliness, and hopelessness upon his enemies. The best way to overcome is to practice the spiritual disciplines the devil hates the most: pray fervently, witness boldly, walk holy, praise thankfully, proclaim God's truth uncompromisingly, and be rich in good works.

SEPTEMBER 13

"The popular gospel of this day, is the laughing-stock of Hell; it dare neither damn the sinner, nor sanctify the saint." Catherine Booth

Though many may hold fast Jesus' name and not deny His faith, yet even those Jesus rebukes, those who tolerate and associate with those who place stumbling blocks before the children of God (Rev 2:13-14). It is essential that Christians separate from such stumbling blocks (2 Cor 6:14-18). Bad company corrupts good morals (1 Cor 15:33) and a little leaven leavens the whole lump of dough (1 Cor 5:6). And we see many such pastoral stumbling blocks today, building entertainment houses out of lego's rather than building spiritual houses out of living stones (1 Pet 2:5). Many religious leaders are quick to embrace compromise and abominations with open hands, and yet pretend to praise God with uplifted hands.

And Jesus would ask such church pastors today: "Who are you applauding" and "What are you eating?" Are you nourished on sound doctrine, on Me, the True Manna, and Living Bread descended out of heaven, or are you feasting on devilish lies and worldly compromise? Are you sacrificing to the god of this world and seeking its riches or serving the Lord in whom are hidden all the treasures of wisdom and knowledge (Col 2:3)? Does your spiritual diet consist of fast food religion or solid food spirituality? Are you drinking from broken cisterns that can hold no water, or from the well of Holy Spirit living water (Ps 34:8; Jn 6:54; Heb 5:13-14; Jn 4:14; 7:37-38; Eph 5:18; Jer 2:13)?

SEPTEMBER 14

"We must come to the place where we can honestly say, 'I'm not afraid of holiness. I'm not going to be afraid of going all the way with God, cost whatever it may." Al Whittinghill

BUILDING LEGO ENTERTAINMENT HOUSES OR SPIRITUAL HOUSES OF LIVING STONES?

Beware of "Christian" leaders who endorse acts of immorality, who listen to, heed and promote devilish and Jezelbellian false teaching that leads astray Jesus' bond-servants (Rev 2:14, 20)? How many holy temples are defiled and rendered incapable of being vessels for honor, sanctified, useful to the Master, prepared for every good work, because of pulpit promoting sins against the Holy Spirit who resides in temples not made with hands and which are created for His purposes (Rev 2:14, 20; 2 Tim 2:21; 1 Cor 3:6; 6:15-20; Eph 2:10, 4:30)?

How many believers will be rejected from being God's priests (Hosea 4:6), though called to be a holy and royal priesthood (1 Pet 2:5, 9), because they do not hear and heed pulpit exhortations to follow Him who is the Way, the Truth, and the Life (Jn 14:6; Rev 1:3) nor make certain their holy calling (2 Tim 1:9; 2 Pet 1:10-11)? Instead they are enticed to follow the god of this world, down the path of lies, deception and dead religion. Many have a name appearing to be alive, but are dead (Rev 3:1). Today many claim to see God and be prosperous, and yet they do not know that they are blind and poor (Rev 3:17). They claim to have need of nothing and to be religious, but are miserable and naked, having need to be clothed with Christ and be spiritual (Rom 13:14; Gal 3:27). They are in need of true riches and spiritual adornment and must return to their first love and devotion to first things (Rev 3:18, 2:4-5).

Though multitudes enter compromising churches and appear religious, yet they are lavishly adorned with the world, walking with soiled garments and not dressed in wedding clothes (Mt 22:11). They are in need of clothing themselves in white garments and fine linen bright and clean (Rev 3:18, 19:7-8). The Lord is calling His own to come out from among them and be the true Church, the pillar and support of the truth (1 Tim 3:15), having the mind of Christ (1 Cor 2:16) and being led by His Spirit (Rom 8:14). The true Shepard is raising up a unified mighty army, His triumphant Church, which He will empower to leap over walls (Ps 18:29), rather than flee in fear like grass hoppers scattering in the grass (Num 13:33). In days ahead, God's judgment fires will spread more rapidly through the churchyard and thorns and thistles will burn (Heb 6:8; 10:26-30; 12:29; 1 Pet 4:17-18). Meanwhile His tailored fiery trials will continue refining His faithful and pruned branches in His true vine (1 Pet 1:6-7a; Jn 15:1-2), which eagerly awaits His return (1 Pet 1:7b; Heb 9:28, 10:37-38; 1 Thess 1:9-10).

SEPTEMBER 15

*The Lord of lords and King of kings is looking for mighty
men and women of valor who want to lead rescued
captives and former sinners into the Promised Land
as saints and overcoming soldiers, rather than lead the
masses into church nurseries where babies crawl and
cry or religious morgues where adults dance, stumble,
laugh and die. He is looking for those who will not
sell out for making false converts at altars of decision,
but making disciples upon the altars of crucifixion.*

TRIED IN THE TRENCHES

In these last days the Lord is raising up those who have been in the trenches for years, but now are rising out of them, battle trained, faith refined, trials transformed, ready to fight and persevere in troubled times. God has washed their past baggage under the bridge. He has turned their mess into a message, their trials into a testimony and their pain into His gain. Now they can carry a suitcase full of spiritual blessings and treasures in Christ and advance over the bridge into His kingdom (Eph 1:3, 3:8; Rom 14:17). Knowing that Jesus sympathizes with their weaknesses (Heb 4:15), and having been comforted by the God of all comfort (2 Cor 1:3-4), and made more holy by His loving discipline (Heb 12:5-11) and stronger by His empowering grace (2 Cor 12:9-10), they are now better equipped to rejoice with those who rejoice and weep with those who weep (Rom 12:15) and to empathize and set captives free from their bondage. Their rescued captives will better understand their language, listen more intently to their message, and will be more easily won by their testimony (Heb 4:15; Lk 7:47; Rev 12:11).

SEPTEMBER 16

Many pastors criticize me for taking the Gospel so seriously. But do they really think that on Judgment Day, Christ will chastise me, saying, 'Leonard, you took Me too seriously'? Leonard Ravenhill

TRUE SPIRITUALITY

Many have been stumbled by churchianity and Christians chasing after treasures at the end of a rainbow. Even the Best Life Now and Prosperity Gossip and Progressive Christianity, pastoral pastries and milk, ear-tickling semonettes and skits, self-help psychology and entertainment are getting old. Their name-and-claim-it promises have failed, their pop-theology and self-centered spirituality and powerless religion haven't delivered. All are contaminated with religious traditions, marketed church growth practices, sinner friendly cheap grace, a worthless and workless faith, and gaiety which offers its victims nothing but perversion, emptiness, hopelessness, false dreams and spiritual poverty. But those willing to drink from God's living well, partake of His Truth, the Living Manna and to fellowship with the Holy Spirit and fear the God of heaven, rather than drink from broken cisterns that can hold no water and listen to deceptive whispers of the god of this world, they will experience the abundant life and the Kingdom of God, enjoy the unfathomable riches of Christ and will inherit unfailing treasures of heaven. They will experience peace in this world that surpasses understanding and perseverance and joy that overcomes all obstacles.

SEPTEMBER 17

"An unholy church! it is useless to the world, and of no esteem among men. It is an abomination, hell's laughter, heaven's abhorrence. The worst evils which have ever come upon the world have been brought upon her by an unholy church." - C.H. Spurgeon

The Lord Jesus Christ purchased for God with His blood men from every tribe and tongue and people and nation and made them to be a kingdom and priest to God and to reign on the earth (Rev 1:6:5:9-10; 1 Pet 2:5, 9). So why is it that so many run from their royal priesthood and live in ruin? Maybe the reason is because many serve another Jesus of their own making, one who is not Lord of all nor Lord at all.

However Paul preached Jesus as Lord: "For we do not preach ourselves but Christ Jesus as Lord" (2 Cor 4:5a). And "for to this end Christ died and lived again, that He might be Lord both of the dead and of the living" (Rom 14:9). Jesus' lordship is an ongoing process beginning at salvation. "If you confess with your mouth Jesus as Lord, and believe in your heart that God raised Him from the dead, you shall be saved" (Rom 10:9). Paul exhorted believers to continue on with that frame of mind: "As you therefore have received Christ Jesus the Lord so walk in Him" (Col 2:6).

Peter likewise exhorts believers: "but sanctify Christ as Lord in your hearts" (1 Pet 3:15a). It is that sincere intent and submission to Jesus as Lord which marks true repentance and brings about mighty conversions, rather than false conversions, and sets one on a course of biblical discipleship. Lordship and obedience are not required prior to salvation, but the sincere intent and practice of both will be evidenced in those who are truly saved. It is a matter of working OUT our salvation in fear and trembling" (Phil 2:12b), not anxiously working FOR our salvation; of practicing the faith that saves, not professing a fruitless faith that is useless and dead (Jam 2:14, 17, 26). It is not a matter of "obey this and that" to get saved, but rather as the famous song lyric says, "Trust and obey" since you are saved. After all, Jesus expected obedience by those who called Him Lord: "And why do you call Me, 'Lord, Lord,' and do not do what I say" (Lk 6:46)?

SEPTEMBER 18

But one thing for sure: the Bible should be the main book we are spending time in and the one we should be intent on living out.

TRIUMPHANT LIVING

"Thanks be to God, who always leads us in triumph in Christ, and manifests through us the sweet aroma of the knowledge of Him in every place" (2 Cor 2:14). Paul identifies "us" earlier in the same epistle. He addresses them: "knowing that as you are sharers of our sufferings [sufferings of Christ, 1:5], so also you are sharers of our comfort (2 Cor 1:7) and "in your faith you are standing firm" (2 Cor 1:24). We see the same triumphant theme expressed in Romans: "But in all these things we overwhelmingly conquer through Him who loved us" (8:37), a positive confession made by those who were being put to death all day long for Jesus' sake and were considered as sheep to be slaughtered (8:36). After all, Jesus told His disciples that they were sent out as sheep in the midst of wolves (Mt 10:16a).

With Christ, God freely gives us all things (Rom 8:32), including the Holy Spirit of truth so "that we might know the things freely given to us by God" (Jn 16:13; 1 Cor 2:12). Believers are also taught to abide in Jesus who is truth in order to experience real freedom (Jn 8:31, 32, 14:6; 1 Jn 2:27). Finally, notice again the promise as well as the condition: "Things which eye has not seen and ear has not heard, and which have not entered the heart of man, all that God has prepared for those who love Him" (1 Cor 2:9). For after all "We know that God cause all things to work together for good to those who love God, to those who are called according to His purpose" (Rom 8:28). But for those who are flesh controlled and self-seeking rather than Spirit led and Kingdom seeking, all things will fall apart.

Triumphant living should be normative for Christians who properly understand their position of being raised up and seated with Jesus in the heavenlies (Eph 2:6). For all who being led by the Spirit of God are sons of God (Rom 8:14), and as such possess divine authority to tread upon serpents and scorpions and over all the power of the enemy (Lk 10:17). The God of peace is crushing Satan under the feet of Christians whose feet are shod with the gospel of peace, rather than man's gospel of prosperity (Rom 16:20a; Eph 6:15). Those who proclaim the full Gospel in demonstration of the Spirit and of power (1 Cor 2:4), even in the power of signs and wonders, are following the example of early Christian ministers of the gospel (Rom 15:19; Acts 8:5-13). And like them we should see much joy in the city and demons fleeing the scene (Acts 8:8, 16:16-18).

Greater is the Holy Spirit who empowers the children of God than the devil and ruler of this world who energizes his sons of disobedience (1 Jn 4:4; 2 Cor 4:4, Eph 2:2; Mt 12:28). Since this same Jesus who came to destroy the works of the devil and to take away sin (1 Jn 3:5, 8) is living in believers, demons will be tormented and flee when they are confronted by Him living in them. (Gal 2:20; Jam 4:7b; Mk 1:24, 5:7). In battling the rulers and authorities of darkness, we overwhelmingly conquer through Him who loved us (Rom 8:37) and arms us (Eph 6:11-12) because He overwhelmingly disarmed and overcame the devil who hates us (Col 2:15).

SEPTEMBER 19

"The chief danger of the church today is that it is trying to get on the same side as the world, instead of turning the world upside down. Our Master expects us to accomplish results, even if they bring opposition and conflict. Anything is better than compromise, apathy, and paralysis. God give to us an intense cry for the old-time power of the Gospel of the Holy Ghost!" A.B Simpson

BOTTLE FED OR BATTLE READY?

Thank the Lord and King of kings that He is raising up more and more Christians who are tired of crawling and sucking the bottle, and are walking and preparing for battle. They are tired of hearing weekly nursery rhymes and are beginning to sing battle hymns. They let the religious dead bury their dead while they go out and proclaim the Gospel that gives life to the dead. Instead of sitting in Americanized churches lamenting "woe is me" looking for another handout, they enter the battlefield declaring: "Awesome is He" with a victory shout. They offer true recovery to bound-up souls as they crush the devil under their feet, by the power of the Spirit who overcomes their foes.

They stare complacency in the face with urgency and stand against heresy with truth and simplicity of devotion. They display brave hearts, not a timid spirit, in the face of danger and deceitful spirits. They expose spiritual compromise with holiness and oppose political corruptness with spiritual correctness. They advocate biblical Christianity not churchianity, preferring to BE the church rather than just go to church. They march on as the true militant Church in the face of religious extremism and religious persecution, rather than hide out in safe, compromising churches, committing treason to God. They are faithful to God, serving the Lord and sharing heaven's only solution.

SEPTEMBER 20

"What are all your kings, all your nobles, all your diadems, when you put them together, compared with the dignity of winning souls to Christ?" C.H. Spurgeon

If all Christians would withdraw their money and support from the world's idolatrous systems they would surely fall. If they would submit to God and resist the devil, he would flee. Jesus told His disciples to shake the dust off their feet before those who didn't want to hear their message. Evangelistic efforts often prove futile when trying to evangelize the unrepentant who have seared consciences, hardened hearts, stubborn wills, closed minds and blinded eyes. Such are not interested in God's saving truth. In these cases one only plant the gospel seed and pray that it may take root before the devil comes to snatch it away (Mk 4:15).

Christians should seek to evangelize those who are responsive to the Lord's drawing (Jn 12:31), the Spirit's convicting (Jn 16:8), and God's teaching (Jn 6:45); those to whom God is granting repentance (2 Tim 2:26) and extending His grace for salvation (Tit 2:11).

One often may say, "I am too tirid to evangelize". But God has not given us a spirit of timidity but of power and love and discipline" (2 Tim 1:7). God desires to work in you, both to will and to work for His good pleasure" (Phil 2:13). God is in the business of transforming timid spirits into brave hearts. "God is not wishing for any to perish but for all to come to repentance" (2 Pet 3:9b). To those who are willing, God transforms lost gutter sinners into heavenly saints, haters of Christ into a fragrance of Christ, religious hypocrites into spiritual giants, worldly captives into heavenly conquerors, lovers of darkness into lovers of light, losers into winners, the downcast into the upbeat, morally bankrupt into holy treasures, and stalkers of darkness into bearers of light.

SEPTEMBER 21

"A man who is intimate with God is not intimidated by man."Leonard Ravenhill

WILL THE REAL APOSTLES AND PROPHETS STAND UP?

The Scripture clearly profiles the character and calling of true apostles and prophets upon which God's household is built (Eph 2:20). And that profile is in stark contrast with today's profile. Today many so-called apostles and prophets are obsessed with seeking mantles, anointings, fame, power and dominion. They stir up people to gain an audience and to make things happen, rather than be led by the Spirit and see God work supernaturally. Paul said: "The signs of a true apostle were performed among you with all perseverance, by signs and wonders and miracles" (2 Cor 12:12). Biblical apostles also experience pain, opposition, persecution and rejection, which modern day apostles and prophets tend to shun.

The apostle Paul elaborates: "For I think, God has exhibited us apostles last of all, as men condemned to death; because we have become a spectacle to the world, both to angels and to men. We are fools for Christ's sake, but you are prudent in Christ; we are weak, but you are strong; you are distinguished, but we are without honor. To this present hour we are both hungry and thirsty, and are poorly clothed, and are roughly treated, and are homeless; and we toil, working with our own hands; when we are reviled, we bless; when we are persecuted, we endure, when we are slandered, we try to conciliate; we have become as the scum of the world, the dregs of all things, even until now" (1 Cor 4:9-13)....."as unknown yet well-known, as dying yet behold, we live; as punished yet not put to death, as sorrowful yet always rejoicing, as poor yet making many rich, as having nothing yet possessing all things" (2 Cor 6:9-10).

Beware of those who come and preach another Jesus or offer a different spirit or preach a different gospel (2 Cor 11:4), "for such men are false apostles, deceitful workers, disguising themselves as apostles of Christ. No wonder, for even Satan disguises himself as an angel of light. Therefore it is not surprising if his servants also disguise themselves as servants of righteousness, whose end will be according to their deeds" (2 Cor 11:13-15).

Are such so-called apostles and prophets faithful servants of God sent by Him to represent the Lord Jesus Christ and to advance His kingdom and gospel? Paul continues: "Are they servants of Christ? I speak as if insane—I more so; in far more labors, in far more imprisonments, beaten times without number, often in danger of death. Five times I received for the Jews thirty-nine lashes. Three times I was beaten with rods, once I was stoned, three times I was shipwrecked, a night and a day I have spent in the deep. I have been on frequent journeys, in dangers from rivers, dangers form robbers, dangers from my countrymen, dangers from the Gentiles, dangers in the city, dangers in the wilderness, dangers on the sea, dangers among false brethren; I have been in labor and hardship, through many sleepless nights, in hunger and thirst often without food, in cold and exposure. Apart from such external things, there is the daily pressure on me of concern for all the churches. Who is weak without my being weak? Who is led into sin without my intense concern? If I have to boast, I will boast of what pertains to my weakness" (2 Cor 11:23-30).

Many contemporary "apostles and prophets" boast of their power, popularity, prosperity and their wisdom and skill.   One must realize that there are apostles and prophets from below as well as from above. Jesus warned of such in the last days. "Beware of the false prophets, who come to you in sheep's clothing, but inwardly are ravenous wolves. You will know them by their fruit…Not everyone who says to Me, 'Lord, Lord,' will enter the kingdom of heaven, but he who does the will of My Father who is in heaven" (Mt 7:15-16a, 21).

SEPTEMBER 22

"When the Lord's sheep are a dirty grey, all black sheep are more comfortable." Vance Havner

A WORD TO THE EMERGING "NEW" KIND OF CHRISTIAN: TEST YOURSELF

There is growing deception and a great falling away from the faith occurring in these last days (Mt 24:4; 1 Tim 4:1). Therefore it would be wise for all believers to test themselves to see if they are in the faith. The apostle Paul warned the saints in the Corinthian church to examine themselves to verify that Jesus Christ is in them, lest they fail the test and find themselves without Him and unknown by Him who is eternal life (2 Cor 13:5; Mt 7:22-23). He had earlier questioned some among the Corinthian believers who may have been deceived and misunderstood regarding their presumed assurance of inheriting the kingdom of God: "Do you not know that the unrighteous shall not inherit the kingdom of God? Do not be deceived….." (2 Cor 5:9-10).

With all the modern day "salvation" pitches thrown by wayward preachers, many may well see themselves struck out, having vainly tried hitting a home run to heaven on the fast pitches of easy believism, hyper grace, effortless Christianity and false religion. That is one test that all entering heaven must pass. There will be no retake when the heavenly bell rings and no curve will be offered when the final grade is given by the holy, righteous, loving and all-knowing Judge and Lord Jesus Christ.

So what does being "in Christ" entail? Persevering in tribulation (Rom 12:12), keeping the faith (Rev 1:9), doing the will of God (Mt 7:21, 12:50) not loving the world (1 Jn 2:15-17), bearing spiritual fruit (Jn 15:1f; Mt 7:20; Gal 5:19-23; 2 Pet 1:8-11), walking in newness of life as a new creature (2 Cor 5:17; Rom 6:14), holding fast to Jesus who is the Head (Col 2:19), living in repentance (Rev 2,3) and out of sin (1 Jn 3:9-10) and possessing sanctification (Heb 12:14) are some of the characteristics.

Though true saints will have tribulation in the world (Jn 15:18-19, 16:33), these citizens of heaven can experience the kingdom of God which is righteousness, peace and joy in the Holy Spirit (Rom 14:17). And persevering in faith rather than falling from faith is necessary to avoid destruction and to preserve the soul (Heb 10:35-39; Mt 24:13; 1 Pet 1:4-9). Don't fail the test, for the Lord desires to pass and has provided all that is needed to make the grade (2 Pet 1:3-4; Rom 8:32).

Indwelling Holy Spirit of Truth, give me ears to hear what you are saying and so I can shut out the falsehoods that the world is screaming. Empower me to walk in the light with Him who is the Light so as not to stumble before the prince of darkness without a fight. Help my spiritual eyes to see what sin blinds me to, so I can live and accomplish what the Lord calls me to.

SEPTEMBER 23

"There wouldn't be so many non-church goers if there were not so many non-going churches." Billy Sunday

IT IS TIME TO STAND UP AND SHOUT THE VICTORY

It is time to become fed up with being shut out, and stand up and give the victory shout: "The LORD has established His throne in the heavens, and His sovereignty rules over all" (Ps 103:19). His kingdom is an everlasting kingdom and His dominion endures throughout all generations (Ps 145:13). "To Him who sits on the throne, and to the Lamb, be blessing and honor and glory and dominion forever and ever" (Rev 5:13). Even though "The kings of the earth take their stand and the rulers take counsel together against the LORD and against His anointed....He who sits in the heavens laughs, the Lord scoffs at them" (Ps 2:2,4).

For "Jesus Christ is the faithful witness, the firstborn of the dead, and the ruler of the kings of the earth; who loves us and released us from our sins by His blood" (Rev 1:5). He has made His true believers to be a kingdom, priests to His God and Father (Rev 1:7). Jesus, as King and Lord is ruling through His believing soldiers, priests and servants seated with Him in the heavenlies, as citizens of heaven. They are no longer incarcerated in this fallen world and captives to its devil and his sons of disobedience. Let the mockers shout what they may, but coming is the day when "every tongue will confess that Jesus Christ is Lord, to the glory of God the Father" (Phil 2:10). Some will do this joyfully from above, others woefully from below.

God's handwriting is on the wall and most ignore it, oblivious to His wake-up call. Those who sit in darkness and read the world's pre-dawn news and sip from their cup must heed the Good News and wake up. Now is the time of salvation. For soon the time will end, and the Bight and Morning Star will arise, and the sleepers, in their mourning, will drink from His cup.

SEPTEMBER 24

"Apostolic preaching is not marked by its beautiful diction, or literary polish, or cleverness of expression, but operates 'in demonstration of the Spirit and of power.'" Arthur Wallis

WHAT IS SAVING FAITH?

The Scripture says: "Now faith is the assurance of things hoped for, the conviction of things not seen" (Heb 11:1). The author of Hebrews demonstrated throughout chapter eleven that true biblical faith results in action. Paul commended the Thessalonian Christians and acknowledged them being chosen by God because he remembered their "work of faith and labor of love and steadfastness of hope" (1 Thess 1:3-4). James says that faith without works is dead (Jam 2:17) and such faith can't save (Jam 2:14) since it is useless (Jam 2:20).

Man is not justified by a faith that never is evidenced by works subsequent to salvation. When John the Baptist saw many of the religious Pharisees and Sadducees coming for baptism, his reply was: "bring forth fruit in keeping with repentance" (Mt 3:8). For one who has truly repented will possess a faith that is accompanied by salvation works (Jam 2:24). They work out their salvation with fear and trembling knowing that God is mightily at work within them (Phil 2:12-13). They are being sanctified or set apart for service to God (Acts 20:32; Heb 10:10). Such ones receive the Gospel of God and are committed to His purpose, having exercised true repentance toward God and saving faith in our Lord Jesus Christ (Acts 20:21, 27).

Paul could not have been more clear about this when he said: "for not the hearers of the Law are just before God, but the doers of the Law will be justified" (Rom 2:13). And Jesus said that every branch in Him, the true vine, which does not bear fruit is cut off and burned (John 15:1f). Jesus said" "Indeed the axe is already laid at the root of the trees; so every tree that does not bear good fruit is cut down and thrown into the fire" (Lk 3:9). Jesus said" You will know them by their fruit" (Mt 7:24). "Not everyone who says to Me, 'Lord, Lord' will enter the kingdom of heaven, but he who does the will of My Father who is in heaven" (Mt 7:21).

Paul said" "For to this end Christ died and lived again, that He might be Lord both of the dead and of the living" (Rom 14:9). That is what Paul preached: "For we do not preach ourselves but Christ Jesus as Lord, and ourselves as your bond-servants for Jesus' sake (2 Cor 4:5). This requires obedience as Jesus said" "Why do you call Me, 'Lord, Lord,' and do not do what I say?"(Lk 6:46).

SEPTEMBER 25

"The opportunity of a lifetime must be seized within
the lifetime of the opportunity." Leonard Ravenhill

The biblical writers warned about the encroachment of a worldly Christianity into true assemblies of believers. Paul forewarned the gathered elders of the church of Ephesus where he had taught for three years saying: "I know that after my departure savage wolves will come in among you, not sparing the flock and from among your own selves men will arise, speaking perverse things, to draw away the disciples after them" (Acts 20:29-30). "For the time will come when they will not endure sound doctrine; but wanting to have their ears tickled, they will accumulate for themselves teachers in accordance to their own desires and will turn away their ears from the truth and will turn aside to myths" (2 Tim 4:3-4)..."holding to a form of godliness, although they have denied its power" (2 Tim 3:5). False teachers and false peoples will arise among those who have received the faith and the true knowledge of the Lord Jesus Christ (2 Pet 2:1-2, 13,15, 20).

Many will follow their sensuality, and because of them the way of the truth will be maligned (2 Pet 2:2), and in their greed they will exploit you with false words (2 Pet 2:3a). Many have crept into the church, their true spiritual nature and agenda unnoticed, who are "hidden reefs in your love feasts when they feast with you without fear, caring for themselves; clouds without water, carried along by winds; autumn trees without fruit, doubly dead, uprooted" (Jude 11-12). Paul warned of "false apostles, deceitful workers, disguising themselves as apostles of Christ", servants of Satan "who disguise themselves as servants of righteousness" (2 Cor 11:13-15).

God says: "In the last days you will clearly understand it. I did not send these prophets, but they ran. I did not speak to them, but they prophesied. But if they had stood in My council, then they would have announced My words to My people, and would have turned them back from their evil way and from the evil of their deeds" (Jer 23:21-22). The apostle Paul's apostolic perspective was quite different from today's popular apostolic movement: "I think God has exhibited us apostles last of all, as men condemned to death; because we have become a spectacle to the world, both to angels and to men. We are fools for Christ's sake, but you are prudent in Christ; we are weak, but you are strong; you are distinguished, but we are without honor. To this present hour we are both hungry and thirsty, and are poorly clothed, and are roughly treated and are homeless" (1 Cor 4:9-11).

However upon God's true bondservants, both men and women, God says: "It shall be in the last days I will pour forth of My Spirit and they shall prophesy. And I will grant wonders in the sky above and signs on the earth below" (Joel 2:17-19). Yet even when God's sanctuary will be temporarily desecrated by Satan and the abomination of desolation in the future, the people who know their God will continue to display strength and take action (Dan 11:31-32). For the great Carpenter never ceases building His Church and the gates of Hades shall not conquer it (Mt 16:18).

SEPTEMBER 26

A true faith in Jesus Christ will not suffer us to be
idle. No, it is an active, lively, restless principle; it
fills the heart, so that it cannot be easy till it is doing
something for Jesus Christ." George Whitefield

WHAT THE SPIRIT IS SAYING TO THE CHURCH(ES)?

In Revelation 2-3 Jesus gave some very important exhortations through the Spirit of God to the churches concerning what they should do, what to repent of and what to expect and practice. It is time for churches to wake up, rise up, repent and start being the overcomers, pillars and supports of the truth, the salt and light and temples of the Living God that they are called to be. Twice the Spirit talks about those who claim to be Jews (true spiritual ones) but weren't (Rev 1:9, 2:9); who loved doing deeds but had left their first love (2:4); who had a name that suggested life, yet were dead (3:1); who claimed to be wealthy and adorned, yet were spiritually bankrupt and naked (3:17-18). Thank the Lord that His will and desire is for those whom He loves, reproves and disciplines to respond properly and become overcomers of all that seeks to overcome them, so they may become partakers of all that He has promised them (Heb 3:6, 14; 10:35-36; Tit 1:2; 1 Pet 1:9).

SEPTEMBER 27

"The great misconception in our day is this: that God isn't concerned to protect His own integrity. He's a kind of wishy-washy deity, who just waves a wand of forgiveness over everybody. No. For God to forgive you is a very costly matter." R.C. Sproul

If only we would receive Him as He is and not perceive Him as we wish. If only we would acknowledge Jesus who is the very image of God and not make Him in our own image. Then we would desire Him all the more rather than desert Him all the quicker. We would walk with Him in victory and see Satan crushed under our feet. If we would follow Jesus who is the Light and Truth, we would not wallow in defeat, being robbed blind by the devil. In Christ are hidden all the treasures of wisdom and knowledge (Col 2:3). Without Him we are left to our foolishness. Abide in Him and we are fruitful. Abandon Him and we are fruitcakes and a nut case to be devoured by the devil.

Jesus is the Way, the Truth and the Life to all who forsake their ways, their lies and their self-life. The one who has died with Christ and is risen with Him should no longer live for self, being down trodden. Jesus gives the invitation: "Come to Me, all who are weary and heavy-laden, and I will give you rest" (Mt 11:28). Only then will one be without worry and not be restless. With Jesus, one is blessed with every heavenly blessing. Without Him, one is cursed with every worldly craving. How much better it is being a slave to the King of heaven and held in His hands (Jn 10:28-29), than being captive to the god of this world and in his clutches (2 Tim 2:26). The great tempter may deceptively offer much to solicit his worship (Mt 4:3f), but He who overcame all temptations surely has more to offer those who worship Him in spirit and truth (Jn 4:24). It's time for all believers to "take up their pallet and walk", to run the race with endurance and to fight the good fight wisely. The final bell is about to ring, the game is near over and the score will be given.

SEPTEMBER 28

"A revival of religion presupposes a declension." Charles G. Finney

DON'T BE BOTHERED BY THISTLES AND THORNS.

Don't be fearful nor be dismayed over those who oppose the Gospel, nor fret over their scoffing words. "Though thistles and thorns are with you and you sit on scorpions; neither fear their words nor be dismayed at their presence, for they are a rebellious house" (Eze 2:6). "But you shall speak My words to them whether they listen or not, for they are rebellious" (Eze 2:7). The GOSPEL saves those who believe (Rom 1:16), and the TRUTH sets free those who abide in it and the Word of God performs its work in those who receive and believe it (1 Thess 2:13). Those who freely choose to refuse both are free to remain in bondage and be held captive by the evil one to do his will (2 Tim 2:26).

SEPTEMBER 29

"A man with God is always in the majority." John Knox

ABANDONED CATHEDRALS

Pay day is coming. It won't be by means of a prosperity gospel. It will be a divine rebuke and purging of flesh anointed, purpose drunken pulpiteers, false shepherds, false apostles and false prophets. The Lord of the Church is beginning to down size the contemporary Church. He will soon begin chasing out the money changers, cleaning out the leaven, and culling out the tares when the divine shaking begins. All those who glory in self behind the pulpit throne and on their performing stage will see their popular "ministries" become of no use, abandoned cathedrals in the eyes of those seeking the Kingdom of God.

Under God's sovereignty, the devil will see that they remain as burned out lamps in the kingdom of darkness, applauded by those who freely choose to sit in darkness and the shadow of death (Lk 1:79), with tickled ears, hardened hearts and blinded minds (2 Tim 4:3; 2 Cor 4:4). The Lord shares His glory with no idolaters. The psalmist reminds us that "The LORD has established His throne in the heavens; and His sovereignty rules over all" (Ps 103:19). He will take center stage "with a view to an administration suitable to the fullness of the times, that is, the summing up of all things in Christ, things in the heavens and things upon the earth" (Eph 1:11) The Lord will have first place in everything (Col 1:18b).

SEPTEMBER 30

"We end up blaming God's sovereignty for the sad state of the church. If there is no revival in the church, we can be very sure that the lack is on our part and not God's!" Al Whittinghill

CHRISTIANS ARE NEW CREATURES

"Therefore if anyone is in Christ, he is a new creature; the old things passed away; behold, new things have come" (2 Cor 5:17). What are a few of the new things that have come? The born again Christian possesses the indwelling Holy Spirit who gives power over sin (Rom 8:13). Jesus' victorious death grants authority over defeated demons, principalities and powers (Mt 28:18-20; Lk 10:19; Col 2:15). Being a new creature includes having a renewed mind that can truly and intimately know God (1 Cor 2:12; Rom 12:1-2), replacing the former depraved mind that was hostile to God (Col 1:21) and unable to understand the things of God (1 Cor 2:14).

The Christian is now led aright by the Holy Spirit of the living God (Rom 8:14), rather than being led astray by the evil spirits to mute idols (1 Cor 12:2). The believer has a new will that can obey the Holy One (1 Pet 1:2), no longer enslaved to the evil one (2 Tim 2:26) and no longer dead in sin and enslaved to sin (Eph 2:1; Rom 6:19-20), but alive in Christ and enslaved to Him (Rom 6:22; Gal 2:20; Col 3:3). The child of God has been made complete in Christ (Col 2:10), even though one may feel inadequate in himself (2 Cor 3:5-6). Though the Christian may feel completely alone, he only has been made complete in Christ (Col 2:10).

Christians are empowered to live for the Lord who died for them (Rom 14:8) since they have died to self and have been raised up with Him (Rom 6:3-4). They have new passions that can enjoy and worship God (Rom 5:5; 1 Jn 1:3; Phil 3:7-8; Jn 4:23-24; Phil 3:3), rather than being alienated from God and enemies to Him (Eph 2:12; Rom 5:10; Col 1:21). They can walk in newness of life rather than wallow in old habits (Rom 6:4). They lay aside the old self and put on the new man (Col 3:9-10). They enjoy being adopted by the Father of light (Jam 1:17; Rom 8:15), no longer abused by the father of lies (Jn 8:44). They are discipled by the grace of God, rather than disgraced by undiscipline (Tit 2:11-13; 1 Tim 4:6-8). Walking as a new creation in progressive sanctification is the wisest choice believers make, because God has done so much in providing for them a salvation that is so great (Heb 2:3). They work out their salvation with fear and trembling knowing that God is working in them both to will and to work for His good pleasure (Heb 2:3; Phil 2:13). They love God by keeping His commandments because He first loved them by sending His Son (1 Jn 5:13, 4:19).

OCTOBER 1

Too many assemble today not in the name of Jesus as one's Lord for life and Savior from sin, but in the name of a performing religious icon to be entertained or in the name of a pulpit moral compromiser in order to remain a friend of sin. Thus religious masses sit not at the feet of Jesus who is the Holy and Righteous One and the Truth, but on the pews before those who are false. "And where two are three or more are gathered in that name, there I am NOT"

GIVE THANKS FOR PASTORS WHO LABOR.

There are several scriptures that describe proper pastoral ministry and how such ministry should be appreciated. "Just as you know how we were exhorting and encouraging and imploring each one of you as a father would his own children, so that you would walk in a manner worthy of the God who calls you into His own kingdom and glory" (1 Thess 2:11-12). "Appreciate those who diligently labor among you, and have charge over you in the Lord, and give you instruction, and that you esteem them very highly in love because of their work" (1 Thess 5:12). "Let the elders who rule well [ie. have stood before you well] be considered worthy of double honor; especially those who work hard at preaching and teaching" (1 Tim 5:17)…"be in subjection to such men and to everyone who helps in the work and labors" (1 Cor 16:16). "Obey your leaders and submit to them, for they keep watch over your souls" (Heb 13:17a).

OCTOBER 2

"If you don't plan to live the Christian life totally committed to knowing your God and to walking in obedience to Him, then don't begin; for this is what Christianity is all about. It is a change of citizenship, a change of governments, a change of allegience. If you have no intention of letting Christ rule your life, then forget Christianity; it's not for you." K. Authur

Saving grace removes sin. Titus says: "For the grace of God has appeared, bringing salvation to all men, instructing us to deny ungodliness and worldly desires and to live sensibly, righteously and godly in the present age" (Tit 2:11-12). Saved Christians do not live in sin, but practice righteousness. This is a major theme of 1 John. "And by this we know that we have come to know Him, if we keep His commandments...Little children let no one deceive you the one who practices righteousness is righteous, just as He is righteous...No one who is born of God practices sin, because His seed abides in him; and he cannot continue to sin (present infinitive), because he is born of God" (1 Jn 2:3, 3:7, 9). Likewise, Paul told the Corinthian believers: "And working together with Him, we also urge you not to receive the grace of God in vain" (2 Cor 6:1). Paul exhorted the Philippian believers saying: "work out your salvation with fear and trembling; for it is God who is at work in you, both to will and to work for His good pleasure" (Phil 2:12b-13).

Christians have been chosen in Christ to be holy and blameless (Eph 1:4). Jesus said: "Therefore you are to be perfect, as your heavenly Father is perfect" (Mt 5:48). James described pure and undefiled religion in the sight of God as comprising works of righteousness like visiting orphans and widows in their distress, as well as keeping oneself unstained by the world (Jam 1:27). Paul admonished Timothy: "I charge you....that you keep the commandment without stain or reproach until the appearing of our Lord Jesus Christ" (1 Tim 6:14). He reminded the Corinthian believers: "For we do not preach ourselves but Christ Jesus as Lord, and ourselves as your bond-servants for Jesus' sake" (2 Cor 4:5). He who properly understands the Lordship of Jesus possesses the mind of Christ and sanctifies Him as Lord of his heart, will display His lordship in his life (1 Cor 2:16; 1 Pet 3:15; Col 2:6).

OCTOBER 3

"Jellyfish Christianity -- A Christianity without bone,
muscle, or sinew, -- without any distinct teaching about
the atonement, the work of the Spirit, justification,
or the way of peace with God -- a vague, foggy,
misty Christianity, of which the only watchwords
seem to be, "You must be liberal and kind. You must
condemn no man's doctrinal views. You must consider
everybody is right & nobody is wrong." J.C. Ryle

We must be on guard against any teaching that undermines the importance and necessity of a holy life and that turns the grace of our God into licentiousness. Such teaching denies our only Master and Lord, Jesus Christ (Jude 4). You cannot serve two masters, sin and the Savior. After being delivered from our Egypt, that darkness and dominion of Satan's world and domain (Col 1:13; Acts 26:18), Christians must continue to trust and obey as citizens of heaven. Jesus has become "to all those who obey Him the source of eternal salvation (Jude 1:5; Heb 5:9b).

Many are familiar with the "faith-promise" of John 3:16: "For God so loved the world that He gave His only begotten Son, that whoever believes in Him should not perish but have eternal life". But many also fail to follow the command to "faith practice" of Jn 3:36: "He who believes in the Son has eternal, but he who does not obey the Son will not see life, but the wrath of God abides on him". When the Lord returns, He will deal out retribution "to those who do not know God and to those who do not obey the gospel of our Lord Jesus Christ (2 Thess 2:10).

The apostle Paul asks believers who have been saved by grace: "Are we to continue in sin so that grace may increase? May it never be!" (Rom 6:1-2a). "For this is the will of God, your sanctification" (1 Thess 4:1a). Without sanctification no one will see the Lord (Heb 12:14). For the outcome of sanctification is eternal life. For it is written: "But now having been freed from sin and enslaved to God, you derive your benefit, resulting in sanctification, and the outcome, eternal life" (Rom 6:22). It is the one who does the will of God who lives forever with Him (1 Jn 2:17b). Conversely, the wages of sin is death, for "if you are living according to the flesh, you must die; but if by the Spirit you are putting to death the deeds of the body, you will live. For all who are being led by the Spirit of God, these are sons of God" (Rom 8:13-14).

OCTOBER 4

*"We should no more tolerate false doctrine
that we would tolerate sin." J.C. Ryle*

HOLINESS IS NOT OPTIONAL FOR CITIZENS OF HEAVEN.

There is a growing tendency today for many Christian leaders to deny or undermine the pursuit of holiness. They may even suggest that holiness is optional for heaven bound believers. After all they say all our sins of any kind past, present and future have already been forgiven. When God sees us, He sees the righteousness of Christ, not our sins, even unconfessed sins. So there is no need for repentance. Live as you wish for God doesn't see you as you are. Such faulty teaching promotes ungodliness and turns the grace of our God into licentiousness. (Jude 4a). Such ones by their wayward teaching and behavior deny our only Master and Lord, Jesus Christ (Jude 4b). He appeared in order to take away sins (1 Jn 3:5) and to destroy the works of the devil (1 Jn 3:8).

To the contrary John wrote: "By this the children of God and the children of the devil are obvious; anyone who does not practice righteousness is not of God, not the one who does not love his brother" (1 Jn 3:10). After all, did not the apostle Paul describe the "beloved of God" as "saints" rather than sinners (Rom 1:7)? No one who abides in Christ continually sins in the sense of living a life of unrepentance and habitual sin, being indifferent about carrying out the will of God which is our sanctification or progression in holiness (1 Jn 3:6a; 1 Thess 4:3).

This sanctification involves not only abstaining from sexual immorality but also maintaining one's own vessel [body] in sanctification and honor (1 Thess 4:3-4). As Paul exhorts: "do not go on presenting the members of your body to sin as instruments of unrighteousness; but present yourselves to God as those alive from the dead, and your members as instruments of righteousness to God" (Rom 6:13). Paul warned that "he who rejects this is not rejecting man but the God who gives His Holy Spirit to you" (1 Thess 4:8). This holy living is accomplished by relying on the power of the Holy Spirit by which one puts to death the deeds of the flesh and inherits eternal life (Rom 8:13). Paul said" "walk by the Spirit, and you will not carry out the desire of the flesh (Gal 5:16) for "those who practice such things will not inherit the kingdom of God" (Gal 5:21). "The wages of sin is death, but the free gift of God is eternal life in Christ Jesus our Lord" (Rom 6:23).

Notice that Paul calls Jesus "our Lord". Serving Jesus as Lord was Paul's life passion and teaching. For he said: "I count all things to be loss in view of the surpassing value of knowing Christ Jesus my Lord" (Phil 3:8a). After all, that was the Lord's call on his life. Jesus' call on Paul's life is clear: "...for this purpose I have appeared to you, to appoint you a minister and a witness to open their eyes so that they may turn from darkness to light and from the dominion of Satan to God, that they may receive forgiveness of sins and an inheritance among those who have been sanctified by faith in Me" (Acts 26:18).

Sanctification is an ongoing spiritual transformation, a world renouncing process accomplished by having the mind renewed by the Spirit of God and enlightened by the truth of God, rather than allowing the body to be conformed to this world (Rom 12:1-2). Those progressing in sanctification are seeking the better, heavenly kingdom as lovers of God rather than returning to their love affair with the world. "God is not ashamed to be called their God" (Heb 11:13-16).

John warns those to whom he writes who "believe in the name of the Son of God" (1 Jn 5:13) to guard themselves from idols (1 Jn 5:21), "for all that is in the world, the lust of the flesh and the lust of the eyes and the boastful pride of life, is not from the Father, but is from the world. The world is passing away, and also its lusts; but the one who does the will of God abides forever" (1 Jn 2:15-17). John later made it clear that the "marriage of the Lamb would come for His bride who made herself ready by being clothed in fine, bright and clean linen which he describes as the "righteous acts of the saints" (Rev 19:7-8). Such separated, sanctified holy ones are those belonging to Jesus, the divine Bridegroom.

OCTOBER 5

"Everyone recognizes that Stephen was Spirit-filled when he was performing wonders. Yet, he was just as Spirit-filled when he was being stoned to death." Leonard Ravenhill

EVANGELISM THAT WINS

If one feels called to evangelize in very hostile places it is wise that intensive spiritual warfare prayer, Holy Spirit power and godly praise precede and prevail throughout such activity. Hostility to the true Gospel is Satan instigated and must be countered by exercising Holy Spirit power with divine authority and proclaiming the name of Jesus. Only in this way may evil principalities and powers be effectively resisted and routed. Though one may see little fruit prolonged preaching to stiff-necked haters of truth, proper evangelism should engage the wicked spiritual forces which energize such opponents of the gospel.

Jesus never spent much time preaching in extremely hostile environments occupied by those who hate God and His truth. We read: "The Pharisees went out, and counseled together against Him, as to how they might destroy Him. But Jesus, aware of this, withdrew from there. And many followed Him, and He healed them all" (Mt 12:14-15). Jesus left the truth bashers alone and attended to the Truth seekers. Jesus instructed His evangelists saying: "Do not give what is holy to dogs, and do not throw your pearls before swine, or they will trample them under their feet, and turn and tear you to pieces" (Mt 7:6). "Any place that does not receive you or listen to you, as you go out from there, shake the dust off the soles of your feet for a testimony against them" (Mk 6:11; Mt 10:14; Lk 9:5, 10:11).

They would depart such hostile, unreceptive areas and go "throughout the villages, preaching the gospel and healing everywhere" to apparently more receptive crowds who were attracted to their message and powerful healings (Lk 9:6, 11). Jesus taught that those who would come to Him were those affected by the conviction of the Holy Spirit (Jn 16:8-11), were drawn by Him (Jn 12:31) and were being taught by the God of heaven (Jn 6:45).

But when the deceived and hostile unbelieving Jews incited support for their cause and instigated a persecution against the early church preachers like Paul and Barnabas driving them away, these preachers in turn "shook the dust off their feet in protest against them and went to Iconium" to evangelize in more fruitful environments (Acts 13:52, 4:1). When opposition arose, the gospel preachers spoke boldly of God's grace and preached the good news about the kingdom of God and the name of Jesus Christ and casting out demons and performing signs and great miracles to those who were receptive (Acts 8:5-7,12-13; 14:3).

Likewise, Jesus rebuked proud religious leaders and upset their demons as He arrived. He didn't ignore their sin but called them blind guides, hypocrites, serpents, brood of vipers and sons of the devil (Mt 23:24, 25, 33, Jn 8:44). Jesus knew what inspired and energized His opponents as did the apostle Paul who taught that "our struggle in not against flesh and blood, but against the rulers, against the powers, against the world forces of this darkness, against the spiritual forces of wickedness in the heavenly places" (Eph 2:1, 6:12; 2 Tim 2:26).

The New Testament gives many examples of biblical, effective and power evangelism. Jesus instructed His disciples to preach saying: "the kingdom of God is at hand'" (Mt 10:6-7). The apostle Paul later elaborated on this kingdom as encompassing the righteousness of God, peace with men if possible, and joy of heart all accomplished by the power of the Holy Spirit (Rom 14:17; 3:24-26; 12:18; Gal 5:22). This often included the Spirit's delivering power over demons (Mt 12:28). And to demonstrate such kingdom preaching Jesus told His sent out evangelists to "heal the sick, raise the dead, cleanse the lepers, cast out demons" (Mt 10:8). The early Pentecostal preachers like Philip likewise preached the good news about the kingdom of God and the name of Jesus Christ, performing signs and great miracles, including the departure of unclean spirits and healing of the paralyzed and lame (Acts 8:4-8, 12-13; Rom 15:18-20).

Thus the early church evangelistic preaching campaigns were not conducted with persuasive words of wisdom, apologetic expertise or by throwing gospel tracks into the wind. Rather they were performed "in demonstration of the Spirit and of power" (1 Cor 2:4). Such truth and power encounters would encourage those who believed not to rest their faith on the wisdom of men but on the power of God (1 Cor 2:5).

OCTOBER 6

"You can have all of your doctrines right, yet still not have the presence of God." Leonard Ravenhill

DISCIPLESHIP THAT LASTS

Biblical discipleship is perhaps the most neglected spiritual discipline practiced today in spite of it being Jesus' last and most important mission command to His disciples. Jesus described discipleship this way: "Go therefore and make disciples of all the nations, baptizing them in the name of the Father and the Son and the Holy Spirit, teaching them to observe all that I commanded you; and lo, 'I am with you always, even to the end of the age'" (Mt 28:19-20). The apostle Paul after directing Titus in the appointment of elders in every city, (Tit 1:5), later reminded him saying "the grace of God has appeared, bringing salvation to all men, disciplining us to deny ungodliness and worldly desires and to live sensibly, righteously and godly in this present age" (Tit 2:11-12). The early church apostles and disciples obeyed, for "After they had preached the gospel to that city and had made many disciples, they returned to Lystra and to Iconium and to Antioch, strengthening the souls of the disciples encouraging them to continue in the faith, and saying, 'Through many tribulations we must enter the kingdom of God'" (Acts 14:21-22).

Such committed disciples "upset the world" rather than being conformed to the world (Acts 17:6). They had been properly instructed and were prepared for opposition for they knew "it had been granted for Christ's sake, not only to believe in Him, but also to suffer for His sake" (Phil 1:29). A very good picture of how Paul discipled is seen in his training of Timothy: "But you followed my teaching, conduct, purpose, faith, patience, love, perseverance, persecutions, and sufferings" (2 Tim 3:10-11a). They were not seeking their "best life now", but were obedient to the Lord's command to teach His followers the importance of obeying all that He commanded. They knew that Jesus is the source of eternal salvation to those who obey Him (Heb 5:9). For Jesus taught that without obedience to Him, one cannot claim Him as Lord (Lk 6:46), and without confessing Him as Lord, one is not saved out of the world (Rom 10:9a).

Satan is ever so busy, disguising his own sent ones, his false apostles, who parade as servants of righteousness (2 Cor 13-15), conjuring up speculations and every lofty thing raised up against the knowledge of God (2 Cor 10:5a). Such last day demonic doctrines and lying thoughts must be taken captive "to the obedience of Christ (1 Tim 4:1; 2 Cor 10:5b). Such false preachers are not interested in changing your character, but only in the change in your pocketbooks, preaching a prosperity gospel and other ear tickling messages, full of hype, but devoid of hope, with disdain for the true gospel and heart piercing sermons.

True change in character and discipleship occurs when we work out our salvation with fear and trembling, knowing that God "is at work in us, both to will and to work for His good pleasure (Phil 2:12-13). This is not self righteousness, but God reverence, for the Psalmist says: "If You, LORD, should mark iniquities, O Lord, who could stand? But there is forgiveness with You, that You may be feared" (Ps 130:3-4).

OCTOBER 7

"The Prince of the power of the air seems to bend all the force
of his attack against the spirit of prayer." Andrew Bonar

An example of warfare praying, anointed praising and promise claiming while evangelizing in hostile environments may resemble this: Lord Jesus, I am thankful that You rescued me from the domain of darkness and have transferred me to your kingdom (Col 1:13). I praise You that I have been empowered by the Holy Spirit sent from on high (Lk 24:49) to be your witness to this lost world (Act 1:8). Lord, it is by your authority and as your ambassador I go out to evangelize and make disciples of those who believe (Mt 28:18-20). God, direct me to where the Lord is drawing and where the Spirit is convicting. Help me to correct with gentleness those who are in opposition if perhaps You may grant them repentance leading to the knowledge of the truth and they may come to their senses and escape from the snare of the devil, having been held captive by him to do his will (2 Tim 2:25-26). May their eyes be opened and their wills be enabled to turn from darkness to light and from the dominion of Satan to God so they may receive forgiveness of sins and an inheritance among those who have been sanctified by faith in Jesus (Jn 12:31-32; 16:8; Acts 26:18), rather than resist Your grace that brings salvation to all (Tit 2:11). Lord, I realize that the god of this world has blinded the minds of the unbelieving to the light of the gospel (2 Cor 4:4). Train my hands for war and by fingers are battle (Ps 144:1), so I can use the sword of the Spirit properly, seeing your desire accomplished (Eph 6:17; 1 Tim 2:4).

Lord, You came to take away sins (1 Jn 3:5), so that the lost may have life and have it abundantly and eternally (Jn10:10b; Rom 6:22-23), by not living in sin but dying to sin (1 Pet 2:24; Rom 6:11). Lord, You are not wishing for any to perish, but for all to come to repentance (2 Pet 3:9). Lord, You came to set free those who are oppressed and to bring release to the captives (Lk 4:18). Help me to be filled and led by the Holy Spirit, walking wisely, making the most of my time in exposing the unfruitful deeds of darkness because the days are evil (Eph 5:11,15-18). I know that even in hostile environments, I will overwhelmingly conquer through the Lord who loved me (Rom 8:37). For greater is the Holy Spirit who resides in me, that the devil who is in the world (1 Jn 4:4). I will be strong in the Lord and in the strength of His might (Eph 6:10). Heavenly Father, I put on all your supplied spiritual armor and stand firm against the devil, resisting him in this evil day so that he will flee (Eph 6:11-13; Jam 4:7). Deliver your evangelistic servants from the evil one, for Yours is the kingdom and the power and the glory forever, Amen (Mt 6:13).

OCTOBER 8

"Rightly understood, faith is not a substitute for moral conduct but a means toward it. The tree does not serve in lieu of fruit but as an agent by which fruit is secured. Fruit, not trees, is the end God has in mind in yonder orchard; so Christ-like conduct is the end of Christian faith." A.W. Tozer

DISCIPLESHIP: THE GREAT OMISSION AND WHY

Jesus commanded it: "All authority has been given to Me in heaven and on earth. Go therefore and make disciples of all the nations, baptizing them in the name of the Father and the Son and the Holy Spirit, teaching them to observe all that I commanded you; and lo, I am with you always, even to the end of the age" (Mt 28:18-20).

Jesus lived it: "Follow Me, and I will make you fishers of men" (Mt 4:19).

The early church practiced it: "After they had preached the gospel to that city and had made many disciples, they returned to Lystra and to Iconium and to Antioch, strengthening the souls of the disciples encouraging them to continue in the faith, and saying, 'Through many tribulation we must enter the kingdom of God" (Act 14:21-22).

Paul modeled it: "Now you [Timothy] followed my teaching, conduct, purpose, faith, patience, love, perseverance, persecutions, and sufferings... to live godly in Christ Jesus" (2 Tim 3:10-12).

The devil despises it: "Be on guard...I know that after my departure savage wolves will come in among you, not sparing the flock; and from among your own selves [elders] men will arise, speaking perverse things, to draw away the disciples after them" (Acts 20:28-30). "For we wanted to come to you—I, Paul, more than once—and Satan thwarted us" (1 Thes 2:18).

Many church leaders shun it, because it takes time, work, knowledge and commitment. Most today are too busy with administration, too lazy in spiritual discipline, too unskilled in discipleship and too uncommitted to the great commission to become effective disciplers. Every God fearing, Jesus serving, Bible believing, Spirit-filled pastor should encourage and call those sitting on the pews to come forward and get discipled. That is a real altar call. Be baptized into discipleship and your life will never be the same.

OCTOBER 9

"If a man will stand before God he will never kneel before men." Leonard Ravenhill

MODERN HYPER GRACE IS A DISGRACE.

The modern hyper grace is a product of the increasing deception in these last days in which false and faddish religious teachings abound. Biblical illiteracy and not being Holy Spirit taught nor properly equipped for Christian service leaves new borns "to be tossed here and there by waves, and carried about by every wind of doctrine, by craftiness in deceitful scheming" " (Eph 4:14a). Consequently, New Age religion, emergent theology, contemplative spirituality, prosperity preaching, progressive Christianity, ecumenical Chrislam and other false teachings are blowing through the Church. The hyper grace movement and its "effortless" Christianity brainchild is refuted by 1 John in particular and biblical spirituality in general. Concerning last day deceptions and myths, Paul warned: "For the time will come when they will not endure sound doctrine; but wanted to have their ears tickled, they will accumulate for themselves teachers in accordance to their own desires, and will turn away their ears from the truth and will turn aside to myths" (2 Tim 4:3-4). "But the Spirit explicitly says that in the later times some will fall away from the faith, paying attention to deceitful spirits and doctrines of demons" (1 Tim 4:1).

John warned of last day deception that undermines righteous living. He wrote: "These things I have written to you concerning those who are trying to deceive you...If you know that He is righteous, you know that everyone also who practices righteousness is born of Him" (1 Jn 2:26, 29). "Little children, make sure no one deceives you; the one who practices righteousness is righteous, just as He is righteous" (1 Jn 3:7). Righteous living demands repeated confession of sin and repentance or turning away from sin. Thus John's promise and exhortation: "If we confess our sins, He is faithful and righteous to forgive us our sins and to cleanse us from all unrighteousness" (1 Jn 1:9).

Paul exhorted: "keep the commandment without sin or reproach until the appearing of our Lord Jesus Christ" (1 Tim 6:14). There will be many false apostles, deceitful workers, disguising themselves as apostles sent by Christ appearing to be servants of righteousness (2 Cor 11:13-15). Such will be effective in drawing away masses from hearing and practicing the "whole purpose" of

God, particularly concerning repentance toward God and faith and ongoing obedience to our Lord Jesus Christ and the gospel of the grace of God (Acts 20:21, 24, 27, 30). The followers of false hyper grace don't like hearing about righteousness, self-control and the judgment to come which the apostle Paul discussed when speaking about exercising faith in Christ (Acts 24:24-25). The true grace of God has appeared, "bringing salvation to all men, instructing us to deny ungodliness and worldly desires and to live sensibly, righteously and godly in the present age" (Tit 2:11-12).

Any teaching that undermines holiness, confession of sin and repentance from sin is another ear tickling message that will not equip Christians for the Lord's work. The Bible often stresses the importance of being cleansed from all sin. Paul exhorted the Corinthian believers saying: "Therefore, having these promises, beloved, let us cleanse ourselves from all defilement of flesh and spirit, perfecting holiness in the fear of God" (2 Cor 7:1). Such behavior is required for one to be most effectively used by God: "Therefore, if anyone cleanses himself for these things, he will be a vessel for honor, sanctified, useful to the Master, prepared for every good work" (2 Tim 2:21). Jesus exhorted the church at Sardis: "Wake up, and strengthen the things that remain, which were about to die, for I have not found your deeds completed in the sight of My God. So remember what you have received and heard; and keep it and repent. Therefore if you do not wake up, I will come like a thief, and you will not know at what hour I will come to you: (Rev 3:2-3).

In light of the soon return of the Lord it is foolish to take confession of sin and righteous living lightly. On the other hand, we must be careful to make the most of our time, because the days are evil, time is short, the will of God is clear and the Lord's return is near. The will of God is our sanctification, separation from the world and personal holiness produced by the ministry of the Holy Spirit (1 Thess 4:3-4, 8). After all, God chose us in Christ before the foundation of the world that we should be holy and blameless before Him (Eph1:4). Such a spiritual state requires continual confession of sin and repentance from sin, for we can not say we never sin, lest we become deceived and speak lies. (1 Jn 1:8, 10).

Any teaching that redefines the grace of God into something that under-mines holy living and takes sin lightly is a teaching contrary to our Master and Lord Jesus Christ (Jude 4). Any teaching that does not take ongoing sin seriously by undermining the necessity of confession of sin and repentance from sin will only bring the judgment of God, insult to the Spirit of grace and obstruction to the believer's sanctification (Heb 10:26-30). When the time comes that God ceases to get angry at sin, He will no longer be holy, and He will no longer be a God worth serving. He will no longer be the God of the Bible, but a figment of man's carnal imagination.

OCTOBER 10

"It is either all of Christ or none of Christ! I believe
we need to preach again a whole Christ to the world
- a Christ who does not need our apologies, a Christ
who will not be divided, a Christ who will either be
Lord of all or will not be Lord at all!" A.W. Tozer

JESUS AS LORD AND SAVIOR

Or to say it another way: Is the Lord Jesus Christ on the throne of your heart (1 Pet 3:15) or is the "Self" still on the throne? Are you walking in newness of life as a new creature in Christ, as a sober and alert newborn citizen of heaven (Rom 6:4; 2 Cor 5:17; Jn 3:3, 5; Phil 3:20; 1 Thes 5:6-8; 1 Pet 5:8) or you still sleeping in the bed with the world, living the old same way? "Therefore if anyone is in Christ, he is a new creature, the old things passed away; behold, new things have come" (2 Cor 5:17).

What passed away and what is new? We passed away, having died to sin and to self. It is written: "And He died for all that they who live might no longer live for themselves, but for Him who died and rose again on their behalf" (2 Cor 5:15). That is how Paul preached, for he said: "For we do not preach ourselves but Christ as Lord" (2 Cor 4:5a). Satan hates such hard preaching. He prefers the soft preaching that tickles ears rather than pierces hardened hearts (2 Tim 4:3; Acts 2:37).

Paul elaborates on Satan's opposition to such holiness preaching regarding sin: "And even if our gospel is veiled, it is veiled to those who are perishing, in whose case the god of this world has blinded the minds of the unbelieving so that they might not see the light of the gospel of the glory of Christ, who is the image of God" (2 Cor 4:3, 4). But in spite of the devil's efforts, "whenever a person turns to the Lord", the veil is taken away, so that the true Lord can be seen, understood and followed (2 Cor 3:16-18).

Let us arise from the dead (Eph 5:14) and walk in newness of life (Rom 6:4). For we are risen with Christ and clothed with Him (Gal 3:27). He has become to us, "righteousness, and sanctification, and redemption" (1 Cor 1:30). Don't neglect our so great a salvation for a lazy salvation (Heb 2:3). Remember the apostle Paul's passion: "My children, with whom I am again in labor until Christ be formed in you" (Gal 4:19). If the true and all sufficient Lord lives in us, we will not be deceived and deficient.

OCTOBER 11

"The only fear I have is to fear to get out of the will of God. Outside of the will of God, there's nothing I want, and in the will of God there's nothing I fear, for God has sworn to keep me in His will." A.W. Tozer

There is no need for any demon to overpower you, temptation to control you, lie to deceive you, situation to discourage you, trial to stumble you, lack to concern you, sin to ensnare you, accusation to condemn you, nor worry to trouble you. You belong to the King of kings and Lord of lords, to the Shepherd and Guardian of your soul; to the Wonderful Counselor, Mighty God, Eternal Father, Prince of Peace and the Holy and Righteous One (Is 9:6; Acts 3:14). God continues to reign supremely on the earth (Ps 103:19; Acts 4:28) and desires to rule supernaturally and triumphantly in your life (Phil 2:13; Rom 5:17, 8:37; 2 Cor 2:14). Our heavenly Father is still making all His enemies a footstool for His feet, submitted under those who bring good news of good things to bad people in these evil days (Heb 1:13; 10:13; Rom 10:15; Acts 8:12).

So let's get to stepping, for God has "given you authority to tread on serpents and scorpions and over all the power of the enemy, and nothing will injure you" (Lk 10:19).

"His divine power has granted to us everything pertaining to life and godliness, through the true knowledge of Him who called us by His own glory and excellence. For He has granted to us His precious and magnificent promises, so that by them you may become partakers of the divine nature, having escaped the corruption that is in the world by lust" (1 Pet 1:3-4). "But in all these things we overwhelmingly conquer through Him who loved us" (Rom 8:37). "For whatever is born of God overcomes the world; and this is the victory that has overcome the world—our faith" (1 Jn 5:4).

OCTOBER 12

"The winter prepares the earth for the spring, so do afflictions sanctified prepare the soul for glory." Richard Sibbes

GRACE THAT ENABLES

God's supernatural enabling and saving grace is seen throughout the Bible. Christians must not receive the grace of God in vain by not relying on His grace for holy living (Tit 2:11-12). They must resist insulting the Spirit of grace by persistent sinning (Heb 10:26-29) and stand on His grace in holy living (1 Pet 5:12; 1:15-16). Scripture exhorts believers to follow the apostle Paul's example and consider his teaching on the subject of grace (1 Cor 4:16; 11:1; 2 Cor 8:9; Col 2:6). "But by the grace of God I am what I am, and His grace toward me did not prove vain; but I labored even more than all of them, yet not I, but the grace of God with me" (1 Cor 15:10). "For this reason, I endure all things for the sake of those who are chosen, so that they also may obtain the salvation which is in Christ Jesus and with it eternal glory" (2 Tim 2:10).

Those who inherit eternal life walk in Holy Spirit enabled obedience (Heb 5:9) and perseverance (Heb 10:35-39). The Holy testifies and gives assurance to such ones, for Paul wrote: "The Spirit Himself testifies with our spirit that we are children of God" (Rom 8:16). Peter exhorted those had received the faith to make certain of their calling: "Therefore, brethren, be all the more diligent to make certain about His calling and choosing you, for as long as your practice these things, you will never stumble; for in this way the entrance into the eternal kingdom of our Lord and Savior Jesus Christ, will be abundantly supplied to you" (2 Pet 1:1, 10-11). So thanks ought to be given to God whose grace not only saves but also enables and keeps those who receive, walk and stand on it.

OCTOBER 13

"A man who loves you the most is the man who tells you the most truth about yourself." Robert Murray M'Cheyne

IS OBEDIENCE OPTIONAL FOR ENTERING HEAVEN?

Biblical faith and obedience are inseparable in the Bible. John says it this way: "He who believes in the Son has eternal life; but he who does not obey the Son will not see life, but the wrath of God abides on him" (Jn 3:36). Merely hearing or talking without obeying and walking is not a sign of one possessing eternal life. John records Jesus saying: "Truly, truly, I say to you, he who hears My word, and believes Him who sent Me, has eternal life, and does not come into judgment, but has passed out of death into life" (Jn 5:24). Paul taught salvation by faith as well as the necessity of continuing on in faith, when it comes to inheriting eternal life. This righteousness of God is obtained through faith in Jesus Christ (initial saving act of believing), and kept by all those who believe (present participle indicated ongoing practicing faith)" (Rom 3:22). Elsewhere Paul said concerning the promise of eternal life: "But the Scripture has shut up everyone under sin, so that the promise by (saving) faith in Jesus Christ might be given to those who believe (have persevering faith) " (Gal 3:22).

The writer of Hebrews makes this same clear distinction speaking of those who enter eternal rest having heard and received the gospel. He says: "For indeed we have had good news preached to us, just as they also, but the word they heard did not profit them, because it was not united by faith in those who heard. For we who have believed enter that rest" (Heb 4:2, 3). The defining characteristic marking those entering eternal rest is the life of faith and obedience. Thus the same author says Jesus having been made perfect, became "to all those who obey Him the source of eternal life" (Heb 5:9). It is not merely a one time altar confession, but life long obedience that characterizes those who will enter heaven. God will render to every person according to their deeds: "to those who by perseverance in doing good seek for glory and honor and immortality, eternal life; but to those who are selfishly ambitious and do not obey the truth, but obey unrighteousness, wrath and indignation" (Rom 2:6-8).

Eternal life is a present result and future reward of a sanctified life. It is not received out of a mere empty, temporary and fruitless confession. Paul says: "But now having been freed from sin and enslaved to God, you derive your benefit, resulting in sanctification, and the outcome, eternal life" (Rom 6:22). John was clear in describing how one could be assured of possessing eternal life. It was by practicing continual faith: "These things I have written to you who believe in the name of the Son of God, so that you may know that you have eternal life" (1 Jn 5:13). Peter also understood this well. Speaking to the chosen of God who continue to believe in God during bad times, such ones obtain as the outcome of their faith the salvation of their souls (1 Pet 1:1, 9). Such are protected by the power of God through faith for a salvation ready to be revealed in the last time (1 Pet 1:5). God says: "My righteous one shall live by faith; and if he shrinks back, My soul has on pleasure in Him" (Heb 10:38). The author of Hebrews clearly characterizes himself and his heaven bound believers as those persevering in faith: "But we are not of those who shrink back to destruction, but of those who have faith to the preserving of the soul" (Heb 10:39).

Persevering faith does not mean sinless perfection or that the believer never sins. Rather it characterizes on-going sanctification or the progressive removal of sin. Fortunately, when we sin, the blood of Jesus our Advocate cleans up our mess when we confess ours sins and walk in the light (1 Jn 1:7,9, 2:1-2). The Christian's pursuit of holiness is a lifelong forward progress achieved by the power of the Holy Spirit (Rom 8:13-14; Gal 5:16). The mind is transformed by the Word of God when taught by the Spirit of God so we will abide in the Son of God (Rom 12:1-2; 1 Jn 2:20, 27). The sanctified believer is promised ultimate and eternal perfection. The Scripture states that God "has perfected for all time those who are being sanctified" (Heb 10:14). For without sanctification no one will see the Lord" (Heb 12:14)

Consequently, Paul labored so the chosen of God would indeed obtain final salvation from God: "For this reason I endure all things for the sake of those who are chosen so that they also may obtain the salvation which is in Christ Jesus and with it eternal glory" (2 Tim 2:10). Peter likewise warned and urged believers saying: "Therefore, brethren, be all the more diligent to make certain about His calling and choosing you; for as long as your practice these things (godly traits listed in 1:5-8), you will never stumble; for in this way the entrance into the eternal kingdom of our Lord and Savior Jesus Christ will be abundantly supplied to you" (2 Pet 1:10-11). In Hebrews we read: "And we desire that each one of you show the same diligence so as to realize the full assurance of hope until the end, so that you will not be sluggish, but imitators of those who through faith and patience inherit the promises" (Heb 6:11-12).

It was Paul's desire that those who possessed the hope of eternal life which God promised long ago (Tit 1:2), those justified by God's grace, would also be made (aorist passive subjective, denoting possibility) heirs of such a hope (Tit 3:7). The devil has always sought to deceive and obstruct those hoping to obtain the promise of eternal life. He often does this by deceiving such ones into thinking they are securely saved while yet remaining unrepentant and serving sin (1 Jn 2:25-26, 3:7; cf. Rev 2,3).

Such ones "want their cake and eat it too". But the cake of Jesus' wedding will only be eaten by those who "have made themselves ready... clothed in fine linen, bright and clean...the righteous acts of the saints" (Rev 19:7-9). Eternal rest and the New Jerusalem will not be inhabited by the unbelieving (Heb 3:19; Rev 3:8), but by those who overcome; those who believe in the name of the Son of God (Rev 21:7; 1 Jn 5:4, 13), the risen Lord and Savior (Rom 10:9, 10; 2 Cor 4:5). "Behold, I am coming quickly and My reward is with Me, to render to every man according to what he has done...Blessed are those who wash their robes, so that they may have the right to the tree of life, and may enter by the gates into the city" (Rev 22:12,14).

OCTOBER 14

It is not enough to know the word of God. You must also know the God of the word.

JESUS AS LORD...."OH LORD, PLEASE TELL ME: IT AIN'T SO!"

Believers in the early Church had it right. When asked: "Sirs, what must I do to be saved" (Acts 16:30). Paul and Silas did not respond with "say this little prayer and ask Jesus into your heart". But instead: "Believe in the Lord Jesus, and you will be saved" (16:31). Paul preached that "if you confess with your mouth Jesus as Lord, and believe in your heart that God raised Him from the dead, you will be saved" (Rom 10:9). This was the apostle Paul's practice: "We do not preach ourselves but Christ Jesus as Lord" (2 Cor 4:5). "Therefore as you have received Christ Jesus the Lord, so walk in Him" (Col 2:7). Peter wrote: "Sanctify Christ as Lord in your hearts..." (1 Pet 3:15). Evangelism and altar invitations for salvation must make clear the necessity for the repentant sinner to be willing to submit himself or herself to Jesus as Lord as well as receiving Him as Savior. The lordship of Jesus is rejected by many today because it requires obedience which is a four letter word in contemporary churchianity with its easy believism, cheap grace and effortless Christianity. But true Christianity calls for a fruitful faith and changed behavior. Jesus said: "Why do you call Me, 'Lord, Lord,' and do not do what I say? (Lk 6:46) and "you will know them by their fruits" (Mt 7:20).

OCTOBER 15

"God's will is hard only when it comes up against our stubbornness, then it is as cruel as a ploughshare and as devastating as an earthquake." Oswald Chambers

There is too little fear of God and too much fear of men. There is too much intimidation and too little confrontation. Instead of running the race, too many "believers" run away from the race. The course many are concerned with finishing is the five course meal. The only faith many keep is the "saving" faith they once expressed once upon a time during a little prayer. More often than not, that bold life "changing" gesture of bravely slipping up the hand with every eye closed, every head bowed and no one looking around, proves to be nothing more than a timid lifting up of the hand. That "Sinner's Prayer" which never resulted in any change of behavior, proves to be nothing more than a prayer of an unrepentant sinner. Much more is required of the lost sinner if one is to have the right to the tree of life (Rev 22:14). "But the day of the Lord will come like a thief… what sort of people ought you to be in holy conduct and godliness, looking for and hastening the coming of the day of God…" (2 Pet 3:10a, 11b-12a). "The eyes of the LORD move to and fro throughout the earth that He may strongly support those whose heart is completely His" (2 Chron 16:9a).

OCTOBER 16

"We are never, never so much in danger of being proud as when we think we are humble." C.H. Spurgeon

We need an old time revival by God-called prophets who grieve the devil. In these last days God will raise up Spirit anointed prophets who are not afraid to rock the boat nor hesitant to cleanse the Temple of prosperity preachers, demonic poachers, false prophets and religious pro-moters. "Surely the Lord God does nothing unless He reveals His secret counsel to His servants the prophets" (Amos 3:7). One reason the house of God is in such a mess, is that false prophets, priests and teachers have invad-ed the Church. "The kings of the earth did not believe, nor did any of the inhabitants of the world, that the adversary and the enemy could enter the gates of Jerusalem, because of the sins of her prophets and the iniquities of her priests" (Lam 4:12-13a). And many prophets not sent by God promote themselves as God's special agents in this late hour. But God said: "If they had stood in My council, then they would have announced My words to My people, and would have turned them back from their evil way and from the evil of their deeds" (Jer 23:22).

Unfortunately, many arm chair theologians mistakenly believe God's prophets have all packed their bags and left town long, long ago. However, true Spirit filled New Testaments prophets still speak and are heard and are received by those who acknowledge God's true messengers. And these New Testament prophets will not be caught up with predicting the future or in reading someone's mail or with dispensing gold dust, angel feathers and dominion proclamations. Rather, they will "speak to men for edification and exhortation and consolation...so that all may learn and be exhorted" (1 Cor 14:3, 31). In some cases they may proclaim not so good news to those hiding secret sins (1 Cor 14:24-25). And don't hold your breath waiting for sin-loving pew dwellers so addicted to church junk food religion and pasto-ral devil's food cake to jump for joy when such prophets wake them up (Jer 23:21-22; Isa 30:9-11).

"As for them, whether they listen or not—for they are a rebellious house---you shall speak My words and they will know that a prophet has been among them" (Eze 2:5, 7). "And you, son of man, neither fear them nor fear their words, though thistles and thorns are with you and you sit on scorpions; neither fear their words nor be dismayed at their presence, for they are a rebellious house" (Eze 2:6). The time will come when "disaster will come upon disaster and rumor will be added to rumor; then they will seek a vision from a prophet, but the law will be lost from the priest and counsel for the elders" (Eze 7:26).

Beware of false prophets who tickle ears and console sinners, who proclaim peace when there is no peace; who breathe out eternal security to entombed sinners, when imminent judgment is knocking on the door. Those who value the Holy Spirit's anointing prophets will take up their holy mantle. Those who understand the times will properly line up for spiritual battle (1 Chron 12:33,38). Those who are wise will make the most of their time. Those who have faith will overcome the world. Those who persevere will be delivered in the end. Those who run the race will see the vision for the appointed time. Those with holy zeal will return to the great commission. Those who are holy will attend the heavenly wedding.

OCTOBER 17

"The essence of idolatry is the entertainment of thoughts about God that are unworthy of Him. The heaviest obligation lying upon the Christian Church today is to purify and elevate her concept of God until it is once more worthy of Him." A.W. Tozer

REWARDS FROM GOD OR RIGHT STANDING WITH GOD?

Many Christian leaders speak only of losing a few rewards in the future. So don't be overly concerned about living righteously today. You have a reserved seat in heaven so live as you please. You said "the prayer" and so you are good to go, so they say. The most common passage that clearly talks about rewards for service is 1 Corinthians 3 which addresses the right and wrong ways a Christian may build on the right foundation. We have to be careful how we go about building up the body of Christ. We are to walk in the works which God prepared beforehand allowing the divine Carpenter to build His Church, rather than relying on our own wisdom and strength, building with wood, hay and straw (Eph 2:10; Mt 6:18; 1 Cor 3:11-15).

Many of the Corinthian believers were carnal minded, remaining babes in Christ rather than having the mind of Christ (1 Cor 2:16; 3:1-3). They were following after men rather than after Christ (1 Cor 3:4-6). But to also read mere loss of rewards in other New Testament warning passages is unscriptural, for they mostly deal with one's right standing with God, not one's performance for Him.

2 Tim 4:7-8 is a fine example which clearly shows that it is the crown of righteousness, the true believer's acceptable and secure standing before the holy God for holy living that is in view and not a reward that may be lost because of carnal building. To say that one can choose not to fight the good fight nor to finish the course and nor keep the faith, and yet only lose a reward or two and yet still inherit eternal life cheapens saving grace beyond description. The Scripture says whoever makes himself a friend of the world makes himself an enemy of God (Jam 4:4) and only the one who does the will of God will live with God forever (1 Jn 2:15-17). The most important and enduring reward is eternal life to those who endure to the end (Mt 24:13), working out their salvation with fear and trembling (Phil 2:12-13). Such ones produce spiritual fruit, remain in the True Vine and perform deeds appropriate to repentance (Jn 15:1-8; Acts 26:20). They receive forgiveness of sins and an inheritance having been sanctified by faith in Him (Acts 26:18; Heb 10:14, 12:14).

Otherwise all that is expected for a Christian to inherit salvation is to only say a little sincere prayer, mentally repent for a little while, intellectually assent to Jesus as Savior, and maybe obey for a season. One is safe and secure in spite of how one lives. Such ones deny the importance of repentance, obedience, holiness and receiving Jesus as Lord. They would read Paul's statement in 2 Cor 5:17 this way: "If anyone is in Christ, he is a new creature, at least for a little while, if following Him becomes too hard". The Lord expects more, requires more, and will accept nothing less than for the true disciple to take up the cross and follow Him. For such followers Jesus promises a place in His mansion in heaven for those who served Him on earth. Jesus promised: "In My Father's house are many dwelling places; if it were not so, I would have told you; for I go to prepare a place for you… and where I am, you may be also…He who loves his life loses it; and he who hates his life in this world shall keep it to life eternal. If anyone serves Me, let him follow Me; and where I am, there shall My servant also be (Jn 14:1-2, 12:25-26a).

OCTOBER 18

*"It was the greatest honor God did to man that he
made man in the image of God; but it is the greatest
dishonor man has done to God that he has made
God in the image of man." Matthew Henry*

DON'T LET TRUTH DECAY DECEIVE YOU.

Jesus said "I am the way, the life and the truth" (Jn 14:6) and "the truth will make you free" (Jn 8:32). He prayed to His Father saying: "Sanctify them in the Truth, Thy Word is Truth" (Jn 17:17). He promised to send the

Spirit of Truth to guide His followers in all the truth (Jn 16:13) so that they might know the things of God and have the mind of Christ who is Truth (1 Cor 2:12, 16). The Holy Spirit is the true anointing that teaches us about all things (1 Jn 2:27). We are to love in deed and truth (1 Jn 3:18). Believers should expect God's truth to be available and discernible by simply reading what the inspired Scriptures say, without always having to interpret them to find out what they mean, or to misinterpret them to say what they want them to say.

Although God still gives to His Church teachers, prophets, and exhorters we must not be overly dependent on those Spirit gifted individuals when we have the indwelling heavenly gift of the Holy Spirit as our Teacher and Guide (1 Jn 2:27). Maybe if we would more often practice the presence of God (Is 57:15; 40:31; Ps 91:1-2), and "sit" at the feet of Truth (Lk 10:39) and enjoy fellowship with His Spirit of truth (2 Cor 13:14; Jn 16:13), we would not feel so distant from God and His truth.

OCTOBER 19

Like a mighty army moves the Church of God. Brothers,
we are treading where the Saints have trod. We are
not divided, all one body we are. One in hope and
Doctrine, One in charity. (words of a hymn)

The Kingdom of God which is "righteousness and peace and joy in the Holy Spirit" will not be accomplished through the political, judicial, educational, religious, economic, military systems of this fallen world. The Lord will claim final victory over the god of this world and his demons who energize the sons of disobedience (Eph 2:2) and who are held captive by him doing his will (2 Tim 2:26). This will be accomplished through His triumphant Church, sanctified by the Word and led by the Spirit. Such a repentant, cleansed and triumphant Church will overcome when He who overcame has finally crushed all His enemies under the feet. Those who proclaim the Good News of His Kingdom are under the headship of the Lord Jesus Christ (Heb 1:13; 10:12-13; Rom 16:20; Eph 5:23; Col 1:18). Jesus, the reigning King is soon to return and be married to His holy and blameless Bride, having no spot or wrinkle or any worldly leaven. So rejoice, lift up your heads for your redemption is drawing near.

OCTOBER 20

"Some preachers ought to put more fire into their sermons or more sermons into the fire." Vance Havner

HOW TO STAY SPIRITUAL IN SATAN'S WORLD

Jesus is the Head of the true Church (Eph 5:23; Col 1:18). Peter writes: "sanctify Christ as Lord in your hearts, always being ready to make a defense to everyone who asks you to give an account for the hope that is in you, yet with gentleness and reference" (1 Pet 3:15). If we give Him His proper place and have His mind, then His body, the Church corporately and Christians individually, will function biblically, properly, powerfully and victoriously (Eph 4:16). "For to this end Christ both died and lived again, that He might be Lord both of the dead and living" (Rom 14:9). The Lord Jesus Christ is to have first place in everything (Col 1:17).

With "Christ in you, the hope of glory" you have no need to be hopeless and in despair (Col 1:27). Having the mind of Christ your mind will not be led astray by false teachings and doctrines of demons (1 Cor 2:16). When experiencing true spiritual transformation you are no longer being conformed to the world, walking in darkness pleasing the god of this world and serving his idols Rom 12:2; 1 Cor 12:2, 10:20; Mt 4:3-10; 1 Jn 2:15-17). Instead, you can walk in newness of life, taste of the fruit of the Spirit and experience the Kingdom of God. (Rom 6:14; Gal 5:22-23; Rom 14:17).

Christians can't grow up as mature believers nor function as good soldiers unless they desire the sincere milk of the word like newborn babes (1 Pet 2:2), practice the strong meat of the word (Heb 5:14) and skillfully use, with the Holy Spirit's enablement, the word of God, their spiritual sword (Eph 6:17). God has chosen us in Christ "before the foundation of the world, that we should be holy and blameless before Him" (Eph 1:4). "How can a young man keep his way pure? By keeping it according to Thy word...Thy word I have treasured in my heart that I may not sin against Thee" (Ps 119:9, 11). "The steadfast of mind Thou wilt keep in perfect peace, because he trusts in Thee" (Is 26:3).

The battle is in the mind, "for the weapons of our warfare are not of the flesh, but divinely powerful for the destruction of fortresses, destroying speculations and every lofty thing raise up against the knowledge of God, and taking every thought captive to the obedience of Christ" (2 Cor 10:4-5). Those who properly guard their minds will experience greater victory in taking captive demonic thoughts, controlling the fiery restless tongue and better resisting devilish temptations. We can control these three terrible T's if we stay spiritual in Satan's world and let the risen Christ rule our mind and be the Lord of our heart.

OCTOBER 21

*"The Bible definitely is infallible, how else could it survive
so many years of bad preaching?" Leonard Ravenhill*

Easy believism, loose living, sin loving hyper grace, avoidance of repentance and the obsession to obtain "decisions" rather than making disciples, has filled churches with false converts. Paul had to remind the Christians in the churches of Galatia of their true Christian identity: "For all of you who were baptized into Christ have clothed yourselves with Christ" (Gal 3:27) and "those who belong to Christ Jesus have crucified the flesh with its passions and desires" (Gal 5:24). In Revelation 2 and 3 Jesus addressed many problems occurring in the churches, calling them to repent and return to being His Church. And even though the learned and sold out apostle Paul had taught night and day for three years in Ephesus and did not shrink from declaring anything that was profitable and teaching publicly and from house to house, solemnly testifying of both repentance toward God and faith in the Lord Jesus Christ, he still had to gather together and warn the elders about false teachers (Acts 20:20, 21, 27, 31). He forewarned them saying: "I know that after my departure savage wolves will come in among you, not sparing the flock; for from among your own selves men will arise, speaking perverse things, to draw away the disciples after them" (20:29-30).

So the New Testament is filled with exhortations to godly living and walking in newness of life (Rom 6:4), being led by the Spirit of God (Rom 8:14), being taught by the Spirit to abide in Christ (1 Jn 2:20, 27) and bearing real fruit, for a tree is known by its fruit (Jn 15:1f; Mt 7:20). Progress in sanctification is important because Christ is the source of eternal to all those who obey Him (Heb 5:9). He has perfected for all time those who are being sanctified (Heb 10:14). Without sanctification no one will see the Lord (Heb 12:14). For those who do not obey the gospel of our Lord Jesus (2 Thes 1:8) and who do not receive the love of the truth (2 Thess 2:10), will pay the penalty of eternal destruction away from the presence of the Lord (2 Thess 1:9).

Jesus said: "Why do you call Me Lord, Lord, and do not do what I say" (Lk 6:46)? Paul made it clear that not the hearers of the Law are just before God, but the doers of the law will be justified (Rom 2:13). You will know them by their fruit, not by their talk. Though you may have few friends and many a foe, in the end those who persevere in holiness will surely know where they will go. When He returns, they will be caught up to meet Him in the air.

OCTOBER 22

"Whenever, in any century, whether in a single heart or in a company of believers, there has been a fresh effusion of the Spirit, there has followed inevitably a fresh endeavor in the work of evangelizing the world." A. J. Gordon

Good morning, America, the Son has risen, the Spirit is raining on the Gospel seeds planted and God is bringing about His final harvest (Mt 24:14; 1 Cor 3:6). The devil hates to see such true fruit produced by truth abiding, Spirit filled believers, because such fruit exposes the unfruitful deeds of his darkness and sets his captives free. The devil loves to produce fruit attractive on the outside, but inside is rotten and full of worms. But the one who abides in the Tree of Life will not be tossed here and there by the winds of demonic doctrine so prevalent in these last days. Rather than being a tumble weed blown about by New Age winds from ancient Desert Fathers and contemporary Emergents, one can be a fruitful branch of the unmovable Tree of Life and worshiper of the heavenly Father in Spirit and Truth.

What Millenials are truly seeking today is not a new definition of Christianity but a new and bold demonstration of biblical Christianity. The lost will not be attracted to a fancy "Re-invented" Christianity, but to a fiery "Re-ignited" Christianity, one baptized with Holy Spirit fire from above, not with strange fire from below. Such a true revival may come when the lukewarm, complacent and deceived stop being bottle fed by best-selling professing Christian authors and New Age channelers who supposedly have "Conversations with God". Such ones who profess to be wise and enlightened have instead become fools stumbling in the dark. They reject the Truth and the Author and Perfector of Faith, the Lord Jesus Christ. They have exchanged the indwelling Spirit of Truth in favor of false inner guides. They take their stand on visions and appearances of "who knows what", rather than standing on the Rock and Him who knows all. One has to wonder how such a "Re-invented" Christianity which denies hell, Christ's substitutionary atonement and a future day of judgment will stand on Judgement Day, when the Judge of the living and the dead crashes their Emergent Party.

OCTOBER 23

"The Holy Ghost does not come upon methods, but upon men. He does not anoint machinery, but men. He does not work through organizations, but through men. He does not dwell in buildings, but men. He indwells the Body of Christ, directs its activities, distributes its forces, empowers its members." Samuel Chadwick

A WORD OR TWO ON SPIRITUAL WARFARE AND HAND-TO-HAND COMBAT

Spiritual warfare is a personal assault on the individual believer. Though the devil never ceases attacking the universal Church and local churches, he gains his stronghold through individual believers who aren't trained in spiritual warfare and who are ignorant of their spiritual enemies. Though corporate prayer and intercession by others is helpful, an individual can't rely on others to guard himself and secure victory in spiritual warfare. Every speculation or thought raised up against the knowledge of God has "to be taken captive to the obedience of Christ" in the battlefield of the believer's mind (2 Cor 10:5). We see an example of such an unguarded mind when Peter began to rebuke Jesus for talking about going to the cross. Jesus said to Peter: "Get behind Me, Satan! You are a stumbling block to Me; for you are not setting your mind on God's interests, but man's" (Mt 16:23).

Also the picture of putting on the divine armor mentioned in Ephesians 6 makes little sense if one doesn't consider "solo" combat. The Sword of the Spirit, the Word of God, is used by individuals in hand-to-hand combat. Satan, who is called "the accuser of our brethren" (Rev 12:10), always prowls about like a roaring lion seeking someone to devour (1 Pet 5:8) and anyone he can to falsely accuse and condemn (Rom 8:33-34; Zech 3:1-2). The combat strategy for the individual is to put on each piece of spiritual armor, including the shield of faith to extinguish Satan's fiery darts (Eph 6:16a) and the sword of the Spirit, the word of truth to destroy his lies (Eph 6:17; Jn 8:44; Jn 17:17). Each one must stand firm in the faith (1 Pet 5:9). Speaking the truth is the best way to combat the devil, just as Jesus did when tempted in the wilderness by telling the devil three times "it is written" (Mt 4:4,7,10).

Believers have to be on the alert lest savage wolves come, even amongst elders of churches, not sparing the flock (Acts 20:17, 29-31). Paul warned the gathered elders saying: "Be on guard for yourselves and for all the flock" (Acts 20:28a). Such wolves are demonically energized sons of disobedience (Eph 2:2) and often are held captive by the devil to do his will (2 Tim 2:26). Every bondservant of the Lord must act properly and wisely when confronting the devil's captives (2 Tim 2:24-25; Mt 10:16).

It surely is not up to the corporate church or the pastor only, to enter the spiritual battlefield. The believer wages battle against the schemes of the devil which may involve unforgiveness (2 Cor 2:11), conceitedness (1 Tim 3:6), reproach (1 Tim 3:7), lack of self-control in marriage (1 Cor 7:5), demonic doctrines (1 Tim 4:1), anger, (Eph 4:26-27), idolatry (1 Cor 10:7, 14, 20), materialism (Jam 4:4; 1 Jn 2:15-17, 5:19), and many other temptations and strongholds. Every individual is responsible for making wise use of all the supplied armor in spiritual warfare.

The overcoming Christian must know how to use the full of armor of God listed in Ephesians 6:10-18, as well as the weapons of love (1 Thess 5:8) and the weapons of righteousness (2 Cor 6:7). A well-guarded heart, not weighted down with dissipation and drunkenness and the worries of life (Lk 21:34) and a lifestyle disentangled in the affairs of everyday life are both vital for the overcoming soldier of the cross (2 Tim 2:3-4). This often neglected topic of spiritual warfare is one spiritual discipline that takes time to learn and self-discipline to master.

OCTOBER 24

*"I have nothing and possess all things.... The church today
has everything yet possesses nothing." Leonard Ravenhill*

HOW TO JUMP-START A STALLED CHURCH.

It is important that church leadership strongly encourages and equips the congregation to implement real discipleship training, devotion to corporate and individual prayer, effective altar and one-another minister within the church and loving outreach to the lost outside the church. Destruction of idols will prove to be greatly blessed such as replacing television with reading of revival books and biographies and family devotions. Biblical teaching on spiritual warfare and holiness and implementing lay-driven, Spirit-led, home fellowships could help many to break down strongholds, celebrate true recovery and properly function as holy and royal priests in the local assembly.

OCTOBER 25

*If 21st century churchianity would only follow the model of
the first century apostles, the modern day church wouldn't be
so lost. Reading 1 Thessalonians 1-2 would be a good place
to start, rather than a best seller by a church growth expert.*

THANK GOD THAT HE DIDN'T LEAVE THE HUMAN RACE DEAD IN SIN.

A part from God's love and grace, we would choose to stay in our depraved mess. Because lost sinners are alienated from God and are dead in their trespasses and sin, God had to make the first move (Rom 5:12; Eph 2:1). So the Bible says that while we were ungodly, helpless, sinners, and enemies of God (Rom 4:5, 5:6,8,10), His grace appeared making the gift of salvation available to all (Tit 2:11).

Everyone who has received the abundance of grace and of the gift of righteousness will reign in life through the One, Jesus Christ (Rom 5:17). Jesus draws all to Him (Jn 12:32). The Holy Spirit convicts the world concerning sin and righteousness and judgment (Jn 16:8). Jesus said: "It is written in the prophets, 'and they shall all be taught of God.' Everyone who has heard and learned from the Father, comes to Me" (Jn 6:45). "The heavens are telling of the glory of God; and their expanse is declaring the work of His hands" (Ps 19:1). "He has also set eternity in their heart" (Eccl 3:11). "For since the creation of the world His invisible attributes, His eternal power and divine nature have been clearly seen, being understood through what has been made, so that they are without excuse" (Rom 1:20). Even their conscience bears witness of God's moral laws (Rom 2:16).

Saving faith does not entail just a one-time confessional, but also a lifestyle of trusting. John says: "These things I have written to you who believe in the name of the Son of God, in order that you may know that you have eternal life" (1 Jn 5:13). The Greek verb construction denotes a lifestyle of faith. And John associates faith with obedience in Jn 3:36, by using two distinct verbs: "He believes in the Son has eternal life; but he who does not obey the Son shall not see life, but the wrath of God abides on him". Likewise, the author of Hebrew says concerning Jesus: "And having been made perfect, He became to all those who obey Him the source of eternal salvation" (Heb 5:9). The Lord does not impose His will and Gospel upon sinners, but extends His grace toward them, enabling them to respond. He draws them and proposes to them. When they receive His Gospel invitation and truly experience His visitation, the wise without hesitation will follow Him without reservation. God's prevenient grace enables lost sinners to receive or reject that gracious gift of salvation. Those who receive and believe He gives the right to become His children (Jn 1:12); to those who believe in the name of Jesus. And His name is Jesus: Lord and Savior.

OCTOBER 26

The One who raised you up will never let you down.

Though true Christians may feel out of place in today's world, they are in place for heaven's future rewards. Though a Christian may at times feel completely alone, he can be assured that in Christ he alone has been made complete (Col 2:10). In Christ he has been made a new creature (2 Cor 5:17) and in Christ he has been blessed with every spiritual blessing (Eph 1:3).

Sanctified or set apart believers rightly feel out of place, as strangers and aliens to the devil's wicked world and his governments (1 Pet 2:11). Even though they are hunted down by the politically correct and hated by the religiously corrupt, they are citizens of heaven and seated with Jesus who triumphantly overcame (Phil 3:20; Eph 2:6). They are loved and accepted by the Holy and Righteous One (Gal 2:20; Rom 5:5; Acts 3:14).

He is coming soon to finish crushing all His enemies under His feet. Though the masses may ridicule, the media brainwash and mainline religion compromise, it is only for a season. God will have the last laugh "He who sits in the heavens laughs, the Lord scoffs at them. Then He will speak to them in His anger and terrify them in His fury" (Ps 2:4-5). Man's foolishness will be revealed, his pride humbled, his excuses denied, his entitlements ended, and his rebellion rewarded. Because God "has fixed a day in which He will judge the world in righteousness through a Man whom He has appointed, having furnished proof to all men by raising Him from the dead" (Acts 17:31). The saints will judge and reign with the King, Jesus the Lord and Ruler of all (Phil 3:20; Jn 16:1-3).

OCTOBER 27

"If rich men only knew when they died, how . . . their relatives would scramble for their money, the worms for their bodies, and the devil for their souls, they would not be so anxious to save money!" William Tiptaft

THANKFULNESS IS MY DUE, BECAUSE JESUS PAID WHAT I OWED.

I am thankful that wherever I go He is there (Mt 28:20; Ps 139:7-10). Whenever I am down He lifts me up (Mt 11:28). Whenever I feel incomplete, He is my completeness (Col 2:10). Whenever I feel lack, He is my all (Eph 1:3, 3:8; 2 Cor 8:9). Whenever I feel overcome, He is my Overcomer (Rev 3:21; Jn 19:30; Col 2:15). Whenever there appears no way, He is the way (Jn 14:6). When my world falls apart, He holds it together (Col 1:17). Whenever I fall into the pit of sin, He raises me up to sit with Him (Eph 2:6). When it looks like Satan is winning, I am reminded that he was defeated (Col 2:15). When the devil tries to scare me and say

...mind him that Jesus said: "It is finished" (Jn 19:30).

...ike complaining He gets me praising (Eph 5:20). Praise

OCTOBER 28

"There is no rowing to paradise except upon
the stream of repenting tears. Till sin be bitter,
Christ will not be sweet." Thomas Watson

Just as Jesus healed all who were oppressed by the devil and cast out demons by the power of the Holy Spirit so are His followers to do likewise (Acts 10:38; Mt 12:28, Acts 8:4-13). Just as Jesus proclaimed: "Repent, for the kingdom of God is at hand" (Mt 4:17), His followers will do likewise, seeking first His kingdom and His righteousness (Mt 6:33), not selfish wants and powerless religion. "For the kingdom of God is not eating and drinking, but righteous, peace and joy in the Holy Spirit" (Rom 14:17). For what truly matters, is not seeking to have the Best Life Now, but seeking to know now Jesus Christ who is eternal life (Jn 17:3)

We are not to be anxious for tomorrow (Mt 6:34) nor fear those who kill the body, but are unable to kill the soul (Mt 10:28a), but fear God who will deliver us from every evil deed, and bring us safely to His heavenly kingdom (2 Tim 4:18). Of course this is accomplished by those who are submitted to the Lordship of the Son of God, empowered by the Spirit of God and nourished on the Word of God. These essential spiritual disciplines are much ignored by the popular megachurch of God. But God has always worked though His unpopular mighty Church.

OCTOBER 29

You will never begin to do the supernatural and walk on water while you stay in the pleasure cruise ship of institutional religion.

GET A SPIRITUAL LIFE. DON'T LET THE DEVIL STEAL YOURS.

Even if you are poor and miserable and wretched and blind and naked, God says: Repent and return unto me, and I will heal your backslidings (Hosea 14:4; Rev 3:17-19). Your forgiving and restoring heavenly Father opens blinded eyes, enlightens darkened minds, cleanses polluted hearts, washes dirty hands and puts praise back on silent lips. "And if you do well, will not your countenance be lifted up (1 Jn 1:9; Is 1:18; Is 42:3; Gen 4:7a)?

If your days seem to be consumed in smoke, your bones scorched like a hearth, your heart smitten like grass which withers away, and your groaning deafening to your ears, and you resemble a pelican of the wilderness (Ps 102:3-5); remember, His light will dispel the darkness, His fire will evaporate the fog and His wind will clear the smog. Then you can mount up with wings like an eagle and soar to the Son (Is 40:31).

OCTOBER 30

*"The devil is not fighting religion. He's too smart
for that. He is producing a counterfeit Christianity,
so much like the real one that good Christians are
afraid to speak out against it." Vance Havner.*

IMITATE AND MEDIATE, DON'T CAPITULATE TO FALSE RELIGION.

We need to practice both: imitate the godly and meditate on the Word. Know Christ in whom are hidden all the treasures of wisdom and knowledge (Col 2:3). Follow Him who is the Way (Mt 4:19; Jn 14:6). Preach Him who is the Truth (Col 1:28; Acts 8:12; Jn 14:6). Imitate Him who our Life (1 Cor 11:1; Col 3:3-4). Meditate on the written Word of God, which is our food (Ps 4:4; 119:148; Jer 16:15; Ps 119:103; Jn 1:1, Mt 4:4; 1 Tim 4:6; 1 Pet 2:2). "Finally, brethren, whatever is true, whatever is honorable, whatever is right, whatever is pure, whatever is lovely, whatever is of good repute, if there is any excellence and if anything worthy of praise, let your mind dwell on these things" (Phil 4:8). "Therefore if you have been raised up with Christ....set you mind on the things above, not on the things that are on earth" (Col 3:1-2). It is through the perseverance and the encouragement of the Scriptures we have hope (Rom 15:4).

Thus says the LORD, "Stand by the ways and see and ask for the ancient paths, where the good way is, and walk in it; and you shall find rest for your souls" (Jer 6:16a). In this way Christians can avoid being deceived by New Age, novel end time religion and demonic doctrines and avoid unnecessary discipline by God's hand. Yet many today fail to do this and don't walk on the narrow and straight path. "But they said, 'We will not walk in it.'

And I set watchmen over you, saying 'Listen to the sound of the trumpet!' But they said, 'We will not listen,'" (Jer 6:16b-17). So what would a true watchman of God proclaim against such a people? He would surely not say that peace and prosperity and the "Best Life Now" are here for the grabbing. He would not lie saying there is no need for correction. He would not promise that mega-churches, mighty mantles, magnificent anointings and Super Apostles will regain dominion and bring in the Kingdom. A watchmen who has eyes to see and ears to hear would warn and proclaim God's announced judgment. "Therefore hear, O nations, and know, O congregation, what is among them. Hear O earth; behold, I am bringing disaster on this people, the fruit of their plans, because they have not listened to My words, and as for My law, they have rejected it also" (Jer 6:18-19).

OCTOBER 31

"Sometimes your medicine bottle has on it, "Shake well before using." That is what God has to do with some of His people. He has to shake them well before they are ever usable."Vance Havner.

MILLENNIALS WANT TO RUN THE RACE NOT TREAD WATER.

The millennials are looking for the real thing. They are tired of powerless religion, circus shows, skits, hype, clowns running loose in the sanctuary or pulpit promoters full of hot air and yet are frozen; counting noses and nickels while courting demons. Many churches today, in seeking to become big, fish for the lost using circus nets. They catch the naive fish, never clean them, and allow them to swim in their religious murky waters, Sunday after Sunday, until finally they are swallowed by the piranha swimming outside the door. Modern churches and mega churches often become mega shallow pools where children play in the water, but never get out and run the race. Millennials want to go somewhere and run the race, not tread water going nowhere.

NOVEMBER 1

"I consider that the chief dangers which will confront the twentieth century will be: Religion without the Holy Spirit; Christianity without Christ; Forgiveness without regeneration; Morality without God and Heaven without Hell." William Booth.

Why be brainwashed by false teachers, whitewashed by false religious leaders, and remain unwashed of the world's dirt? Why be abused by ravenous wolves who have invaded the Laodicean Church, who see false visions, utter lying divinations, twist truth and peddle the Word? Instead, why not have your mind truly renewed by the Spirit of Truth (Rom 12:1-2; Eph 3:16), your self cleansed from all defilement of flesh and spirit (2 Cor 7:1), your life fully washed by the Word of God (Eph 5:26; Ps 119:9, 11) and your soul lovingly cared for by true Shepherd and Guardian (1 Pet 2:25)? "Her prophets have smeared whitewash for them, seeing false visions and divining lies for them, saying, 'thus says the Lord God,' when the LORD has not spoken".... "I searched for a man among them who would build up the wall and stand in the gap before Me for the land, so that I would not destroy it; but I found no one" (Ezekiel 22:28, 30).

NOVEMBER 2

"The devil doesn't mind how many sermons
we preach or prepare if it will keep us from
preparing ourselves." Vance Havner

As it was in Israel in days of old, so it is among God's EKKLESIA (Church) today: "There is a conspiracy of her prophets in her midst like a roaring lion tearing the prey. They have devoured lives; they have taken treasure and precious things; they have made many widows in the midst of her. Her priests have done violence to My law and have profaned My holy things; they have made no distinction between the holy and the profane, and they have not taught the difference between the unclean and the clean; and they hide their eyes from My Sabbaths, and I am profaned among them. Her prophets have smeared whitewash for them, seeing false visions and divining lies for them, saying, 'thus says the Lord God,' when the LORD has not spoken" (Ezekiel 22:25-26, 28).

There is a devilish conspiracy among many "Christian" prophets, compromising pastors and false teachers today, tearing their prey, devouring lives, and robbing saints of their heavenly blessings. Keeping the risen Christ and heaven's Bride Groom in the grave, they make the heavenly bride feel like a worthless widow; while soiling her bright and clean clothing with spots and wrinkles (Eph 5:27; Rev 3:4, 19:7-8). God's laws are broken, commandments are disobeyed, and holy things are made carnal.

Contamination restrains sanctification, happiness replaces holiness and compromise rules the day.

Everyone does what is right in his own eyes and what is pleasing to his flesh, thereby profaning the Lord's name, rather than proclaiming it; painting religious whitewash over sin-tarnished souls. Many prefer to see a false vision rather than seek after His true mission. Because many are so busy working and playing they fail to enjoy waiting and resting with their Shepherd, Lover and Creator (Mt 11:28).

NOVEMBER 3

"If Jesus Christ be God and died for me, then no sacrifice can be too great for me to make for Him." C. T. Studd.

GOD MOCKERS AND GOD ROCKERS

The devil is mad at God's saints because they are seated in the heavenlies with their Winner and King of kings and Lord of lords (Eph 2:6). The poor devil has been thrown down to the earth to dwell with his demon losers, all waiting for their appointed place in hell below; to entertain fellow sinners and God mockers, forever dreadfully recalling the God rockers warning: "I told you so".

"For this reason, rejoice O heavens and you who dwell in them. Woe to the earth and the sea, because the devil has come down to you, having great wrath, knowing that he has only a short time". (Rev 12:12). It is obvious if one looks at the last day signs, growing apostasy, globalism, proliferation of abominations, laboratory tinkering with creation, unrestrained civil and religious violence, persecution of Jews and Christians along with prohibition of expression of their beliefs and exercise of their rights, that we are witnessing the final gasps of a dying world. Those who have eyes to see will make the most of their time while they have the time, valuing and pursuing that which has eternal value.

NOVEMBER 4

"But what is the use of preaching the Gospel to men whose whole attention is concentrated upon a mad, desperate struggle to keep themselves alive?" William Booth

Political band-aids can't heal spiritual cancers. Too many only want to receive handouts from Uncle Sam rather than seek the face of their Heavenly Father. Fortunately, every obedient, God-fearing, Bible believing, Christ-imitating, Spirit-led Christian can now live in victory because we have been elected to win, reigning in life now and soon to be raptured to heaven with Him (Rom 5:17; 1 Thess 4:16-17). There will be no election fraud before that True and Holy One, for He will secure His election of His saints and the perdition of lost sinners.

It's not enough to cast a vote at the pole. We must also cast our self on the cross. Only after the old self has died on the cross will the new self arise and carry the cross (Rom 6:3-5). Only when one has died with Christ to sin, can one live again free from sin's bondage (Rom 6:9-14). Since God's people are called the "pillar and support of the truth", only when the Lord sees the sanctuary full of repentance, will law and order return to society (1 Tim 3:15; 2 Chron 7:14). The gospel is the power of God for salvation from the guilt and power of sin to those who truly believe and trust in Him (Rom 1:16; 10:9-10).

NOVEMBER 5

"It is impossible to be a true soldier of Jesus Christ and not fight." J. Gresham Machen

All God's saints ought to be "looking for and hastening the coming of the day of God" (2 Pet 3:11). On that day finally all the enemies of the Lord are made a footstool for His feet (Heb 1:13) when "at the name of Jesus every knee will bow, of those who are in heaven and on earth and under the earth" (Phil 2:10). So, go on mocking you Christ haters, for "He who sits in the heavens laughs, the Lord scoffs at them" (Ps 2:4). "Now therefore, O kings, show discernment; take warning, O judges of the earth" (Ps 2:10). Your day in heaven's court is imminent and that Righteous Judge will not be bribed nor will He be lenient.

NOVEMBER 6

"Shout, 'Get thee behind me, Satan,,,' and you will have the best time on earth. Whisper it, and you won't." Smith Wigglesworth

Spiritual warfare is both an individual and a corporate church endeavor. The many verses dealing with resisting the devil and putting on the armor are directed to individuals (Eph 6; Jam 4; 1 Pet 5; 2 Cor 10). But the corporate assembly also has an importance role in spiritual warfare through corporate intercession. The Lord said the gates of hell would not prevail against the Church (Mt 16:18). He never promised individual immunity from devilish attacks and their consequences. The devil can prevail over individuals who don't resist. He won't flee from those who do not resist him (Jam 4:7), but will prowl about to devour them (1 Pet 5:8).

However, lone ranger Christianity is never the best plan of action when engaging in ministry in a fallen world, under the influence of the devil (1 Jn 5:19). Jesus "called the twelve together, and gave them power and authority over all the demons, and to heal diseases. And He sent them out to proclaim the kingdom of God, and to perform healing" (Lk 9:1-2). After that, "the Lord appointed seventy others, and sent them two and two, ahead of Him to every city and place where He Himself was going to come …to tread upon serpents and scorpions, and over all the power of the enemy" (Lk 10:1, 19). In the New Testament there are many passages showing the people of God asking for prayer support from other believers as they contend earnestly for the faith.

NOVEMBER 7

"If it is in the Bible, it is so. It's not even to be prayed about. It's to be received and acted upon. Inactivity is a robber which steals blessings. Increase comes by action, by using what we have and know. Your life must be one of going on from faith to faith." Smith Wigglesworth

LET'S QUITE FOOLING AROUND AND GET
HOLY SPIRIT FILLED UP.

Let's get back to the Acts of the Apostles, so we can see the Acts of the Saints. We will get back to doing such divine activity when we start doing the work of our apostleship, that is, when we start doing what we have been "sent out" to do. And that mission is to make disciples, to BE the Church: the pillar and support of the truth (1 Tim 3:15; Mt 28:18-20). True Jesus followers will be the salt of the earth, preserving sound doctrine and creating a thirst for right doctrine (Mt 5:13).

The Church needs to return to her first love and her first deeds (Rev 2:4-5): to be continually devoted to the apostles' teaching, to fellowship, to the breaking of bread and to prayer (Acts 2:42). Only cleansed vessels are suitable for God's use (2 Cor 7:1; 2 Tim 2:21). Only fully armored and good soldiers are in God's overcoming army (2 Tm 2:3; Eph 6:11f). Only lamps filled with Holy Spirit oil can be bright lights that expose Satan's darkness (Mt 5:14; Eph 5:11-14).

The chosen of God need to see themselves as adopted and born again children of God and citizens of heaven. Christians are not to be stressed out sinners overcome by the world, but called out saints and overcomers. They are commissioned soldiers of God and ambassadors of Christ, the King of kings, (Rom 8:15; Gal 3:26; 2 Cor 5:20; Rev 19:16). We have all received grace, apostleship, authority and power to bring about the obedience to the true faith (Rom 1:5, 16:26; Mt 10:1, Lk 9:1, 10:1; Mt 28:18-20; Acts 1:8). The Lord will entrust to His committed followers His confirming mighty miracles, when they enlist themselves to carry out His almighty mission.

NOVEMBER 8

*"A revival of real praying would produce a
spiritual revolution." E.M. Bounds*

"Now as they observed the confidence of Peter and John and understood that they were uneducated and untrained men, they were amazed, and began to recognize them as having been with Jesus" (Acts 4:13). One is far more equipped for ministry by spending time with Jesus, who is the Truth, than being committed to an institution arguing and debating philosophy, religion and ism's. After all, in Christ are hidden all the treasures of wisdom and knowledge (Col 2:3). Digging, not diplomas, uncovers hidden treasures. One becomes hotter for the things of God by acquiring the fire of the Spirit rather than degrees of man.

NOVEMBER 9

*"All it takes to make a preacher is a sermon - but it takes
an altar to make a man of God." B.H. Clendennen*

TODAY'S VISION OF SLAUGHTER

A timely lesson can be learned by reading God's instruction to Ezekiel regarding how He views abominations, even those committed by religious leaders in defiled sanctuaries. And we also see God's protection for those who mourn over such abominations. "The LORD said to him, 'Go through the midst of the city, even through the midst of Jerusalem, and put a mark on the foreheads of the men who sigh and groan over all the abominations which are being committed in its midst'. But to the others He said in my hearing, 'go through the city after him and strike; do not let your eye have pity and do not spare. Utterly slay old men, young men, maidens, little children, and women, but do not touch any man on whom is the mark; and you shall start from My sanctuary.' So they started with the elders who were before the temple" (9:4-6).

In the first century, the Great Shepherd cleansed the Temple. In the twenty first century, many shepherds only expect their pew dwellers to play, to be entertained and cut their teeth on pastoral pastries. They do not preach repentance, expect holiness nor sigh and groan over sin. Instead, they let their coveted tithers and loyal admirers continue to play, sing on, ignore sin and disdain true piety. Meanwhile, the devil is given authority and opportunity to continue to slay, in his own way, bringing destruction to marriage, family, person, and society operating through his own demonic forces and their disguised captive puppets (Eph 2:2; 2 Tim 2:26; 2 Cor 11:13-15).

NOVEMBER 10

"I must honestly declare my conviction that, since the days of the Reformation, there never has been so much profession of religion without practice, so much talking about God without walking with Him, so much hearing God's words without doing them..." JC Ryle.

THE TRUE PROSPERITY GOSPEL

Don't let the false prosperity gospel rob you blind. Beware of false preachers who fleece pockets for money instead of filling hearts with Truth, leaving behind a trail of loose change rather than a testimony of permanent change.

God's true children have been blessed with every spiritual blessing in Christ (Eph 1:3). They are commissioned to preach the unfathomable riches of Christ to others (Eph 3:8). The love of God is experienced by those who fear God and keep His commandments (Jn 14:21, 23; 1 Jn 2:5, 5:3). The joy of the Holy Spirit is experienced by those who are filled with the His power, instructed in His teaching and possessors of His fruit (Gal 5:22; Lk 10:21; Jn 16:13; Rom 15:13; 1 Jn 2:27). Spiritual blessings, peace, joy and friendship with Christ envelopes those who follow Him and practice what He preached and obey what He commanded (Jn 13:17, 14:26-27, 15:14 16:33, 17:13). Now that is the true Prosperity Gospel.

NOVEMBER 11

"People do not believe lies because they have to, but because they want to." Malcolm Muggeridge

When professors of Christ become possessors of Christ supernatural things happen (1 Cor 6:11; Gal 3:5; Jn 14:12). "Old things passed away; behold, new things have come" (2 Cor 5:17). The old man which was dead in trespasses and sins is now buried and the new man is raised up and united with the risen Christ, walking in newness of life and dead to sin

(Eph 2:1; Rom 6:3-12; Eph 2:6). Such a one becomes God's workmanship and begins the supernatural and wonderful journey of walking in the works which God prepared beforehand (Eph 2:10).

By contrast, the life of many contemporary Christians is static, mundane, powerless and much like the world and void of the supernatural working of God. Such a life is a poor witness to true faith and does not draw the attention of the lost to authentic Christianity. It is subnormal, unbiblical and reflective of much of the contemporary, institutional and bankrupt religion. This counterfeit religion displays little of the Lordship of the Son of God (Lk 6:46; Rom 10:9; 2 Cor 4:5), the fellowship of the Spirit of God (2 Cor 13:14) and the power of the Word of God (Heb 4:12; 2 Tim 3:16-17). But praise the Lord, a new wind is blowing through the house, cleansing the Temple of God, replacing dead wood with living stones (1 Pet 2:5).

NOVEMBER 12

If we aren't being led by the Holy Spirit sent
from above, we will be led astray by the evil
one of this world sent from below.

Christians must put on the full divine armor of God, resist the devil and fight the good fight if they are going to destroy the works of the devil as Jesus did and be overcomers of this world just as Jesus overcame the world (1 Jn 3:8; cf. Acts 10:38; 1 Jn 5:4; Jn 16:33). Did not Jesus say: "Peace be with you; as the Father has sent Me, I also send you" (Jn 20:21)? And He promised saying: "Truly, truly I say to you, he who believes in Me, the works that I do shall he do also; and greater works than these, shall he do; because I go to the Father" (Jn 14:12). But today, there appears to be more nudist assemblies or naked churches as Jesus called them than churches filled with overcomers (Rev 3:17). Such assemblies contain many not clothed with power from on high (Lk 24:49) nor outfitted with the full armor of God (Eph 6:11) nor have taken up the breastplate of faith and love, and as a helmet, the hope of salvation (1 Thess 5:8). They are not clothed with the Lord Jesus Christ (Rom 13:14) nor "clothed in fine linen, bright and clean which is the righteous acts of the saints (Rev 19:8).

Rather they are dressed for success, wanting to win friends and influence people, wanting to be entertained by the world rather than be engaged in combat with the world. And we wonder why the devil is having so much success in church and even more victory in society. At best, we have some who feel sorry over sin, whenever sin is addressed. But few are those who are truly repentant over sin and fewer still who have stopped allowing sin to reign over and master them (Rom 6:12-13). Yet the Scripture addresses vividly how to deal with sin: "You have not yet resisted to the point of shedding blood in your striving against sin" (Heb 12:4). "Let us lay aside every encumbrance, and the sin which so easily entangles us" (Heb 12:1a). "Consider yourselves to be dead to sin" (Rom 6:11). "Let us cleanse ourselves from all defilement of flesh and spirit, perfecting holiness in the fear of God" (Cor 7:1). "Like the Holy One who called you, be holy yourselves also in all your behavior" (1 Pet 1:15).

Instead, the popular religious culture is often clothed with religious fig leaves provided by institutional churches filled with those who are fed pastoral pastries from ear tickling preachers. They prefer an "effortless" Christianity rather than "working out their salvation with fear and trembling" (Phil 2:12). But only vessels cleansed from sin and corrected by the Scripture are useful to the Master and prepared for every good work (2 Tim 2:21, 3:16-17). They will prove to be the faithful and overcoming remnant and showcase of God's sanctifying workmanship, walking in the good works He which prepared beforehand (Eph 2:10). They will enjoy fellowship with the Holy Spirit (2 Cor 13:14), and Christ living in them (Gal

2:20), relying on the grace of God laboring with them (1 Cor 15:10) and the power of God mightily working within them (Phil 2:13; Col 1:29).

NOVEMBER 13

"A man who spoke little English gave this description of a sermon he had heard: he said 'Big wind. Much lightning. Loud thunder. No rain!'" Author unknown

THIS IS THE DAY THE LORD HAS MADE, LET US REJOICE AND BE GLAD IN IT.

After all, as Saints of God, the ekklesia, the divinely called and chosen, redeemed and persevering peoples of all races, have been blessed with every spiritual blessing in the heavenly places in Christ (Eph 1:3). They fully know that "God causes all things to work together for the good to those who love God, to those who are called according to His purpose" (Rom 8:28). They are fully persuaded that what God has promised He is able also to perform (Rom 4:21).

In trying situations we overwhelmingly conquer through Him who loved us (Rom 8:37). We persevere in trials knowing that "momentary, light affliction is producing for us an eternal weight of glory far beyond all comparison" (2 Cor 4:16). After we have suffered for a little while on earth, the God of all grace, who called us to His eternal glory in Christ, will Himself perfect, confirm, strength and establish us (1 Pet 5:10). To the degree that we share the sufferings of Christ, we keep on rejoicing, knowing that at the revelation of His glory we will rejoice with exultation (1 Pet 4:13; 2 Cor 1:5, 7). We will be "heirs of God and fellow heirs with Christ, if indeed we suffer with Him in order that we may also be glorified with Him" (Rom 8:17). For "if we endure, we shall also reign with Him" (2 Tim 2:12a).

The love of God has been poured out in our hearts through the Holy Spirit who was given to us (Rom 5:5). This same Holy Spirit caused us to be born again to a living hope (Jn 3:5; 1 Pet 1:3), to walk in newness of life (Rom 6:4) as citizens of heaven (Phil 3:20). We are no longer captive to the god of this world (2 Tim 2:25-26; Lk 4:18; Gal 5:1).

The body of our humble state will be transformed into conformity with the glorified body of our Lord Jesus Christ (Phil 3:20). This mortal will put on immortality and this perishable will put on the imperishable (1 Cor 15:53-54). We will obtain an inheritance which is imperishable and undefiled and will not fade away, reserved in heaven for us (1 Pet 1:4) who persevere in faith. We are protected by the power of God through faith for a salvation ready to be revealed in the last time...obtaining as the outcome of our faith the salvation of our souls (1 Pet 1:5, 9).

So, when the world becomes more evil and its grey becomes fifty shades darker, know that the return of JESUS, the Light of the World and the Holy One, is drawing near. Then we will be like Him, because we will see Him just as He (1 Jn 3:3), will be married to Him just as He promised (Rev 19:7-8) and will dwell with Him in His' Father's house which He has prepared (Jn 14:1-3; 12:24-26). This heavenly mansion will be occupied by those who knew that they could not serve two masters, loving and serving self while claiming to also love and serve Him (Mt 7:21-13; Lk 16:13).

NOVEMBER 14

"This life is a dressing room for eternity -
THAT'S ALL IT IS!" Leonard Ravenhill

Jesus is the divine Carpenter, sure Foundation and only Head and Builder of the holy Church. If anyone claims to follow after Him, he must deny himself, not delight in self, take up his cross daily not Sundays only, and follow Him, not men (Lk 9:23). Today, we have too many heads, exalting themselves, building happy churches on crumbling foundations rather than holy churches on the Sure Foundation because they please men rather than Him. Meanwhile, the Carpenter's A-team continue following Him in the highways and byways, being the Church, rejoicing in hope, persevering in tribulation and devoted to prayer (Rom 12:12). These servants of the Lord preach the gospel in demonstration of the Spirit and of power (1 Cor 2:4), doing good and healing all who are oppressed by the devil just as Jesus did (Acts 10:38), with signs and wonders following, just as they followed Him (Jn 20:30-31; Mt 4:24; 11:1-6; Acts 3:16, 8:4-13; Rom 15:19). They exercise faith in the Son who is exalted (Phil 2:9). They are baptized into Him who has risen (Gal 3:27; Rom 6:6-3-5). They are empowered by the Spirit who was given (Acts 1:8; Eph 3:16). They draw near to God's throne of grace because they are forgiven (Heb 4:16).

NOVEMBER 15

*The devil knows he faces a fierce battle, a tough fight
and sure defeat when the Lord's soldiers use the divine
sword, the Word of God on the real battlefield. He would
much prefer that we rely on human babble, butter knives
and spit wads and remain in the church playground.*

To call sin a sin is not sin. This is not judging but merely declaring the truth and honestly telling it like it is. God is judge of all and judges sinful behavior. Christians are commanded to expose the unfruitful deeds of darkness as well as to separate from wickedness. They don't condemn individuals as Jesus didn't come to condemn but to save. But that is not the same as calling sin sin. Christians have too long turned their head away from sin to ignore it or buried their heads in the sand to claim ignorance of it. That time has gone. Their light must shine to expose all darkness. And that applies to all sins, those inside as well as outside the church, in others as well as in themselves.

NOVEMBER 16

"The law shows the distance that exists between
God and man; the Gospel bridges that awful chasm
and brings the sinner across it." C.H. Spurgeon

IN CASE YOU HAVEN'T NOTICED, GOD'S CHOSEN AND HIS TRUE CHURCH IS MARKED.

It is that spiritual body made up of members who do the will of God (Mt 7:21, 12:50), who bear much fruit (Jn 15:8), who confess Jesus as Lord and Savior (Rom 10:9), who have genuinely repented (Acts 2:38; Rev 2,3), who have believed and continue to believe in Jesus as Lord and Savior (Gal 3:22, Rom 3:22, 1 Jn 5:13; Rom 10:9; 2 Cor 4:5; Col 2:6; 1 Pet 3:15), which is God's true Church. They hold fast to the Head of the Church (Col 2:19) and are separated from the world (1 Cor 1:2 Cor 6:17-17; 1 Jn 2:15-17). They work out their salvation with fear and trembling (Phil 2:12). They pursue sanctification and are sanctified (Heb 10:14, 12:14). They practice love in deed and in truth (Jn 13:35; 1 Jn 3:18, 4:7). They are led by the Spirit (Rom 8:14) and have crucified the flesh in regard to its passions and desires (Gal 5:24). They are partakers of Christ and hold fast to the beginning of their assurance firm unto the end (Heb 3:14; Mt 24:13; 2 Tim 2:12). They share in the sufferings of Christ (Rom 8:17; 2 Cor 1:5, 7) and are devoted to prayer (Col 4:2; Acts 2:42, 6:4) and to the Word of God (Acts 2:42, 6:4, 2 Tim 4:2).

They are diligent to make certain about God's calling and choosing of them (2 Pet 1:10-11). They are wise to test themselves to see if they are in the faith (2 Cor 13:5), remembering Jesus' warning: "Not everyone who says to Me, 'Lord, Lord,' will enter the kingdom of heaven; but he who does the will of My Father who is in heaven. Many will say to Me on that day, 'Lord, Lord, did we not prophesy in Your name, and in Your name cast out demons, and in Your name perform many miracles.' And then I will declare to them, 'I never knew you; depart from Me, you who practice lawlessness'" (Mt 7:21-23).

NOVEMBER 17

As the world becomes more evil and its grey becomes fifty shades darker, know that the return of Jesus, the Light of the World and the Holy One, is drawing nearer.

SHAKEN BUT NOT MISTAKEN

When the Lord is given His proper place, one doesn't have to fear what might take place. For all things will work together for good, though some things may appear bad (Rom 8:28). When those who are in Christ think that they are left completely alone, they can rest assured that they alone have been made complete (Col 2:10). The Bright Morning Star will rise daily to shine on them who die daily. Darkness will be cast aside, when Jesus the Light, is standing at your side.

When the heavenly shaking starts, all churches build on shifting sand and doctrines of men will crumble to the ground, while the true Church will rise to take her stand and shout the victory sound. Then, heavenly focused Christians will mount up with wings like eagles; they will run the race to the finish but not get tired, walk the narrow walk and not become weary. Those who truly know their God will display strength and take action. Those who only know about God will manifest their weakness and take cover.

NOVEMBER 18

If Christ lives in us and God is for us, why be
down on ourselves and beside ourselves?

If God is for us, who can be against us? (Rom 8:31)? If God is at work in us, what circumstance can work against us (Phil 2:13)? If the Spirit of God empowers us, what force can overpower us? (Acts 1:8; 1 Jn 4:4)? If the victorious Son of God lives in us, why live in defeat? (Gal 2:20)? If we are citizens of heaven, why live as captives in the world (Phil 3:20)? If Jesus has bruised the serpent on the head (Gen 3:15), and the God of peace wishes to crush Satan under our feet (Rom 16:20), why allow the devil to hold us under his thumb? If Christians are called saints, why be characterized as sinners (Rom 1:7)? If God wants to father us, why walk as prodigals (Rom 8:15; 2 Thess 2:16-17)? If the Spirit wants to walk in fellowship with us, why walk without Him (2 Cor 13:14)? If Christ, the hope of glory is in us, why be gloomy (Col 1:27)?

Maybe it is because we do not allow the Spirit to give us newness of life by teaching us how abide in the Word of Life (Jn 6:31; 1 Jn 2:27; Rom 6:4,8:14). Or maybe it is because Jesus is Lord of little rather than Lord of all. Or maybe it is because we have never died on the cross with Jesus in order to live in resurrection life for Him. For "unless a grain of wheat falls into the earth and dies, it remains alone; but if it dies, it bears much fruit" (Jn 12:24). Or maybe is it because we are more concerned about "the best life now" than we are taking taking hold of the eternal life to which we were called (1 Tim 6:12). Maybe we are more in love with self than with the Savior, more interested in being happy and holy. Why settle for so little when we have been blessed so greatly (Eph 1:3; Rom 8:32; Phil 4:19)?

NOVEMBER 19

Revival need not tarry.

R evival on a local and personal scale has been, is and should be experienced and will be experienced whenever its conditions are met. The children of God have been commanded to experience such a personal revival, as saints, as overcomers, as those walking in newness of life and as new creatures in Christ. They are to give thanks in all things and overwhelmingly conquering in all circumstances. For to those who separate themselves from lawlessness, darkness and idolatry God promises: "I will dwell in them and walk among them; and I will be their God and they shall be My people...I will be a father to you, and you shall be sons and daughters to Me" (2 Cor 6:14-18).

To them God has granted by His divine power everything pertaining to life and godliness, through the true knowledge of Him who called them by His own glory and excellence (2 Pet 1:3). He has granted to you His precious and magnificent promises, in order that by them you might become partakers of the divine nature, having escaped the corruption that is in the world by lust (2 Pet 1:4). And His promises are not "I hope so" but "I know so" proclamations. "For as many as may be the promises of God, in Him they are yes; wherefore also by Him is our Amen to the glory of God through us" (2 Cor 1:20).

Christians are to believe the Bible wholly, take their call seriously, proclaim the Gospel boldly, pursue holiness seriously, practice effective prayer continually, die to self completely, worship God reverently, fellowship with the Spirit intimately, serve the Lord wholeheartedly, resist the devil vehemently, despise the world passionately, maintain their faith uncompromisingly and practice agape love sincerely. A personal heaven sent revival only awaits a heart-rent repentance.

NOVEMBER 20

*Many Christians today are being tempted to go the
path of least resistance, to forsake the narrow way,
to embrace an "effortless" Christianity, to lay down
the cross, to embrace demonic doctrines and distorted
gospels and to read the best sellers of men rather
than the living and inspired Word of God.*

PASTORAL PASTRIES DON'T CUT THE MUSTARD.

We should expect most of God's Word, the Truth, to be available and discernible by simply reading what the inspired Scriptures say, without always having to interpret them to find out what they mean or to misinterpret them to say what we want them to say. What's on your plate: religious junk food or sound spiritual doctrine? False teachers have set up camp in the sanctuary to roast marshmallows, tickle ears, and entertain lukewarm souls. "An appalling and horrible thing has happened in the land: the prophets prophesy falsely, and the priests rule on their own authority; and My people love it so! But what will you do at the end of it?" (Jer 5:30-31).

Pastoral pastries hot off the pulpit don't cut the mustard. God's people must become obedient to the Lord's commandment to live on every word that proceeds out of the mouth of God (Mt 4:4) and become equipped by reading Scripture (2 Tim 3:16; Joshua 1:8) and being nourished on solid food and sound biblical doctrine (Heb 5:14; Tit 2:1). If they choose rather to be malnourished on spiritual fast food, spoiled milk and pastoral devil's food cake, they will continue to be deceived by the devil (1 Tim 4:1; Col 2:8), devoured by the lion (1 Pet 5:8), destroyed for lack of knowledge (Hosea 4:6), and taken captive by the powers of darkness (Isaiah 5:13). When all else fails in life because one is following vain imaginations of men and false interpretations of the religious, one would be wise to become led and taught by the Holy Spirit (1 Jn 2:27).

NOVEMBER 21

"We're suffering from a believism that never has believed and a receivism that never has received and it leads to deceivism." Vance Havner

UNITY IN WARFARE AND CAUTION IN AIMING

Christians don't have time to waste debating theology with made-up minds. We need to keep declaring what the Bible clearly teaches to those seeking to possess the mind of Christ (1 Cor 2:16). Those who have spiritual ears to hear will hear. Christian soldiers must speak and write precisely and predominantly on first principles pertaining to victorious Christian living. This will encourage and equip true kingdom seekers rather than discourage and extinguish their zeal with irrelevant doctrinal controversies. Christian soldiers would be wise to labor with all who are fellow-workers and fellow-soldiers "being diligent to preserve the unity of the Spirit in the bond of peace" (Eph 4:3) if at all possible (Rom 12:18), though they may often differ in minor details of doctrine.

We have a battle to fight, and don't have time to sit in the barracks bickering over what translation caliber of ammo or denomination color of uniform our fellow Christian soldiers may wear, while our enemy the devil and his false teachers roam about to steal, kill and destroy. Of course, in these last days of great deception and increasing apostasy, we must expose false teachers who preach false and distorted gospels and doctrines of demons. But there are those who are very orthodox in their foundational doctrine but who have taken upon themselves the role of the Holy Spirit in being the spiritual teacher and sanctifier in the lives of genuine believers.

I am referring to those who believe that embracing a particular theological system or following a certain legalistic protocol is more important that simply loving God by keeping His commandments, pursuing holiness and loving others in deed and in truth. Some Christians become heresy hunters and trigger happy, seeing other true believers as heretics who have fallen from the faith when such ones are likely those who either do not fully understand the faith or have not matured in their walk.

NOVEMBER 22

*"The first step towards the evangelizing of the world
is the christianizing of the church." Vance Havner*

SNAKE OIL OR HOLY SPIRIT OIL?

It is impossible to keep up with the myriads and myriads of false teachers today. It is time consuming to expose the many dangerous and yet popular religious band wagons which are circling the modern church selling their newest brands of snake oil. The devil will infiltrate any church today that opens the door to him (Acts 20:29-30). The devil is no respecter of persons or of denominations. He loves to disciple pastors who will listen and infiltrate churches which will compromise. His deceitful spirits love to preach to the pew dwellers just enough distorted gospel to get them "saved", and sell just enough religious drugs to keep them high and happy, and dispense just enough prosperity gospel to keep them spiritually bankrupt (2 Cor 11:13-15; Jude 4,12).

Ultimately, each Christian is responsible to know and practice the Truth, to follow Jesus, obey His commandments and be Holy Spirit taught (1 Jn 2:20, 27, 3:23-24). It is by knowing and abiding in the truth that one is set free (Jn 8:31-32) and by practicing solid food that one discerns falsehood (Heb 5:14). Christians who stand on Christ the Cornerstone (Is 28:16; Eph 2:20) and on the foundation of biblical apostles and prophets (Eph 2:20) will stand strong and not be blown about by every wind of doctrine nor deceived by false apostles and prophets (Eph 4:14; Col 2:8; Mt 24:4-5, 11, 24). Those who take their stand on the shifting sands of popular religious opinions, false prophetic proclamations, ear-tickling sermons, vain imaginations and man-made theology will never mature in sound doctrine.

NOVEMBER 23

*"Religion is hanging around the cross; Christianity
is getting on the cross." Steve Hill*

FIFTY SHADES OF CHRISTIANITY

"Progressive" Christianity, a "New" Christianity, a "Redefined"
Christianity, an "effortless" Christianity. Oh, the many shades of
gray the devil invents in his vain efforts to dim the light of biblical Christianity (2 Cor 4:4-6). The good news is that the Son is rising and shining
through His own vessels of light (Mt 5:14-16; Eph 5:8-14); bright shining
lamps filled with Holy Spirit oil, baptized with the Holy Spirit and with
fire.

Such ones seek a new demonstration of Christianity not a new definition of it. They are committed to displaying biblical Christianity rather
than hiding it; proclaiming it rather than denying it and living it rather
than talking about it.

We need more than what we are seeing in too many churches today, the
religious ritual: "Come as you are, Sing 'just as I am', Now go as you were". I
thought the apostle Paul declared: "Therefore if any man is in Christ, he is a
new creature; old things passed away; behold, new things have come" (2 Cor
5:17). I thought he taught: "Therefore we have been buried with Him through
baptism into death, in order that as Christ was raised from the dead through
the glory of the Father, so we too might walk in newness of life" (Rom 6:4).

The militant (aggressive) and triumphant (overcoming) Church is
assured that neither the gates of hell nor the striking of man's gavel

will overpower it (Mt 16:18). For we have not been sent on a "mission impossible" but on a mission invincible. All that is needed for good to triumph is for the saints to do something, and that something is to BE the Church.

NOVEMBER 24

"When there's something in the Bible that churches don't like, they call it legalism."Leonard Ravenhill

Since Christians are called holy brethren, partakers of a heavenly calling (Heb 3:1), led by the Holy Spirit (Rom 8:14) and are to be holy as He is holy (1 Pet 1:15), why is it that many fail to cleanse themselves from all defilement of flesh and spirit, perfecting holiness in the fear of God (2 Cor 7:1)? Why is holiness is taboo? There is little fear of God and of the Lord Jesus Christ, the Holy and Righteous One, who is often disowned by popular religion (Acts 3:14). They do not hold fast to Him who is the Head but delight in the worship of angels, taking their stand on false visions, having their minds contaminated with deceitful spirits and doctrines of demons (Col 2:18-19; 1 Tim 4:1). They are blown about by every wind of doctrine, jumping on religious bandwagons to be entertained, rather than standing strong on the Solid Rock to be equipped (Eph 4:14). Rather than stand on foundation of the Lord Jesus Christ and be fed by the teachings of His apostles and prophets (Eph 2:20), they sink down in quicksand, being misled by American idols and falling stars, by false apostles and false prophets (Matt 24:4, 5,11, 24) and by fleshly annointings and flashy mantles.

Many contemporary Christians only want smooth sermons, spoiled milk and gummy morsels rather than hard truth, solid food and sound doctrine. Peter exhorted: "Like newborn babes, long for the pure milk of the word, that by it you may grow in respect to salvation" (1 Pet 2:2). The author of Hebrews rebuked such babes: "For though by this time you ought to be teachers, you have need again for someone to teach you the elementary principles of the oracles of God, and you have come to need milk and not solid food" (Heb 5:12). Too many just "want their cake and eat it to". But they are being served Devil's Food Cake. And when the candles burn out and the party is over in this life, the fire may just begin in the next.

NOVEMBER 25

"The last word of our Lord to the church was not the Great Commission. The last thing He said to the church was 'Repent.' He said that to five out of seven." Vance Havner

The founder of Salvation Army, General William Booth once said: "The chief danger that confronts the coming century will be religion without the Holy Ghost, Christianity without Christ, forgiveness without repentance, salvation without regeneration, politics without God, heaven without hell". The greatest danger today is that General William Booth's prophetic warning is being fulfilled by intellectuals who have no brains, by politicians who have no sense, by religionists who have no morals, by philosophers who have no clue and by the depraved who have no conscience in the face of Christians who have no backbone.

In a time such as this it is important that Christians believe and practice this God-inspired truth and exhortation: "God has not given us a spirit of timidity, but of power and love and discipline. Therefore do not be ashamed of the testimony of our Lord or of me His prisoner, but join with me in the suffering for the gospel according to the power of God" (2 Tim 1:7-8). "Who will stand up for me against evildoers? Who will take his stand for me against those who do wickedness" (Ps 94:16)?

NOVEMBER 26

"There was a time when ministers spoke forthrightly and named things. We don't name anything anymore. Finney had a sermon on How to Preach so as to Convert Nobody. He said 'Preach on sin but never mention any of the sins of your congregation - that will do it.'" Vance Havner

Today many are falling away from the faith for many reasons. First, contemporary Christianity is a farce. It tickles the ears but does not feed the soul. It's offers lethal hype but no living hope and religion without power rather than a relationship with the godhead. It proposes a redefined Christianity without the true Christ rather than true Christianity built upon Christ. It sells a false grace that does not bring deliverance from sin's power but rather a denial of its danger. It speaks of a faith that only entails an intellectual assent and but no obedience. It preaches a repentance that occurs in the mind but is not required to be demonstrated in the life.

Second, many are falling away from the faith because they are paying attention to deceitful spirits and doctrines of demons (1 Tim 4:1). They fail to take spiritual warfare seriously, allowing Satan to ensnare them unconsciously. They don't understand and heed biblical instruction regarding protecting the mind, making it a playground for evil. Paul was careful to explain to the Corinthian believers: "For though we walk in the flesh, we do not war according to the flesh, for the weapons of our warfare are not of the flesh, but divinely powerful for the destruction of fortresses. We are destroying speculations and every lofty thing raised up against the knowledge of God, and we are taking every thought captive to the obedience of Christ" (2 Cor 10:4-5).

Third, many fail to realize the danger of deception. When Jesus was asked by His disciples to elaborate concerning end time events, His first response was: "See to it that no one misleads you" (Mt 24:4). The devil is deceiving and drawing away all he can, using every scheme he can, often operating through his professing Christians as well as through his lost puppets in the world whom he energizes (Eph 2:2; 2 Tim 2:26). And because most Christians don't read their bibles and don't practice what little they read, but listen to religious pulpit babble they are destroyed and go into exile for lack of knowledge (Hosea 4:6; Isa 5:13), or maybe even into the cemeteries to suck up some anointings of the dead. The way is indeed narrow and the road is rough, and few are those who are willing to travel down it and fewer still are those who seem to stay on it.

NOVEMBER 27

"And so it had gotten down to the place where salvation was nothing more than the assent to a scheme or a formula." Paris Reidhead

"When they bring you before the synagogues and the rulers and the authorities, do not worry about how or what you are to speak in your defense, or what you are to say; for the Holy Spirit will teach you in that very hour what you ought to say" (Lk 12:11-12). So Christ-minded, Spirit taught believers are blessed to have an answer for religious and political opponents and depraved civil authorities whom the god of this world inspires and energizes (Eph 2:2; Jam 3:15-18). They are at odds with Him who is the Truth and in whom are hidden all the treasures of wisdom and knowledge (1 Cor 2:16; Jn 14:26; 1, Jn 2:27; Lk 10:17-20; Col 2:3). God has chosen the foolish things of the world to shame the wise. On judgement day the Lord will come to "bring to light the things hidden in darkness and disclose the motives of men's hearts" (1 Cor 1:27, 4:5). Jesus has forewarned: "Behold, I am coming quickly, and My reward is with Me, to render to every man according to what he has done" (Rev 22:12).

NOVEMBER 28

"You may say, 'God doesn't hate anybody. God is love.' No, my friend. You need to understand something. Jesus Christ taught, the prophets taught, the apostles taught this: that apart from the grace of God revealed in Jesus Christ our Lord the only thing left for you is the wrath, the fierce anger of God because of your rebellion and your sin." Paul Washer

Believers who are not progressing in sanctification as commanded in Scripture (Heb 10:10; 12:14; Jn 17:17) are at risk of following away when God's great shaking increases in intensity (Heb 12:25-29). Their religious figs leaves will blow away and their spiritual nakedness will be exposed, as Jesus warned of in Rev 3:17. And their constant diet of pastoral pastries and polluted waters will not sustain them during the tough times ahead. Only those who are nourished on sound doctrine and filled with Holy Spirit will have the faith to overcome and the power to endure.

But the good news is: "God makes a home for the lonely; He leads out the prisoners into prosperity, only the rebellious dwell in a parched land" (Ps 68:6). True spiritual prosperity, even in times of cultural spiritual drought, comes to those citizens of heaven who view themselves as aliens and strangers to this evil world (Phil 3:20; 1 Pet 2:11). They are not willing to be conformed to this world (Rom 12:2). Through obedience to the Lord they drink from the well of living water (Jn 7:37-38, 4:10) and are filled with the Holy Spirit "whom God has given to those who obey Him" (Acts 5:32; Eph 5:18).

NOVEMBER 29

*"The world has lost the power to blush over
its vice; the Church has lost her power to
weep over it." Leonard Ravenhill*

Modern Christianity in too many assemblies has robbed faith of its works, repentance of its fruits, conversion of its commitment, the Lord's house of its prayer, God's household of its disciples, religion of its power, the Word of its place, Christians of their high priestly calling, the Savior of His glory, the Lord Jesus of His Lordship, and many sanctuaries of God's presence. And worst of all, most of this devilish robbery has not even been noticed.

Many professing Christians in contemporary churches are naive and deceived because they have been drinking from polluted wells, broken cisterns and feasting on fast-food religion and flesh-feeding sermons. They have itching ears scratched by soft lies, rather than burned with hard truth. They have hearts hardened by the deceitfulness of sin (Heb 3:8, 13), rather than hearts pierced by preaching against sin (Acts 2:36-40). They are too busy having a good time for themselves, rather than redeeming their time for Him.

NOVEMBER 30

"The man who remains in his sin will be damned
just as surely as the sun comes up in the east
and goes down in the west." A.W. Tozer

To many preachers either cannot listen because they are lost or do not listen because they are carnal, to the God's warnings through His prophets. They have been sounding the alarm, but preachers are too busy building churches and tickling ears to hear the bell. The institutional church will be shaken to the ground. But the true remnant Church will remain strong on its sure foundation, confessing the Lord Jesus Christ. They will exit the buildings to meet in homes more and more as persecution increases, ministering to one another and encouraging one another to BE the Church.

Jesus: "Behold, an hour is coming, and has already come, for you to be scattered, each to his own home, and to leave Me along; and yet I am not along, because the Father is with Me. These things I have spoken to you, that in Me you may have peace. In the world you have tribulation, but take courage; I have overcome the world" (Jn 16:23-24).

DECEMBER 1

Head knowledge that never makes it into
the heart tends to give more headaches to the
proud than heartaches for the poor.

SUGGESTIONS ON HOW TO KEEP THE ALTAR FIRES BURNING

First, church leaders have to be cleansed from sin if they are to be vessels of honor, "sanctified, useful to the Master, prepared for every good work" (2 Tim 2:21). They need to be cleansed from all defilement of flesh and spirit (2 Cor 7:1). They should diligently labor among the flock over which they have charge and give them instruction (1 Thess 5:12). They should follow biblical leadership like that modeled by the apostle Paul who was approved by God to be entrusted with the Gospel. He did not seek to please men nor did he make use of flattering speech. He did not have a pretext for greed nor did he seek glory from men, but was committed to being a good steward of God's grace given to him for ministry (1 Thess 2:4-6; Eph 3:2, 7; 1 Cor 9:17). He behaved devoutly and uprightly and blamelessly toward believers willing to impart not only the gospel but his own life because of his love for them (1 Thess 2:7-11). He did not tickle ears but exhorted, encouraged and implored believers to walk worthy of God who calls all to kingdom living (1 Thess 2:7-12).

Second, church leaders need to get away with their staff for an extended period of time to pray and discuss which spiritual disciplines would be most suitable and helpful for their congregations. Some of the more crucial ones to stroke the altar fire would be the following: developing a committed prayer team and ministry; incorporating biblically functioning home cell groups; having a biblical men's ministry [not just fellowship] that would equip men to become more fruitful within the church and serve in the community through project outreach teams or in mentoring younger men. Other suggestions could include having an ongoing evangelistic outreach, a discipleship program and maybe an alternative worship service that would be "lay" driven to encourage participation and spiritual gifts. An anointed altar ministry including follow-up with a view to discipleship would be very fruitful.

The discussed, selected and approved ministry objectives would be presented and suggested to the congregation by church leadership with a great sense of urgency, excitement and expected participation. Those preferring to continue sleeping in the pews, remain lukewarm or babes in the faith and doing nothing should be encouraged to find a place more comfortable for them; perhaps a Resthaven Community Church down the road. There is no time to play. We are in war for the souls of the lost, the sanctity of marriage, the preservation of the family, the equipping of the saints, the pursuit of holiness and the expansion of the kingdom of God.

DECEMBER 2

"Is prayer your steering wheel or your spare tire?" Corrie Ten Boom

SPIRITUAL DECEPTION WON'T DELIVER.

"We are a fragrance of Christ to God among those who are being saved and among those who are perishing; to the one an aroma from death to death, to the other an aroma from life to life" (2 Cor 2:15-16a). To those whom Jesus is drawing, whom the Spirit is convicting, whom God is calling and saving, we are a breath of fresh air, of Holy Spirit life (Jn 12:32; 16:8; Rom 8:11).

But what about those who fail to hear and learn from the Father (Jn 6:45), who are unwilling to come to the Son for eternal life (Jn 5:40), who insult the Spirit of grace which brings salvation to all men (Heb 10:29; Tit 2:11), and who stubbornly refuse to repent before God and believe in the Lord Jesus Christ (Rom 2:4-5a; Acts 20:21)? Don't be surprised that the Jesus haters who love the world and serve its god, also hate and reject the gospel of truth. They are storing up wrath for themselves in the day of wrath and revelation of the righteous judgment of God, who will render to every man according to his deeds (Rom 2:5-6), because they did not receive the love of the truth so as to be saved (2 Thess 2:10). "He who believes in Him is not judged; he who does not believe has been judged already, because he has not believed in the name of the only begotten Son of God" (Jn 3:18). Unless God grants them repentance and they come to their senses and respond to God's grace and receive Jesus as Savior and Lord, they will continue to be held captive by the devil to do his will (2 Tim 2:25-26; Tit 2:11), and remain blinded by him to the light of the gospel (2 Cor 4:4).

Thus the apostle Paul tells the Corinthians: "And working together with Him, we also urge you not to receive the grace of God in vain—for He says, 'At the acceptable time I listened to you and on the day of salvation I helped you'; behold, now is the acceptable time, 'behold, now is the day of salvation'" (2 Cor 6:1-2). God our Savior "desires all men to be saved and to come to the knowledge of the truth" (1 Tim 2:4). Peter writes to "those who have received a faith of the same kind as ours" (2 Pet

1:1), and warns them saying: "God is patient toward you, not wishing for any to perish but for all to come to repentance" (2 Pet 3:9b). Jesus often addressed spiritual deception: "Why do you call Me, 'Lord Lord,' and do not do what I say?" (Lk 24:46). "Not everyone who says to Me, 'Lord, Lord,' will enter the kingdom of heaven; but he who does the will of My Father who is in heaven" (Mt 24:21).

The devil is no respecter of persons when it comes to deception. He deceives the lost as well as those who think they are saved. In these lasts days of great deception, imposters are deceiving and are being deceived (2 Tim 3:13). Many false christs and false prophets are arising and performing false signs and wonders, (Mt 24:24). Many are falling away from the faith and truth and turning aside to myths and doctrines of demons (1 Tim 4:1, 2 Tim 4:3-4). Many preachers have a disdain for preaching repentance toward God and faith in our Lord Jesus Christ (Acts 20:21). Ear tickling writers and preachers preach from their own private interpretation, not from Scripture (2 Tm 4:3; 2 Pet 1:21), who peddle and adulterate the word of God (2 Cor 2:17, 4:1), rather than handle it accurately (2 Tim 2:15).

They are sending deceived multitudes to a place they never dreamed of going, many clutching religious security blankets thinking they were ever so secure. Such ones don't live and confess Jesus as Lord (Rom 10:9; 2 Cor 4:5, Col 2:6), though they may have once upon a time professed Him as Savior. They do not die to sin, but live in sin (1Pet 2:24; Gal 5:24 1 Jn 3:9-10). They choose not to follow after Him, who is the Way, the Truth and the Life (Jn 14:6). But Jesus gives eternal life to those who hear His voice and not the voice of hirelings; those who follow after Him, not after them (Jn 10:8, 27-28). Eternal life is not promised to those hold to a sin-friendly spirituality based on false grace, but to those who stand firm on the true grace of God (1 Pet 5:12), and continue exercising true faith in the name of the Son of God (1 Pet 5:12; 1 Jn 5:13; Rom 3:22; Gal 3:22).

DECEMBER 3

*"Going to church doesn't make you a Christian any more
than going to the garage makes you a car." Laurence J. Peter*

What has Jesus Christ done for you lately? Do you know that He came to set the captives free, to deliver from bondage (Lk 4:18), to bring peace to those who are troubled and rest to all who are weary and heaven-laden (Mt 11:28). He came to offer an abundant life now by being our loving Lord as well as eternal life hereafter by being our personal Savior (Jn 10:10b). He came to deliver the religious from religion. He came to call out an army of saints to destroy the works of the devil who seeks to kill, steal and destroy (1 Jn 3:8; Jn 10:10a).

Just as His heavenly Father sent Him into the world, so Jesus has sent His own into the world (Jn 17:18). The glory which His Father gave Him, He has given to those who follow Him (Jn 17:22). He said, "The Spirit of the LORD is upon Me, because He anointed Me to preach the gospel to the poor. He has sent Me to proclaim release to the captives, and recovery of sight to the blind, to set free those who are oppressed, to proclaim THE FAVORABLE YEAR OF THE LORD" (Lk 4:18-19). He was anointed with the Holy Spirit and with power and went about doing good, and healing all who were oppressed by the devil, for God was with Him" (Acts 10:38). And the works that Jesus did, greater works will those do who believe in Him (Jn 14:12), because He ascended into heaven in order to send the Holy Spirit to empower them (Jn 16:7; Lk 24:49; Acts 1:8).

Now is that acceptable time, behold, now is the day to proclaim salvation (2 Cor 6:2), rather than neglect our so great a salvation (Heb 2:3). Now is the time for Christ to live in you, the hope of glory (Col 1:27) and for the Holy Spirit to fill you, manifesting His glory.

DECEMBER 4

*"Be ready to cut off everything that would hinder, and
cast it from you. Be ready and willing to suffer the loss of
possessions, of friends, of health - of all things on earth - so
you may enter into the kingdom of heaven." John Wesley*

How well have Christians been outfitted for spiritual victory? The inspired Scriptures makes us adequate and prepared for every good work (2 Tim 3:16-17). The abundance of God's grace is fully adequate for us to stand strong (2 Cor 8:9). The indwelling Spirit of God is greater than any power coming against us (1 Jn 4:4). Our biblical faith overcomes the world (1 Jn 5:4) and extinguishes all the fiery darts of the evil one (Eph 6:16). God's great and magnificent promises secure for us all that is needed for life and godliness (2 Pet 1:3-4).

Christ's intercession keeps us in fellowship with God (1 Jn 2:1-2; Rom 8:33-34). The Spirit's prayers keep us on the path of sanctification (Rom 8:26-27). The love of God keeps us encouraged (Rom 5:5; 2 Cor 5:14) and the faithfulness of God keeps us hopeful (1 Cor 1:9; 1 Jn 1:9; 1 Thess 5:23-24; 2 Tim 2:13). Our future inheritance, redemption and eternal bliss keep us fighting and persevering (Rom 8:18, 24-25; 1 Cor

15:51-58; 2 Cor 4:16-17; 1 Pet 1:3-9). Our righteous indignation and fear of God keeps us hating evil and warring in the heavenlies against wickedness in the world (Prov 8:13; Eph 6:12f); launching prayers that pierce his darkness and declaring truths that expose his lies. If more Laodicean Christians and others would begin realizing how well they have been outfitted, maybe the shame of their nakedness would not be so revealing (Rev 3:17).

DECEMBER 5

"When a prophet is accepted and deified, his message is lost. The prophet is only useful so long as he is stoned as a public nuisance calling us to repentance, disturbing our comfortable routines, breaking our respectable idols, shattering our sacred conventions." A. G. Gardiner.

When we break God's promises we often stoop down to pick up the pieces. These may be His partial blessings because of His mercy and grace, even though we did not fulfill the conditions to His promises to be fully blessed. At other times, the pieces may be His blessing of fatherly discipline so we won't be swept away by His judging floods, or blown about by His judging winds and stumble and fall about under His mighty earthquakes. And yet how often do we still fail to stop and listen to His still small voice which says: "Why do you keep ignoring the conditions?

DECEMBER 6

"Those whom God calls to such a ministry [of a true prophet]
- and a call is essential - must be prepared for a pathway
of unpopularity and misunderstanding. "You troubler of
Israel" was the way Ahab addressed Elijah." Arthur Wallis.

There is the every present temptation to seek the Lord for what we can receive, rather than for how we can serve. The tendency for many is to first seek His supernatural signs and wonders, rather than seek first His kingdom and His righteousness, and wait for His signs and wonders to follow. Such signs confirmed His divine mission and nature. Jesus wants us to seek Him because of who He is, not for what He has to give. "Jesus answered them and said, 'Truly, truly, I saw to you, you seek Me, not because you saw signs, but because you ate of the loaves and were filled" (Jn 6:27). The challenge today is to get believers away from the religious church's buffet line of easy believism, hyper grace and "effortless" Christianity, pastoral pastries and prosperity gossip, long enough to seek and partake of true spiritual food. Jesus said: "My food is to do the will of Him who sent Me and to accomplish His work" (Jn 4:34).

DECEMBER 7

"A hundred years ago they read less about the Bible and
more out of the old Book itself!" Charles L. Goodell

SPIRITUAL INTENT AND SANCTIFICATION

Spiritual intent as well as progressive sanctification is sabotaged when sin is courted, the Spirit is quenched and the mind is left unattended. Or to say it another way: the practice of holiness, the promise of entire sanctification and the procuring of total cleansing of one's temple (2 Cor 7:1) is only accomplished when the God the Father is allowed to work (Phil 2:13), the Son of God allowed to live (Gal 2:20), and Spirit of God allowed to sanctify the blood bought and redeemed vessel (1 Thess 4:7-8; Rom 8:13; 1 Pet 1:16,18; 1 Cor 6:19-20).

The evil spirit of the age says: "Bah, humbug: eat and drink and be merry". But the Holy Spirit of the ages exhorts us to: Look at the cloud of witnesses, the Scripture's present commands, your future accounting before the Chief Shepherd and Supreme Judge. For He is coming quickly to "both bring to light the things hidden in the darkness and disclose the motives of men's hearts" (1 Cor 4:5). He will bring His reward with Him "to render to every man according to what he has done" (Rev 22:12). Thus Paul prayed with anticipation for those chosen by God: "Now may the God of peace Himself sanctify you entirely, and may your spirit and soul and body be preserved complete, without blame, at the coming of our Lord Jesus Christ" (1 Thess 5:23, 1:2-4).

DECEMBER 8

Holiness is not attained by dancing with wolves but by crushing them under our feet. And that is done by exercising the Holy Ghost' two step dance of repentance toward God and faith in the Lord Jesus Christ (Acts 20:21).

The one who exercises faith to receive eternal salvation, rests easy; but the one who works hard to earn salvation, never rests at all (Eph 2:8-9; Rom 4:4-5; Heb 4:1-3). True faith results in godly fruit and is demonstrated by works in one's life. It does not relish in mere theological debates in one's mind. And persevering, keeping faith that obtains eternal life, likewise never ceases believing and obeying. John clearly believed this: "He who believes in the Son has eternal life; but he who does not obey the Son shall not see life, but the wrath of God abides on him" (Jn 3:36).

The apostle Paul never ceased to teach this. He spoke of the saving righteousness of God obtained "through faith (initial act of saving faith) in Jesus Christ for all those who believe (present participle indicating a continuing lifestyle of believing) (Rom 3:22). We see this again in his teaching to the Galatian believers: "But the Scripture has shut up all men under sin that the promise by faith in Jesus Christ (bringing salvation) might be given to those who believe (present participle)" (Gal 3:22). And John said later: "These things I have written to you who believe (present participle) in the name of the Son of God, in order that you may know that you have eternal life" (1 Jn 5:13).

One is assured of possessing of eternal life not because once upon a time he believed a truth about Jesus Christ, but because that saving faith continued believing, trusting and obeying Him. Hebrews teaches the same truth: "Although He was a Son, He learned obedience from the things which He suffered. And having been made perfect, He became to all those who obey Him the source of eternal salvation" (Heb 5:8-9).

So the apostle Paul warns all who disobey: The Lord Jesus shall be revealed from heaven with His mighty angels in flaming fire, dealing out retribution to those who do not know God and to those who do not obey the gospel of our Lord Jesus" (2 Thess 1:7-8). "If anyone loves God, he is known by Him" (1 Cor 8:3). And what is the evidence of such a true love for God that assures one that he is personally know by Him? John says: "The one who says, 'I have come to know Him,' and does not keep His commandments, is a liar, and the truth is not in him" (1 Jn 2:4). "For this is the love of God, that we keep His commandments; and His commandments are not burdensome" (1 Jn 5:3). Jesus said: "If you love Me, you will keep My commandments" (Jn 14:15). So those who speak against the need for obedience and keeping Jesus' commandments are offering up irrational service to God and one not acceptable to Him (Rom 12:1-2).

DECEMBER 9

"Pride is God's most stubborn enemy! There is no sin so much like the devil as pride. It is a secret and subtle sin, and appears in a great many shapes which are undetected and unsuspected." Jonathan Edwards

We serve the God who girds us with strength and makes our way blameless. He sets us upon high places so that we can pursue our spiritual enemies and overtake them, and shatter them so that they are not able to rise (Ps 18:32, 33, 37, 38). By the power of God we leap over walls, not hide under pews (Ps 18:29), destroy the works of the devil (1 Jn 3:8), not to be devoured by him (1 Pet 5:8), resist the devil in spiritual combat, not assist him with spiritual compromise (Eph 6:13, 5:11), allow no advantage be taken of us by Satan, by not being ignorant of his schemes (2 Cor 2:11; Eph 6:11). Then our walk will be blameless and His victory obvious.

DECEMBER 10

"Before a man can bind the enemy, he must know there is nothing binding him." Smith Wigglesworth

Spiritual warfare is an essential spiritual discipline today. Scripture is full of teaching, commands and warnings concerning the necessity for a Christian to be wise in the art of spiritual warfare. This means knowing the strategies of the devil and his fallen demonic co-workers as well as possessing knowledge and skill in our warfare against such spiritual principalities and powers and their schemes (2 Cor 2:11; Eph 6:11). There are many Scriptures showing how the devil and his demons steal, kill and destroy family, marriage, health, society, godly values, life and truth.

The devil seeks to compromise Christian values, undermine Christian duties and oppose spiritual disciplines. These include evangelism (Mt 13:19; Acts 13:5-12), discipleship and followup (Acts 20:29-31; 1 Thess 2:18), holy living (Job 1:6-12), prayer (Act 16:16), worship (Mt 4:8-10) and fellowship with God (Mt 16:23; Acts 5:3). We ignore such to our peril. To ignore the devil or to live as if he doesn't exist, and not rely on God's grace and spiritual provisions to assist us in our warfare causes individuals, families, churches, and nations to suffer needlessly at the hands of the devil. He shows no mercy to those who fail to resist and stand against him.

Though spiritual warfare can be complex, the evil strategies of the devil usually fall in the areas of our temptations, thought life, treasures, and time. The wise Christian can overcome these strategies of the god of this world by resisting this tempter (Mt 4:3; Jam 4:7), taking every thought captive to the obedience of Christ (2 Cor 10:5), not loving the world nor the things in the world (1 Jn 2:15), and by not giving place to the devil nor attention to his demonic idols (Eph 4:27; 1 Cor 10:14, 20).

DECEMBER 11

"A Theologian has nothing on a man who has experienced God." Paul Washer

THE CHRISTIAN'S "BEST LIFE NOW" IS THE VERY BEST AND IS ETERNAL

Since Christians are uniquely blessed with every spiritual blessing in the heavenly places in Christ, they don't feel deprived (Eph 1:3). Since they are seated with Him in the heavenlies, they don't sit in the world's gutters (Eph 2:6). Since they alone have been made complete in Christ, they never feel completely alone (Col 2:10). Since they can do all things through Him who strengthens them, they don't believe they are incapable of doing anything (Phil 4:13). Since they drink from the fountain of living waters, they don't hew for ourselves cisterns which can hold no water (Jer 2:13; Jn 7:37-38). Since they partake of the Living Bread from heaven, they never go hungry (Jn 6:35), by grasping for the world's fallen crumbs. Since the great I Am lives in them, they don't complain "woe is me" (Jn 8:58; Gal 2:20). Since they abide in Him who is the truth, in whom are hidden all the treasures of wisdom and knowledge, they are not bound up in the devil's lies and bankrupt by his deception (Jn 8:31-32; Col 2:3). Since they follow Him who is the Light of the World, they don't walk in darkness with the god of this world (Jn 8:12). Since they are in Him, the hope of glory, they never feel hopeless without Him (Col 1:27). Since Jesus invites them to come to Him to find rest, they don't feel rejected, weary, heavy-laden and restless and without Him (Mt 11:28).

Since they know that their Creator is lovingly watching over them, they never worry about anything coming against them (Rom 8:31, 35, 39). Since the Sustainer of everything holds them, they don't fret when their world seems to fall apart before them (Col 1:16-17). Since they know the Lord is always at their side, they never have to feel beside themselves (Mt 28:20). Since He intercedes for them when they fail, they can continue on and prevail (1 Jn 2:1-2). Since they follow Him who is the Way, they don't stray and lose their way. Since they are rooted in Him who is the truth, they can resist the devil, the father of lies (Jn 14:6; Col 2:6-7; Jn 8:44; Eph 6:14).

So even at times when they are not what they ought to be, maybe they just failed to remember what they are called to be. Maybe they have begun to hold on to what is worthless rather than cling to Him who is priceless. Maybe that's why the apostle Paul, when he was on his back and saw the Light, got up and never looked back. He was determined to forget his terrible past and kept reaching forward to His terrific future (Acts 9:3-4; Phil 3:13). He was no longer zealous for his ancestral tradition and dead religion, but was anxious for a living relationship and filled with holy ambition (Gal 1:13-14; Phil 3:6-8; 2 Cor 5:9). Such ones experience the true "Best Life Now", that is Jesus, the only Life there is (Col 3:4).

DECEMBER 12

"The devil's not fighting churches today,
he's joining churches." Vance Havner

BE SET FREE

Believe the Lord's statement that He came to set captives free (Lk 4:18). You can be free from sinful bondage, emotional turmoil, mental madness, soulish depression, demonic oppression and fleshly struggles. Otherwise you make the statement that Jesus was just joking or that God is not willing (Gal 5:1,13) or His Spirit is not capable (Phil 4:13; Eph 3:16) or His Scriptures are not adequate (2 Tim 3:16-17) or His promises are not valid (2 Cor 1:20; 2 Pet 1:3-4) or His Son's intercession is not effective (1 Jn 2:1-2; Jn 11:22, 42) or His Good News Gospel is not so good after all (Lk 2:10-11). Don't live in defeat because of your past failures, but trust in God's future victories (Phil 3:13). Don't be paralyzed by your sense of inadequacy, but be energized by God's divine adequacy (2 Cor 3:4-6). Hope in God's ability and commitment to work everything out for your good as you continue to love Him and fulfill His purpose (Rom 8:28). You can walk in the good works which He prepared beforehand for you (Eph 2:10). You don't have to fear any such threats to the liberty you have in Christ. "You shall not dread them, for the LORD your God is in your midst, a great and awesome God" (Deut 7:21).

DECEMBER 13

*"Many people in the world have not rejected
Christ. They have rejected the Christ they've seen,
projected by Christendom." Zac Poonen*

WARFARE PRAYER

The apostle Paul asked the Roman Christians: "strive together with me in your prayers to God for me" so that he would be rescued from the disobedient ones who were energized by the devil and his demons (Rom 15:30-31; Eph 2:2). Wise Christians will do likewise, praying that those being attacked would be delivered from the evil one (Mt 6:13), be filled with all spiritual wisdom and understanding (Col 1:9) and be fully clothed with spiritual armor (Eph 6:11f), resisting the devil firm in the faith (1 Pet 5:8-9) and crushing under their feet all the power of the enemy (Lk 10:19).

Believers don't have to be "afraid of the terror by night or of the arrow that flies by day" (Ps 91:5). Though many are the afflictions of the righteous, the Lord delivers them out of them all (Ps 34:19). The psalmist says: "A thousand may fall at your side and ten thousand at your right hand, but it shall not approach you. You will only look on with your eyes and see the recompense of the wicked" (Ps 91:7-8).

The Lord continues to crush spiritual enemies under the feet (Ps 91:7-8; Romans 16:20) of those who have made the LORD their refuge, even the Most High, their dwelling place (Ps 91:9). Believers can joyfully taste of the fruit of the Spirit (Gal 5:22-23) and let the victorious Christ living in them answer the door when the defeated devil comes knocking. There is no reason for Christians seated in the heavenlies with Christ to allow the devil to get them sitting with him in the gutters of his world (Eph 2:6).

DECEMBER 14

"A church with apostolic foundations is that body of people whose central impulse and principle of life, being and service is one thing only, namely, a radical and total jealousy for the glory of God." Art Katz

THE FIVE-FOLD MINISTRY THE DEVIL HATES

There are many ways that biblical Christian ministry can be summarized and categorized. Here is another way to describe a five-fold ministry which the devil surely fears and hates:

Sinners delivered: Luke 2:20-11, 9:1-2; 10:1-3; Gal 1:4, 5:1, 13; 2 Tim 2:25-26; Tit 2:14

Self dethroned: 1 Pet 3:15; Jn 12:24-26; 1 Pet 4:1; Gal 2:20; 1 Cor 15:10; Rom 15:17-19

Saints discipled: Mt 28:18-20; Acts 14:21-23; 20:27; Gal 4:19; 2 Tim 3:10-11; Tit 2;11-14

Servants devoted: Lk 6:46; Mt 7:21; Rom 12:10-13; 14:7-8; Eph 3:1-2, 4:1; Phil 1:21; Gal 6:14

Soldiers deployed: 2 Tim 2:3,4; Eph 6:11; 2 Cor 6:4,7; 1 Thess 5:5-8; 1 Pet 4:1, 2

DECEMBER 15

*"It is better to have a sore than a seared
conscience." Thomas Brooks*

BANK ON GOD'S WORD AND YOUR LIFE WILL
NEVER BOUNCE

Though the stock market may fall, God's word never fails. "Forever,
O LORD, Your word is settled in heaven" (Ps 119:89). "So will My
word be which goes forth from My mouth; it will not return to Me empty,
without accomplishing what I desire, and without succeeding in the matter for which I sent it" (Ps 55:11). Lord, "I have rejoiced in Your testimonies
as much as in all riches" (Ps 119:14). "The Law of Your mouth is better
to me than thousands of gold and silver pieces" (Ps 119:72). "Therefore I
love your commandments above gold, yes above fine gold" (Ps 119:127).
May I ever be nourished on your inspired words rather than the babblings
of man, for only such God-breathed nourishment is capable of bringing
about spiritual growth (Mt 4:4; 2 Tim 3:16-17). "How sweet are Your
words to my taste! Yes, sweeter than honey to my mouth" (Ps 119:103).
"My eyes anticipate the night watches that I may mediate on Your word"
(Ps 119:148).

I will not meditate on some New Age god within but will worship the
God above, for the Lord has "established His throne in the heavens, and
His sovereignty rules over all" (Ps 103:19). "I will rejoice at Your Word
as one who finds great spoil" (119:162). For the butter knife of mankind
and the pitchfork of the devil is no match for the Sword of the Lord (Eph

6:17). Holy Spirit of Truth open my eyes that I may behold wonderful things from God's Law (Ps 119:18). Help me to study and practice God's word that produces faith which overcomes the world's enticements and discernment that exposes the devil's lies and deceptions (Rom 10:17; Heb 5:14; 1 Jn 5:4).

Not seven minutes a day, but seven times a day I praise You, because of Your righteous ordinances (Ps 119:162). "Your commandments make me wiser than my enemies, for they are ever mine" (Ps 119:97). Lord, alert me to the many religious leaders who profess to be wise but have become fools (Rom 1:22). Guard my mind against their ignorant speculations, contemplative ravings, and esoteric terminology spewed out by those who are "always learning but never able to come to the knowledge of the truth" (2 Tim 3:7). Lord, "establish Your word to Your servant, as that which produces reverence for You" (Ps 119:38). For I know that "the fear of the LORD is the beginning of wisdom, and the knowledge of the Holy One is understanding" (Prov 9:10).

DECEMBER 16

"The 'flesh' is too bad to be cleansed; it
must be crucified." Watchman Nee

A TERRIBLE PAST CAN BRING A TERRIFIC FUTURE.

Lord, I am convinced that a terrible past only prepares me for a terrific future. Though the evil one, whom I despise, may attempt to bring my past mistakes against me for evil, this will only result in good because of the Holy One whom I serve (Gen 50:20). For I know that "God causes all things to work together for good to those who love God, to those who are called according to His purpose" (Rom 8:28). I claim Your promise: "For I know the plans I have for you, 'declares the LORD,' plans for welfare and not for calamity to give you a future and a hope" (Jer 29:11). You turn the curse into a blessing (Neh 13:2). The psalmist relates what God says to the one who trusts in Him as His refuge and fortress: "I will not be afraid of the terror by night or of the arrow that flies by day; of the pestilence that stalks in darkness, or of the destruction that lays waste at noon. A thousand may fall at your side, and ten thousand at your right hand; but it shall not approach you" (Ps 91:5-7).

Lord, help me love You truly, to know You intimately, to serve You devoutly, and to worship You properly. For I know that your blessings are great and your lovingkindness is enduring to those who fear You. You promise such a one: "Because he has loved Me, therefore I will deliver him; I will set him securely on high because he has known My name. He will call upon Me, and I will answer him; I will be with him in trouble; I will rescue him, and honor him" (Ps 91:14-15). So Lord "turn to me and be gracious to me, after your manner with those who love your name" (Ps 119:132). O LORD, You are forever, "a stronghold for the oppressed, a stronghold in times of trouble, and those who know Thy name will put their trust in Thee; for Thou, O LORD, hast not forsaken those who see Thee" (Ps 9:9-10).

My heart rejoices in You because I trust in Your holy name (Ps 33:21). For Your holy Word says, "the people who know their God will display strength and take action" (Dan 11:32). I choose to be strong in the Lord and in the strength of His might. I will put on the full armor of God so that I can take action and overcome evil spiritual forces (Eph 6:10-12). I will count on your everlasting lovingkindness which is shown to whose who fear You, to those who keep Your covenant and who remember Your precepts to do them (Ps 103:17-18). It is written: "Blessed are those who hear the word of God and observe it" (Lk 11:28). For better is sincere obedience than religious sacrifice (1 Sam 15:22); a faithful walk, than frivolous talk. Lord,

I claim the promise: "And after you have suffered a little while, the God of all grace, who called you to His eternal glory in Christ, will Himself perfect, confirm, strengthen and establish you" (1 Pet 5:10).

DECEMBER 17

We must have true Repentance from sin, a cleansing
Revival in the church, a spiritual Revolution in the
nation and a wholehearted Return to the Bible.
These are the absolute Requirements for today or
we will experience awful Ruin tomorrow.

FRUITLESS BRANCHES ON DEAD TREES

Many churches today lack the manifest power, presence and peace of God because they have quenched the Spirit of God, denied the Son of God and have adulterated the Word of God. They do not worship God in spirit and truth because they have no fear of God (Jn 4:24). They do not walk by the Spirit of God because they are not filled with the Spirit (Eph 5:18; Gal 5:16, 25). They do not love the Son of God because they do not keep His commandments (Jn 14:15). They despise the Word of God because they do not submit to its divine authority (Prov 13:13; 2 Tim 3:16; Heb 5:12; 1 Thess 2:13).

When this happens all that is left are powerless religious traditions, vain imaginations of men and marketing strategies by which many contemporary churches are built. They may have many offering plates, but few living and holy sacrifices (Rom 12:1). Some may raise a hand while no one is looking around, but few will raise a voice to declare that Jesus is Lord of all. A few may walk to the altar and say a little prayer, but few will die at the altar and pay the ultimate price. Though many quick and sincere confessions may be said, few long lasting and genuine disciples will be made.

We need to BE the Church which Jesus is building, upon the solid rock confession that Jesus is the Christ, the Son of the living God. We don't need to GO to man-made churches built on the shifting sands of another Jesus or receive a different spirit or a different gospel (2 Cor 11:4). The perishing don't need to be invited to a church which isn't holding fast to the Head (Col 2:19), but to Christ, the Head the Church; the Church which is the pillar and support of the truth (Eph 5:23; Col 1:18; 1 Tim 3:15). Those alienated from God need to be brought into the household of God which is built upon the foundation of the apostles and prophets, Christ Jesus Himself being the corner stone (Eph 2:19-20).

True revival is awaiting a Church that overcomes the world, not one being overcome by and conformed to the world. Such a Church consists of members working out their salvation with fear and trembling (Phil 2:13). They abide in Jesus who is the True Vine (Jn 15:1). By bearing much fruit they prove to be His disciples (Jn 15:8). By obeying Him they prove that He is their Lord (Lk 6:46). By keeping His commandments they demonstrate that they have come to know Him (1 Jn 2:4). And by not practicing lawlessness they prove that He knows them (Mt 7:23).

Beware of fruitless branches which hang on dead trees. "They profess to know God, but by their deeds they deny Him, being detestable and disobedient, and worthless for any good deed" (Tit 1:16). They are deceived disciples of the evil one and slaves of unrighteousness and of sin (Mt 7:22-23; 1 Jn 2:26, 3:7). Such ones hold to a form of godliness without power (2 Tim 3:5), proclaim a distorted gospel which cannot save (Gal 1:6-7) and will depart into the eternal fire which will not be quenched (Mk 9:45-46). They have a hope which will only disappoint because they have not "fixed their hope on the living God who is the Savior of all men, especially those who believe" (Rom 5:5; 1 Tim 4:10). Such ones judge themselves unworthy of eternal life (Acts 13:46), because they rejected God's purpose for themselves (Lk 7:30), being unwilling to come to and receive Jesus who is eternal life (Jn 1:12, 5:40, 17:3). Instead, they freely choose to go away into eternal punishment which they denied (Mt 25:46) and into the eternal fire prepared for the devil and his angels (Mt 25:41).

DECEMBER 18

"A man's most glorious actions will at last be found to be but glorious sins, if he hath made himself, and not the glory of God, the end of those actions." Thomas Brooks

PURPOSE DRIVEN PROPERLY

The things of God are understood by those who love God (1 Co 2:9-10). Those who love God obey His commandments (Jn 14:21-23) and are Jesus' friends (Jn 15:14). Those who love the world are enemies of God (Jam 4:4) and will not inherit eternal life (1 Jn 2:17). Jesus said that one cannot serve two masters (Lk 16:13). If we are seated in the heavenlies, why live in the world? (Col 3:1f). The unrepentant are held captive by sin (Jn 8:34-35) and in the devil's snare (2 Tim 2:25-25). The repentant are held captive by God's love and experience the blessings of His care and have as their ambition to be pleasing to Him (2 Cor 5:9).

Paul, Silvanus and Timothy, though apostles of Christ, did not seek glory from men (1 Thes 1:1, 2:6). Instead they behaved devoutly, uprightly and blamelessly toward believers in Thessalonica. They were exhorting and encouraging and imploring each one of them as a father would his own children, so that they would walk worthy of the God who was calling them into

FINDERS OF TRUTH

His own kingdom and glory (1 Thess 2:10-12). Now that is real Christian leadership in action and a divine purpose worth following.

It is much better to be Purpose Called to God's desire than Purpose Driven to our carnal dreams. Our God and Savior desires all men to be saved and to come to the knowledge of the truth (1 Tim 2:4), not wishing for any to perish but for all to come to repentance (2 Pet 3:9b). "For to this end Christ died and lived again, that He might be Lord both of the dead and of the living" (Rom 14:9). Jesus didn't die so we could pursue God's dream of an enhanced Self-Esteem or for a greater enlightenment to our inner divine nature. The Scripture says: "He Himself bore our sins in His body on the cross, that we might die to sin and live to righteousness; for by His wounds you were healed" (1 Pet 2:24). You are no longer dead in trespasses and sins, but have been born again, raised up from the dead, to live and reign with Him (Jn 3:3, 5; Eph 2:1, 5-6; Rom 5:17, 8:37).

DECEMBER 19

Time is running out. Which way are you running? Make the most of your time because the days are evil. Make the very most of your time because the days are short.

YOU WILL KNOW THEM BY THEIR FRUIT, NOT THEIR LIPS.

There is a common religious opinion that a sinner gets saved and is "good to go" for heaven by simply asking Jesus to "come into one's heart" or by simply acknowledging for a moment, even sincerely, that Jesus is one's Savior. This and only this is all that is stated as necessary for receiving eternal life. There is often no mention of the necessity of repentance or the need of confessing Jesus to become one's Lord in life. Though one may become saved this way, for only God knows the heart, yet subsequent fruit of repentance and some evidence of Jesus' lordship must be present if one wants biblical assurance of true salvation. The author of Hebrews says, "Without sanctification no one will see the Lord" (12:14) and "He has perfected for all time those who are being sanctified" (Heb 10:14).

By not mentioning repentance and receiving Jesus as Lord, such pulpit and altar "evangelists" lead their "converts" to believe that saving faith doesn't ever have to be demonstrated by subsequent works of faith nor is repentance toward God required for salvation. That is, one doesn't have to commit to, obey and decide to live for Jesus or stop living for self or begin dying to sin (Acts 20:21; 26:18, 20; Rom 10:9; 2 Cor 4:5; Col 2:6; Col 3:1; Gal 5:25). Such "belief in" Jesus never has to "work out" in one's life. Jesus who is to be our Life (Col 3:4), becomes another Jesus who is only "a confession". All the lost sinner has to do is to exercise a verbal confession of faith and intellectually assent to Jesus as being Savior; no need to receive and submit to Him as Lord.

Nothing can keep the lost sinner farther from Him who is the Truth. For the book of Hebrews which defines and profiles true faith, also spoke of "things that accompany salvation" (6:9) and describe works of saving faith throughout the book, especially in chapter 11. James taught in agreement: "But are you willing to recognize, you foolish fellow, that faith without works is useless" (2:20)…"a man is justified by works, and not by faith alone (without works) (2:24). And Paul said" "For not the hearers of the Law are just before God, but the doers of the Law will be glorified" (Rom 2:13). Paul knew that the Thessalonian believers he addressed were chosen of God because of their "work of faith and labor of love and steadfastness of hope in our Lord Jesus Christ (1 Thess 1:3-4).

So put aside religious opinion, easy believism and cheap grace and receive true saving faith and sanctifying grace that not only qualifies and enables sinners to obtain salvation and escape hell, but also empowers them to overcome the world, conquer sin and live for Him (Tit 2:11; 1 Jn 5:4; 1 Pet 1:4, 5, 9; Jn 1:12, 3:36; Heb 5:9). After all, Jesus didn't say "You will know them by the fruit of their lips". Jesus expected obedience from those who truly claimed Him as their Lord. He asked: "And why do you call Me, 'Lord, Lord,' and do not do what I say" (Lk 6:46)? He expected life bearing fruit from His followers who truly believed in Him for eternal life. "By this is My Father glorified, that you bear much fruit, and so prove to be My disciples" (Jn 15:8).

DECEMBER 20

"More than 2 billion people who do not know Jesus head toward hell to perish for eternity, while the church laughs its way to hysteria, claiming this is the sign of the last days' outpouring of the Holy Spirit...My brothers and sisters, this is not Christianity". K.P. Yohannan

CHRISTIAN IDENTITY IN CHRIST

To the born again child of God and new creature, Christ has become: wisdom from God, and righteousness and sanctification, and redemption (1 Co 1:30, 2 Cor 5:17). This new creature who has been made complete in Christ (Col 2:10) and has been redeemed from sin's condemnation (Rom 8:1, 34) can walk in newness of life (Rom 6:4), being liberated from sin's controlling power (Rom 6:12,14), cleansed from sin's defilement (1 Jn 1:9; 2 Cor 7:1) and sanctified or set apart from sin's presence (Heb 10:14). He has been adopted into God's family and can enjoy being an overcomer and citizen of heaven (Col 2:10; Rom 8:15, 37; Phil 3:20; 1 Jn 5:5; Rev 2:7, 11, 17, 26-28, 3:5, 12, 21; 12:11). However, without Christ one remains a son of the evil one (1 Jn 3:10; Eph 2:2), a captive of the devil (2 Tim 2:26) having no hope and without God in the world (Eph 2:12).

Those who have heard and received the Word of God, as the life-giving Word coming from God and not from men (1 Thess 2:13), will find that the Word of God performs its saving and creative work in those who believe (1 Thess 2:13; Rom 1:16; Heb 4:12; Jn 6:63). So we see that this is a faith venture; but surely one that will prove valid by a subsequent new creation for those who are truly born again. Every religion is a faith venture, except for the sceptic who refuses to believe or the atheist who believes it is foolish to believe. Only Christianity offers a religion whose founder is alive, resurrected and ascended above the heavens, rather than being a pile of dead bones buried beneath the earth. That is why Christianity is rightly called "a living relationship" rather than a dead religion.

DECEMBER 21

"Most Christians don't hear God's voice because we've already decided we aren't going to do what He says." A.W. Tozer

JESUS HAS NO APPETITE FOR PROSPERITY PREACHING

Jesus warned the church in Laodicea: "Because you are lukewarm...I will spit you out of My mouth. Because you say, 'I am rich, and have become wealthy, and have need of nothing,' and you do not know that you are wretched and miserable and poor and blind and naked, I advise you to buy from Me gold refined by fire so that you may become rich and white garments so that you may clothe yourself, and that the shame of your nakedness will not be revealed; and eye salve to anoint your eyes so that you may see" (Rev 3:16-18).

So why settle for a prosperity gospel of fools gold when God has already granted you His precious and magnificent promises enabling you to become a partaker of divine nature (2 Pet 1:3-4)? You have already been blessed with every spiritual blessing in Christ (Eph 1:3), in whom are hidden all the treasures of wisdom and knowledge (Col 2:3). And with Him, God will give you all things needed to make certain His calling and choosing of you (Rom 8:32; 2 Pet 1:10-11). The God of peace Himself is able to sanctify you entirely and preserve your spirit and soul and body complete, without blame at the coming of our Lord Jesus Christ (1 Thes 5:23-24).

DECEMBER 22

"There is a common worldly kind of Christianity in this day, which many have, and think they have enough. "This cheap Christianity offends nobody, requires no sacrifice, costs nothing, and is worth nothing!" J.C Ryle

ARE YOU IN BONDAGE TO YOUR FREEDOM?

I sn't it wonderful to be enlightened by the multicultural age and to live in the land of the free and home of the brave, as long as you don't disturb Mother Earth or become patriotic? You are totally free to go wherever you wish if you can afford the gas. You can live as you wish as long as you don't live as if God is alive. You can say whatever you wish, as long as it is politically correct and isn't hateful and isn't Christian. You can be whatever you wish: male, female or both, and you can even change that daily. You can marry whatever or whoever you wish, as often as you wish for as long as you wish. You can work at whatever you wish, if you can find a job. You can charge up all your credit cards as much as you wish, and keep your change. You can be religious, self-righteous or unrighteous as much as you wish, just don't be truly spiritual. You can worship wherever, however and or whatever you wish, as often as you wish, if you wish. Just don't worship the God of the Bible in spirit and truth. You are free to make God in your own image, to think of Christianity in your own way, to serve a Christ of your own liking and accept a gospel that suits your tastes. You can tithe as little as you wish, be carnal as much as you wish and be lazy all that you wish.

Then God's grace brings you to your senses and you become spiritually enlightened (2 Tim 2:25-26; Eph 1:18, 5:14). You realize that you are in bondage to your great freedom and deceived by your great wisdom. You discover that the devil has blinded you to the light (2 Cor 4:4) and has conformed you to his world (Rom 12:1). You are bound up by strongholds of the flesh (Heb 12:1; Jn 8:34), have been lied to by the devil (Jn 8:44) and are held captive to do his will (2 Tim 2:26). You open your eyes and you realize you were so free to be a slave of the god of this world (2 Cor 4:4; 1 Jn 5:19), living under the dominion of Satan (Acts 26:18) and walking under the authority of his darkness (Col 1:13), even being energized by his power (Eph 2:2).

Then you decide to abide in Jesus who is the way, the truth and the life (Jn 14:6). You begin to walk in newness of live, overcoming the world, the flesh and the devil, knowing that you can do all things through Him who strengthens you (Phil 4:13). The sanctifying Holy Spirit brings to your memory Jesus' statement that "everyone who commits sin is the slave of sin" (Jn 8:34, 14:26) and is a captive son of the evil one (1 Jn 3:8, 10). You realize that true and lasting freedom is only possible to the one who is born again from above (Jn 3:3, 5), who walks by the Spirit of God (2 Cor 3:17; Gal 5:16), who abides in the Word of God (Jn 8:32) and is enslaved to the will of God (Rom 6:22). You lay aside falsehood and abide in the truth and become free indeed (Jn 8:32-36).

DECEMBER 23

"The Church did the most when the Church was the least like the world." G. Campbell Morgan

Don't fret if you seem to be an outcast in the eyes of the world. The world may see you as a dysfunctional misfit, but God sees you as foolish for Him and perfectly fit for His service (2 Cor 5:13; 1 Cor 1:27-28). Everyone who remains on the Potter's wheel will prove to become mighty in the Potter's hand. The one who has been purified by fiery trials (1 Pet 1:6-7), pruned by the Vinedresser (Jn 15:2), and disciplined by the Father (Heb 12:11) will bear much fruit and be a trophy of His grace.

Those who walk as citizens of heaven are never well received by the world any more than Jesus was received. The world was made through Jesus, yet it did not know Him (Jn 1:10). He came to His own and they did not receive Him (Jn 1:11). Initially, even His brothers were not believing in Him (Jn 7:5). Many of His disciples withdrew from Him (Jn 6:66). The world hated Him (Jn 15:18), religious leaders tested Him (Jn 8:6) and the devil tempted Him (Mt 4:3-11). Even one of His own chosen ones betrayed Him (Jn 18:2).

"Consider it all joy, my brethren, when you encounter various trials" (Jam 1:2). "For just as the sufferings of Christ are ours in abundance, so also our comfort is abundant through Him" (2 Cor 1:5). You who abide in Him are in good company. For just as Jesus said "It is finished" (Jn 19:30), we can say to all our enemies "you are finished". God will soon make all Jesus' enemies a footstool under His feet (Heb 1:13). God is still on the throne and reigns over the earth, for "the LORD has established His throne in the heavens, and His sovereignty rules over all" (Ps 103:19). For soon Christ is returning and "then comes the end, when He delivers up the kingdom to the God and Father, when He has abolished all rule and all authority and power. For He must reign until He has put all His enemies under His feet" (1 Cor 15:24-25). "But thanks be to God, who gives us the victory through our Lord Jesus Christ. Therefore, my beloved brethren, be steadfast, immovable, always abounding in the work of the Lord, knowing that your toil is not in vain in the Lord" (1 Cor 15:57-58).

DECEMBER 24

"The first duty of believers is to say yes to God; the second is to say no to idols." Os Guinness

IDOLATRY DEPRIVES, BUT THE GREAT I AM PROVIDES.

David's devotion and reliance on his LORD is clearly seen in many of his psalms. "I have set the LORD continually before me; because He is at my right hand, I will not be shaken. Therefore my heart is glad and my glory rejoices; my flesh also will dwell securely. You will make know to me the path of life; in Your presence is fullness of joy; in Your right hand there are pleasures forever" (Ps 16:8-10, 11). However, "the sorrows of those who have bartered for another god will be multiplied" (Ps 16:4).

Christians are called to be bright lights of the world shining on those who walk in the world's darkness (Mt 5:14-16; Eph 5:7-15). They are to glorify their Father in heaven, the Father of lights (Jam 1:17). They are to expose the unfruitful deeds of darkness. Unfortunately more and more Christians are having their candles blown out by the ever increasing winds of false and demonic doctrine (Eph 4:14; 1 Tim 4:1). Too many love the world's presents and are amused by its idols to keep their lamps trimmed and their flasks full of Holy Spirit oil (Mt 25:1-7).

But those who give themselves to God are persuaded of the scriptural promises: "He who did not spare His own Son, but delivered Him up for us all, how will He not also with Him freely give us all things?" (Rom 8:32) and "My God shall supply all your needs according to His riches in glory in Christ Jesus (Phil 4:19). Another psalm says: "No good thing does He withhold from those who walk uprightly" (Ps 84:11b).

So there is no need to worry about experiencing lack. And it makes no sense to listen to those who preach an enticing and false prosperity gospel. Instead give attention to those who preach the unfathomable riches of Christ (Eph 3:8). Don't let a distorted prosperity gospel rob you blind. The devil always leaves you with loose change and counterfeit bills. The God of heaven endows you with eternal riches and true wealth. Lay up for yourselves treasures in heaven not on Wall Street. You can take that to the bank in heaven.

DECEMBER 25

There are more important battles to fight than that
of pin pointing the exact day of the Savior's birth.
You will know them by their love, by their unity and
by their fruit, not by their correct calendars.

"But an hour is coming, and now is, when the true worshipers will worship the Father in spirit and truth; for such people the Father seeks to be His worshipers. God is spirit, and those who worship Him must worship in spirit and truth" (Jn 4:23-24). The Spirit of truth was sent to testify about the Son (1 Jn 5:7-8; Jn 15:26) and to glorify Him who is the Truth (Jn 14:6, 16:14). However, religious leaders have a tendency to transgress the commandment of God for the sake of tradition and to worship God in vain by teaching as doctrines the precepts of men (Mt 15:4, 9).

You have to wonder how much true worship exists in the so-called houses of God, where the Son of God is not exalted, the Word of God is not preached and the Spirit of God is not welcomed (Jn 4:23-24, 14:6, 15:26; 17:17; Mk 7:7). Today, we have church growth contractors who build colossal churches to which the religious multitudes come. But Jesus, heaven's Carpenter, is building His Church (Mt 16:15-18) with living stones to practice a holy and royal priesthood (1 Pet 2:5, 9).

DECEMBER 26

"For a small reward, a man will hurry away on a long journey; while for eternal life, many will hardly take a single step." Thomas a' Kempis

Because God is…we can…
Because God is eternal we can possess eternal life.
Because God is immutable we are not consumed.
Because God is holy and just we can be assured of justice.
Because God is merciful we don't lose hope.
Because God is omniscient He knows our needs.
Because God is love we are loved.
Because God is omnipresent we can pray.
Because God is sovereign we don't have to worry.
Because God is omnipotent He can take care of us.
Because God is for us, who can be against us?

DECEMBER 27

"The coming revival must begin with a great revival of prayer. It is in the closet, with the door shut, that the sound of abundance of rain will first be heard." Andrew Murray

In these last days, only those who are led and taught by the Spirit of truth to abide in the truth will know the truth, and be set free from powerless religious tradition (1 Jn 2:27; Jn 8:31-32; Gal 5:1,13,16). When Jesus was baptized the Holy Spirit descended upon Him (Lk 3:21-22). He was later led by the Spirit (Lk 4:1), rejoiced in the Spirit (Lk 10:21) and cast out demons by the Spirit (Mt 12:28). It would seem that we should likewise experience the ministry, power and fellowship of the Holy Spirit (2 Cor 13:14). Could it be today there is so much disunity in the body of Christ because so many Christians do not know intimately the Holy Spirit who was sent from the Father by the Son to be our divine Helper (Jn 14:26) and to preserve unity within His body (Eph 4:3)?

Jesus prayed that this divine Helper would perfect unity in His disciples (Jn 17:23). The apostle Paul encouraged the believers in Ephesus to be diligent to preserve the unity of the Spirit in the bond of peace (Eph 4:3). Concerning this unity Paul prayed that the believers at Philippi would conduct themselves in a manner worthy of the gospel of Christ by "standing firm in one spirit, with one mind striving together for the faith of the gospel" (Phil 1:27). He also stated that his complete joy rested on them "being of the same mind, maintaining the same love, united in spirit, intent on one purpose" (Phil 2:2).

If the battle to keep the faith, to conquer our spiritual enemies and to become a unified body of believers isn't won in the mind, it seems to be all but lost or greatly compromised in the walk. No wonder the Word says to set the mind on things above not on things below (Col 3:1-2), on the spiritual not the carnal (Phil 4:8). The mind is to be renewed not corrupted (Rom 12:2), having the mind of Christ (1 Cor 2:16). So the word of God says to take every thought captive, not every other thought (2 Cor 10:5). Taking every thought captive is the great battle. But the greater challenge is being spiritually alert and disciplined and Holy Spirit empowered to successfully engage in such a battle.

DECEMBER 28

It is altogether doubtful whether any man can
be saved who comes to Christ for His help with
no intention to obey Him". A.W. Tozer

In days of old, God's saints enjoyed and proclaimed the glory and majesty of God's kingdom and experienced His power, saw His works, meditated on His words and praised His name. Today, too many spend their time watching American Idols, living their powerless religion and laboring for that which perishes. Many in Churchianity today continue relaxing in their pews, soaking up entertainment, snacking on a pastoral pastry, preferring it over a heart piercing and life changing exposition. But those who prefer to hear God's Word and Truth expounded and choose to abide in it, they will experience true freedom and the spiritual fruit that comes from it (Jn 8:32-36; 15:1-8). Those who follow Jesus who is the Way, the Truth and the Life, doing what He commanded rather than just thinking what He would do, they will experience the abundant life which the Good Shepherd came to offer and will avoid the detours of life which the father of lies loves to whisper (Jn 10:10b; 14:6; 8:44; 2 Cor 10:3-5).

DECEMBER 29

"What is Christianity all about? It is about an intimate
relationship with God. And I HATE a christendom, a

churchianity that God is not big enough and glorious enough
so that we have to give them other things." Paul Washer

Today there is need for quick, massive, wise and effective evangelism. I am talking about Wisdom Evangelism, Prayer Evangelism, Power Evangelism and Warm Market Evangelism in places where most are not frozen solid and hard against the Gospel as those who are marching in parades hand in hand with the devil or even those sitting inside churches being entertained by the devil. One can walk any streets of America and find that most are lost as a goose. Churches themselves have also become a vast mission field in America because many are led by lost preachers who are preaching a gospel that sends people to hell, to pews filled with those who think they are heaven bound. Thank the Lord that He is raising up true and bold gospel preachers today who are wise to often plant gospel seeds on soils of all conditions inside and outside of churches. Those who are led by the Spirit preach everywhere, making the most of their time, not leaving any lost behind, paying special attention to those whom the Lord is drawing. God speed to all bravehearted street preachers.

DECEMBER 30

"It is easier to speak about revival than
to set about it." Horatius Bonar

The Lord reveals His Word and carries out His will in all who are hungry for Truth, who are living sacrifices for Him. That is a reasonable service of worship to those who are being taught and led by the Holy Spirit of Truth, without discrimination regarding one's age, gender, education, spiritual gifting, troubled past, miserable wanderings and moral failures or sins (Rom 12:1-2). "We all stumble in many ways" (Jam 3:1)..."if we say that we have no sin, we are deceiving ourselves" (1 Jn 1:8). So there is the need for confession of sin (1 Jn 1:9, Jam 5:16). But with sincere confession and true repentance, one is forgiven of sin (1 Jn 1:9). Thus we are told to forget the past and reach forward to what lies ahead (Phil 3:13), in the power of the Holy Spirit and sanctified by His Truth, cleansing ourselves from all defilement of flesh and spirit (Rom 8:13; 2 Cor 7:1; Jn 17:17).

DECEMBER 31

*"Any manipulation of the Scriptures to make
them speak peace to the natural man is evil
and can only lead to ruin." A. W. Tozer*

DIRT CLODS OR TROPHIES OF DIVINE GRACE?

A true gospel preacher challenges the present faddish addiction to uncommitted service, diluted preaching, workless faith, "effortless" Christianity and carnal living. Our calling is clear, our Leader is proven, our mission is divine, our weapons are proven, our victory is certain and our spiritual enemies are terrified because more and more Christians are rising up to BE the Church, rather than just go to church.

Oh Christians, your adversary the devil, the god of ruin roaming the world, prefers that you be dirt clods crushed into dust under his feet, rather than God's feet bringing glad tides of good things to the lost (Rom 10:15). But the Lord of peace, ruling from heaven, has called you to be the living stones He uses to build up His spiritual house not dry bricks in a church building. And the Father's house is not only to be called a house of prayer (Mt 21:13). It is also to be a place to offer up spiritual sacrifices and reasonable worship, in light of His saving grace (Rom 12:1-2; Mt 16:19; Lk 19:46; 1 Pet 2:5, 5:8). The God of peace will soon crush Satan under your feet (Rom 16:20). Until then, His hands will continue molding you into His trophies of grace. The new year is upon you. Become a trophy of God's grace not a dirt clod of disgrace.

ABOUT THE AUTHOR

R OBERT KLOUS holds a master's degree in theology from Dallas
  Theological Seminary. He presently resides in Tennessee and publishes
works that promote biblical literacy helping Christians find truth, keep
faith, leading to personal renewal, corporate revival and cultural revolution.
He is passionate about replacing contemporary Churchianity with biblical
Christianity by encouraging private devotion, public demonstration of the
Gospel and bold proclamation of the Truth.

Email: rklous@hotmail.com
Facebook page:
https://www.facebook.com/rklous
For bulk order discounts for distribution contact author.
Additional copies of the book can be purchased at www.amazon.com

SUBJECT INDEX

Subjects listed by month and day